TOWARD THE TWENTY-FIRST CENTURY
IN CHRISTIAN MISSION

Toward the Twenty-first Century in Christian Mission

Essays in honor of

Gerald H. Anderson

Director, Overseas Ministries Study Center,
New Haven, Connecticut
Editor, International Bulletin of Missionary Research

edited by

James M. Phillips *and* Robert T. Coote

WILLIAM B. EERDMANS PUBLISHING COMPANY
GRAND RAPIDS, MICHIGAN

Copyright © 1993 by Wm. B. Eerdmans Publishing Co.
255 Jefferson Ave. S.E., Grand Rapids, Mich. 49503

Printed in the United States of America

Library of Congress Cataloging-in-Publication Data

Toward the twenty-first century in Christian mission: essays in honor of Gerald H.
Anderson, director, Overseas Ministries Study Center, New Haven,
Connecticut, editor, International bulletin of missionary research /
edited by James M. Phillips and Robert T. Coote.
p.   cm.
Includes bibliographical references.
ISBN 0-8028-0638-4
1. Missions — Theory. 2. Missions — History — 20th century.
I. Anderson, Gerald H. II. Phillips, James M., 1929-
III. Coote, Robert T., 1932-
BV2063.T688 1993
266'.001 — dc20   92-39052
CIP

Contents

III. FOUNDATIONAL DISCIPLINES OF MISSION

Foreword

The purpose of this book is to give a comprehensive survey of the status of Christian mission among its many families, in all parts of the world, relating it to its basic disciplines, and with regard to the special challenges it faces. The writers deal with their diverse topics as they have developed to this point, but always with an eye to the new century that is about to dawn upon us.

We have sought to meet the needs of several groups of readers who are concerned with the present and future of Christian world mission: students in college and seminary; mission planners and mission board administrators; pastors, church members, and people of all sorts who want to become better informed on mission. Our aim has been not simply to meet academic needs, but above all to present our topics in such a way that the joys and the challenges of Christian mission may be caught by our readers.

The particular period during which this book was compiled saw a number of far-reaching changes in our world, including the collapse of Communist regimes in Eastern Europe and the Soviet Union, with the many repercussions that have followed. We have tried to keep the final text as up to date as possible, but change is an unavoidable element in the world in which we live. The century just ahead of us will bring far more changes with it, but it is worthwhile for Christians to take stock of the legacies with which we enter the new era.

It goes without saying that a book of this size could not cover everything exhaustively. We hope that these essays present incentives for further explorations of the topics dealt with here. To that end, we asked each of the writers to include a list of ten to twenty items "For

Further Reading." Some of them provided much longer lists. Christian mission remains a topic about which there is always more to be said.

We wish to express our deep gratitude to the writers of these pieces for the time and vision they have given to this book. Thanks are also due to the William B. Eerdmans Publishing Company for their advice and encouragement. We hope that this volume will be a fitting tribute to Dr. Gerald H. Anderson, director of the Overseas Ministries Study Center, for his many contributions to Christian mission. In the words of the hymn written by Dr. William Howard Doane, in whose honor the Overseas Ministries Study Center was founded, "To God be the Glory!"

JAMES M. PHILLIPS AND ROBERT T. COOTE
Overseas Ministries Study Center
New Haven, Connecticut

Preface

Lesslie Newbigin

As we look forward into the next century of the Christian world mission, it is good to pause long enough to look back. In the closing decade of the nineteenth century, a great movement of spiritual renewal was sweeping through the universities of Europe and North America, giving birth to a passionate conviction that the world could — and therefore should — be evangelized "in this generation." Of course, these ardent young men and women were not so foolish as to dream of the conversion of all the human race in one generation. But they did believe that the time had come when it would be possible to bring the name of Jesus Christ into the consciousness of every nation. Thousands of them signed the famous declaration "It is my purpose, if God permit, to be a foreign missionary" and went forth into the farthest corners of the world. In due course they inspired and led the World Missionary Conference of 1910 with its detailed planning for the fulfillment of this vision.

To an amazing extent, their dream has come true. The Christian church is now, for the first time in history, a truly global fellowship, present — in however humanly weak a form — in every part of the

---

Lesslie Newbigin was for many years a missionary and bishop of the Church of South India in Madras. He is now retired in Birmingham, England, where he taught for several years on the faculty of Selly Oak Colleges. Among his books are *The Other Side of 1984* (1983), *Foolishness to the Greeks: The Gospel and Western Culture* (1986), and *The Gospel in a Pluralist Society* (1989).

1

world, and including in its shared life a vast variety of human cultures, races, and languages. And that is our problem! As Walter Freytag noted at the 1958 Ghana Assembly of the International Missionary Council, Christian mission has experienced a loss of "directness." It is no longer a matter of the simple command to go to the ends of the earth and preach the gospel where it has not been heard. In every nation there are already Christian believers. The church is already there, and its integrity must be honored. The missionary who simply ignores the church and goes ahead to "do his own thing" dishonors it. Perhaps, then, as some have concluded, his or her duty is rather to help the church everywhere fight the battle against evil in all its forms. The missionary calling is thus merged (or dissolved) into the general obligation of all Christians everywhere to fight injustice, challenge evil, and side with the oppressed. "Mission" becomes everything that the church is to do and to be in the world.

If we regret the loss of "directness," we must also remember that the old "directness" had a great deal to do with the colonial expansion of the European powers. Some of the confidence of the missionary movement, and some of the power of its thrust, derived from the confidence that "civilization" was a blessing in which all the world should share. The three-volume work of James S. Dennis, *Christian Missions and Social Progress,* was a massive documentation of the role of missions in bringing to the rest of the world what Europeans in the first decade of this century understood to be "progress." This was accomplished through a vast network of schools, colleges, hospitals, agricultural programs, and technical training. Missions were, in fact, among the main bearers of "civilization" so understood.

In this respect nineteenth-century missions were very different from the model found in the New Testament or in the first thousand years of the expansion of Christendom. St. Paul did not offer to provide schools and hospitals for the citizens of Rome. When came the difference? It came, of course, in the eighteenth century from that profound conversion experience called — by those who lived through it — "enlightenment." It was the Enlightenment that launched Europe into its program of worldwide conquest.

At the heart of the Enlightenment was the conviction that the true explanation of all things was now, in principle, accessible through the use of human reason and that the conscience was set free from the shackles of tradition and superstition. Human reason, it was believed, is fundamentally the same everywhere, and if liberated, it can ensure the advancement of the whole human race as one "family of man." The prime means of achieving this was to be education, the program by which young people were removed from their families, where old traditions dominate, and placed for their formative years in schools where the new science and the new understanding of history would be taught. The school was to be the great agent of enlightenment, and it is a token of the degree to which missionaries accepted the ideas of the time that they gave schools such an important place in their work. For William Carey the teaching of science in the new college at Serampore was an integral part of his work as a Christian missionary. The pioneer Scottish missionaries in the area of South India where I worked opened schools in many places, even where there was no Christian teacher, in the belief that schools — provided the Bible was part of the curriculum — were missionary agencies. And, as is well known, the products of these schools and colleges have provided most of the leadership for the process of decolonization. A very large proportion of those who have led the nations of the Third World to national independence have been graduates of Christian schools.

But the Enlightenment provoked a reaction in Europe that was to have worldwide consequences. Tradition, which Enlightenment thinkers had seen as the oppressive power from which human reason was to be liberated, reentered the battle under the name of "national culture." The Romantic movement, in reaction to the "Age of Reason," affirmed the supreme value of the spirit of a people as it is embodied in its traditional culture. Insofar as the universal claims of reason effectively dissolved traditional cultures in what Lippmann called "the acids of modernity," these cultures were stimulated into a powerful reassertion of their validity. This happened in Europe in the nineteenth century, and it has happened in former colonies in the twentieth. This has placed Christians in these countries in a difficult position, caught between the universal claims of a Christianity that has been deeply involved in a syncretistic alliance with Enlightenment beliefs, and the particular claims of the national traditions they have inherited, claims that have been powerfully reawakened by the colonial experience.

At the end of the twentieth century, the concept of Christian civilization as something owed to the whole world is no longer viable. Europe, at least, has lost the confidence that inspired the Edinburgh gathering of 1910. After two devastating wars and the division of Europe for seventy years into two ideological camps, there is no longer the confidence that the civilization developed in Europe is for the whole world. The opening up of travel and communication has brought both the peoples and the ideas of Latin America, Asia, and Africa into the consciousness of Western Christians. We no longer use the kind of language that was natural for Christians in 1910. We feel a proper sense of guilt about the wrongs done in the name of our "Christian" civilization, and we are impressed by what other cultures have to teach us.

Yet we continue without embarrassment to export our science and technology, and the rest of the world not only receives it eagerly but surpasses us in its development. The modernization that so many nations seek is, of course, the adoption of the culture developed in Europe and its cultural offshoots since the Enlightenment. The irony of the situation is captured in the advice tendered recently to the French government by the savants of the Collège de France. They laid down as the first principle that must govern education: "The unity of science and the plurality of cultures." Human understanding of the reality with which all human beings have to deal is thus split into two separate domains: a world in which universal truths of reason prevail, and a world in which they do not. "Culture" becomes separated from human understanding as a whole, exempt from universal norms. Of culture one does not say "true or false," or "right or wrong," but only "This is our culture." And religion is widely seen as part of culture.

The experience of European churches suggests that the synthesis between Christianity and the Enlightenment, which was inherent in much of the missionary thrust of the last century, is not sustainable forever. If religion is relegated to a sphere where the question "True or false?" does not arise; if, in other words, religion is seen only as a solace and spur for the individual soul, and therefore a matter of purely personal choice; if universal norms of truth and right do not operate in the sphere of religion; then the disenchantment of which Weber spoke will ultimately eat into the fabric of Third World Christianity as it has done in the older churches. Missionary expansion is currently taking place mainly in areas where the old religious attitude toward life is still strong and where the Christian churches still share much of this attitude. But it seems probable that the same process of disenchantment will be repeated as the churches of the Third World become more fully involved in and committed to the process of modernization.

The Enlightenment was, among other things, a vision for the unity of the human race. It has bequeathed to us a world that is, in one sense, more unified than could have been conceived two hundred years ago. Every part of the world is in contact with every other. No part of the human race can now live in seclusion from the rest. But we do not have to study the behavior of rats in a cage to know that crowding people

4

together does not create unity. What it does create, however, is a situation in which unity is a matter of life or death.

The gospel of Jesus Christ is an invitation to human unity on another basis. "I, when I am lifted up from the earth, will draw all people to myself," says the one who is the creative Word incarnate. The Christian church exists to be the sign and foretaste of that unity. The Enlightenment, with its roots deep in the thought of the later Middle Ages, was a development within the Christian society that brought much good to the world but that also became a source of falsehood and disaster. It placed the autonomous human reason and conscience where God alone belongs. I have suggested that it was an explosive mixture of Christian faith and Enlightenment ideals that fueled the amazing expansion of the church in the past two centuries. The result is a world-wide community of Christians, a multicultural community in which the Christian faith is expressed and lived out in many different styles, but a community everywhere caught in a triangular pattern of tensions. There is the pull of the traditional culture with its normally powerful religious components; there is the pull of modernization that always means involvement with the science, technology, and political ideas that the Enlightenment let loose in the world; and there is the call to faithful discipleship of Jesus Christ.

If we are thinking of world mission in the twenty-first century, this is where we start. Mission, wherever it is, must be seen to be the invitation to join, in the adventure of discipleship, the One who has promised to draw us all together. Nothing else will measure up to the realities of our global neighborhood. I take this to mean in practice that missions must be multidirectional and that we must work rapidly toward a situation where it is as normal for a missionary to travel from Asia to Europe or from Africa to North America as for missionaries to travel the other way. But I do not think that this by itself will measure up to the real need. What is needed is a serious attempt to disentangle the alliance between Christian faith and Enlightenment ideas that has existed for so long, so that the word of the gospel can be heard distinctly in its own right and not as part of the worldview into which it has been so generally domesticated. This is a long-term enterprise. It will require the sustained intellectual effort of Christian thinkers in every culture where Christianity has taken root. Certainly it must enlist the effort of Western churches for whom this long alliance has been part of normal experience.

There is, I think, a danger at the present time of a kind of unjustified euphoria in the nations of the West. For a long time it has been said that the great challenge to Christian civilization came from the ideology of Marxism and its embodiment in the Soviet empire and its satellites. This was always an illusion. But now, in the wake of the collapse of faith in that ideology, some think that those who call themselves "the free world" have won the victory. Freedom was the great gift of the Enlightenment, and we must be thankful for the liberations of thought and of conscience that were won against the resistance of the church. But the deep spiritual problems of the free world, above all in the inner cities where human beings are most tightly packed together, demonstrate that freedom as an absolute is empty. Freedom is only real as the freedom to exercise choice among realities, where every choice made precludes a range of other possibilities. The one who does not choose that reality from whom our freedom comes is made the slave of illusion. Our contemporary modern culture massively demonstrates that fact. The old heartland of the Western missionary movement is now among the mission fields in which the faithful communication of the gospel is most urgently needed, and the task is made very difficult by the long confusion between two different concepts of freedom.

This task calls for the best intellectual efforts that can be mobilized for its discharge. Missiology is increasingly accepted as a legitimate area of study. Unfortunately academia has imposed its own rules, and these studies tend toward the historical and descriptive. They deal with what missions have been and are. Normative missiology, that is to say a kind of study that is directed under the Word of God to seeking what mission ought to be in the coming century, raises questions with which the academy is uncomfortable precisely because they threaten to undermine the foundations on which the modern academy stands. It is not the least of the good gifts which Gerald H. Anderson has given to the churches that he has tirelessly sought to enlist the intellectual and spiritual energies of Christians from many traditions in the development of a normative missiology. It is a privilege to be able to join with the contributors to this volume in his honor. May God continue to prosper his ministry.

I. Christian Families in Mission

Evangelical Missions

Arthur F. Glasser

It has been commonplace to claim that the twentieth century dawned
in 1914, the year in which World War I broke out. Ever since the
downfall of Napoleon in 1815, the West's industrial growth and colonial
expansion, broken only by minor wars, poured a spirit of optimism into
the churches and into their plans for missionary expansion. When their
leaders gathered in Edinburgh in the summer of 1910 for a World
Missionary Conference, no speaker gave the slightest intimation that a
most ruinous war would soon break out in Europe and that it would
engulf the world. I have often wondered how radically reshaped the
missionary movement would have been had its leaders realized in 1910
that within a short time millions of people would be destroyed, the
morale and economies of many nations shattered, and the seeds of
nationalism sown throughout the colonial world.

Now, eighty years later, the missionary movement stands on the
threshold of what promises to be an even more significant period in
world history. During World War I the lure of a secular revelation
brought social and political revolution to war-weary Russia. In no time
at all Marxist-Leninism was being ardently embraced by the disenchanted, and churches worldwide found themselves challenged by a
savage adversary whose zealots were determined to change the world

---

Arthur F. Glasser is Dean Emeritus, School of World Mission, Fuller Theological Seminary, Pasadena, California. He was a missionary to China (1946-
51) with the China Inland Mission, and later was home director for Overseas Missionary Fellowship in the United States.

and capture the allegiance of all peoples. Crisis followed crisis, but their zeal for social revolution remained undiminished, stimulated by the West's economic collapse (1929-34), by Japan's occupation of Manchuria (1931), Italy's invasion of Ethiopia (1935), the Spanish Civil War (1936-39), Japan's invasion of China (1937), and particularly by World War II (1939-45). Following the collapse of Germany's Third Reich, the military power of the Soviet Union and Eastern Europe became steadily more formidable and kindled revolutionary movements in Latin America, China, parts of Africa, and southeast Asia.

But just as the world reached the threshold of the 1990s, this élan suddenly began to evaporate. Mounting economic problems and social unrest diminished Soviet power at home, her dominance over Eastern Europe, and her ability to export social revolution. Marxist-Leninist ideology was increasingly scorned, and its "command economy" was repudiated as totally unworkable. These economic and political crises awakened long-oppressed peoples within the former USSR and among the nations of Eastern Europe. Has there ever been a period to equal November-December 1989, when country after country rejected its communist leaders, pressed them to humiliating confessions of failure, and began the radical overhaul of their economies? An unprecedented spiritual vacuum became evident among peoples long indoctrinated in militant atheism.

This is the background against which we examine evangelicals and their mission prospects in the twenty-first century. Will evangelicals manage to shift gears and devise new approaches to their understanding of the world and of Christian mission? True loyalty to the great essentials of "the faith which was once for all delivered to the saints" (Jude 3) requires a "translation" of that faith into the particular type of missionary obedience demanded by the tumultuous days through which the world is passing. It is my deepest belief that evangelicals will play a prominent role in the worldwide missionary enterprise of the twenty-first century, but the pitfalls ahead are many.

Who Are the Evangelicals?

In discussing evangelicals we confront a classification of Christians that defies precise definition. They do not represent a particular institution but rather an amorphous movement that all agree exists in practically every tradition within the worldwide Christian church. In terms of numbers, evangelical mission agencies are formidable and growing, their missionary personnel significantly outnumbering the personnel deployed by conciliar agencies. Many evangelical missionaries are actually members of denominations related to the World Council of Churches (WCC) but have found it more congenial to serve in agencies independent of denominational control. Other large numbers serve in the agencies that have grown out of the life of evangelical denominations. Still others serve in interdenominational and independent agencies.

Years ago Max Warren, leader of the Church Missionary Society, came closest to an adequate definition when he said that evangelicalism consisted of "a particular balance" of the following cluster of theological postulates: (1) unquestioned submission to the trustworthiness and authority of Scripture as the Word of God; (2) the essentialness of the atonement of Christ if anyone is to be made fit for the presence and fellowship of God; (3) an existential saving encounter with the Holy Spirit; and (4) a concern for the proper scriptural use of the sacraments. Most evangelicals would add the obligation to evangelize non-Christians throughout the world.

The intensity with which evangelicals adhere to these theological postulates should not be underestimated. They are not negotiable. As a result one can confidently predict that in the decades ahead there will be no erosion of commitment from an unqualified acceptance of Chalcedonian Christology: the mystery of the incarnation of the preexistent Son of God. Evangelicals are trinitarians through and through. Jesus of Nazareth is both *vere Deus* and *vere Homo*. The confidence evangelicals have in Scripture binds them unalterably to Jesus' claims concerning himself and to the early church's confession of him before the world.

On other levels, however, evangelicalism is exceedingly complex. Robert Webber identifies at least fourteen major evangelical subcultures (1978:32). I will attempt a classification of only five, reflecting particularly the evangelical community in the United States, though the pattern is widely echoed in other parts of the globe.

First, the separatist fundamentalists who are still in the trenches of the fundamentalist-liberal struggles of the 1920s and 1930s, with their hostility currently focused on the WCC and on those evangelicals who fail to march to the beat of their drum. They are also anti-charismatic. Their negativism keeps them from growing significantly.

Second, the low-key dispensational evangelicals who fight shy of ecumenical encounter find charismatics a problem, but fill the ranks of both the independent "faith" missions and those of some smaller evangelical denominations.

11

Third, the charismatic evangelicals, who range from traditional Pentecostals to the newer mainline church charismatics. Not a few tensions exist among them. For their part, the newer mainline charismatics are burdened to bring renewal to all churches, whether within or outside the WCC, and to the Catholic Church. In contrast, Pentecostals tend to feel that these charismatics have not gone all the way in their pursuit of life in the Spirit. Generally speaking, both Pentecostals and charismatics outdistance all other evangelicals in growth and vitality.

Fourth, the ecumenical evangelicals. They are cautiously open to the positive values of critical scholarship and feel obligated to pursue ecumenical relations. Because of their desire to obey Scripture, they promote renewal and express the oneness of "the One, Holy, Catholic and Apostolic Church." They are also concerned to stimulate the social responsibility of all evangelicals. Their numbers are steadily growing, although they are often attacked by the more conservative members of the other evangelical subgroups.

Finally, there are nonconciliar, traditionally orthodox communions. Their historic roots are so highly cherished that the dominant thrust of their concern is to preserve these values, whether Reformed or Lutheran, Mennonite or Plymouth Brethren. They tend to be ingrown, having largely lost the concern for the renewal of the larger church that originally brought them to birth. Their growth patterns tend to be static.

A somewhat more theologically oriented classification will be found in *The Future of Evangelical Christianity*, by the noted theologian Donald G. Bloesch (1988). Bloesch's sixfold classification ranges from Fundamentalism to Neo-Evangelicalism (ex-fundamentalists) to Confessional Evangelicalism (within creedal Protestantism) to Charismatic Religion (within and outside the WCC) to Neo-Orthodoxy (Barthianism) to Catholic Evangelicalism (distinctly charismatic).

Organizational Associations

When we attempt to evaluate the worldwide missionary outreach of evangelicals, it soon becomes apparent that attention first must be given to the associations within which they identify themselves. In 1917, in North America, the Interdenominational Foreign Mission Association (IFMA) was formed to strengthen those who filled the ranks of the "faith missions." IFMA drew evangelicals who were independent in spirit, wary of denominational control, and largely noncharismatic and pro-dispensationalist in their understanding of the Bible. Almost one hundred Canadian and American agencies with well over eight thousand missionaries, plus more than three thousand from other countries, currently make up its growing membership.

In 1945 the Evangelical Fellowship of Mission Agencies (EFMA; formerly the Evangelical Foreign Missions Association) was formed to perform a similar service to North American denominational missions affiliated with the National Association of Evangelicals (NAE). Its theological consensus is broader than that of the NAE in that it is open to charismatic expressions of evangelicalism. At present it serves more than nine thousand missionaries drawn from evangelical denominations as well as independent churches and more than three thousand non–North American missionaries. It also is growing in member organizations and in missionaries. Collaboration between IFMA and EFMA, initiated in 1957, augurs well for their future usefulness, although many wonder why these two associations do not merge. Indeed, this demonstrates evangelicalism's great weakness — its toleration of division.

Separatist fundamentalist groups are found in the Fellowship of Missions (FOM), formed in 1972 as a breakaway movement from the Associated Missions, organized in 1948 by the militantly antiliberal International Council of Christian Churches. The goal of FOM is "to further the testimony of separation from all apostasy and perversion of the truth" and to accomplish this by "the formation of Bible-believing missionary or church fellowships, in as many countries as possible." Today FOM serves more than three thousand missionaries working in fifty-two countries and belonging to thirteen societies.

In 1985 the Association of International Mission Services (AIMS) was founded by charismatic leaders "to further world evangelization through a consortium of member churches, mission agencies and training institutions." The sphere of its anticipated service is the "tens of thousands of new churches in North America" that have emerged "during the past thirty years." The estimated number of these churches ranges from seventy thousand to a hundred thousand independent renewal congregations in the United States alone. It is significant that both IFMA and EFMA encouraged the founders of AIMS. More than two hundred agencies have joined this rather dynamic association, which in the aggregate includes thousands of missionaries. At this point AIMS seems to be indifferent to organizational walls, wanting to identify with the whole household of faith and eager to promote the missionary cause as widely as possible, both at home and overseas.

In spite of the impressive services of mission associations such as these, there are some significant evangelical missions that have remained independent. The "Open" Plymouth Brethren are served by a coordinating body called Christian Missions in Many Lands, dating from 1921. This association sees itself as bridging the gap between missionaries on the field (more than 1,200) and hundreds of autonomous Plymouth Brethren congregations in Canada and the United States.

The Lutheran Church Missouri Synod operates in a similar fashion. Its Board for Mission Services, organized in 1893, serves 310 missionaries working in nineteen countries.

The Southern Baptist Convention has also pursued the pattern of avoiding all formal association, even with other Baptist denominations. Even so, in recent years Southern Baptists have been consistently active in what can only be described as an informal pattern of ecumenical activities, including almost all of the many diverse segments within the worldwide Christian movement. At present almost 3,900 missionaries serve in 113 countries around the world.

Wycliffe Bible Translators International was formed in 1942 along with its sister organization, the Summer Institute of Linguistics (WBT/SIL). There is no segment of the worldwide church with which WBT/SIL does not cooperate to achieve its goal of making the Bible available to all peoples in their separate languages. At present it has almost six thousand members working in more than fifty-five countries; half of its personnel are citizens of countries other than the United States and Canada.

Another sizable independent group with a high level of non–North American members is Youth With a Mission (YWAM). This is a worldwide organization that has deliberately sought to avoid the image of an American-centered operation. The leader of its work in Asia is a Tongan, in Southern California a New Zealander, in the midlands of England a Zimbabwean, in Tongo a Swiss, in the Ivory Coast a citizen of Burkino Faso. Its full-time staff worldwide is approaching the seven thousand mark.

Finally, mention should be made of Campus Crusade for Christ International. In 1989 it reported "16,000 staff members and volunteers of most nationalities." They serve "in virtually every major country," with nearly four thousand working in the United States. All must be actively engaged in the life and worship of a church in the locale where they serve. Evangelism and discipleship training are the main components of the forty major sub-ministries in which Campus Crusade is involved.

The departure from the older pattern of monocultural mission agencies is a growing phenomenon. Indeed, one can confidently state that those organizations reluctant to become both multiracial and multinational in membership will fade in the days ahead. This follows because today's most dynamic missions are increasingly finding themselves interacting with and hence identifying with the varied mission movements currently emerging in the Two-Thirds World. Already more than a thousand such agencies exist, sponsoring more than thirty-five thousand Third World missionaries around the globe (Pate 1989).

The World Evangelical Fellowship and the Lausanne Movement

Fortunately, the World Evangelical Fellowship and what is known as the Lausanne movement have led the way in bringing about East-West, North-South collaboration among evangelicals on a worldwide scale.

The World Evangelical Fellowship, with roots going back to the middle of the nineteenth century in England, was formed in 1951 at an international gathering in Woudschoten, Netherlands, with representatives present from twenty-one countries. Forty years later, the WEF claims more than sixty national evangelical alliances, the great majority of which are in the Third World. WEF member alliances take a cautious stance toward other Christian communities, often being adamantly separatist in relation to the Roman Catholic Church, the World Council of Churches, the Orthodox churches, and the charismatic movement.

The Lausanne movement came into existence as a result of the vision and support of the most respected evangelist in our day, Billy Graham. Graham put the considerable resources of his organization behind a succession of world congresses on evangelism, the first being held in Berlin in 1966. Sponsored jointly with *Christianity Today* magazine, its rubric was "One Race, One Gospel, One Task." More than 1,200 attended from almost a hundred countries. In his opening address Graham stated: "Within the conciliar movement deep theological differences make it almost impossible to form a definition of evangelism and to give authoritative biblical guidelines to the church. This is one of the purposes of this congress — to help the church to come to grips with this issue, and to come to a clear understanding of the evangelistic and missionary responsibilities of the church for the remainder of this

15

century" (1967:24). Regional conferences followed in Singapore (1968), Minneapolis (1969), and Amsterdam (1971).

But more was needed. Graham saw the need for a "working congress" that would deal specifically with nothing less than world evangelization under the rubric: "Let the Earth Hear His Voice." In July 1974 almost four thousand gathered in Lausanne, Switzerland, from more than 150 nations, representing (though not officially) more than 135 denominations. In his opening address Graham sounded the keynote: "We are enthusiastic about all the many things churches properly do, from worship to social concern" (1975:27). But he then went on to express his conviction that since "evangelism and the salvation of souls is the vital mission of the Church, the whole Church must be mobilized to bring the whole gospel to the whole world" (31).

This congress proved to be the much-needed catalyst evangelicals of all sorts had been praying for, following their rapid growth after World War II. They heard that they should not "drive a wedge" (René Padilla) between evangelistic outreach and the discharge of social responsibilities. They were challenged to be done with triumphalism, cultural imperialism, and missionary paternalism. Lausanne's call was to biblical evangelism, radical discipleship, social involvement, sacrificial living, genuine partnership, and venturesome faith. The two lasting achievements of Lausanne were the drafting of a covenant that gave biblical support to the central truths to which evangelicals are committed and the launching of an ongoing organization, the Lausanne Committee for World Evangelization (LCWE). The Lausanne Covenant has proved to be a remarkable, unifying statement. It has given evangelicals a worldwide sense of their identity within the framework of historic, biblical Christianity. Since LCWE welcomed all evangelicals, the Committee has been open to the strong influence of Christians both within and without the historic churches identified with the WCC. During the period 1974-1988 the LCWE sponsored fifty-four separate conferences and eleven national congresses, and initiated more than twenty-five networks focused on the evangelization of specific people groups. Even so, LCWE leaders became convinced that much unfinished business remained.

As a result, in July 1989 Lausanne II was convened in Manila under the rubric: "Proclaim Christ Until He Comes: A Call to the Whole Church to Take the Whole Gospel to the Whole World." This gathering of some 4,500 participants, staff, and observers, from 168 countries, was remarkable in many ways. It sought to respond to its pre-congress mandate: "to assess our world . . . evaluate our progress . . . face key

16

theological issues . . . coordinate worldwide strategies . . . unite in worship of the Lord Jesus . . . recognize the role of women and lay people . . . cooperate and eliminate duplicated efforts . . . encourage and energize the whole church."

The Manifesto produced at Manila reflected the impact of strong representation from the Two-Thirds World (40%). Furthermore, traditional evangelicals were eclipsed by the evangelical charismatics. Of the four hundred workshops offered, the top ten (rated by attendance) were all related to the Holy Spirit, to spiritual warfare, to prayer. When it was proclaimed that by the year 2000 at least fifty percent of the world's population would be urban — and poor — this also captured popular imagination and shaped the document. Such crucial issues as the work of Christ as the only basis of salvation; the necessity of unity in Christ if our witness to the gospel is to have credibility; social responsibility, including responsibility for the physical environment; the AIDS epidemic; youth ministry; and women's concerns were included.

When it came to the WCC, the Manifesto was quite explicit: "All of us urge the World Council of Churches to adopt a consistent biblical understanding of evangelism." Behind this concern is the awareness that the central theological issue of the 1990s is the person of Jesus Christ. In May 1989, in San Antonio, Texas, the WCC's Commission on World Mission and Evangelism convened its twelfth in a series of ecumenical global mission conferences (the first was at Edinburgh in 1910). The theme was "Your Will Be Done: Mission in Christ's Way." Among the more than five hundred participants from almost a hundred countries were 152 evangelicals who signed a letter calling the Lausanne Movement to "share ways in which many have come to faith in Jesus Christ from other religious traditions, and how the Gospel has been shared with integrity with those of other faiths." The reply that came out of Manila noted that Lausanne II had devoted attention to some of the themes discussed at San Antonio: good news for the poor; the social responsibility of Christians; the gospel and culture; and the call to a simple life style. Then Lausanne went on to appeal to WCC leaders to explore at the forthcoming Seventh WCC General Assembly (Canberra, 1991) the christological stance of the 1982 document "Mission and Evangelism — An Ecumenical Affirmation." Most pointed was its exhortation that the WCC give due regard to the uniqueness of the salvation solely provided in Jesus Christ.

Evangelical leaders wish to take at face value two significant WCC documents: the aforementioned "Mission and Evangelism," and the "Stuttgart Statement on Evangelism" (1987). Yet sections of the conciliar

17

movement continue to project views that challenge the basic postulates of these documents. A case in point is the WCC sub-unit, Dialogue with People of Living Faiths. The publications of this unit fail to take seriously the christological basis of the WCC, that Jesus Christ is "God and Savior according to the Scriptures." Furthermore, in essence they deny Christ's expressed command that disciples be made of all peoples through the proclamation of his gospel.

To be specific, one need only call attention to the erosion that has taken place in conciliar churches over whether the Jewish people should be evangelized. In 1927 the International Missionary Council made the following affirmation:

> Our message to the Jews is the love of God revealed in Jesus Christ; crucified, risen, glorified, the fulfillment of the Law and the true Messiah. He is the incarnate Word, the Redeemer of the world, the Savior from sin, who is bringing Israel to her destiny — viz., to become a blessing to all humanity. (1988:125)

At the founding Assembly (1948) of the World Council of Churches, this position was reaffirmed: "We have . . . in humble conviction to proclaim to the Jews 'The Messiah for Whom you wait has come.' The promise has been fulfilled by the coming of Jesus Christ" (1988:129). The tragedy is that over the years this commitment has become so eroded that by 1988 WCC leaders could state: "The next step may be to proscribe all proselytism of Jews on the theological ground that it is a rejection of Israel's valid covenant with God" (186).

In contrast, when evangelicals encounter the synagogue, they recognize that the church is being tested as to whether or not she is truly the church of Jesus Christ. At Lausanne II the following statement was incorporated into the Manifesto:

> It is sometimes held that in virtue of God's covenant with Abraham, Jewish people do not need to acknowledge Jesus as their Messiah. We affirm that they need him as much as anyone else, that it would be a form of anti-Semitism, as well as being disloyal to Christ, to depart from the New Testament pattern of taking the gospel to the Jew first . . ." We therefore reject the thesis that Jews have their own covenant which renders faith in Jesus unnecessary.

Evangelicals grant that an abiding covenant exists between God and Israel (Rom. 11). However, they are quick to add that this fact did not lessen in the slightest the Apostle Paul's prayers and evangelistic efforts to lead Jewish people into a saving relationship with the Lord Jesus Christ (Rom. 10, etc.). Apart from the WCC's getting its house in order on this issue, I see little possibility of the Lausanne Committee for World Evangelization responding positively to the friendly overtures emanating from the WCC headquarters in Geneva. And as long as salvific potential is granted to other religious systems, apart from Jesus Christ, this gulf will steadily deepen and widen.

Tragically, from the standpoint of concerned evangelicals, the Seventh WCC General Assembly (Canberra, 1991) not only ignored the question of Christology, but further diffused its theological stance by permitting dubious — even reckless — overtures to its member churches to see the spiritual powers of traditional religions as expressions of God's own Spirit. As a result, one can fully expect further disengagement of evangelicals from the WCC. *yes.*

A.D. 2000 and Beyond

Many evangelicals have become fascinated with the year A.D. 2000. Entrepreneurs are multiplying all sorts of plans to make possible a "last big push" to evangelize the world. Over fifty such plans are multimillion-dollar programs of awesome dimensions. Yet when one realizes that a third of the countries of the world are closed to expatriate evangelistic activity, that vast sums of money will be needed to carry out these plans, and that few of the plans are in touch with one another, questions arise.

Even so, one should neither downplay nor underestimate the desire of evangelicals to obey their Lord's last command. Behind the A.D. 2000 hype serious thought is being given to the reevangelization of Western Europe. Furthermore, many are taking note of the unprecedented spiritual vacuum that has suddenly beckoned to evangelical activism in Eastern Europe. I have been impressed with the creativity of new approaches in reaching Muslims. And never before has the desire to prevail through prayer in achieving these goals been so widespread in evangelical circles. Then too, missionaries from the Two-Thirds World will increasingly occupy center stage. Indeed, the internationalization of the missionary movement is "the great new fact of our time." Under the Spirit's sovereignty, evangelicals show every evidence of growing in numbers and maturity and being major partners in tomorrow's missionary obedience.

For Further Reading

Bloesch, Donald G.
1983   *The Future of Evangelical Christianity: A Call for Unity Amid Diversity.* Garden City, NY: Doubleday and Company, Incorporated.

Graham, Billy
1967   "Why the Berlin Congress?" In *One Race, One Gospel, One Task,* Vol. I, World Congress on Evangelism, Berlin, 1966. Official Reference Volumes: Papers and Reports. Edited by Carl F. H. Henry and W. Stanley Mooneyham. Minneapolis: World Wide Publications, pp. 22-34.

1975   "Why Lausanne?" In *Let the Earth Hear His Voice,* International Congress on World Evangelization, Lausanne, Switzerland. Official Reference Volume: Papers and Responses. Edited by J. D. Douglas. Minneapolis: World Wide Publications, pp. 22-36.

Pate, Larry D.
1989   *From Every People: A Handbook of Two-Thirds World Missions.* Monrovia, CA: MARC Publications.

Webber, Robert E.
1978   *Common Roots: A Call to Evangelical Maturity.* Grand Rapids, MI: The Zondervan Corporation.

World Council of Churches
1988   *The Theology of the Churches and the Jewish People.* Statements by the World Council of Church and its member churches. Commentary by Allan Brockway, Paul van Buren, Rolf Rendtorff, and Simon Schoon. Geneva: World Council of Churches.

Conciliar Missions

Eugene L. Stockwell

"Conciliar missions" has a strange ring in the ears of those involved in the life and work of councils of churches, for though such councils are very much concerned with Christian mission in its widest meaning, they seldom speak of "missions" in the plural form.

Councils of churches are not churches, though some would argue that they have an "ecclesiastical character." Councils, as we know them in today's ecumenical world, do not generally send out "missionaries" as many churches do. They do in some instances engage and send out persons with special skills, for example, technicians or development workers. But only seldom do councils employ evangelists, it being assumed that the churches themselves will do that. Nor do councils generally describe their activities as "missions." Symbolic of this is the change in the name of the World Council of Churches' journal, which until the mid-1960s was called the *International Review of Missions*, but (in the face of distinguished opposition, notably from Bishop Lesslie Newbigin) became the *International Review of Mission*, dropping the last *s*.

If for the purpose of this chapter, however, we understand "conciliar missions" to include the mission activities of churches that are members of the councils, then the panorama is vast, and it is quite

---

Eugene L. Stockwell was for ten years a Methodist missionary in Uruguay, followed by twenty-seven years of work in denominational and ecumenical organizations, most recently as Director of the World Council of Churches' Commission on World Mission and Evangelism from 1984 to 1989. He currently is living in Buenos Aires, where he serves as Rector of the Evangelical Higher Institute of Theological Studies (ISEDET).

proper to speak of "missions" as specific tasks, activities, or projects of the churches, carried on under an overall concept of ecumenical Christian mission. The variety of such missions is so great, both among different churches and within any one church, that it is dangerous to indulge in broad generalizations. It is even riskier to try to peer into the future and suggest lines of development that may appear in the twenty-first century.

Here we shall hazard a look at the future from two perspectives: (1) conciliar ecumenical understandings of mission, particularly as expressed by the WCC, and (2) one promising trend in mission activities of churches that define themselves as "ecumenical" which may portend future directions. From the outset it must be recognized that what "is" today is a shaky basis from which to prophesy what "may be" in the future, given the many surprises and unexpected turns of events that continually plunge into our history. Nevertheless, a Christian can look forward to the future with great hope, for even if we do not know what the future holds, our faith does tell us who holds the future.

Ecumenical Understandings of Mission

The most succinct understanding of Christian mission, from an ecumenical perspective, is "Mission and Evangelism — An Ecumenical Affirmation," a statement that was approved by the Central Committee of the World Council of Churches in July 1982. This affirmation, though far from perfect, has received wide appreciation and support from a broad spectrum of Christian leaders: evangelical, "mainline" Protestant, Anglican, Orthodox, and Roman Catholic. The heart of the document sets out seven "ecumenical convictions" focused on these themes:

1. Conversion.
2. The Gospel to All Realms of Life.
3. The Church and Its Unity in God's Mission.
4. Mission in Christ's Way.
5. Good News to the Poor.
6. Mission in and to Six Continents.
7. Witness among People of Living Faiths.

Though these seven areas by no means exhaust the many aspects and concerns of Christian mission, they do point to some of the central mission emphases of churches within today's ecumenical movement, and they dovetail quite remarkably with some of the trends we shall discuss below. At the risk of omitting some important elements, it seems that these convictions lift up four matters that are of particular concern in contemporary ecumenical thinking about mission, all of which will be of much significance in future conciliar study and activity: unity, the poor, mission to the West, and relations to people of other living faiths.

Unity

Several years before the 1989 San Antonio WCC World Mission and Evangelism Conference, a questionnaire was circulated requesting people across the world to suggest possible overall themes for the conference. Repeatedly a concern was expressed that unity in the Christian family was essential as a basis for more effective Christian mission. The many evidences of disunity in and among Christian churches was seen as a serious drawback to presenting the one Christ to the world. Many of the responses dealt not only with the obvious division among Christian churches, but with the more elusive and profound search for both spiritual and structural unity in the body of Christ. Discussions often centered around Ephesians 1, with the vision of everything in the cosmos coming together in Christ.

Looking toward the future of Christian mission, we do not doubt that the ecumenical and conciliar world will continue to emphasize the necessity of working toward Christian unity. Guided by the WCC's Faith and Order Commission, it will stress *visible* unity, but that does not impede the search for every kind of unity possible within the Christian family. There was a time in the twentieth century when considerable enthusiasm surrounded the idea of actual structural union among churches. The creation of the Church of South India was a striking example of what could occur, and there were other unions similar to it. In the United States there were several unions within confessional families — Methodist, Presbyterian, Lutheran, and others. The Consultation on Church Union process points toward a major union of several denominations in the future, though it is quite uncertain whether or when it might become a reality.

Evangelical groups talk more of spiritual than of structural unity. Ecumenically minded churches talk about visible unity but are somewhat stalled in the area of structural union, though they continue to urge joint activity in councils, joint action groups, and other cooperations.

There appears to be a considerably greater sense of urgency about the need for unity as a basis for Christian mission in the Two-Thirds World than in the North Atlantic world. The scandal of denominational divisiveness is more evident in those parts of the world where the Christian community is a minority within the population. The fact that many of the divisions, perhaps most, have been imported from the West highlights the problem even more. It is to be hoped that in the years to come there will be a growing sense of the need for a more significant and visible unity at every level.

The Poor

In recent years the phrase "preferential option for the poor," attributed to Roman Catholic leaders, has become widely accepted in ecumenical circles. At the 1980 Melbourne WCC World Conference on Mission and Evangelism, a central theme was "Good News to the Poor," and there was widespread recognition that the unevangelized peoples of the world are by and large also the economically poor of the world. The struggle for justice by the poor, and by the whole Christian community in solidarity with the poor, is increasingly seen within the ecumenical world as inseparable from Christian mission at its very heart. Evangelistic efforts that are not predicated on a genuine identification with the struggle for justice and that fail to take account of biblical prophetic witness and of Jesus' radical identification with the lost, the last, and the least, lack credibility.

As the world moves into the next century, the gap between wealthy and poverty-stricken nations will increasingly highlight the plight of the poor. Instant worldwide communications bring to the attention of all, the realities of discrimination, oppression and poverty. What does this portend for the Christian church? Two relatively new things can be mentioned: (1) If, as seems probable, the plight of the poor is more and more tied to the exploitation of the earth and the ecological devastation of creation, the church will have to link its concern for the well-being of the poor with an attack on all actions, systems, and structures that exploit the earth for private or national gain. Hence, Christian mission will tend to give an ever greater place and importance to what currently is summed up in the phrase "justice, peace and the integrity of creation." (2) An emphasis on the poor may accentuate conflict within the church, especially in the affluent world. One result could be that churches in affluent areas may decrease in membership, though that need not be the case; churches that identify with the poor may well grow in numbers. But faithfulness to God and to God's poor is not usually a prescription for numerical success nor for "church growth" in population terms. The poor with whom the church will identify, already crucified in so many ways, may lead the church to a crucifixion of its own.

Mission to the West

At the 1963 Mexico City WCC World Mission and Evangelism Conference, the whole idea of "mission to six continents" was affirmed, making clear that unidirectional mission efforts from North to South, or from West to East, had to be accompanied by "reverse mission" from former "receiving" areas to the former "sending" areas. Christian mission is multidirectional. In recent years there have been quite a few practical efforts to implement such a concept. There has evolved growing clarity that at the heart of mission to six continents is a "mission to the West." Bishop Lesslie Newbigin has underscored this in a series of writings. In the West (referring mainly to North Atlantic countries) Christian faith is under heavy attack or in frank retreat. Many find no attraction to Christian faith. Social disarray, evidenced particularly by widespread crime and drugs, prevails. Pessimism, instead of hope, characterizes much thought about the future. So, the argument goes, if the Christian church is to be faithful to its Lord at this time in history, it must accept as a major priority the task of converting the West. Whether the churches of the world will take up this challenge remains to be seen, but there are some indications of resolve in this direction.

Churches in the Two-Thirds World understandably have ambivalent feeling about this emphasis. Is the emphasis just one more evidence that the West cares more about itself than about the rest of the world and its peoples? Will this emphasis signify a withdrawal of resources now devoted to support worldwide mission efforts in order to channel them to Western concerns? They fear a renewed Western isolationism. On the other hand, some across the Two-Thirds World recognize that many of their problems in society and in the church are "made in the West," so they welcome any effort by which Western societies and churches endeavor to put their own houses in order on the basis of greater respect for justice, human dignity, and fairness in community relationships.

Predicting how this emphasis on mission to the West will develop in years ahead is very hazardous. Surely the emphasis will not go away in any near future, but its impact on the West itself and on the Two-Thirds World is difficult to foresee. If present trends continue, it is likely that the emphasis will be greater within the "ecumenical" world than in the "evangelical" world, but that could change. What can be affirmed is that the older concept of "mission fields" will no longer exclude the West. Christian faithfulness cannot be limited geographically to one area or another; in every land, those in the West included, the Word must be proclaimed by word and deed, dire needs must be faced, hope must be reignited.

Relations to People of Other Living Faiths

In a shrinking world, where people of many different nations and faiths come into closer touch with each other, persons and churches involved in Christian mission are faced, ever more urgently, with the question of how they should relate to adherents of other great religious communities. Is the Christian imperative solely to do everything possible to convert persons of other faiths to the Christian faith? Is sensitive and kindly discussion the proper stance, still hoping for conversion to result? Is dialogue with no ulterior motive save to engage in a mutual sharing of faith the best way, leaving it to God's Holy Spirit to act in the midst of the dialogue as the Spirit so wills?

Currently this topic is a very controversial one within the Christian community. The ecumenical community leans to the dialogue position, not without much internal debate, but without desiring for a moment to sacrifice its conviction that Jesus is Lord of all, and that Christian mission is an imperative for the church that cannot be watered down or forgotten. Thus, dialogue is seen as part and parcel of Christian mission; all mission efforts, whether among persons of other faiths or not, should be dialogical in nature.

What is surely ahead is a greater search for theoretical understandings, based on biblical teachings and theological analyses. For example, is a pluralism of faiths God's intention, or does God intend that everyone on earth should be a Christian, the sooner the better? What is our theology of religion itself, as we try to understand the multiplicity, complexity, and greatness of the religions of the earth? What do we understand by the oft-used phrase "the uniqueness of Christ"? These and many other issues demand much discussion and thought, and within ecumenical circles at least this pursuit of understanding will hopefully take place in discussions that include representatives of other faiths willing to engage in the conversations. At stake here is not merely a search for good relationships, but more profoundly a search for a deeper Christian understanding of the/ nature of our faith, of the meaning of Christian mission, and of the meaning of faithfulness to Jesus Christ.

The ecumenical task of dialogue will not be easy, particularly in areas where fundamentalist adherents of other faiths make life especially difficult for Christians (as indeed Christians historically have sometimes done so for adherents of other religions). One can hope that the destruction or burning of churches, the persecution of new converts to Christianity, the imposition of laws that violate the freedom of religious conscience, and the like, might be a thing of the past. That is not yet the situation in contemporary history, even if such actions are isolated and occasional. Christian faith requires that Christians engaged in direct contact with persons of other faiths be faithful to the best of their own faith, whatever others may do. Love, forgiveness, sensitive understanding, and patience are as essential in the difficult moments of relationship as in situations where such difficulties are absent. One can only hope that future relationships among the major religious communities of the world will develop in a spirit of sincere mutual respect and a genuine search for mutual understanding rather than for victory or gain by one faith over another.

One Promising Trend

In a critical assessment of the WCC San Antonio Conference David J. Bosch of South Africa concluded that the conference "did not succeed in making any significant contribution to missionary thinking, and has, in fact, led to some confusion" (*Missionalia* 17, no. 2 [August 1989]:126). There could well be some argument about that critique, particularly if one realizes that the intention of the conference was not to come up with some new refinement in missiology but rather to press the churches of the world to faithfulness to the missiological imperatives of the gospel already well-known. Be that as it may, Bosch concluded his article by indicating that in the conference reports there was one recurrent theme never before so explicit, the idea of community. "Perhaps," he wrote, "the search for community will turn out to be a major missiological theme during the 1990s" (ibid.:137).

This is a most important insight. Could it be that underlying the issues stated above there is a growing sense in the Christian world family that anything of significance it does in mission will depend on the nature of the Christian community itself, a community responsive to God's purposes for the church and for the world at large? Here there surely is a trend. After long years of male domination in the churches (still too prevalent in some churches), a new conviction has evolved that the church is a community of men and women where all, regardless of sex, have an equal and important place. Women themselves, out of their own sense of hurt, have helped the churches toward this new understanding, and with it have come new patterns of relations within and among the churches. The prominence of the poor, or at least concern about the poor, has led many churches into solidarity actions that enlarge their sense of community, and has brought into church forums oppressed people who used to be outside the church community. The Orthodox family, well represented in the WCC structures, has grown in influence and importance not just as another confessional body, but as a tradition with contemporary contributions to make to the Christian community, even though for long ages past other branches of the Christian family have looked upon the Orthodox as strange and separated from the mainstream Christian community. Racial and cultural groups often excluded from many sectors of the community are demanding, and attaining, their rightful places in Christian churches.

Participation in Christian mission today, and surely in the decades ahead, cannot be limited to a self-appointed few who exclude large portions of the human family, no matter how righteous or theologically orthodox they may appear to themselves or to others. As those who participate in decision-making about mission increasingly diversify and come to represent more realistically the panorama of the whole world community, traditional ways of doing mission will have to change. New perspectives will emerge. New insights will abound. New freedoms will be claimed. There are those who see in all this, as I do, the action of God's Holy Spirit, alive and well. In it the hope for Christian mission in the twenty-first century is great indeed. We can expect, with eyes of faith, to be surprised at the new mission community that is growing in the coming ecumenical world family, open to God and open to the world.

For Further Reading

Bevans, Stephen B., and James A. Scherer
    1992   *New Directions in Mission and Evangelization, 1: Basic State-
                ments, 1974-1991.* Maryknoll, NY: Orbis Books.

Bilheimer, Robert S.
    1989   *Breakthrough*. Grand Rapids, MI: Wm. B. Eerdmans Publishing Company.
Castro, Emilio
    1985   *Freedom in Mission: The Perspective of the Kingdom*. Geneva: World Council of Churches.
Commission on World Mission and Evangelism.
    1982   *Mission and Evangelism — An Ecumenical Affirmation*. Geneva: World Council of Churches.
Costas, Orlando E.
    1982   *Christ Outside the Gate*. Maryknoll, NY: Orbis Books.
Cragg, Kenneth
    1987   *The Christ and the Faiths*. Philadelphia: Westminster Press.
Gill, David, ed.
    1983   *Gathered for Life*. Official Report of VI Assembly of World Council of Churches. Geneva: World Council of Churches.
International Review of Mission
    1989   "The San Antonio Conference." *International Review of Mission*, Vol. 78, nos. 311/312.
Newbigin, Lesslie.
    1986   *Foolishness to the Greeks: The Gospel and Western Culture*. Grand Rapids, MI: Wm. B. Eerdmans Publishing Company.
    1987   *Mission in Christ's Way*. Geneva: World Council of Churches.
Scherer, James A.
    1987   *Gospel, Church, and Kingdom: Comparative Studies in World Mission Theology*. Minneapolis: Augsburg Publishing House.

Roman Catholic Missions

Mary Motte, F.M.M.

Introduction

The understanding of mission among Roman Catholics has undergone a major reorientation since the time of the Second Vatican Council (1962-65). While the beginnings of many changes occurred before 1962, the Council was to be an important catalyst for implementing wide-scale change. The shape of these changes has become clear only gradually, and it would seem this process of reorientation will continue on into the twenty-first century.

Following the Council increasing attention has been given to contextual influences, and therefore, a greater appreciation of faith's integration with everyday life. One of the best testimonies of this trend has been the emergence of contextual theologies, the best known being Latin American Liberation Theology (Schreiter 1985). Contextual theological reflection takes life with all its ramifications as the starting point for communicating with God. Present situations, the fiber of history, become an important basis for understanding salvation. Contextualization calls for an attitude of listening as the missionary's first stance upon entering a new place, a listening that tries to learn through the

---

Mary Motte, a Sister of the Franciscan Missionaries of Mary (F.M.M.), is Director of the Mission Resource Center of the F.M.M. in North Providence, Rhode Island. She is a member of the board of the United States Catholic Mission Association and formerly Roman Catholic Consultant to the Commission on World Mission and Evangelism of the World Council of Churches.

lives and actions of the people what God is doing among them. The Council set the direction for this approach by calling attention to the necessity of reading the signs of the times. The Conciliar Document *Gaudium et Spes* states that "the people of God" recognize in faith that the Spirit "fills the whole world," and therefore they try "to discern in the events, the needs, and the longings which [they share] with other people of our time, what may be genuine signs of God's presence or purpose."

There are two areas in the life of the church that in post-conciliar development have particularly affected the understanding of mission among Roman Catholics. These are (1) the relation between Christian faith and other systems of religious belief, and (2) the self-understanding of the church. These are interrelated, but for purposes of analyzing their impact upon the understanding of mission, I will discuss them separately. The way of looking at mission that I will describe has developed largely through the life experience of missionizing women and men, and their collective experience as missionary societies within the Roman Catholic Church. These are mainly religious and priests, but the experience of a growing number of laity is also reflected.

The Relation between Christian Faith and Other Systems of Religious Belief

Prior to the Second Vatican Council, it was commonly held among Roman Catholics that an individual who adhered to another system of religious belief could attain salvation through a desire to pursue truth according to the possibilities available. However, the missionary activity carried out by the Church aimed at penetrating as many situations as possible so that everyone would have access to the truth as revealed in Christ and as witnessed to by the Church (Mueller 1987; Shorter 1972). A by-product of this approach, which flourished in the context of colonialism, was an emphasis on establishing the role of the church through various structures. This direction in missionary activity resulted in a certain de-emphasis on developing an awareness of God as Creator of the universe. One has only to recall the Pauline hymn in Ephesians 1:3-14, or Francis of Assisi's Canticle of Brother Sun, to recognize that there was an earlier tradition that was not so focused on implanting the church and its auxiliary structures.

Missionaries geared toward implanting the church tended to equate salvation with baptism and membership in the church. Such emphasis did not lead to insights about the meaning of religious belief outside the Christian tradition. This is not to suggest that missionaries should not have implanted the church, but simply to note, with the benefit of historical hindsight, that this emphasis led to one way of understanding mission rather than another way. Vatican II introduced a corrective that is still seeking a balance.

When the Roman Catholic Church began to examine itself and its relation to the world of human persons, it did so with the various historical developments of the mid-twentieth century in mind. It therefore recognized the integral relationship between God's self-revelation and historical development in the world. Advances in human sciences helped to shape these theological discoveries. The Council acknowledged the intention of God as revealed historically, namely to save all persons (*Ad Gentes*, #5; *Lumen Gentium*, #11). It further understood that freedom is constitutive of the human person, which accounts for the intimate relation between the God of truth and human conscience seeking truth (*Dignitatis Humanae*, #2, 3). The Decree on Missionary Activity (*Ad Gentes*) clearly states that there are "ways" to reach God outside the Christian community. Since the time of the Council, however, theologians have struggled to interpret the relationship between Christian faith and other faith traditions in the light of the new insights recognized by the Council. This ongoing struggle has been filled with illuminations and difficulties (cf. *Dialogue and Proclamation*, no. 4, c). In general, research in dialogue has improved relationships among followers of the different systems of religious belief and Christians. Moreover, it has opened the way to explore more deeply how these relationships can be lived out and further developed in the context of a world that continually poses new questions. The pivotal question at the heart of any attempt by Christian theologians to describe interreligious dialogue is the person of Christ and his uniqueness in history (Knitter 1985).

Space does not allow an examination of the various theories evolved to date about this matter. I wish, rather, to look at how these new insights, their interpretation, and the continued search for greater clarity have affected the Roman Catholic understanding of mission. In the late sixties there was a loss of missionary impetus among Roman Catholics that coincided with the emphasis that God's salvation extends to all persons. The motif of saving souls from damnation, which had so often accompanied missionary motivation, no longer seemed appropriate. However, once the initial debate and confusion had subsided, the need for Christians to bear witness to the mystery of Christ, even

while respecting the integrity of other beliefs, was reaffirmed by missionaries who lived in the midst of communities of other faith traditions. Catholics, confronted by huge populations belonging to other
faith traditions, as in Asia, discovered the critical importance of an
approach that would provide a starting point for relationships other
than the question of uniqueness, and that would open the way to the
future. This is the "dialogue of life" approach to mission.

Dialogue of life is described as the "daily practice of brotherhood
[sisterhood], helpfulness, openheartedness and hospitality," and joint
commitment to "whatever leads to unity, love, truth, justice and peace"
(Federation of Asian Bishops' Conferences, #49, 1987). This way of
understanding sees dialogue as a lifestyle that entails "living in harmony with people of other faiths, forming an open attitude toward
other religions, sharing religious experiences and working together
with peoples of other faiths." Awareness of the dynamics of societal
components in the interaction of communities inserted in distinct cultural and historical realities, places a new constraint upon relations.
Interpersonal relationships, culture, and history are now more clearly
acknowledged to be components of faith and integrally part of salvation
history. Through its development in concrete situations, the dialogue
of life is leading to a commitment to build human community directed
not so much to the growth of the church as to the coming of the
kingdom. Nevertheless, the church has a clear role in this process, which
is witnessed by the involvement of missionaries in dialogue.

Living out a dialogue of life in Asia and elsewhere has produced
a new set of inquiries into the meaning of mission and dialogue. Here
the pivotal question concerns the meaning of evangelization. There are
those who see dialogue as one reality and evangelization as another,
related but separate in intent, with evangelization being the ultimate
goal in all situations. There are others who stress the interrelation of
dialogue and evangelization, insisting that the effort to engage in dialogue of life is evangelization. It is a way of proclaiming the message
of the gospel (Motte 1987).

Dialogue and Proclamation, a joint document published by the
Pontifical Council for Interreligious Dialogue and the Vatican Congregation for the Evangelization of Peoples (1991) reflects the developments in official understanding of Dialogue and other expressions of
the mission outreach of the Church. This document recognizes the
mystery and complexity of the relationship between the Church, "sign
and instrument of the Divine Plan of salvation," and the Kingdom of
God (cf. no. 33). It situates the Church's relation to those of other faith

traditions in the context of the "mysterious presence of the Kingdom in the sacrament of the Church" (cf. no. 35). Present understandings of this relationship are blurred, however, for as the document indicates, "the Church's transparancy as sacrament of salvation is blurred" (no. 36). Continued exploration is clearly indicated.

> In this dialogue of salvation, Christians and others are called to collaborate with the Spirit of the Risen Lord, who is universally present and active. . . . (no. 40)

There are some clear indications of an understanding of mission that is emerging in actual experience, particularly among those who see dialogue as a way of evangelization, namely, that it is a way of living out the gospel imperative of announcing the kingdom of God. This understanding of mission insists upon quality presence to the other, a presence that in itself proclaims to other persons the primacy of Christ in the missionary's life, the experience of God's love, a commitment to justice, truth, and peace, and the role of human life in the evolution of God's kingdom. The inviolable freedom of the human person to follow the dictates of conscience requires an openness to the mystery of God at work in the other, even though that work of salvation remains a mystery. There is a deepening commitment to contemplation among missionaries engaged in the dialogue of life. And this contemplation is expressed by a standing before the mystery of God's saving presence in human history, concretely manifested in human persons. These missionaries are constantly encountering an aspect of mystery in their efforts to understand how salvation is wrought, and there is a growing willingness among them to give up the need to understand, and to be present to that mystery until God shall uncover it for them.

The final word has not been said about the relationship between Christian faith and other traditions of religious belief. However, it is clear that Vatican II proved to be a watershed in situating this relationship in a new context, namely that of universal salvation. As a result the Church has set out to explore what this relationship implies for its understanding of mission. While theologians continue to inquire into mission and the relationships it implies, missionary congregations have especially followed the directions emerging from the experience of the Church in Asia and have committed themselves to a dialogue of life. This commitment makes possible relationships based on values recognized by all as essential for justice and peace. These same values are basic to the gospel message. This approach begins from pluralism in society. It can be hoped that this experience of building human community will lead to realizations of how God effects salvation for all, as well as to a clearer understanding of the role of the church as sign and sacrament of this salvation within pluralistic communities (Federation of Asian Bishops' Conferences, #49, 1987; FABC Theological Advisory Commission, 1989).

Self-Understanding of the Church

The understanding of the church that emerged from the Council was particularly underscored in two of its decrees: *Lumen Gentium,* which considered the inner life of the church, and *Gaudium et Spes,* which considered the church in its relation to the world. The understanding expressed in these documents imaged the church as a pilgrim people, a community of believers in which the dynamic interaction between gospel and community constituted the reality of its mission. For the Catholic Church, which prior to the Council had a limited understanding of universality, this meant that there was a new focus on the local context. A new understanding of universal also emerged, which was not so much a geographical concept, but one based on theological, ecclesial, and sociological foundations, for example, common faith in Jesus Christ, unity around the Bishop of Rome, and communion among local churches (Arns 1981).

Base Christian Communities emerged in the concrete life of the Church at the local level, first in Latin America, and then in other places with appropriate adaptations. These communities began among the poor in northeastern Brazil. In their initial phase they gave the poor and oppressed, who ordinarily vied with one another for the favor of the rich, the opportunity to discover how to trust each other. The organizational impetus for these communities was focused upon shared reflection on the Word of God and its implications in the context of present history. As people came together around the Word, were converted, and formed community, they were gradually led to an expression of the missionary dynamic, namely moving beyond the community with the message of salvation and transformation (*Evangelii Nuntiandi,* 1975; Libanio 1982).

Another important aspect in the self-understanding of the church for Roman Catholics has been the preferential option for the poor. This option has been part of the tradition from earliest Christian times, but in the late sixties when the Latin American bishops gave fresh expression to this option; it came as a moment of conversion in modern history. The call to hear the cry of the poor emerged from within a new historical consciousness that now grasped the continuity of revelation. The poor are those who stand at the intersection between being and non-being, at the critical junction in creation between life and death. Therefore where one stands in relation to the poor is indicative of one's intention in proclaiming the gospel message.

Following the publication of the document "Justice in the World" from the 1971 Synod of Bishops, with its clear statement regarding the essential relationship between justice and evangelization, missionary and religious congregations took unambiguous stands regarding justice as related to their efforts in evangelization. Further, these choices gradually evolved into stated preferential options for the poor. In the living out of missionary activity this has meant insertion among the poor, expressions of solidarity with the poor, and a walking with the poor and oppressed in their efforts to achieve integral human salvation (Gutiérrez 1983; Motte 1987).

The post–Vatican II understanding of the role of the church in relation to the modern world has led to less separation between expressions of faith and political activity. This growing integration between faith and politics has meant that standing with the poor has been, in and of itself, interpreted as political action. In a number of cases this choice has resulted in imprisonment and/or death.

In all of the above, Roman Catholics do not possess exclusive ownership but experience a shared reality with Christians of other communions, Protestant, Orthodox, and Anglican. And that leads to another aspect of the new self-understanding of the Roman Catholic Church that has emerged from the Second Vatican Council and which has affected its understanding of mission: a commitment to search for Christian unity.

Common Witness, a study document developed by the Joint Working Group of the World Council of Churches and the Roman Catholic Church (1970, revised 1980), points the way to greater collaboration in efforts to proclaim the gospel message in today's world. Here the pivotal question is often that of church membership. However, once again, as in the case of interreligious dialogue, a different starting point is directing the Church toward deeper collaboration. Greater efforts have been made to unite around projects that call out for Christian witness in human suffering as well as in happiness. And in these, prayer for Christian unity and efforts for solidarity with the poor and oppressed are showing ways in which collaboration around a common faith bridges barriers to communication and understanding.

A major factor in Roman Catholic mission history has been the activity of missionary congregations of priests, sisters, and brothers. Up until the time of the Council, there had only been a limited involvement of laity in mission. Vatican II inaugurated a change in direction that has been slowly taking hold. Today a number of laypersons are involved in cross-cultural, overseas mission. These laity are also assuming a greater role in the inner life of the Church, as can be seen in the Base Christian Communities, where they hold responsibility for a variety of ministries. Their participation in shaping the life and mission of the Church is gradually changing the self-understanding of the Church, and moving it toward a more community-based expression.

In summary then, the new self-understanding of the Church is reshaping the understanding of mission through an emerging consensus about localness in the Church, a concept derived directly from the contextualization spoken of at the beginning of this chapter. Further, the Church now has a wider concept of universality, based directly on theological, ecclesial, and sociological expressions of communion, unity, and inclusiveness. The latter is an issue urgently demanding attention, especially in the areas of racism and sexism. Ministerial expressions of mission, and those bearing the responsibility for these, are emerging from within the local church, and, in a special way, from within the community models developed from the Base Christian Communities. The preferential option for the poor determines to a large extent the way missionaries go out to others; the insistence is on insertion, solidarity, and walking with the people. A growing consensus among Orthodox, Protestants, and Roman Catholics about common witness in relation to mission challenges a former exclusiveness that limited the understanding of mission (Commission on World Mission and Evangelism 1983). Finally, the gradual emergence of the laity, with its increasing role in the life and mission of the Church, promises a continued shaping of our missionary understanding.

Conclusion

The understanding of mission as it has developed among Roman Catholics after the Second Vatican Council emerges as a way of interacting with the process of salvation immersed in the history of the world. The incarnation of God's Son in a particular history and society is the model on which missionary activity is based. This understanding of mission underscores a quality presence to the other that recognizes the mystery of God at work in the lives of peoples and societies. It is a way of standing before the other with respect, and of waiting to discover how one is called to interact and further proclaim that which has been seen and heard as part of the missionaries' experience of God's love as revealed in Jesus Christ.

Mission immersed in history has to start with the poor, those who stand in the critical juncture of creation and history, if it is to be credible good news. Relationships built upon truth and justice are the groundwork upon which missionaries build community, which in Christian situations is a primary ecclesial unit, and in religiously plural situations is a primary human unit that brings society toward unity and vision.

While the women and men of religious and missionary congregations continue to contribute to the work of the church's mission, there has been a move toward greater inclusiveness, with the laity increasingly assuming its responsibility. This is a new movement among Roman Catholics, and it is leading to a new way of being the church. This greater inclusiveness has also effected a growing collaboration among Orthodox, Protestant, and Roman Catholics in a genuine search to proclaim together the good news that they share through a common faith in Jesus Christ.

As each of these shaping factors has emerged, a series of critical questions has been raised in the encounter of the coordinates of history, namely past tradition, present reality, and future vision. The struggle to grasp these questions, and to collaborate in a process of growth more directly grounded in history, has led and continues to lead to pain, difficulty, and misunderstanding. Yet, fidelity to continue the process set in motion by the Second Vatican Council is the great challenge today. If one can venture a vision for the future, it will be a greater communal participation in the realization of mission. And this communal participation will call for a deeper probing of the meaning of the Eucharist in our common journey in salvation history, for the Eucharist is bread for the missionary journey (Commission on World Mission and Evangelism 1980). The future calls us beyond our limited understandings of how we are to interact with the mystery of salvation at work in the world. The willingness to become instruments of salvation for others requires an openness and a freedom to hear the gospel imperative with a disciple's ear that is always ready to learn anew.

For Further Reading

Arns, Paulo Evaristo
1981 "The Communion of Churches in Society." In *Concilium: Tensions between the Churches of the First World and the Third World.* Edited by Virgil Elizondo and Norbert Greinacher. New York: Seabury Press.

Bevans, Stephen B., and James A. Scherer, eds.
1992 *New Directions in Mission and Evangelization 1: Basic Statements 1974-91.* Maryknoll, NY: Orbis Books.

Bosch, David J.
1991 *Transforming Mission: Paradigm Shifts in the Theology of Mission.* Maryknoll, NY: Orbis Books.

Commission on World Mission and Evangelism
1980 *Your Kingdom Come: Mission Perspectives.* Geneva: World Council of Churches.
1983 *Mission and Evangelism: An Ecumenical Affirmation.* Geneva: World Council of Churches.

Evars, Georg
1987 "The Joint Consultation on Interreligious Dialogue: A Report." In *FABC Papers*, No. 48, *Living and Working Together with Sisters and Brothers of Other Faiths.*

Flannery, Austin, ed.
1975 *Vatican Council II: The Conciliar and Post-Conciliar Documents.* Northport, NY: Costello Publishing Company.

Gremillion, Joseph, ed.
1976 *The Gospel of Peace and Justice: Catholic Social Teaching since Pope John.* Maryknoll, NY: Orbis Books.

Gutiérrez, Gustavo
1973 *A Theology of Liberation.* Maryknoll, NY: Orbis Books.
1983 *The Power of the Poor in History.* Maryknoll, NY: Orbis Books.

Joint Working Group of the Roman Catholic Church and the World Council of Churches
1984 *Common Witness: A Study Document.* WCC Mission Series. Geneva: World Council of Churches.

John Paul II, Pope
1990 *Redemptoris Missio.* Evangelical Letter on the Permanent Validity of the Church's Missionary Mandate. Vatican City: Polyglot Press.

Knitter, Paul
   1985   ✓ *No Other Name? A Critical Survey of Christian Attitudes toward the World Religions.* Maryknoll, N.Y.: Orbis Books.
Libanio, João
   · 1982   "Brazil," in *Mission in Dialogue: The Sedos Research Seminar on the Future of Mission.* Edited by M. Motte and J. Lang, Maryknoll, NY: Orbis Books.
Motte, Mary
   1987   *A Critical Examination of Mission Today: Research Project — Phase One.* Washington, DC: U.S. Catholic Mission Association, pp. 35-43.
Muller, Karl
   1987   *Mission Theology: An Introduction.* Nettetal: Steyler Verlag — Wort und Werk.
Pontifical Council for Interreligious Dialogue and the Congregation for the Evangelization of Peoples
   1991   *Dialogue and Proclamation:* Joint Document by the Pontifical Council for Interreligious Dialogue and the Congregation for the Evangelization of Peoples. Vatican City: Polyglot Press.
Schreiter, Robert
   1985   *Constructing Local Theologies.* Maryknoll, NY: Orbis Books.
Theological Advisory Commission of the Federation of Asian Bishops' Conferences
   1989   "Seven Theses on Interreligious Dialogue: An Essay in Pastoral Theological Reflection." *International Bulletin of Missionary Research* 13:3.

Pentecostal and
Charismatic Missions

Gary B. McGee

Since the beginning of this century, modern Pentecostalism (in its various forms) has come to represent one of the most energetic forces for renewal and evangelization in the history of Christianity. Reflecting on this development, church growth specialist C. Peter Wagner marks three great waves of the power of the Holy Spirit in the twentieth century: first, the Pentecostal movement; second, the charismatic movement; and, finally, "third wave" evangelicals, who practice prayer for the sick, exorcise demons, and manifest spiritual gifts (e.g., prophecy) in the life of the church (Wagner 1988:15-19).

Although Wagner's distinction of third wave evangelicals from charismatics is unconvincing (the similarities outweigh the differences), his categories are widely disseminated in David Barrett's statistical speculations on the number of Pentecostals and charismatics in the world. Reporting well over 350 million participants, Barrett subdivides them under a dizzying array of labels: Classical Pentecostals, Black/Non-White indigenous Pentecostals, Isolated radio Pentecostals, Chinese house-church Pentecostals, Catholic charismatics, and Crypto-charismatics, to name only a few (Barrett in Burgess and McGee 1988:810-30). Whether or not one accepts the accuracy of these historical and statistical interpretations, it is obvious that tens of millions of

---

Gary B. McGee is Professor of Church History at Assemblies of God Theological Seminary, Springfield, Missouri.

Christians identify themselves with renewal movements of the Spirit. By so doing, they form one of the largest segments of believers in Christendom, uniquely transcending the traditional barriers of denominations, councils of churches, and confessional statements.

The global significance of this block of Christians has become apparent as observers note: (1) the Pentecostal spirituality of large sectors of believers in the Two-Thirds World (including China), (2) the vibrant missionary impulse of these Christians and their churches, and (3) the continuing commitment of resources by North Americans and Europeans (Pentecostals, independent charismatics, and charismatics in the historic Protestant churches and the Roman Catholic Church) to world evangelization. Any generalizations and predictions about Pentecostal and charismatic missions, however, must remain tentative, despite the appearance of certain trends.

Pentecostal Missions

The eschatological fervor of premillennialism pervaded the atmosphere of early Pentecostalism. Charles F. Parham and his Topeka, Kansas, Bible school students prayed in January 1901 to experience speaking in tongues (i.e., xenolalia, a form of glossolalia in which human languages previously unknown to the speaker would be given by the Holy Spirit). The bestowal of this gift would then have enabled prospective missionaries to bypass formal language study, thus hastening the evangelization of the world in the "last days" before the return of Christ (Goff 1988:62-79). Through later revivals that Topeka triggered (notably the influential Azusa Street Revival in Los Angeles [1906-09]), Pentecostal missionaries crisscrossed the globe in ever increasing numbers.

So intensely did they expect the Second Coming of Christ that envisioning an additional decade — or even another century — for evangelization would have been inconceivable. But when Christ did not return according to the expected timetable, and desiring to stabilize their mission initiatives, Pentecostals easily adopted the paternalistic policies of their Protestant counterparts. Nevertheless, some read the books of the Anglican missiologist Roland Allen (particularly *Missionary Methods: St. Paul's or Ours?* [1912]) with great interest. Despite his advocacy of episcopacy and sacramentalism, his insights into Pauline methods of church planting accorded with their restorationist notions of the New Testament church.

Pentecostal missiologists, particularly Melvin L. Hodges, followed the paths explored by evangelicals on mission theology and social action, as well as in their antipathy to the ecumenical movement and liberation theology (McGee 1989:157-58). The spiritual bond with evangelicals can be easily traced to formative influences of the last century on the Pentecostal movement. This predilection has been obvious in the membership of several American Pentecostal denominations in the National Association of Evangelicals ([NAE] 1942), its missionary arm, the Evangelical Foreign Missions Association ([EFMA] 1945, which in 1991 changed its name to the Evangelical Fellowship of Mission Agencies), in addition to international Pentecostal participation in the World Evangelical Fellowship ([WEF] 1951) and the Lausanne movement (1974-). Furthermore, recent heightened interest in evangelizing unreached peoples can be traced to the challenge made by Ralph D. Winter to the delegates at the Lausanne Congress on World Evangelization in 1974.

Pentecostal missionaries have always been more adept as practitioners than as theorists, often depending on evangelical missiologists to address pertinent issues in their publications. This has been a marriage of convenience since both parties share conservative doctrinal views regarding the inspiration and authority of the Bible, the lostness of humankind without Christ, and justification by faith. They also generally have believed that evangelism should have priority over social action. Missiological statements by Pentecostals, therefore, often represent traditional evangelical doctrines with the addition of Pentecostal theological distinctives. This is particularly evident in Hodges' *Theology of the Church and Its Mission* (1977). Ironically, this identification with evangelical missiology (also characteristic of many charismatics) partially explains the neglect of Pentecostal perspectives in recent surveys of missiology (e.g., James A. Scherer's *Gospel, Church, and Kingdom* [1987]).

Although conservative evangelicals still view Pentecostal pneumatology with suspicion, Pentecostals have benefited from evangelical missiological expertise. With no signs of dissipating, this alliance will undoubtedly continue into the next century, since for Pentecostals the evangelical connection denotes theological integrity. Notwithstanding, some Pentecostals in the Two-Thirds World (much to the consternation of North American Pentecostal denominations) have moved beyond association with evangelicals and have established ties with the ecumenical movement by joining the World Council of Churches (Sandidge in Burgess and McGee 1988:901-3).

It is noteworthy, too, that certain Pentecostal missiologists have begun to question the compatibility of their pneumatological distinc-

43

tives with evangelical beliefs about the Holy Spirit. For example, Paul A. Pomerville contends that post-Reformation Protestant scholasticism has had a negative impact on evangelicalism. In his view, its strong rationalistic orientation

> has eliminated the "witness of the Spirit" in verifying Christian experience. Biblical theology was, therefore, reduced to the "objective" written Word. Its locus was wrongly conceived as the text of Scripture rather than the *witness of the Spirit* in conjunction with that written Word *in the heart of the Christian.* (Pomerville 1985:83-84)

This deficiency has left many Western Christians with only a limited understanding of the Spirit's work in the life of the believer and evangelism. In contrast, the gospel of the kingdom should be proclaimed with the expectancy of signs and wonders to follow, confirming the truth of the message. Pentecostalism, therefore, serves as a corrective to evangelical missiology. (Nonetheless, Pomerville's argument suffers from not recognizing the complexity of the evangelical heritage [e.g., the historic Wesleyan interest in the work on the Holy Spirit is not considered].)

It is apparent that contemporary questions facing Pentecostals, and other issues appearing on the horizon, will not allow them to sit on the sidelines any longer waiting for others to prepare adequate responses. The exposition of Pentecostal missiology must be a priority item on the agenda if their mission enterprise is to retain its integrity and uniqueness. With an unwavering commitment to the authority of Scripture, they should move beyond the hesitancies of evangelical theology to articulate a theology of mission that does full justice to the biblical text in regard to the work of the Holy Spirit. Pomerville's ground-breaking *Third Force in Missions* (1985) and *Called and Empowered: Global Mission in Pentecostal Perspective* (1991), edited by Murray W. Dempster, Byron D. Klaus, and Douglas Peterson, reflect a growing interest among Pentecostals who are academically equipped in theology, missiology, history, and the social sciences to speak to the challenges of global mission.

Charismatic Missions

Charismatic Christians have until recently been the sleeping giant of the Christian world mission. After almost forty years of growth, their

44

leaders called for the 1990s to be a decade of evangelization in order to convert at least half the world's population to Christ. Their unity in the Spirit, crossing denominational and confessional barriers, points to one of the most important happenings of our time. Author David Shibley maintains that "world evangelization can never be accomplished by charismatics alone. Neither can it be realized without us" (Shibley 1989:29). In his estimation, the readiness to employ spiritual warfare in evangelization will mark the charismatic contribution: power encounter with demonic forces active in non-Christian religions.

Charismatic interest in missions was strongly evident at the North American Congress on the Holy Spirit and World Evangelization in Indianapolis in August 1990. There, a broad range of denominational participants (e.g., Baptists, Christians [Churches of Christ, Disciples], Episcopalians, Lutherans, Mennonites, Presbyterians, Roman Catholics, United Methodists, and United Church of Christ), in addition to independent charismatics and Pentecostals, gathered to focus on evangelism. This event may have signaled the emergence of a major new mission thrust.

Catholic charismatics have already launched several important programs. Training schools have been established, exemplified by the Catholic Evangelization Training Program at the Franciscan University of Steubenville (Ohio). Keith Fournier, the dean of evangelization, asserts that

> our first evangelistic goal must be to bring people to an *explicit commitment* to Jesus Christ. . . . The core of the Christian message is the person of Jesus Christ who must be proclaimed in his fullness in both our lifestyle and our words. (Fournier 1989:13)

Promoting evangelization on an international scale is Fr. Tom Forrest, C.Ss.R. With offices in Rome, Forrest directs "Evangelizacion 2000," a bold initiative contrasting sharply with some of the current, more socially and economically-oriented movements in Catholic missions.

The range of denominational and independent charismatic activities in missions is difficult to survey for many reasons including the wide-ranging mission operations of local congregations, networks of churches, and para-church organizations. To cite but one example, the large North Way Christian Community Church of Wexford, Pennsylvania, has its own missions director and supports over twenty-seven foreign missionaries and national ministers. A growing number of such congregations and agencies are joining the Association of International

Mission Services formed in 1985, potentially a charismatic alternative to the EFMA.

Structures and Strategy

The primary mission strategy of both Pentecostals and charismatics centers on each believer being empowered and guided by the Holy Spirit (Acts 1:8; 2:4). For many, the baptism of the Holy Spirit, accompanied by glossolalia (speaking in unknown tongues) either as initial evidence or as a consequence of the experience, signals a deeper work of the Spirit in the believer (Spittler in Burgess and McGee 1988:335-41). For others, any manifestations of the gifts of the Spirit (I Cor. 12, 14), including glossolalia, testify to the presence of apostolic power. This concentration on the baptism, gifts, and promptings of the Spirit, to be indispensably grounded in Christian love (I Cor. 13), represents the heartbeat of millions of believers. Theologian Russell P. Spittler correctly observes that the history of Pentecostal missions "can be told through stories of persons who sensed the guidance of the Holy Spirit and accordingly took bold, venturesome — some would say foolish — 'steps of faith'" (Spittler 1988:415).

The belief that Spirit-baptism equips every believer for ministry reveals the leveling influence of modern Pentecostalism and the key to its rapid growth. This supernatural emphasis highlights the large campaigns of the West German evangelist Reinhard Bonnke and those of the Argentinian Carlos Annacondia with their spectacular reports of miraculous healings and exorcisms. But the same can be found in the ministry of charismatic Anglicans in the diocese of Singapore and the informal witness of Pentecostals from Burkina Faso traveling (with their Bibles, songbooks, and Sunday school materials) to other West African nations in search of employment.

Despite their homage to the directives of the Holy Spirit, Pentecostals have balanced the experiential dimension by effectively charting strategies for church growth. Charismatics, without a lengthy mission history, could profit from the expertise that Pentecostals have gained through the years.

The contours of Pentecostal and charismatic missions will continue to be modeled after the three traditional systems of church polity. Episcopal structures with sundry degrees of hierarchical control can be found in the mission polity of the Church of God (Cleveland, TN); in the organization and international ministries of mega-churches such as

46

the large Yoido Full Gospel Church in Seoul, Korea, pastored by Paul Yonggi Cho (who now prefers to be known as David Cho); and in the 5,000 Nigerian churches founded under the auspices of "Archbishop" Benson Idahosa (Vaughan 1984:35-49, 91-97). With an appearance of congregationalism, mega-churches function as denominations under the oversight of strong leaders, portraying accepted cultural patterns of administration. Somewhat related is the growing interest in the restoration of the fivefold ministry mentioned by Paul in Eph. 4:11, particularly the role of modern-day apostles as church planters (Watney 1979:248-54).

Churches with a presbyterial/congregational polity such as the Assemblies of God have tended to promote indigenous (self-supporting, self-governing, and self-propagating) national churches on mission fields (e.g., the Assemblies of God of El Salvador). Their organizational designs, however, usually reflect a mixture of Western democratic ideals with local approaches to authority. Implementing indigenous church principles has necessitated the founding of hundreds of Bible training institutions for the preparation of leaders and church workers. The Assemblies of God (USA) has led the way in ministerial training programs. With its fraternally related churches, it supported 329 such schools in 1989, ranging from Bible institutes, to Bible colleges, to three graduate-level institutions. The five transnational ministries of the Assemblies of God (U.S.A.): Life Publishers, International Correspondence Institute, International Media Ministries, Center for Ministry to Muslims, and HealthCare Ministries, also work closely with national churches.

Congregational polity (naturally supportive of indigenous principles) is followed by millions of Pentecostal believers worldwide, from Scandinavians, to the French, to the Brazilians. Missionaries from these countries are entirely responsible to their supporting congregations. Training for prospective church planters is usually provided by the local pastor and/or special seminars, although in some instances Bible training schools have been established.

A considerable number of para-church ministries work with all sectors of Pentecostals and charismatics. Youth With A Mission (YWAM), Evangel Bible Translators, Terry Law Ministries, and International Health Services Foundation are but a few of the independent agencies engaged in differing aspects of world evangelization.

The myriad of ecclesiastical structures and para-church ministries underlines the vitality and pragmatism of Pentecostals and charismatics (both clergy and laity) in their efforts to fulfill the Great Commission.

The urgent calls to take the gospel to unreached peoples and to re-evangelize the West, and growing interest in alleviating the sufferings of the sick and destitute demonstrate their ardor for Christian witness. Even though these are identical to evangelical objectives in mission, the spirituality propelling their advancement is inspired by an eschatological vision coupled with a dynamic pneumatology.

Challenges

Serious challenges loom ahead for Pentecostal and charismatic missions. To participants, the foremost concern is to seek all effective means for reaching every person with the gospel. But important questions can also be raised about the future economic outlooks of North American and European countries whose churches have been the financial mainstays of the mission enterprise. The growing list of missionaries emerging from churches in the developing industrial nations on the rim of Asia, the future of the church in China, and the effectiveness of short-term missionaries abroad constitute only three of many items that merit consideration. The limitations of this chapter, however, preclude extensive study. Nevertheless, three critical challenges warrant examination. Their solutions will severely test the determination of Pentecostals and charismatics to seek the guidance of the Holy Spirit, while at the same time demanding exacting biblical, theological, and missiological analysis.

Defining the Church

The first and paramount challenge for the foreseeable future will center on issues related to the definition of the church: proselytism, relationships with national churches, and the dilemma of affirming so-called indigenous Pentecostals groups. Originally, Pentecostals viewed themselves as a renewal movement within established North American and European churches (Hocken in Burgess and McGee 1988:211-18). But before long they usually found themselves disenfranchised from these churches, prompting strong sectarian sentiments. Rejection led to doubt that any spiritual vitality remained in the historic churches. At the same time, they shared traditional Protestant fears about the Roman Catholic Church. Thus, the coming of the charismatic movement in the late 1950s and 1960s jolted the Pentecostals. While many warmly embraced Protestant and Catholic charismatics, recognizing in them the same dy-

48

namic activity of the Holy Spirit, others have remained skeptical about
the genuineness of their spirituality. Probably the most difficult relationship to address has been that of fellowship with Catholic charismatics, a virtually unthinkable scenario for most European and Latin
American Pentecostals.

Since Pentecostalism has flourished in many nominally Roman
Catholic countries, the appearance of charismatic renewal movements
has prompted missionaries in some quarters to review their attitudes
toward Catholics. The foremost Pentecostal missiologist, Melvin L.
Hodges, while convinced of errors in Catholic theology, nevertheless
positively considered the prospect of Spirit-filled bishops, priests, and
nuns. In his thinking, the mission of the church was not designed to
enhance church affiliation but to extend the kingdom of God (Hodges
1977:96).

The divisive issue of proselytizing also demands serious attention.
Progress will probably begin with Protestant and Catholic charismatics
searching for an amiable accord. If they continue to model humility in
their relationships (reflecting the fruit of the Spirit), and if cooperation
in evangelization follows (testifying to the distribution of the Spirit's
gifts in the universal church), the groundwork will then be laid for a
peaceful resolution to this and other sensitive questions. In the same
spirit, some Pentecostals may be prompted to overcome their hesitancies about broader cooperation, benefiting from and perhaps participating in these developments. Such a direction from the Holy Spirit
could lead to a remarkable transformation and enlargement of the
landscape of Christianity in the twenty-first century.

The arena of indigenous church relationships also requires
scrutiny. With thousands of Western and Two-Thirds World missionaries traveling to other countries, attitudes toward Pentecostal and charismatic churches already located in those areas have created serious
tensions. Conflicts engendered by differing church polities or elitist
attitudes about directives from the Holy Spirit occasionally arise. Unfortunately, the call of Jesus for spiritual unity (John 17) is sometimes
ignored at the cost of competing visions of the church, paternalism,
racial and cultural prejudices, and strategies for reaching the uncon-
verted.

Attitudes toward indigenous Pentecostal sects, frequently the offshoots of mission churches, raise another serious question about the
identity of the church (Hollenweger 1986:9-12; Pomerville 1985:26-35).
Although the rapidly growing African Independent churches (e.g., the
Church of Christ on Earth by the Prophet Simon Kimbangu) have

Pentecostal-like phenomena, they commonly reflect levels of syncretism with traditional religions. While observers have stressed their
basic affinity to Pentecostalism and advocated closer contacts, most
missionaries, mission agencies, and national (mission) churches have
remained wary of their theological integrity.

A Holistic Mission to the World

The second challenge engaging Pentecostals and charismatics in the
next century will be the concept of a holistic mission to the world. If
Pentecostals prophetically challenged social and economic injustices,
would this necessarily dilute the redemptive power of the gospel?
Generally speaking, North American Pentecostals, while historically
responding to charitable appeals, have been reluctant to emphasize
social concerns too strongly, lest it diminish their goal of converting
unbelievers before the imminent return of Christ (McGee 1989:249-54).
In contrast, Scandinavian Pentecostals have been less restrained about
their involvement in such endeavors. For some charismatics, less influenced by dispensational premillennialism, evangelization should be
followed by the Christianization of society (Paulk 1988:151-77). Given
the staggering problems facing the larger part of the world's population
today, many Pentecostals and charismatics will follow the lead of the
Lausanne movement in emphasizing that the preaching of the Word
(proclamation) should be complemented by deeds (social concern) in
announcing the good news of the kingdom of God.

It is noteworthy that Pentecostals in the Two-Thirds World are not
waiting for directives from North American missionaries before speaking forthrightly on social ills. The recent declaration entitled "A Relevant Pentecostal Witness" by certain South African Pentecostals con-
demning apartheid as sinful is a case in point.

Power Evangelism

Pentecostals and charismatics have always been willing to address the
dark side of spirituality: Satanic activity. As a result, establishing biblical
parameters on subjective religious experiences will constitute the third
major challenge. Even though they have traditionally depended on the
Scriptures for information on angels and demons, a tension has always
existed in Pentecostal and charismatic circles between the biblical revelation as authority and revelation through personal experience.
This issue has recently surfaced again in the "signs and wonders

movement" associated with the ministry of John Wimber (Vineyard Christian Fellowship) and the writings of C. Peter Wagner (School of World Mission, Fuller Theological Seminary). Their calls for "power evangelism" (exorcism and manifestations of the gifts of the Spirit) to accompany gospel preaching bear a strong affinity to Pentecostal ideals. Notwithstanding, particular assumptions about "territorial spirits" (evil principalities over specific regions of the world) generate suspicions that knowledge gained from demons in "power encounters" has exceeded what the biblical text warrants (Wagner 1989:282-85). (Demons are an untrustworthy lot!) Unfortunately, hasty claims about the "demonization" of Christians have accompanied this interest in demonology, raising unnecessary doubts about the triumph of Christ as victor over evil forces and the security of the believer (Col. 2:15; 1:13-14).

Although recognizing the threat of Satanic activity in the world, the value of intercessory prayer, and the need for Christians to contend with the forces of evil (Eph. 6:10-18), the theological conclusions of these influential proponents require further scrutiny. Without it, the praxis of power evangelism will become recklessly trivialized.

Final Remarks

When queried as to what Pentecostal missions would be like in the next century, one mission executive responded by asking, "What will the Holy Spirit be doing?" Without doubt, the future vitality and success of Pentecostals and charismatics in evangelization will hinge on their ability to answer that question. Nevertheless, their vigorous enthusiasm to fulfill the Great Commission, sensitivity to the work of the Holy Spirit, and potential for Christian unity must be attended by discerning theological and missiological reflection.

For Further Reading

Burgess, Stanley M., and Gary B. McGee, eds.
    1988   *Dictionary of Pentecostal and Charismatic Movements.* Grand Rapids, MI: The Zondervan Corporation.
Dempster, Murray W., Byron D. Klaus, and Douglas Peterson, eds.
    1991   *Called and Empowered: Pentecostal Perspectives on Global Mission.* Peabody, MA: Hendrickson Publishers.

Fournier, Keith
1989   "Where is Jesus?" *New Covenant,* January.

Goff, James R., Jr.
1988   *Fields White Unto Harvest: Charles F. Parham and the Missionary Origins of Pentecostalism.* Fayetteville: University of Arkansas Press.

Hayford, Jack
1989   "Jack Hayford: The Power of the Holy Spirit in Evangelism." Interview by Steven Lawson. *Charisma and Christian Life,* November, pp. 94-96, 98, 100, 102, 104.

Hodges, Melvin L.
1977   *A Theology of the Church and Its Mission.* Springfield, MO: Gospel Publishing House.

Hollenweger, Walter J.
1986   "After Twenty Years' Research on Pentecostalism." *International Review of Mission* 75 (Jan.): 3-12.

McClung, L. Grant, Jr., ed.
1986   *Azusa Street and Beyond: Pentecostal Missions and Church Growth in the Twentieth Century.* South Plainfield, NJ: Bridge Publishing.

McGee, Gary B.
1986   *This Gospel Shall Be Preached: A History and Theology of Assemblies of God Foreign Missions to 1959.* Springfield, MO: Gospel Publishing House.
1989   *This Gospel Shall Be Preached: A History and Theology of Assemblies of God Foreign Missions Since 1959 — Vol. 2.* Springfield, MO: Gospel Publishing House.

Pate, Larry D.
1989   *From Every People: A Handbook of Two-Thirds World Missions with Directory/Histories/Analysis.* Monrovia, CA: MARC.

Paulk, Earl
1988   *Spiritual Megatrends: Christianity in the 21st Century.* Atlanta: Kingdom Publishers.

Petrella, Lidia Susana Vaccaro de
1986   "The Tension Between Evangelism and Social Action in the Pentecostal Movement." *International Review of Mission* 75 (Jan.): 34-38.

Pomerville, Paul A.
1985   *The Third Force in Missions.* Peabody, MA: Hendrickson Publishers.

Pousson, Edward K.
1992   *Spreading the Flame: Charismatic Churches and Missions Today.* Grand Rapids, MI: The Zondervan Corporation.

Sandidge, Jerry L.
1987   *Roman Catholic/Pentecostal Dialogue (1977-1982): A Study in Developing Ecumenism.* Frankfurt am Main: Verlag Peter Lang.

Shibley, David
1989   *A Force in the Earth: The Charismatic Renewal and World Evangelism.* Altamonte Springs, FL: Creation House.

Spittler, Russell P.
1988   "Implicit Values in Pentecostal Missions." *Missiology* 16 (Oct.): 409-24.

Vaughan, John N.
1984   *The World's 20 Largest Churches.* Grand Rapids, MI: Baker Book House.

Wagner, C. Peter
1988   *The Third Wave of the Holy Spirit.* Ann Arbor, MI: Vine Books, Servant Publications.
1989   "Territorial Spirits and World Missions." *Evangelical Missions Quarterly* 25 (July): 278-88.

Watney, Paul B.
1979   "Ministry Gifts: God's Provision for Effective Mission." D.Miss. diss., School of World Mission, Fuller Theological Seminary.

Wimber, John, with Kevin Springer
1986   *Power Evangelism.* San Francisco: Harper and Row.

II. Christian Mission by Region

Southern Asia

Saphir P. Athyal

The immense population of Asia, and the tremendous variety of peoples, religions, and social conditions, indicate something of the challenge that Christian witness faces in Asia in the twenty-first century. Even when one leaves China and Northeast Asia and concentrates, as in this survey, on the twenty or so countries lying east of Iran and extending through the Indian subcontinent to Indonesia and the Philippines, it is impossible to do justice to the diversity of Southern Asia.

The Southern Asia Context

Every two seconds, five more people are born in the world. Three are Asian, and of these three two are born in Southern Asia. It is not surprising, then, that from the standpoint of population alone, the profile of Southern Asia is overwhelming. Although containing less than seven percent of the land mass of the globe, this region holds nearly thirty percent of the world's population. This concentration of humanity — more than a billion and a half people — outnumbers China by almost half a billion.

One may get a false notion of the immensity of Southern Asia if

---

Saphir P. Athyal served as Principal of Union Biblical Seminary, Pune, India, for fifteen years. A member of the Mar Thoma Church of India, Dr. Athyal is a member of the Executive Committee of the Lausanne Committee for World Evangelization.

one simply reckons it as part of the Two-Thirds World along with the rest of Asia, Africa, and Latin America. India alone, with a population of more than 800 million, though it looks small compared to the rest of Asia, has more people than all the nations of Africa, Central Africa, and South America combined.

Furthermore, we must deal with amazing diversity. There are around four thousand ethnolinguistic groups in Asia, and the great majority are found in the nations of Southern Asia. Almost three thousand are found in India and Indonesia alone.

Social tensions that often accompany such diversity have been intensified by revolutionary changes in politics and economic conditions. All the nations of Southern Asia, with the exception of Thailand, emerged from the experience of colonialism after World War II. Many began with democratic ideals, but today multi-party systems — not just a two-party system but perhaps a dozen or more parties without effective leadership — have led to fragmentation and instability. This in turn has produced in a number of countries totalitarian rule with the accompanying problem of violation of human rights and restriction of the religious freedom of minorities.

Whereas the West took three hundred years to industrialize, many Asian countries have been trying to achieve industrialization in a fraction of the time. Work opportunities take many people away from their families, as for example in the flow of workers into Arab lands. Although rural inhabitants are still the majority, more and more people gravitate to the cities. With some of the largest cities in the world, Asia confronts all the familiar problems of urbanization. Secularization, with its emphasis on the individual and the accompanying disruption of families and breakdown of traditional values, also adds to the difficulty of nation-building and establishing self-identity and self-reliance.

Asia also must deal with tremendous social inequities. Bangladesh is one of the poorest countries in the world, with an average annual family income of less than four hundred dollars. In stark contrast, Singapore averages nearly twelve thousand dollars annual family income. Wherever individuals and communities have prospered, they have become like oases of riches in oceans of poverty. While there is no slavery as such, the poor typically enter into a kind of bonded service. Borrowing from the rich, they pay interest at the rate of forty or fifty percent, and the principal is never reduced. In effect, they are bound for life to a kind of medieval servitude, usually passing their debts onto the next generation.

On the one hand, these forces lead many people to question the

58

religious basis and values of past centuries. Many others, however, are turning back to their religious heritage, resulting in a resurgence of traditional religions in Asia. It appears that we are experiencing a kind of return to the sixth century B.C., when many of the world's great religions took form. At that time, if there had been a parliament of world religions, Gautama Buddha would have stood as a reformer of Hinduism; Mahavira, as a representative of Jainism (another Hindu reform movement); and Zoroaster, to whom modern Parsiism is indebted, would have been there. Confucius, too, would have been present, as well as perhaps Jeremiah and Ezekiel. Today a similar religious ferment exists on a global level, with new forms of ancient beliefs, some of which are characterized by a kind of fundamentalism or right-wing militancy.

This religious resurgence reflects the holistic approach to life that characterizes most Asians, for whom even cultivation of the land is a religious act. With religion at the heart of all social issues and activities, the integration of the sacred and the secular is the hallmark of Asian spirituality. Accompanying this is a strong fatalism running through Islam, Hinduism, and Buddhism: You accept your destiny because that is what you deserve.

Such is the socio-cultural and religious climate confronting the Christian community in Southern Asia.

Why the Poor Returns of Mission?

With the sole exception of the Philippines, Christians form a small minority in all nations of Southern Asia. Only in Indonesia and Singapore do they make up as much as ten percent of the population. India is typical with about three percent. Given the almost five hundred years of Catholic missions and two hundred years of Protestant missions in Asia (not to mention the presence of Christianity in South India possibly from the first century A.D. and in other parts of Asia soon after that) how is it that the results have not been greater?

Obviously it is wrong to measure the fruits of Christian witness merely in terms of the number of people who join the Christian community or by the size of the Christian church. One can hardly fathom the impact of the gospel upon Southern Asia in the areas of socio-cultural values or the ideologies that shape the society and human development at large. Yet we may attempt to identify a few limitations and hurdles that the Christian missions experienced in the past and continue to face today to help explain the relatively limited size of the Christian population.

First, although early colonial policies often forbade evangelization of national populations, Christian faith nevertheless is associated in the minds of Asians with colonialism. When people become Christians they are looked upon as betraying their culture and denying their citizenship. Christianity carries the stigma of being a Western religion that came with the colonialists and should go with the colonialists.

Second, the religious heritage of India and other nations of Southern Asia is so deep that people find it very difficult to leave it for Christian faith. It is quite different from the record of Christian mission among tribals where the great religions never took root. The contrast is illustrated by comparing the animistic Nagaland peoples of Northeast India where the Christian population now approaches seventy percent, to the peoples of neighboring Bangladesh where the Christian population measures only half of one percent.

A third reason is the eclectic mentality of Asians. The tendency is to say, "All ideas are right, all faiths are the same, we simply call the one reality by different names." In India, we come across numbers of people who listen to the gospel with great enthusiasm, but they do not follow through to receive Christ as the one and only Lord and Savior.

The lack of sensitivity on the part of Western missionaries to the cultures they encountered has been yet another impediment. Although some of the early pioneers worked hard to relate the Christian message to the contexts of Southern Asia, most later efforts seem to have taken for granted the superiority of Western forms.

Internal difficulties also help account for the limited results of Christian witness in Southern Asia. To begin with, in a number of countries some other religion is the official religion and Christians are looked upon as second-class citizens. The majority of people in government support policies that tend to discriminate against minority groups like the Christian community. In Malaysia you cannot even have a house-church, let alone get permission to erect a church building. If your neighbors hear singing and other evidence of Christian activity, you are likely to be reported to the police. In a number of states of India, getting permission to build a church can be very difficult and involves going through much red tape.

It is not surprising, then, that an inferiority complex often affects Christians. Outside the protective confines of the church, our people may be fearful and hesitant to acknowledge their Christian faith. Yet other minority groups make their voices heard in these countries; the Christian community must learn to do so as well.

The leadership crisis is another key area. Until the Indian government imposed tighter controls on expatriate workers, sometimes even local leadership was in the hands of Westerners. Once they were gone, it was not always possible to fill their posts with properly trained nationals. In addition, some of our best minds have found greener pastures in the West; others have been attracted by parachurch organizations based in the West that offer better salaries than our local churches.

In addition, within the Christian community there may be an aversion to advanced education. This is very true in the Indian background, where the feeling is that if you are truly spiritual you will avoid any serious exercise of your mind. This may have something to do with the Hindu and Buddhist stance regarding renunciation of worldly concerns such as status, pleasure, and money.

We also have been hurt by ecclesiastical confusion and controversies. People do not know what to make of a Christian community that is divided into literally hundreds of different denominations. Furthermore, instead of developing our own biblical and theological insights related to the uniqueness of the East, we have allowed ourselves to be caught up in the theological agenda of the West.

When it comes to leadership training, denominational rivalries again deter us. Instead of pooling resources and faculty in order to insure sufficient depth and breadth, each group wants to establish and control its own institution. As a result, faculties are spread too thin, libraries are inadequate, and many of our schools struggle along with with only thirty or forty students.

Nominalism in the church is another problem in many instances. By the time the second or third generation of believers comes along, Christian faith may appear to be little more than a set of rituals, prayers, and traditions, that is, a form of religion without any personal deep convictions or inner power. This condition also seems to breed internal disunity and quarrels. I know of many churches and Christian institutions involved in court cases over property, which drains the energy of the Christian community and undermines our witness for Christ.

Indigenous Missions of Southern Asia

Nevertheless, in recent decades the Christian community of Southern Asia appears to be experiencing a new vitality, life, and vision. It also is asserting a new level of self-reliance and independence from the church in the West. Singapore and Indonesia, Nepal, and certain areas of India report significant growth in the Christian churches. Another indication of new vitality is a growing mission to unreached communities and people groups of Southern Asia. A 1988 study reported more than four hundred indigenous mission agencies in the nations of Southern Asia, supporting approximately thirteen thousand missionaries.

Most of the indigenous missions are not composed of denominationally based people. In general, Asian missionaries are sent by local churches or nondenominational groups. Most mainline denominations in Asia do have a committee on mission, but very few are doing anything significant.

The vast majority of Asian missionaries are also distinguished by the fact that they are involved in actual grass-roots level evangelistic work, not Christian services such as health, education, or communications. One reason for this, of course, is that they do not have the resources to establish medical institutions, schools, and other forms of ministry that are capital intensive. For the same reason we are seeing a greater inclination among Asian missions to pool resources and cooperate in evangelism and church planting.

Another characteristic of Asian missionaries is that they are more likely than Westerners to identify with the social and cultural situation of the people. Missionaries from South India, though they may be working among altogether different ethnolinguistic groups in North India, nevertheless find many common values: the concept of the family unit, respect for the aged, hospitality, a common history. Another advantage experienced by Asian missionaries is that they tend to share the same economic position as the people to whom they witness. All of these things bring them together, minimize culture shock, and aid communication.

One of the most striking results of the work of these indigenous missionaries is that the churches they establish are absolutely independent of outside support. They are not looking to any denomination, either in Asia or the West, and not even to their founding mission for support of any kind. Therefore, right from the beginning the new churches are learning stewardship, independence, and self-reliance. Furthermore, this frees them to develop their own theological responses to their situation. The old pattern of theological purity being imposed from above has been broken.

Finally, because of the work of Asian indigenous missions and the churches they establish, the image of Christianity as a Western religion is gradually declining.

To balance the picture, some serious problems with Asian indigenous missions must also be noted. One is in the area of training. We have only two or three missionary training centers, and few seminaries offer even as many as one or two courses in Christian mission. We simply do not have the history, the resources, or the experience of the West. As a result, we are likely to make mistakes that better trained missionaries would avoid.

Another problem is that the majority of Asian missionaries are men. In many places men cannot effectively share the gospel with women; cultural patterns prevent any kind of contact. Women missionaries will be needed. Yet, it seems that most Asian women are reluctant to risk long journeys and go to unknown places. Even if they were prepared to do so for the sake of the gospel, in many places unmarried women are a kind of taboo; single women might not find acceptance.

Some Selected Issues of Mission

It is not easy to single out a few issues of mission as the most critical ones for the church in Southern Asia. They differ with various contexts and conditions. Therefore only a few general issues can be dealt with here, and these only very briefly.

An issue of critical importance for the coming years is the encounter of Christian faith with other faiths of the region. A great majority of the people in the region belong to Islam, Hinduism, Buddhism, or folk religions. With the single exception of the Philippines, Christians in the nations of Southern Asia make up a small minority. These people in general are very religious, and their respective religions have profound influence upon their convictions, cultures, and total life.

Interacting with people of other faiths and seeking to understand them are not optional exercises for us. In communities where people of different religions live together as neighbors, it is inevitable that they will be conscious of their interdependence and seek to promote peace and mutual understanding. It is also necessary for us to be well aware of the beliefs and convictions that shape people if we wish to communicate the gospel effectively to them. These are the considerations that lead to interreligious dialogue.

In the attempt to avoid the problematical aspects of interreligious dialogue, different approaches and theories have been proposed. One approach stresses the personal dimension of one's experience of God and avoids any criticism of the partner's experience. Once I participated in a public meeting in our city's large civic hall that gathered persons from each of the major religions. No one was to compare his faith to that of any other, and no one was to take simply a philosophical or theological approach. Rather, each person was to say, "This is my quest for God and my experience of God." I found this to be a very meaningful experience, speaking on behalf of my Christian faith, and somewhat beginning to understand the sincere desire and search for God among people of other faiths.

From the Christian standpoint, dialogue can serve as a form of pre-evangelism or "bridge-building." For the dialogue to have integrity, we must come to the partner as his or her equals; we must listen just as much as we speak; and an outright criticism and rejection of the position of the other is not proper. This does not mean, however, that I should not desire that the partner be attracted to Christ and the gospel. If Christ is for me the truth, the way, and the life, how can I come to dialogue with integrity unless I am prepared to share what is most precious to me, with the hope and prayer that someday my friend will discover the same riches in Christ?

I see a number of reasons why dialogue is necessary and vital to Christian witness. First, it expresses true respect for people. They are not treated simply as objects or targets of evangelism. We learn to listen with genuine interest and teachableness. As a result, we increase our capacity to be sensitive to and respectful of other people's backgrounds, feelings, and convictions.

Second, a genuine participation in dialogue shows humility. It indicates an acknowledgment that we are not superior and that we come with a willingness to learn from others, whatever their background.

Third, dialogue is a mark of authenticity. We cannot throw the gospel at people from a safe distance on a take-it-or-leave-it basis. We must be willing to expose ourselves to others.

Fourth, dialogue clarifies misunderstandings. We all harbor prejudices and false notions about other religions. The cause of truth can only be served if we are willing to clear away these misconceptions.

A fifth reason for dialogue is our own enrichment. Many times people of other traditions are very earnest and faithful in their spiritual disciplines. The areas of fasting, prayer, and the punctuality by which their religious rites are performed, every morning making sure that they make some offerings to their gods before they go off to work, and so forth — such things can be eye-opening and challenging to us. Many times we Christians have lost the art of spiritual discipline and meditation, and so our lives can be enriched through dialogue with people who excel in such areas.

Finally, dialogue prepares us for effective communication of the gospel. How can we communicate if we do not know our partners well enough, if we do not understand the screen through which they hear and understand?

A second critical issue for us is our unity and cooperation in faith, witness, and service. The Bible is clear as to what our position should be. We say we are all one in Christ, but in actual practice we perpetuate division, duplication of effort, and competition. Our minority position and limited resources should tell us we cannot afford such a state of affairs. The solution is not in creating some sort of superstructure. Unity is more than simply having a common address and a common administrative head. India and other nations of Southern Asia have established conciliar bodies and church unions, but without necessarily achieving the unity mandated in the New Testament.

We cannot set aside this concern. Ephesians 4:3 states that we are to "make every effort to keep the unity of the Spirit." Scripture doesn't assume that because we already have unity in Christ no effort on our part is required. To the contrary: "Stand firm in one spirit, with one mind striving side by side for the faith of the gospel" (Phil. 1:27). Christian mission must exhibit the kind of unity that Christ prayed for, as recorded in John 17, a unity that is visible, "so that the world may believe that thou hast sent me" (v. 21).

Much of the division among the churches of Southern Asia was imported from the West. It is only natural, though regrettable, that our churches reflect the ecclesiology and theological peculiarities of the missions that brought us the gospel. In too many cases, differences that have been rationalized on the basis of doctrinal purity turn out to be matters of a secondary nature. Often they can be traced to conflict between strong personalities or certain historical factors that have little or nothing to do with the issues that are crucial to Christians in the East.

In addition, we tend to import into Southern Asia the theological differences and confessional debates of the West. A few years ago I gave some lectures in the United States at two well-known seminaries representing distinct theological positions. In both cases, when I addressed the faculty, the first question was, "Is your seminary back in India Calvinistic or Arminian?" In both cases I answered in the same way. "OK," I said, "may I ask you a question also, and if you answer my question, then I will answer your question." (I learned this approach from Jesus!) "Tell me, is your seminary Appaswamyian or Chenchayeeian?" Silence. Then somebody started to laugh, and soon everyone got the point. The various churches of Southern Asia may have their own theological schools of

65

thought, but they don't come to Europe and North America and expect the churches of the West to fit into their categories. Why, then, should we be put into the particular categories of the West?

Cooperation among us is often very difficult because of our greater interest in furthering the cause of our own denominations and organizations than in furthering the cause of Christ. But we need to seek practical ways of building full partnership between the church in Southern Asia and the church in the West, between different denominations, between churches and missions, and between churches and parachurch groups. The task before us is so immense and the Christians such a small minority that we have no option but to cooperate with a sense of urgency.

Perhaps it will take some great trauma of suffering, as occurred during the cultural revolution in China, to bring us together. Better still, perhaps the growing vision for evangelistic outreach will lead to greater unity.

A third pressing issue is the socio-economic realities of Southern Asia and our need for a deeper understanding and a more costly obedience to the demands of the gospel in this regard. The gospel we proclaim is the gospel of the kingdom of God. It speaks of the rule of God over all areas of human life. This has far-reaching implications for the bearers of the gospel, especially in the context of Southern Asia with its vast problems of social injustice, suffering, and utter despair. It is often false religious convictions and traditions that lie behind the acceptance and the perpetuation of the miserable plight of the people.

Many lack even the basic necessities of life. The mushrooming of cities that absorb multitudes of people has generated many critical social problems. While responding to people's needs with acts of compassion is relatively easy, we must also try to solve the basic causes of misery, which is a far more demanding and risky task.

The gospel is centered around the Christ-event and the redeeming work of God. Yet its scope embraces wholeness and reconciliation in all aspects of life and relationships. Living the gospel takes the form of loving — loving God and loving our neighbor. The gospel of love should penetrate all areas of the lives of those in distress.

A fourth issue we face, and will continue to face with increasing intensity, is the organized opposition to the gospel and even persecution of Christians in some places. Many Christians in Southern Asia live under severe restraints because of their faith.

In recent decades we have seen how communism, as in Vietnam, Laos, and Kampuchea, ruthlessly represses Christian witness. But during the coming years fundamentalist Islam will prove to be a more militant oppressor of Christianity and other faiths than communism. A number of countries have Islam as their official religion, the most recent case in point being Bangladesh. In them Christian mission is under great pressures and as a rule evangelism is allowed only among those who are not Muslims. Fundamentalist segments of Islam and of other religions are gaining influence in the national governments in many countries. Fanaticism in these religions means more costly evangelism in many parts of the region in the years ahead. We should be prepared for increasing persecution and opposition to the gospel.

Conclusion

There are several encouraging developments in Southern Asia relating to Christian witness. As we noted above, many indigenous missions have begun to send Christian workers to areas where there has been no witness for Christ. Also, the involvement of laypeople in the Lord's work is rapidly increasing. Many professional laypeople go as tent-makers to areas where missionaries as such do not have access. Moreover, the church in Southern Asia now has technological resources and means that it never had before in its work of outreach. Still another very encouraging matter is the movement of the Holy Spirit in all segments of the Christian church, including the Orthodox and Roman Catholic churches, with a new concern for the unreached.

Southern Asia is indeed an immense region, as are the challenges it holds for mission in the twenty-first century. At the same time, the opportunities that we face and the resources that we possess in terms of people and commitment are beyond measure. Therein lies the promise of Christian mission for the future in our region, and the same is true for the entire world.

For Further Reading

Anderson, Gerald H., ed.
    1976   *Asian Voices in Christian Theology*. Maryknoll, NY: Orbis Books.
Cooley, Frank L.
    1982   *The Growing Seed: The Christian Church in Indonesia*. New York: Division of Overseas Ministries, National Council of Churches.

David, M. D., ed.
1985   *The Church in Asia*. Bombay: Himalaya Publishing House.
Mundadan, A. Mathias, general ed.
1984   *A History of Christianity in India*, Vol. 1. Bangalore, India: Theological Publications in India. Other volumes projected.
Neill, Stephen
1984   *A History of Christianity in India: The Beginning to* A.D. *1707*. Cambridge: Cambridge University Press.
1985   *A History of Christianity in India: 1707-1858*. Cambridge: Cambridge University Press.
Sitoy, T. Valentino, Jr.
1985   *A History of Christianity in the Philippines. Vol. 1: The Initial Encounter*. Quezon City, the Philippines: New Day Publishers. One more volume projected.
Smith, Alex C.
1982   *Siamese Gold: A History of Church Growth in Thailand*. Pasadena, CA: William Carey Library.

Note: Population data underlying this article have been drawn from Patrick Johnstone, *Operation World*, fourth edition (1986), Bromley, Kent: STL Publications.

Commonwealth of
Independent States (CIS)

J. Martin Bailey

The change was evident as I stepped off the bus. The front of the
Stalin-era Ukraine Hotel (where I had stayed several times before) was
decorated prominently with Christian symbols. A friend, who met me
at the Moscow airport, had promised visible evidence of *glasnost*.

I had made the journey in 1988 to join in the celebration of the
Millennium of the Baptism of Rus — of the evangelization of Russia. I
knew that the public events that had been announced for months could
not happen without the permission of the State. I had observed a
gradual moderation of the governmental control of the churches and
religious societies in the Soviet Union — as the Commonwealth of Independent States was then called — over a period of six years. But still,
I was unprepared for what happened.

On the broad steps of the Ukraine Hotel a broadcast journalist
was waiting for me. He had been told that I would be the spokesper-
son for the American delegation. On previous visits with church
groups I had preferred to "meet the press" myself, for I knew how
easily reporters from both Soviet and Western media could take a
comment out of context and make one appear to be a "dupe" if not a
"fellow traveler."

J. Martin Bailey is Associate General Secretary of the National Council of
Church of Christ in the USA's unit for Education, Communication, and
Discipleship. He has traveled frequently to the USSR/CIS and reported on
its religious communities.

I wasn't eager to be asked about the state of religious life in the Soviet Union before I had at least talked privately with some of my longtime friends. But there he was, microphone in hand, tape recorder running. It was his question that demonstrated that changes had indeed taken place in the USSR.

"I think you know, Dr. Bailey, that in our country the church has been repressed. Christians are not permitted to speak openly about their faith. They have not been allowed to operate schools or hospitals. I understand that in your country the church is engaged in many forms of social service and that this is a form of evangelism. Could you tell the radio audience about this?"

Since that encounter I have thought a lot about what it represented. The interest in a form of mission that Western Christians take for granted was not just a response to *glasnost*. Even before the 1917 Revolution, Russian Christians put a different interpretation on the word "mission" than Protestants and Roman Catholics. Orthodox Christians outside the CIS do also, for that matter.

One cannot understand the approach of the churches in the CIS to mission without considering the historical context. And that context includes the thousand-year history of Orthodox Christianity, the more recent Protestant, Roman Catholic, and Pentecostal expressions of the faith, and especially the restraints of seventy years under the Soviet political system.

The Russian Orthodox Church and other Eastern and Oriental Orthodox bodies frequently are misunderstood to be anti-mission. Especially in the Middle East and India these ancient churches have reason to be unhappy about Western Protestant efforts to proselytize their members. Several Orthodox churches that trace their origins to apostolic times have experienced the single-minded missionary zeal of uninformed English-speaking Protestants. Often these well-meaning Christians had little awareness of the courageous witness of Orthodox believers whose churches have endured through many persecutions. And, in recent decades, many Western Christians have failed to recognize that pious devotion and patient ministries have done more to keep the faith alive than smuggled Bibles and political rhetoric. During nearly three generations of repression under Soviet rule, the churches did well what churches always do best. They expressed their faith through worship, weekly and even daily.

70

Ancient and Historic Tradition of Mission

That witness was nothing new for them. Their life of worship was a reflection of their origins; Orthodox Christians in the CIS share an ancient and historic missionary heritage. According to tradition, the apostles Thaddeus and Bartholomew responded to the Great Commission by preaching the gospel in what is now Armenia. In 310, during the time of King Trdat III and of St. Gregory the Illuminator, Christianity became the state religion (van der Bent 1982:168). The son of an outlaw, Gregory was raised by a Christian nurse in Caesarea. His devotion led him to return to his native land so that he might atone for his father's sin by preaching the gospel to all the people (Zahirsky 1980:14). St. Andrew-the-First-Called is said to have preached in what is now Georgia (van der Bent 1982:171). There the prayers of a Christian slave girl from Cappadocia led to the healing of the Queen of Georgia, and eventually St. Nina baptized King Mirian in the Kura River in about 330. That led to the conversion of the royal house and the entire population (Zahirsky 1980:5).

All Slavic Christians share another missionary tradition. During the ninth century, Greek and Slavic people mingled freely in the border city of Thessalonica. Two brothers, Constantine (who later took the name Cyril) and Methodius, learned the Slavic tongue from their playmates. Eventually, with classical Greek educations, they traveled to Moravia where they discovered that the Slavs had no written language. The alphabet that they created is known as Cyrillic to this day. They became teachers and translated the Gospels, religious service books, and other important Christian writings. Through their disciples their work was carried into the vast reaches of the Byzantine Empire (Hatch 1980:5).

In the year 988, the Kievan Prince, Vladimir, accepted Christianity. In a dramatic event Vladimir tore down the wooden idols and the people of Kiev were baptized in the Dnieper River. The Orthodox faith that he accepted spread through what was called Rus, northward to Suzdal, Rostov, Moscow, and Novgorod. As it spread it provided the bonding and unifying influence that led to the formation of the country of Russia. Priests, especially monks like Sergius of Radonezh, served the people and provided models of faithfulness. Moreover, the walled monasteries often furnished safety from Mongol invaders. The encouragement that St. Sergius gave to Prince Dimitri at the Battle of Kulikovo Pole in 1360 is regarded as a turning point in the nation's history (Bailey 1987:19).

In more modern times, an energetic and courageous priest, Father John Veniaminov-Popov, went with explorers from the Russian-American Company in 1823 to serve the Aleuts in Aunalakhskha ("This is Alaska"), an island Father John later declared to be "a kingdom of eternal autumn" (Bailey and Tarasar 1987:4). He visited parishioners in outlying islands and over mountainous wastes, sometimes alone in a kayak. He transcribed the sounds of the Aleutian language and slowly developed a vocabulary and understanding of grammar so that he could provide the Gospels and a catechism for the people. He built churches and carved icon screens, so that the villages could have appropriate places for worship. Eventually, after the death of his wife, he returned to Russia and became a monk, taking the name of Innocent. After his own death he was known as the "enlightener and apostle of America," and in 1977 was canonized as a missionary saint by the Russian Orthodox Church (Bailey 1987:31). In Orthodox churches a troparion collect is sung annually to St. Innocent including the affirmation, "You accepted dangers and tribulations/To bring many peoples to the knowledge of truth;/You showed us the way/ And lead us now by your prayers/Into the kingdom of heaven."

The Church as Mission

"The Orthodox concept of mission depends entirely on the understanding of the nature of the Church.... The church is the aim of the mission, and not vice versa.... Therefore, mission is not proclaiming some ethical truths or principles but calling people to become members of the Christian community in a visible concrete form. 'Building up the body' is a very apostolic vocation" (Bria 1980:4). With those words, Professor Ion Bria has described the primary focus of mission among Orthodox Christians, in Russia and elsewhere. The difference between this Eastern approach and Western concepts is significant, though perhaps subtle enough to be confusing.

In part, this is another way of saying that the church, through generations, has been present for people — it has been the place where individuals encounter God and where their spiritual needs are met. In this, there is recognition of the holiness of space. Protestants, on the other hand, generally emphasize that God can be encountered in any setting. Perhaps even more significantly, the Orthodox think of the church as part of the kingdom. History and eschatology are part of a single continuum. The communion of saints is a reality, past, present, and future together. While Protestants may give lip service to this concept, at worship Orthodox believers are, in fact, "surrounded by a cloud of witnesses."

Metropolitan Anthony of Leningrad (now again known as St. Petersburg) and Novgorod wrote that "behind the external beauty and grandeur [of outward forms of Christianity] was hidden an inexhaustible supply of spiritual grace; that in these festive . . . rites the Divine Strength and Wisdom were manifest. . . . Consequently, a reverent priest is a missionary, and his mission, with its uncountable good fruits and results, promotes the salvation of many" (Metropolitan Anthony 1980:477).

One needs only to stand for hours with Orthodox believers in the great cathedrals or the rural churches to sense how the church, with its familiar onion domes and colorful icons, appeals to the spiritual yearning of people. The corner icon in the family's dining room is more than a decorative painting and, I suspect, even more than the crucifix in Roman Catholic homes. I have watched men and women express their devotion during worship. Sometimes they seem oblivious of what is being said or sung; they seem absorbed in their own prayers. They may busy themselves (a Westerner's description) tending the candles, replacing those burned down to stubs with fresh tapers. Or they may stand long moments before a favorite icon as though communicating with an old friend. They may supervise the children — and the foreign visitors who wearily put their hands in their pockets. In all of this they are deeply at prayer. Even their long, trudging journeys to the church seem an act of devotion unlike our often hasty automobile trip to "get to the church on time."

For the Orthodox, "mission is neither primarily nor fundamentally a matter of sociology and statistics," according to Bria. "The church is the power of resurrection, the sacrament of the risen Christ who communicates to humanity and the whole of creation his own resurrection and glorification. The missionary vocation of the church is to induce in the world the process of transfiguration. Therefore, every church is called to be a *dynamic* missionary church" (Metropolitan Anthony, "On Mission," 478).

In an interview with Emilio Castro in 1974, Metropolitan Anthony talked of efforts to "evangelize the neo-pagan man" — the one who has "emerged out of a culture that was very deeply pervaded by Christian thought in art, in music, in style of life — and into a period . . . which, unfortunately, corresponds to the loss of our past while we have not yet attained to a present which is another culture" (Castro 1974:87). The scholarly Anthony, whose father had been a member of the Russian Imperial Diplomatic Corps and who served in the French army as a medical officer during World War II, was cautious about pushing people "back into a rut" from their cultural past. Yet he acknowledged that "we have a chance to appeal to people's past, particularly their cultural past."

I cite two examples from personal experience. A group of American Christians was taken by an Intourist guide to see one of the museum cathedrals within the walls of the Kremlin. She spoke of the architectural significance of the building and provided a cultural, rather than religious, explanation of the restored icons that lined the walls. As we then wandered about, I noticed her standing quietly before one particular icon. Later I asked her about it. "My *babushka*, my grandmother, showed me that icon once. She is a Christian." The guide, I believe, somehow became involved in her own searching. On a later trip, during the Millennial celebration, an English-speaking doctoral student had been employed to assist us. She took us to a number of cultural events and attended, with us, some of the religious programs. As I left Moscow, she came to me and said simply, "*The* God (as nonbelievers customarily use the article to imply a lack of personal relationship with God), *the* God has a new friend in Elena. The God will always have a friend in Elena, now."

Thus the church utilizes its history, its art, and its relation to the culture to make a witness without pressure. It did just that, both instinctively and strategically, during the time when religious propaganda was forbidden.

Liturgy as Mission

Western Christians, especially Protestants, place high value on *kerygma*, the proclamation or preaching of the gospel. Worship is considered to be the center of the church's life. But, in a way that goes beyond either of these two affirmations, the Orthodox believers see the Liturgy as mission. Professor Bria includes this statement in his book: "Two inseparable movements take place in the action of Liturgy, which in fact constitute the rhythm of mission: the gathering and the sending forth. . . . The function of the Liturgy is to initiate us into the Kingdom, to enable us to 'taste' it (1 Peter 2:3). The Liturgy is an invitation to enlist with the Lord and to travel with Him. Hence the worshipping community itself is an act of witness" (Bria 1980:6).

The "sending forth" was described in 1978 by Archbishop Paul, the

Orthodox Primate of Finland. "As we leave the Liturgy the words of the
hymn follow us: 'We have seen the true Light! We have received the
Heavenly Spirit! We have found the true Faith . . .' This is our mission:
to take this Light which we have seen in the Eucharist into the world and
to fulfill the Lord's words: 'Let your light so shine before men that they
may see your good works and give glory to your Father who is in
heaven." As a young monk, Archbishop Paul was forced to evacuate the
Valamo monastic community in Northwestern Russia during the
"Northern War" of 1939 and flee to Finland (Archbishop Paul 1980:65).

Elsewhere Bria has written that "the Liturgy is not an escape from
life, but a continuous transformation of life according to the prototype
of Jesus Christ, through the power of the Spirit" (Bria 1986:38). He sees
this not so much as the transformation of individual lives, but the
transformation of the community. Bria explains that "since the Liturgy
is the participation in the great event of liberation from the demonic
powers, then the continuation of Liturgy in life means a continuous
liberation from the powers of evil that are working inside us, a continual
re-orientation and openness to insights and efforts aiming at liberating
human persons from all demonic structures of injustice, exploitation,
agony and loneliness, and aiming at creating real communion of persons in love" (39).

Monastic Mission

As elsewhere in the East, the spread of Christianity through the
Ukraine, Byelorus, and the Russian republic was closely related to the
development of monasteries and hermitages. Metropolitan Anthony,
who for a number of years participated in the Commission on World
Mission and Evangelism of the World Council of Churches, frequently
pointed to the missionary activity of monasteries and of the monks who
live there. In an article in the *International Review of Mission,* he compared hermits and starets like Ambrose of Optina and Theophan
Zatvornik to the "greatest missionaries and holy apostles of Christ."
Their influence, and their credibility, came from "their constant communion with Christ, from whom they received gracious strength and
wisdom through constant prayer. . . . They went out preaching,
strengthened by their faith in God . . ." (Anthony 1980:478).

One needs only to observe the crowds of pilgrims that come, at
great personal expense and often sacrifice, to such places as the Monastery of the Caves in Kiev or to the Holy Trinity–St. Sergius Monastery in

Zagorsk, to sense the continuing influence of the pious saints and martyrs of Russian Orthodoxy. And the presence, in those and other monasteries and convents, of monks who are sought out both by simple pilgrims and by sophisticated seekers for truth was a fact of life that Soviet leaders reluctantly had to accept. The spiritual witness of men and women like St. Seraphim of Sarov, who in the early nineteenth century counseled an unending flow of pilgrims — sometimes as many as several thousand a day — is an acknowledged part of Russian history comparable to the memory of St. Francis in Italy or St. Patrick in Ireland.

On my first visit to Kiev, the famed Monastery of the Caves was controlled by the State as a kind of museum, a place of historic interest and an architectural monument. Some of the schoolchildren and their parents who visited on holidays were, of course, sightseers. But even among our guides who described themselves as atheists, there was a spiritual curiosity that was real. We walked through the catacombs where for hundreds of years the monks carved niches from the limestone for their own burial places. Their mummified bodies were visible; generally only their leather-like hands were uncovered. I found the long walk on planks, through clammy, dimly-lit passageways, strange, uncomfortable, and rather gruesome. But one Protestant layman in our group sensed better than I the holy significance of the place. From his humming we picked up the lyrics of the hymn, "For all the saints, who from their labors rest." His was a Protestant and perhaps an American response. But it captured at least a hint of the persuasive power of such places for the Russian mind and spirit.

During the Millennial celebrations several monasteries and hermitages, including the Monastery of the Caves, were returned to the control of the church with official participation in ceremonies and rituals that were telecast nationwide. I see this as one more evidence that the patience rooted in Orthodox piety has been vindicated.

Furthermore, the monastery is seen as a holy place — a place reclaimed for its divine purpose, a prototype, as it were, of the kingdom. "For the Orthodox, the main ground of mission is the cosmic dimension of the event of Redemption. . . . The whole of creation is in the process of becoming ecclesia, the Church, the Body of Christ" (Bria 1980:6).

Creative Accommodation to Restraints

The Orthodox and other churches — like other religious bodies in the former Soviet Union — faced severe restraints following the Com-

76

munist Revolution. Many churches were closed, the buildings and contents destroyed or confiscated. On January 23, 1918, a sweeping decree was published on the separation of church and state. Although the decree technically assured freedom of conscience and the right to "confess any religion or no religion at all," these regulations tended to favor those who professed no religion. Religious oaths were abolished, and individuals were prohibited from "evading citizen's duties on the grounds of religion."

One of the most devastating provisions was the separation of the school from the church. The teaching of religion was prohibited in state, municipal, and private schools and was permitted only within the family. Indeed, there were ways of discouraging that as well. Ecclesiastical and religious associations were subject to regulations. Such associations were prohibited from owning property and could not "enjoy the right of legal entity."

Eleven years later a series of religious laws were enacted that further limited the churches. Religious bodies were forced to register with the State and were controlled by the Council for Religious Affairs. Religious associations were prohibited from organizing children, young people, and women for "biblical or literary study, sewing, working or the teaching of religion, etc., excursions, children's playgrounds, libraries, reading rooms, sanatoria or medical care. Only books necessary for the purpose of the cult (worship) may be kept in the prayer buildings and premises." Further, "the activities of clergymen, preachers, preceptors and the like shall be restricted to the area in which the members of religious associations reside and in the area where the prayer building or premises are situated."

There were purges and persecutions as well, and although religious bodies were denied opportunities to propagandize or teach religion, atheistic groups were permitted and encouraged to do so (Beeson 1982:34).

In the face of such severe restraints, the Orthodox and other churches were forced either to go underground, as some did, or to develop the spiritual resources to live creatively within the restrictions. Since the underground churches were illegal, the authorities sought out their members, and many were punished severely. Some who were imprisoned or exiled in Siberia actually began new churches there. They proved, once again, that "the blood of the martyrs is the seed of the church."

The registered churches, including most of the Russian Orthodox churches, emphasized their traditional witness through worship — the mission of Liturgy. Believers discovered new meaning in repetition of biblical passages, which are chanted during the Liturgy. Biblical sermons became prime teaching tools. The services thus became important means for outreach.

Baptism and the Eucharist also took on added meaning. Not infrequently the grandmothers who cared for young children provided Christian education even in the face of parental opposition. Many youngsters were taken to the church for baptism without their parents' knowledge. The lives of ancient saints and martyrs were marked at special events and celebrations, and beloved icons told their stories of faith and sacrifice and victory. Like the stained glass windows of medieval Europe, they were the textbooks of the masses.

During the most difficult times of World War II, when German troops were at the outskirts of Moscow, Stalin was forced to acknowledge that he needed the support of the church in order to claim the loyalty and continued sacrifices of the people. The church, emphasizing its own history, once again provided a base for national identity. In strategic centers like Leningrad, church leaders stood courageously with the suffering and starving people. When the war was over, the church ministered to survivors and, without blessing the evils of the regime under which it had been persecuted, found ways to affirm the positive contributions of the social order.

One area in which the churches played a significant, and relatively visible role was in relation to the work of the quasi-official peace committees. In this the churches walked a very fine line, most of the time successfully. They welcomed opportunities to state publicly the Christian concern for peacemaking, and they avoided becoming too closely identified with Soviet propaganda.

Acting on behalf of other religious bodies, the Russian Orthodox Church called a major international conference in 1982: "Religious Workers for Saving the Sacred Gift of Life from Nuclear Catastrophe." This was followed by several international round table discussions on related topics. Thus the churches not only became more prominent in the society but they also established significant ecumenical ties with Western churches and religious figures, including Dr. Billy Graham.

In association with the National Council of the Churches of Christ in the United States, the Soviet churches sponsored prayer vigils during each of the several summit conferences between Presidents Reagan and Gorbachev. At the initial conference, held in Geneva in 1985, Russian church leaders for the first time were introduced to reporters and producers from the Soviet electronic media. This in turn led to another first, the appearance of church officials on Soviet television.

Among the Soviet church leaders who took advantage of these new opportunities for public visibility was the head of the Publishing Department of the Moscow Patriarchate, Metropolitan Pitirim of Volokolamsk and Yuriev. As a liturgical scholar, Metropolitan Pitirim assembled high fidelity equipment to record church music and make it generally available. A workshop that he developed produced quality reproductions of significant icons for sale to pilgrims at Zagorsk.

Himself a skilled photographer, the Metropolitan also brought together a group of professionals to provide remarkable documentation on the church's worship and ecumenical activities. On one occasion several years ago, Metropolitan Pitirim invited me to review a display of photos in the reception area of the congregation where on Sundays he regularly conducts the Liturgy. "It is a quiet form of education," he explained, "observed by those who come into the church for special events." After I had marveled at the quality and variety of the photographs, I asked what he would say if the authorities questioned this pro-active form of communication. With a characteristic twinkle in his eyes, the bearded hierarch said to me, "I would simply say that they are modern icons!"

In Moscow and several other cities, the Russian Orthodox Church has gradually increased its visibility in churches located on the grounds of convents and monasteries that the government had earlier confiscated. It has done this in order both to preserve and restore religious art and architecture in such places as the Novodevichei Convent, and to make itself available to the tourists and visitors who come to the historic sites and cemeteries. Considerable effort has been devoted to providing daily Liturgies with excellent choirs.

The churches in the former USSR also used their association with the United States National Council of Churches to gain public recognition in a variety of ways. The NCC's travel seminars took hundreds of American Christians to numerous cities. Each time this provided opportunity for some attention in the public media. Also, as a result of negotiations with the Intourist Travel Office, the locations of open "working" churches and their times of service were publicized. That, in itself, corrected an earlier disinformation campaign that implied that all churches were now only museums.

It would be a mistake, however, to see such efforts in purely mechanical or pragmatic terms. In these and in other cases, "integration into the ethnic culture (indigenization) was not considered simply as a

79

missionary tool, but rather as a 'transfiguration' of the richness of the human culture and history by the light of the gospel" (Bria 1980:10).

Protestant and Pentecostal Mission Activity

The illustrations offered so far have been mostly from the dominant religious body in the CIS, the Russian Orthodox Church. Yet Pentecostal bodies and Protestants — especially the All Union Council of Evangelical Christians, Baptists — have also been active. With approaches that more closely resemble the efforts of Western Christians, these groups have grown significantly as a result of dedicated work that sometimes closely skirted the borders of legality.

The Baptists, for example, have utilized music groups to engage both adults and youth in religious expression. Congregations are known as singing churches and have large choirs. Practice sessions become important gatherings in which young people often participate and provide orchestral accompaniment. Rehearsals themselves become an opportunity for Christian education and lively fellowship. Choir leaders in Baptist churches frequently are trained in biblical studies and theology as well as music; seventy have graduated from Bible correspondence schools.

I recall a visit in 1984 when our group of American and Canadian Christians were invited to the Moscow Baptist Prayer House for a special service featuring a new cantata for the massed choirs and orchestra. The music director of the church had composed the music for "Life and Peace." It was magnificent. But more important, it provided the members of that congregation an opportunity to express their faith directly and forcefully.

Alexei Bichkov, then general secretary of the All Union Council, said that Baptists had a special department to carry on their work of evangelism. "We direct our evangelism to family members, friends and co-workers," he told me. "We say to church members, 'Use any possibility to witness to the love of Jesus'" (Bailey 1987:55). The members seem to make the most of their contact with nonbelievers. People are invited to the churches, and if they are converted they are baptized — sometimes as many as seven or eight at a time, eight to ten thousand a year.

Bichkov's own model for ministry is Billy Graham. Speaking of his grandfather Stephan, who was "converted" to the evangelical faith while a German prisoner during World War I, Bichkov described the "eloquent preacher" as "the first small Billy Graham in our family." Having visited the United States several times, Bichkov was instrumental in the three visits that Graham made to the former Soviet Union. On each occasion the American evangelist preached in Bichkov's Moscow church, and during his extended second visit he led a national seminar for Baptist pastors.

He told the preachers that "there is another way to preach: by the Holy Spirit producing the fruit of the Spirit in our lives. In some parts of the world you may not verbalize your faith, but we can love, we can have tenderness, and as the Scripture says, 'Against such there is no law.' No one can tell you that you cannot love your neighbor" (Terrell 1985:80).

During the decade of the 1980s the All Union Council established three hundred new congregations, and more than a hundred prayer houses were built or renovated in such cities as Leningrad (St. Petersburg), Rostov, Alma-Ata, Kishinev, and Minsk. They are strongest in the Ukraine, where there were more than 1,500 congregations and nearly 300,000 members; there were also congregations in far-off Tashkent, in the heart of Muslim territory.

Among Baptist families, especially in Siberia, is a phenomenon called the "household church." In these families the father often serves as the home pastor and the mother functions as a deacon. Bible correspondence schools have made it possible for several hundred local church pastors to be trained in recent years. In the mid-1980s 150 new pupils were enrolling and fifty students were graduating each year. Thus believers were allowed to study the Scriptures systematically for three years in their homes — a practice that the government permitted even when Sunday schools and organized classes for youth and adults were prohibited.

Methodists and Lutherans are most numerous in the Baltic nations of Latvia, Lithuania, and Estonia, where their churches have helped to preserve the national identity of those republics. Even before the restraints on Christians were relaxed, the churches in those areas found ways to help the people express their humanity with dignity and courage. It was, for them, an important form of evangelical witness.

The Effects of *Glasnost* and *Perestroika*

If the openness demonstrated by the broadcast journalist on the steps of the Ukraine Hotel surprised me, what followed that week amazed

81

me, and what has taken place in recent months has been an answer to the prayers of millions. During the Orthodox Millennial celebrations, some of which took place in the Bolshoi State Theatre (of all places!), there were live national telecasts, the return of monasteries including the highly significant Monastery of the Caves, and the laying of the foundation stone of a new cathedral on land provided by the State. Hundreds of church buildings have now been returned to churches, millions of Bibles have been imported, and some CIS leaders even use references to God in their public speeches. Several ranking clergy have held legislative posts. At the time of the tragic earthquake in Soviet Armenia, Church World Service and other foreign church organizations were permitted to provide direct aid for the first time and churches were encouraged to begin work in hospitals and care centers.

These events have enormous import for the missionary approach of the Orthodox and other churches. The public attention given to religious events on television, for example, has the effect of freeing people to practice their faith openly. Christian educational programs and events are held publicly. The churches are training new pastors as fast as the now-crowded seminaries will permit; the new pastors will serve the reopened and new churches. There is excitement. And there is worry. Can the churches maintain the pace? Can the churches afford the costs of such opportunities?

Two other major concerns trouble thoughtful Christians in the CIS. Much of the attention during the Millennial Celebrations focused on the Russian Orthodox Church — the historic and long established church. The sudden official attention gives that church an enormous advantage. It is not the "state church" of Czarist times. I know of no one who would want that. But the publicity and even friendliness of the government give the enormous Orthodox Church a quasi-official status. Even though the minority churches also have new freedoms, they are likely to be overshadowed and could even suffer from benign neglect or unintended prejudice.

The other concern relates to the Ukrainian Catholic problem. Stalin forced a significant number of Roman Catholic churches to become Orthodox. Reversing that historic and tragic fact will not come easily. Russian Orthodox leaders, some with a measure of influence, can hardly be expected to welcome the change. The political and spiritual costs will be felt for years and are likely to impede both the ecumenical spirit and the outreach of the churches.

Change has indeed come rapidly. But the changes that lie ahead may be more difficult.

For Further Reading

Anthony, Metropolitan
1980   "On Mission and Evangelism." *International Review of Mission*
            69 (276-77):477-80.
Bailey, Betty Jane, and Constance J. Tarasar
1987   *Eyes to See, Ears to Hear.* New York: Friendship Press.
Bailey, J. Martin
1987   *One Thousand Years.* New York: Friendship Press.
Beeson, Trevor
1982   *Discretion and Valour.* Philadelphia: Fortress Press.
Bria, Ion
1980   *Martyria/Mission: The Witness of the Orthodox Churches Today.*
            Geneva: World Council of Churches.

1986   *Go Forth in Peace: Orthodox Perspectives on Mission.* Geneva:
            World Council of Churches.
Castro, Emilio
1974   "Interview with Metropolitan Anthony." *International Review
            of Mission* 63 (249):87-95.
Hatch, Janene Pinchot
1980   *New Apostles of Christ.* Syosset, NY: Orthodox Church in
            America.
Paul, Archbishop
1980   *The Faith We Hold.* Crestwood, NY: St. Vladimir's Seminary
            Press.
Terrell, Bob
1985   *Billy Graham in the Soviet Union.* Minneapolis: Billy Graham
            Evangelistic Association.
van der Bent, Ans, ed.
1982   *Handbook of Member Churches.* Geneva: World Council of
            Churches.
Zahirsky, Valerie G.
1980   *Enlighteners of Ancient Kingdoms.* Syosset, NY: Orthodox
            Church in America.

Africa

Lamin Sanneh

In these reflections on the consequences of Christian mission and some policy implications for the future, I am not concerned with whether missions have a future in Africa, or whether such a future must be safeguarded, but with what might happen should churches decide to embark on such a task. As such I examine the challenges and issues in that context. Finally, I offer some guidelines for action, not in any systematic or exhaustive fashion, but, for want of better, of what could reasonably be stated.

There is no doubt that we have entered a new age in the life of the church. The translatability of Christianity has created national churches and forged deeper connections at the level of cultural self-understanding. The churches in the Third World today are strong or weak in proportion to the depth of their vernacular roots, roots that mission had nurtured through attention to scriptural translation. I am not, of course, pretending that these churches are secure, or that everywhere the vernacular task has been accomplished. There are too many Westernisms in the church to make that uniformly possible. It is the case, however, that Christian confidence is nearly everywhere a function of the vernacular principle, hinging as it does on cultural self-

---

Lamin Sanneh is Professor of History and of Missions and World Christianity, and Chairman of the Council on African Studies, Yale University. He is the author of *West African Christianity: The Religious Impact* (1983), *Translating the Message: The Missionary Impact on Culture* (1989), and *The Jakhanke Muslim Clerics: A Religious and Historical Study of Islam in Senegambia* (1989).

understanding. Thus the translatability of Christianity under missionary aegis has brought into being national churches who see their work in the context of national development. Although delicate issues are involved, including the desire of national Christian leaders to act independently of foreign church agencies, the success or failure of church projects for national renewal determines whether or not the church anywhere and everywhere has a credible mission.

Two major strands are intertwined in the national question. The first is the unquestioned responsibility of churches in Africa to proclaim the gospel to their own people, whose safety and advancement are priorities of the first order. Unlike most governments in Africa, the churches have their credibility with men and women whose roots are in the soil. Yet the gospel is not the monopoly of any one nation or culture. Hence, to introduce the second consideration, the reality of the worldwide fellowship of the church should prevent the absolute domestication of the gospel lest it become nothing more than a national ideology. It is important to build networks of understanding and partnership into the exigencies of history and nation in recognition of who, and whose, we are.

Necessity of Continued Western Engagement

Similarly, in the nature of the case, the Western church cannot now turn its back on Third World Christians, although for a variety of reasons, including the strong urge to withdraw the apron strings of dependency, a good case can be made for leaving Third World Christians to work out their own salvation in fear and trembling.

In view of that sentiment, the mainline Protestant churches in the West are by and large reluctant to be engaged in explicit ways in the life of the Third World churches, arguing that the worthy goals of self-reliance and self-propagation would be set back by Western missionary meddling. This is not, in my view, a persuasive argument, although as an historian of religion I am aware of, and share concern about, the paternalism it seeks to combat. It is scarcely a remedy to substitute for the injuries of paternalism the indifference of moratorium. If Christians wash their hands of each other's affairs, then a menacing gulf of indifference will open up between them and within them, with sinister implications for the worldwide witness of the church. The only responsible way forward is to accept the consequences of the history of our interrelatedness and to proceed on the basis of mutual support and interest. Our very cultural differences should help us appreciate the richness of our common heritage, so that we may claim our particular roots as the strands in an interconnected universal fellowship, not as trophies of national exclusiveness.

One of the realities of today's changed circumstances is the sensitiveness of Third World Christians to Western control and influence. The Western church as the moral and spiritual arbiter of Western values has been particularly vulnerable (though not necessarily answerable) to charges of neo-colonialism. I suggest that a profound misunderstanding has complicated our understanding of the church's role here. The process of Westernization has been so confused with that of Christianization that evidence of the one is seen as proof of the other. I am not against the idea of Western culture as a positive stimulus for the church abroad; for such a formula, if it could work, would help clarify our responsibility today. In fact it does not work, and yet we persist as if it does, with guilt serving as both evidence and interpretation of foreign meddlesomeness.

In the present mood of criticism of the Western missionary enterprise, it is hard to encourage people that much can be learned from past labors. Our reluctance to look to the past restricts our freedom to move into the future, and leaves us with a consuming sense of guilt. That guilt has produced a deep sense of futility. Condemned in our past actions, we are afraid to act any more, with inaction becoming a subjective source of Christian evasiveness. It is as if missionary efforts in the past confirm Western perfidy for which retreat and denial make suitable restitution. That response, however, still leaves the West as the center of the problem and its solution, rather than a provisional instrument of God's purpose.

In a different connection the Yale historian C. Vann Woodward notes that the preoccupations and problems that constitute our knowledge of blacks are predominantly those of whites. "His conscience burdened with guilt over his own people's record of injustice and brutality toward the black man, the white historian often writes in a mood of contrition and remorse as in expiation of racial guilt or flagellation of the guilty. In this connection it is well to recall Butterfield's observation that 'since moral indignation corrupts the agent who possesses it and is not calculated to reform the man who is the object of it, the demand for it . . . is really a demand for an illegitimate form of power'" (Woodward 1989:34).

We may extend this by analogy to the situation of missionary vision and scholarship. It is for that reason that we need to shift from

86

viewing mission chiefly as the wrongs and injuries the Western world perpetrated on non-white races. For the tenacity of the caricatures of mission are a form of Western self-centeredness. To paraphrase Vann Woodward, the Western critics of mission might pretend to be defending Africans and others, but in fact the history of these native peoples is assumed to be the record of what the whites believed, thought, legislated, did, and did not do *about* them and their societies. In this scheme the African is a passive agent, the one to whom things happened, the object rather than the subject of history. Such history "is filled with the infamies and philanthropies, the brutalities and charities, the laws, customs, prejudices, policies, politics, crusades, and laws of whites *about* blacks" (Woodward 1989:35).

There are indeed many areas of painful ambivalence toward Africans, the condescension and racism that infected relations and twisted attitudes. But let me not be understood as saying that the whole history of mission consists only of what missionaries said and did. Unless we are convinced that the real story of Christian mission is the story of white cultural and political impact, as I am sure it is not, we have to recognize an original role for Africans, and, behind that, for the God of all history. After all, it was the Africans' language that missionaries adopted for the Scriptures of Christianity, their god who became the God of Abraham, Isaac, Moses, and Jesus, their music the hymn of the Savior, and their rituals the vessel of the Holy Spirit. A rather momentous shift of focus is involved in such massive projects of indigenous transposition.

Fortunately, the ongoing work of the churches in Africa has not had to wait for a shift in Western attitudes to enable it to move forward. We may rejoin the enterprise at any of its various points: in demands of primary evangelism in points of growth; in responsibility for leadership training; in prospects of ecumenical collaboration; in educating and equipping women and youth; in programs for health and social welfare; in the creation of cooperative societies; in agricultural schemes and animal husbandry; in problems of migrant labor; and in opportunities for national reconciliation and reconstruction, among others.

Pliny, the Roman historian, said of Africa that "it always offers something new," which in the postwar era took the form of what Lord Hailey described as "the manifestation of the spirit of Africanism which is one of the most distinctive features in the picture of postwar Africa. . . . It envisages the attainment of a government dominated by Africans and expressing in its own institutions the characteristic spirit of Africa as interpreted by the modern African" (Hailey 1957:252). This

African sentiment was opposing the view that justified Western colonialism on the continent, as Sir Harry Johnston, the British colonial pioneer and administrator expressed it in 1899. The vast territories of Africa, he argued, were "to be governed as India is governed, despotically but wisely, and with the first aim of securing good government, and a reasonable degree of civilization to a large population of races inferior to the European" (Johnston 1899). However, Ndabaningi Sithole, an African nationalist, observed appropriately that, "No thinking African can deny that Africa very badly needs Western help, but no thinking African accepts this as justification for being European ruled" (Beetham 1960:7-8).

Although colonialism has disappeared in most of Africa, the legacy of white onslaught on black pride and dignity is too fresh in the minds of Africans to be forgotten. The view of some people that Africans should turn their backs completely on Europe and North America in order to escape that legacy is unrealistic and impractical, for how do you separate the technology and market economy introduced with Western colonialism from its exploitative mechanism; or the eradication of yaws and sleeping sickness from the intrusive impact of the poll tax on bedazzled villagers; or even literacy in Western languages from the disdain for African "dialects" so-called that accompanied it? It is this mixed bag of the Western legacy that remains a motivating force in Africa's modern struggles.

Tom Beetham observed that in retrospect European opinion in both church and state failed to understand how the pace for change in Africa would quicken in the first half of the twentieth century, there being such a slow appreciation for the value of indigenous agents and institutions. Europeans tended to equate right qualification for leadership with technological competence. "Neither in Church nor in State," he writes, "was there yet a grappling with the problem of giving authority in leadership to those who were a people's natural leaders even if they were not personally seized of the methods of Western technology; maturity is too readily equated by Anglo-Saxons with an acquaintance with water-borne sanitation" (Beetham 1960:5).

It is the same problem that today besets development-minded churches in the West in their drive to put toilets before television as a Third World priority. It would be well to recall the story of the Spanish Capuchin missionaries who arrived at the court of Benin in Nigeria in 1651. Finding it difficult to gain an audience with the king, the prefect of the mission decided through a messenger to present his royal host with the novelty of a chiming clock. Impressed, the king returned it *c h a *

with a request for the missionary to explain how it worked. However, the clock was intercepted by the king's wary Lord Chamberlain, who saw through the ruse, handing back the clock to the missionaries with the message that the king and his people could manage without it (Sanneh 1983a:46). In later centuries Africans received significant technological wares without that altering their attitude on the harm of dependence on the West. Technology is a Western Trojan horse with a resilient centuries-old life expectancy.

It is well to bear in mind that while Africans admitted the superior material advantages of continued colonial tutelage, they nevertheless opted for the little-tested and long-begrudged prospect of self-responsibility. For instance, when the British government floated the kite of a Central African Federation of Rhodesia and Nyasaland on grounds of its generally recognized economic advantages, the African opponents rejected it as incompatible with political freedom. To the disbelief of colonial authorities, Africans were undercutting the patently clear benefits of economic progress in a stable political framework, preferring political restoration of lost dignity and identity to acquired tastes for material enhancement. Even today, people in the West find it hard to appreciate why grinding need fails to produce the logical consequence of market-oriented societies in Africa, so strong is the spell of the materialist worldview.

No doubt this matter will continue to be a debating point in the future, but rather than continuing to grin through gritted teeth at a sanguine West and an intransigent Africa, we should for our purposes look elsewhere at the vernacular springs of revitalization in African societies, for that is also the level of creative innovation and hope, one that development projects disregard.

Impact of Christian "Translatability"

African societies carry much deeper marks and more enduring roots from the systematic exposure of their languages and culture to missionary attention than from the shock of Western colonial overrule, here today and gone tomorrow. The close connection between language and culture in these societies meant that language study and development such as occurred under missionary sponsorship touched off a ripple effect throughout society.

One effect was the democratic leveling of scriptural translation, a neglected aspect of the study of the missionary enterprise. The vernacular languages that missionaries developed were, of course, the property of ordinary people, yet in making them the preeminent medium of religion, missionaries detached these languages from the notion of religious exclusivism, thus enfranchising men and women normally excluded in traditional religions and offering them a decisive, if at first limited, role in the Christian movement. People no longer had to observe rules of ritual cleanliness to possess and use the vernacular Bible, as they would in the old dispensation. Such desacralization of religious language had necessarily a corresponding impact on access in the wider social sphere. For it is scarcely conceivable that men and women who should consider themselves without stigma before God should not feel an identical unbarring before Caesar.

The second effect was that culture as human creativity was assumed into the higher process by which God fashioned tribal populations into tribes of the New Israel. This had a twofold impact on culture. For the one part, culture was purged of the sin of deification, and, for the other, the eloquence of the tribal assembly was employed in proclamation and witness. Tribal cultures, regardless of how profane or despised, were constituted into expressions of God's living purpose through the vernacular Scriptures. By the same token, these cultures, whatever their preeminence and achievements, were stripped of their self-sacralizing tendencies by being made aware that regarding Jew and Gentile "there is no respect of persons with God" (Rom. 2:11). Tribal self-awareness became only a frontier of the gospel's historic course. It was from this source that cultural freedom became a reality and the precursor of the political variety.

A third ripple effect concerns the nature and purpose of mission. The idea of Christian mission as Western religious export was challenged as Africans perceived in vernacular translations vindication for indigenous primacy. The current Western dilemma about how, in a previous age, in the name of faithfulness missionaries committed wrongs against others, may be mitigated by knowledge of indigenous appropriation superseding the export version of the faith. Western Christians may, for their part, repay Third World assurances with humble acknowledgment of the instructive value of indigenous appropriations. In the end this should nurture a sorely needed sense of universal fellowship across cultures and nations.

Third World Christian leaders and scholars can facilitate this process by themselves becoming clearer about what they perceive as wrong with mission. Much of our discussion in this area has become fixed in repetition and raised voices. I understand quite well the sense of wrong and injustice from which we all speak; indeed, this became clear in flaring nationalist rhetoric and the feeling of battered national pride. Nevertheless, we live in a unique time of challenge and opportunity, and our inclination to exclude outsiders from our affairs is untrue to the genius of the gospel and to the pressures of world community. In isolation our wounds become ironically only ours, unable to be shared. As such they suppurate and defy mediatory intervention. Exclusiveness is inimical to reconciliation and hope.

Role of the Church in a Renewed Africa

And now for a reappraisal. First, in any meaningful future enterprise of the church, we cannot afford to be churlish about the missionary roots of Christian renewal in Africa. We should recognize today's immense vernacular gains as springing out of the translation ferment of the previous missionary era and the anticolonial sentiment it nursed. Christian mission was the force that thrust upon the contemporary scene the new societies with their sense of self-awareness, although individual missionaries may have opposed African advancement as an offshoot of that self-understanding. In some of the most significant instances, Africans came to their sense of cultural and national self-awareness through the grammars, dictionaries, and the vernacular literacy of Christian missions. The missionary contribution of outsiders to the modern reawakening of Africa has few parallels, and should stand as a monument to the scaling down of cross-cultural barriers. We should give praise and honor to God that he raised in the Western church servants of his cause in Africa and elsewhere. The dry bones of many of these missionaries, rising from their unmarked graves, gave voices to our ancestors. This was, in fact, the substance of the tribute that J. B. Danquah, a leading Ghanaian nationalist, paid to the Basel missionary, Rev. J. Christaller. Danquah called Christaller an ancestor *(Nana)* of the Akan for ensuring that the Akan take their place as progressive members of the wider human family (Danquah 1944:186ff.).

Second, we need to recognize that any future dispensation will require a form of pluralism that expresses fully the genius of our peoples. Such a future must carry the signs of a new Pentecost where we hear for ourselves God's mighty acts, "each of us in his own native language" (Acts 2:8). This is a warrant for pluralism as the framework for cultural particularity rather than for homogenous conformity. Pluralism in this sense is more radical than many current projects for

91

abandoning Christian distinctiveness, since such projects leave intact confidence in Western historical and intellectual experience as universally normative. The pluralism of Pentecost, by contrast, includes *all* cultures in their distinctiveness within the *one* scheme of God's universal purpose for human life, while excluding in them exclusive and self-absolutizing tendencies, such as those of powerful cultural traditions, whether Hellenist, Western European, or Victorian imperialist. What we regard as the center of human affairs will, from the pressure of God's unfolding plan, come to acquire a peripheral and marginal status.

The pluralism of vernacular translation extends the logic of Pentecost into modern Africa, and indicates that cultural and linguistic uniformity cannot be a requirement of the coming kingdom. Christians of today have an enormous stake in the pluralism of the missionary heritage, and we should spare no effort to claim and augment that heritage.

In effect we should moderate the emphasis on institutionalization, encouraging particularity within the framework of mutual interdependence. The church is often caught between two extremes: either lurching toward a single administrative instrument as an expression of unity or else succumbing to fragmentation as an answer to free choice. Neither is desirable. The unitary instrument is fraught with elements of compulsion and is deeply destructive of creativity, while fragmentation merely repeats the coercion of uniformity by making the fragments exclusive norms of the truth.

The vast and often bewildering array of the worldwide Christian fellowship, vivid and aloud in its sundry parts, is in unity only according to the pattern of the One who came not to be served but to serve and to lay down his life (Mark 10:45).

Third, in view of the accelerating pace of world solidarity we should investigate how ecumenical cooperation might advance the search for the new humanity. Whatever forms such cooperation takes, the exercise will undeniably involve some retracing of the pattern of the cross in demands for self-denial, humble service, and trust in divine self-vindication. No one will be exempt from the pressures of that new humanity, but Christians may have a special clue to the mystery by which God has always composed a new world from the lives of those on the margins and in excluded pockets of society. Christians must grasp the delineations of the new humanity in the role being assumed in our midst by new waves of refugees, immigrants, and other transitory elements, seeing how a bold new world is coming into being to challenge old certainties and the symbols that enshrine them. Churches with any future must claim the role of the sojourner as the paradigm-filled condition of the emerging new world order.

Coming nearer to home, the churches in Africa will find themselves being drawn into consequences of the operations of the post-colonial state. Or, perhaps, one should speak of the inoperativeness of the state. At any rate, the great swirl of renewal that has engulfed communist states in the former Soviet Union and Eastern Europe is unlikely to spare self-avowed Marxist states in Africa, as early indications prove. In those circumstances the churches will be challenged to respond to meaningful discussions about ethics and public policy, and about the nature and limits of state power. One line of inquiry will address the unexamined notion of the state as an exclusive unitary instrument in both the private and public domain. The Christian insight that pluralism has a status in the divine providence undergirds the safety of state and society too. Like culture, the state in the Christian view is a human contrivance, existing by our will and changing at our choice. There is nothing absolute or immutable about it, and it must answer to the limited criteria of justice and morality or forfeit its right to be. For Christians only God is absolute, and our earthly affairs stand under his sovereign rule and justice. This conviction safeguards the integrity of the relative and instrumental sphere where the state properly belongs. Christians should be uneasy about religious/political syncretism, because from it political corruption and religious hypocrisy arise. Yet the separation of church and state does not mean that the civil magistrate is unaccountable before the moral law, or that the prelate is an ascetic disembodiment. The autonomy of the political sphere should be a sign of its instrumental character, not the rule of self-divinization. Historical experience suggests that the state functions better when it is stripped of the self-assumed attributes of religion, and that the church's prophetic credibility grows from abjuring the political instrument to advance itself. When Jesus declared that we should render unto Caesar the things that are Caesar's and unto God the things that are God's, he actually gave the kiss of life to a state that was suffocating from self-deification.

This is a large and pressing issue. It calls us to consider the setting up of a working party whose members would determine the most practicable and expeditious way of tackling the subject of political reconstruction in the context of Christian renewal and responsibility. The first step would be to produce a working draft on the lines of church and society. This initially would be a Christian reflection, but ultimately it would draw on interreligious resources as well as historical and anthropological materials. As a by-product it would recognize the significant work being done by national institutes of church and society and would add significantly to the ecumenical cause in general.

Another issue likely to vex mission planners and policymakers is the relationship between economic development and social progress. The global impact of new transnational corporations is likely to include a fresh tension between urban industrial complexes and the sources of rural productivity. Consequently, rural development projects might look attractive to churches whose social base is predominantly rural. Yet rural development might only result in reducing villages and farms to structural dependence on urban industrial forces, with local produce liable to sequestration by the export sector. Yet there are forms of appropriate technology and the requisite education that churches might undertake to mitigate whatever distortions urban industrial projects might introduce.

Two basic problems have held back our peoples. One is the fundamental truth that life is more than meat and the body more than raiment (Luke 12:23). Losing sight of that has driven our leaders into irrational greed. There is a spiritual hunger on the continent far deeper, even if less tangible, than the famine crisis. The new waves of conversion that have threatened to overwhelm the churches signify an extraordinary awakening and demand a bold, imaginative moral initiative to harness their force. It is *the one thing needful* for public leaders, and churches must step confidently, if at times perilously, into the role of moral guides. The situation in Africa today may be compared to the breakup of the Western medieval world in the sixteenth and seventeenth centuries and to twentieth-century attempts at public theology, suggesting the complexity of the present task.

The second problem has to do with the substitution of the promise of material abundance for God's promises. Ordinary people who were taken in by the rhetoric of economic salvation felt betrayed as corruption ate away at our spiritual foundations. As a frustrated highly trained African professional put it to me once, "*Nyii gomuñ yalla,*" "These (our leaders) do not trust in God," the context being open and persistent economic corruption. The apparent intractability of material deprivation has compelled the kind of fundamental reckoning compatible (and identical) with the spiritual quest.

These two problems find their institutional focus in the doctrinaire state, the notion that the political kingdom precedes and supersedes the heavenly kingdom. Insofar as Africans have become disenchanted with the rhetoric of economic abundance, they have been in incipient

94

rebellion against the idea of the all-competent state, more and more persuaded that people must work out their own salvation unfettered by state oversight. This is in part the reason why churches have played an increasingly active public role, chiding, admonishing, counseling, and exhorting, giving people hope.

Beside these two areas of concern, the mission of the churches will increasingly face the issue of a politically active Islam. I think it is fair to say that African Christians have in the main learned to get on well with their Muslim counterparts religiously and socially, in spite of Western claims that Christians have been slow or unwilling to accept Muslims. However, a politically articulate Islam is a new phenomenon for church leaders who find the old assurances of religious tolerance and social harmony inadequate. In Uganda, the Sudan, Nigeria, and elsewhere, Muslim political activism has sent the churches scrambling. The churches' attitude of believing that their worldly "foolishness" of disinterested vigilance will be counted as wisdom in the hereafter does little to deter the new political militancy, and the pressure is on to develop a fresh understanding of religious pluralism to embrace its political variety.

This calls for a new kind of theological leadership. In the competition between the state and private sector for educated Africans, the church has the added handicap of demanding more in the form of the strongest possible academic credentials allied to an uncommon commitment to the mission of the church. The church will thus have added to the deepening problem of manpower scarcity that of rising expectations. If, in the meantime, the church is compelled to set its sights lower in order to respond to recruitment pressures, it must nevertheless for the long duration continue to uphold exemplary standards. Theological training for the relatively few who feel so called must, consequently, nurture the ideal of hearts astir and minds ablaze for God and the righteous kingdom.

For Further Reading

Barrett, David B.
    1968   *Schism and Renewal in Africa: An Analysis of Six Thousand Contemporary Religious Movements.* Nairobi: Oxford University Press.
    1982   *World Christian Encyclopaedia.* Nairobi: Oxford University Press.

Beetham, T. A.
1960   *A New Order in Africa.* Beckly Pamphlets, New Series, no. 2.
1968   *Christianity and the New Africa.* New York: Praeger Publishers.
Blyden, Edward W.
1967   *Christianity, Islam and the Negro Race.* Edinburgh: Edinburgh
        University Press. Originally published 1887.
Curtin, Philip D.
1964   *The Image of Africa: British Ideas and Action 1780-1850.* Madison: University of Wisconsin Press.
Danquah, J. B.
1944   *The Akan Doctrine of God.* London: Lutterworth Press.
Delavignette, Robert
1964   *Christianity and Colonialism.* New York: Hawthorn Books.
Hailey, Lord
1957   *An African Survey Revised 1956.* Oxford: Clarendon Press.
Johnston, Sir Harry H.
1899   *A History of the Colonization of Africa by Alien Races.* Cambridge: Cambridge University Press.
Lugard, Lord
1922   *The Dual Mandate for Tropical Africa.* Edinburgh: Blackwood and Sons.
Moorhouse, Geoffrey
1973   *The Missionaries.* Philadelphia: J. P. Lippincott Company.
Nida, Eugene A.
1952   *God's Word in Man's Language.* New York: Harper & Brothers.
1954   *Customs and Cultures: Anthropology for Christian Missions.* New York: Harper & Brothers.
1960   *Message and Mission.* New York: Harper & Row.
Paden, John
1986   *Ahmadou Bello: Sardauna of Sokoto.* London: Hodder & Stoughton.
Oliver, Roland
1970   *The Missionary Factor in East Africa.* London: Longman.
Sanneh, Lamin
1977   "Christian-Muslim Encounter in Freetown in the 19th Century." *Bulletin of the Secretariat for Non-Christian Religions* 12:1-2.
1978   "Modern Education among Freetown Muslims and the Christian Stimulus." In *Christianity in Independent Africa.* Edited by E. Fashole-Luke, Richard Gray, Adrian Hastings, and Godwin Tasie. Bloomington: Indiana University Press.

1979	"Muslims in Non-Muslim Societies of Africa." In *Christian and Islamic Contributions Towards Establishing States in Africa South of the Sahara*. Stuttgart: Council for Foreign Relations, Federal Republic of Germany.
1980	"The Domestication of Islam and Christianity in Africa." *Journal of Religion in Africa* 11:1.
1983a	*West African Christianity: The Religious Impact*. Maryknoll, NY: Orbis Books.
1983b	"The Horizontal and Vertical in Mission." *International Bulletin of Missionary Research* 7 (4).
1987	"Christian Missions and the Western Guilt Complex." *The Christian Century*, April 7.
1989	*Translating the Message: The Missionary Impact on Culture*. Maryknoll, NY: Orbis Books.

Woodward, C. Vann

1989	*The Future of the Past*. New York: Oxford University Press.

North America

Keith R. Crim

Statistics and extrapolations, even in a context of faith in the One who is the same yesterday, today, and forever, cannot give a guarantee of reliability. But they can be a record of hopes and aspirations for the future of our world and a suggestion of how we might contribute to that future.

First, we will look at the churches that serve as the base for mission in the twenty-first century in terms of some of their strengths and some of their weaknesses. Second, we will look at aspects of the society in which the mission must be carried out. Third, we will consider movements in opposition and in competition to mission. Then as we plan our mission we need to remind ourselves of the wealth of resources that have served us well in the spiritual warfare of the past. And finally, we will look at means and methods that will continue to be called upon when the twenty-first century has become the present.

The Church as the Base for Christian Mission

Protestantism in North America continues to change. The 1980s saw the merging of long separated bodies, resulting in new structures for Lutherans and Presbyterians. New tensions emerged in those two de-

Keith R. Crim is a Presbyterian pastor in Concord, Virginia. Formerly an editor at Westminster Press, Philadelphia, he was a Presbyterian missionary to Korea from 1952 to 1966 and was involved in both evangelistic and educational ministries.

nominational families, and in many others as well. The complexities encountered in building new denominational headquarters and restructuring administrative staff have probably been enough to convince all but the most optimistic that contemplating any further such unions is hardly worthwhile. The missionary task is to revive in these and other denominations a commitment to evangelism and to the worldwide mission of the church. Other issues can be either hindrances or helps to that goal. The issues raised by feminism and by social concerns, by ethnic diversity, concern for the unborn, poverty, the struggle for peace and justice, ecology, crime, and drug abuse now seem fragmented with single-issue constituencies playing the role of advocates. Yet all of these have been and continue to be part of the missionary vision.

In addition to traditional denominational structures there are major areas of Protestantism where independent congregations and a wide range of nondenominational organizations carry out the work of mission. With their great strength in numbers, evangelicals, both within denominations and functioning independently, are able to carry on mission enterprises that will continue unabated into the next century.

In spite of the debates and tensions within the Catholic Church, mission continues to be vigorous. Especially by championing the cause of the poor and the dispossessed, the Church has gained new strength. In the next century the current crisis in religious vocations will probably have been resolved, and new structures for mission will bring a revival on many fronts, some totally unexpected at this point. Did anyone foresee the work and the world renown of Mother Teresa?

One of the developments resulting from the Second Vatican Council is the cooperation between Protestants and Catholics in biblical studies. This is seen most clearly in the work of the Catholic Biblical Society and in that of the Bible Societies. *The Jerome Biblical Commentary* (1968) marked the new maturity of Catholic biblical scholarship and its place in the mainstream of biblical studies. In 1990 *The New Jerome Biblical Commentary* was published, an even more outstanding work that will provide a sound basis for mission and for education. Sponsored by the Catholic Biblical Society, this new commentary is the work of a cross section of both younger and older Catholic scholars.

The Bible Societies have drawn together Catholic and Protestant translators to produce new translations in Spanish, French, English, and many other languages. These "common language versions" were especially designed for evangelistic use and have enjoyed striking success in reaching people of varied backgrounds previously unfamiliar with the Bible message.

Such scholarly work on commentaries and Bible translations has been a major factor in the biblical renewal that now is revitalizing the churches. Wherever the Bible is being studied and cherished, new foundations are laid for mission in the next century.

Yet another sign of hope and promise is the emphasis on social justice as an essential element in mission. The work of Orbis Press and other Christian publishing houses has provided insights into the needs of the poor in countries around the world, including North America. In terms of concrete action, Habitat for Humanity, a Christian organization that works with people in need of decent low-cost housing to help them build their own homes, is one of the particular signs of successful evangelism (James 2:14-17).

On the other hand, a dark shadow is cast on the work of the churches by the declining membership in so many denominations. Dean Kelley's book *Why Conservative Churches Are Growing* (1972) surveyed the wide scene of American religious life and demonstrated that those groups which take their religion seriously grow in membership, while those who regard it as optional steadily lose members. The older Protestant denominations, sometimes called "mainstream," have been conspicuous for decline in membership. There are, however, many signs that their complacency is being shaken, and a new commitment to mission is emerging.

The Society to Which We Witness: The Changing Family

A special edition of *Newsweek* (Winter/Spring 1990) was devoted in its entirety to "The 21st Century Family." The issues it raised are crucial for our witness in North America.

We take for granted the decline of the extended family in our society and the prevalence of the nuclear family. On the other hand we have become increasingly aware of the "blended family," now a dominant family form. How do we witness to members of families of stepfather or stepmother, stepbrothers and sisters? *Newsweek* (1990:24) states, "Some demographers predict that as many as a third of all children born in the 1980s may live with a step-parent before they are eighteen."

How will the churches witness to single-parent families in which the child or children were born after the mother was artificially inseminated, and how can we make them feel at home in the church? An even more difficult group for the church to deal with are lesbian couples

100

raising children together. The churches must examine their responsibility to witness to Christ in such situations. The problems are somewhat similar to those which missionaries have faced in the past as they proclaimed the gospel in societies where plural marriage was the norm.

Throughout the cities of North America the problem of poverty threatens our mission. It is estimated that of the 33 million people living in poverty in the United States, 13 million are children, and 500,000 of those children are homeless (*Newsweek* 1990:49). Furthermore, the number of children addicted to drugs from their mother's womb steadily increases. James 2:14-17 reminds us that something must be done, but the extent of poverty and homelessness seems to place their eradication beyond the power of the churches. Many feel that their sense of mission requires them to work through political structures in order to deal with these problems.

Most of our traditional churches are less touched by the problems of poverty than they are by the problems of affluence. Children born to affluent parents seem to mature emotionally and socially long after they mature physically. *Newsweek* (1990:69) cites the problems caused by the desire for immediate gratification — sexually as seen in widespread cohabitation and unwanted pregnancies, and economically as seen in unrealistic levels of "discretionary spending," which force many of them to continue to live with their parents after they are otherwise on their own. The words of Jesus seem hard to bear in such situations: "Go and sell all you have and give the money to the poor . . ." (Matt. 19:21, TEV).

Mission to the aging is another area that requires new thinking. We cannot take it for granted that everyone who grows old has a religious commitment. Our concerns usually center on the needs of the elderly for health care and adequate housing, but there is a large mission field among elderly persons who have never committed their lives to Christ and those who have failed to develop a mature faith.

Mission to Ethnic Groups

During the 1970s, and especially during the 1980s, immigration from East Asia and many other parts of the world has greatly increased. With the anticipated return of Hong Kong to China before the end of this century, many Chinese are moving from Hong Kong to Canada, and many more are expected to do so. This highly educated and motivated population presents a significant opportunity for mission, and it demands skills in cross-cultural understanding and communication. In the United States every city of any size has a Korean community in which large numbers are already Christian. The Southern Baptist Convention has done such effective work in church development and evangelism among Koreans in this country that its Korean constituency now ranks with the older Korean constituencies of Methodists and Presbyterians (Synod of the Trinity 1989). Other Protestant groups, as well as outstanding Catholic leaders, are also part of the picture. God is bringing to our continent Christian leaders who are sharing in the work of evangelism as well as many non-Christians to whom we are privileged to witness.

Larger in numbers than the Chinese and Korean communities, and often hampered by their disadvantaged position in society, the Hispanic communities also present a challenge not always recognized by the churches (Recinos 1989). The challenge presented by the black community is complicated by the barriers that still are placed in their path by the white majority and by the chaos in the cities. Here again it is evident that the churches, black and white, cannot carry out their mission without also being involved in solutions to the larger social problems. And our lives must agree with our words. It is not easy to live simply in an affluent society and witness to the poor. Nor is it easy to avoid the materialism and greed that characterized the 1980s. Whatever the century, it still is not possible to serve God and Mammon.

The issues of ethnic diversity confronting Canada may take different forms than those of the United States, but they bring equal challenges to the churches. The long-standing assumption that a federal policy of bilingualism would be adequate to safeguard the particular interests of the nation's French-speaking citizens in Québec and elsewhere has been brought into question by the failure in 1990 of the Meech Lake accords. It is yet possible that since Canada's Catholic and Protestant churches both have members from both linguistic and cultural communities, the churches may in the twenty-first century be a greater part of the solution to these vexing issues, rather than part of the problem.

Opposition and Competition

Materialism and greed are not our only competitors in the contest for the allegiance of women and men. New religious groups are constantly emerging and the old religions of Asia are demonstrating new energy and self-confidence.

The late twentieth century has witnessed the rise and fall of a number of religious movements new to North America. Some of them provoked reactions of fear and distrust far beyond what might be justified by their strangeness. The Hare Krishna movement and the Unification Church of Sun Myung Moon were the objects of various lawsuits and often had difficulty obtaining their constitutional rights. Many parents of converts to these groups have charged that their children have been "brainwashed," a charge regarded by most competent social scientists as unfounded (Shinn 1987). As the power of these groups wanes, other equally "strange" groups will probably arise. The best defense against their blandishments is to lead present Christians into a deeper, more mature faith, and to help new Christians grow spiritually and intellectually so that they will no longer be "tossed to and fro and carried about with every wind of doctrine" (Eph. 4:14).

Movements rooted in the superstitions of Western culture are much more formidable competitors. The "New Age Movement" of the 1980s has been both anti-intellectual and anti-Christian. But because it carries the glamour of pop culture and the prestige of Hollywood, it can proclaim reincarnation and the value of astrology and sway millions. It is not enough to wring our hands and denounce these movements. The churches must find ways to carry out their mission and win the followers of the "New Age" to Christ.

Just as the new immigration brings opportunity for mission, it also brings sophisticated and articulate proponents of Islam, Buddhism, Hinduism, and other faiths. It has long been the case that the mission fields of distant lands have come to North America. It is now much more of a reality. To minister to such groups requires education and commitment to Christ. Yet commitment to the uniqueness of Christ does not require disrespect for other religions. It requires respect and sensitivity as we make our witness.

The problem of mission to Jews continues to cause anguish. So much unites Christians and Jews that sensitive persons in both faiths feel our closeness to each other, as well as the depth of issues that divide us. But the inescapable responsibility to witness to all who do not know Christ as Savior cannot be denied. Arthur F. Glasser has written in reference to those who oppose mission to Jews (IBMR 1989:159), "[Hebrew Christians] will undoubtedly raise the final question that if Judaism can manage without Christ . . . do the churches really need Christ?" Glasser's article states the issues clearly and succinctly and will repay careful study.

Old rivals are also still very much with us. Mormons, for example, are now part of the North American mainstream, but their understanding of Christ and the gospel is still contrary to Scripture and to the historic Christian faith. Yet while many Christian denominations continue to decline in membership, the Mormons and other groups continue to grow. Their firm faith and strong commitment bring them the success that eludes the complacent. Most Christians are either ignorant of and indifferent to such groups, or are fired by indiscriminate and zealous opposition to them. Neither attitude is a help to mission. Other groups are also a challenge to our mission, and will continue to be so in the twenty-first century.

The Resources for Mission

The resources available for North American mission in the twenty-first century are incredibly rich, but at present quite obviously underutilized. With our schools and theological seminaries, thinktanks and research institutions, mission organizations and boards, committees at every level of church life, well-trained personnel, and the vast resources of literature and mass media, we can do better than we are doing now.

Scholarly Bible study has already been mentioned. Today there is also increased focus on Bible study that brings renewal to laity and clergy alike. These efforts are enriched by new translations, new study resources, and newly organized programs. Roberta Hestenes (1985) and others emphasize new methods of group study, and both formal and informal groups are popular. More and more Christians are discovering the joy of knowing the Bible and living its teachings. In addition, most Protestant groups have not yet assessed adequately the impact of the Bible's role in the Catholic Church underscored in the Second Vatican Council. The full effects of this movement have yet to be felt, and we all have much to learn from it.

The Pentecostal churches and movements have imparted a sense of rejuvenation to many outside their bounds, and charismatic Christians in mainline denominations have influence beyond their numbers. Other renewal groups are more traditional, but no less effective. Toward the end of the 1980s two formerly separate groups working to bring new spiritual life to the Presbyterian Church (U.S.A.) merged and are now working within their denomination for lasting spiritual renewal. The sense of denominational loyalty in such groups is impressive. It seems to be the nature of denominational structures to ossify and to perpetuate the informal power structures that control them, but that is

104

not inevitable. The exciting fact is that enthusiasm, prayer, and a sense of mission are at work to overcome spiritual lethargy.

One of the many developments that hold promise but also threaten the church is the multiplication of electronic devices that make communication easier. Church and church organizations have computer networks, broadcast and television ministries, and FAX machines and will have whatever new tools become available. The greatest scandals involving church ministries have of course been associated with television evangelists and the abuse of money and power created by television. Fortunately, however, there are associations of Christians pledged to financial integrity and to assuring that their members act according to the highest ethical standards. Great things will happen in the twenty-first century if people of honesty and integrity continue to be in high positions.

The two Christian doctrines with us here are the doctrine of sin, "all have sinned and fall short of the glory of God" (Rom. 3:23), and the doctrine of forgiveness of sin, "If we confess our sins, he is faithful and just, and will forgive our sins" (I John 1:9). Perhaps the greatest of all our resources for mission is the knowledge that we are forgiven and that we are commanded to forgive.

The Means and Methods of Mission

Mission at its best has always had the two foci of proclamation of the gospel and ministry to human need. The great works of mercy and compassion carried on in the name of Christ will continue in every century. The ways in which they are expressed will change.

What is the role of our proclamation? Without the witness of our deeds we are inadequate, but there must also always be our words, our theologically informed message. Theological education faces a genuine crisis, the tension between the academy and the church. Is a seminary's main responsibility to contribute to scholarly research and publication, or to train women and men for ministry? How are the two to be reconciled? Who makes the decisions?

In keeping with the increasing ethnic and ideological pluralism of North America, everyone engaged in ministry needs to learn to think in cross-cultural terms, to understand how others think, and to recognize the shortcomings that they find in our culture. Missionary anthropologist and pastoral counselor David Augsburger (1986) describes three stages in our response to people in other cultures, applicable to people of other faiths or no faith at all. Sympathy, he says, is when we see our picture of others and see it in our own frame of reference. Empathy is when we truly see the picture that they see, but see it still in our own frame. A third stage, which he calls "interpathy," is reached when we see their picture and see it as they see it, coming as close as is humanly possible to identifying with them and feeling what they feel. Then we can begin to share our faith in Christ. We will be "like a householder who brings out of his treasure what is new and what is old" (Matt. 13:52).

For Further Reading

Augsburger, David W.
 1986   *Pastoral Counseling Across Cultures*. Philadelphia: Westminster Press.
Catholic Biblical Association of America
 1968   *The Jerome Bible Commentary*. Englewood Cliffs, NJ: Prentice-Hall.
 1990   *The New Jerome Bible Commentary*. Englewood Cliffs, NJ: Prentice-Hall.
Glasser, Arthur F.
 1989   "Responses." *International Bulletin of Missionary Research* 13:158.
Hestenes, Roberta
 1985   *Using the Bible in Groups*. Philadelphia: Westminster Press.
Kelley, Dean
 1972   *Why Conservative Churches are Growing*. New York: Harper & Row.
Newsweek
 1990   *The 21st Century Family Special Edition*. Winter/Spring.
Recinos, Harold J.
 1989   *Hear the Cry! A Latino Pastor Challenges the Church*. Philadelphia: Westminster Press.
Shinn, Larry D.
 1987   *The Dark Lord: Cult Images and the Hare Krishnas in America*. Philadelphia: Westminster Press.
Synod of the Trinity, Presbyterian Church (U.S.A.)
 1989   "A Glance at the Korean-American Churches in the U.S.A.," 4 pp.

Oceania

Darrell L. Whiteman

Numerically the church in Oceania[1] is a mere drop in the ocean when compared with the size of the Christian church around the world. Missiologically, however, the Pacific church is far more significant than its relatively small size of five million islanders would indicate. The vast majority of the population claim allegiance to Christianity, and there are no "hidden peoples" here who have not heard the gospel. In the few cases where people have chosen to remain within their traditional religion, it has been a conscious choice, one made with the knowledge of Christianity's existence in their region, if not with an adequate understanding of it. Moreover, it is interesting to note that the few who have rejected Christianity have also frequently rejected Western technological and modernizing influences. But these rejectors represent a

---

1. Australia and New Zealand are excluded from discussion in this chapter by virtue of the fact that culturally they belong to the Western world more than they do to the world of the Pacific Islanders. For discussion of the church in Australia cf. Kaldor et al. (1988) and Smith (1989); for New Zealand cf. Nichol and Veitch (1983).

Darrell Whiteman teaches missiological anthropology in the E. Stanley Jones School of World Mission and Evangelism at Asbury Theological Seminary in Wilmore, Kentucky. He has had research and mission experience in Central Africa and in Melanesia, where he served on the staff of the ecumenical Melanesian Institute researching issues of Christianity and culture. He is the author of *Melanesians and Missionaries* (1983) and *Introduction to Melanesian Cultures: A Handbook for Church Workers* (1984), and is the editor of the journal *Missiology*.

small minority in the Pacific, a remnant of a bygone era before the impact of World War II and other events that brought the Pacific Islands into the orbit of geopolitics and global economics. While the challenge of mission in Oceania in the nineteenth century was the evangelization of Pacific Islanders, it is clear that this will not be the main challenge of mission in the twenty-first century.

Geographic and Cultural Distribution of Pacific Islanders

There are about twenty thousand islands in Oceania scattered over an immense area from Belau in the west to Easter Island in the east and from Hawaii in the north to New Zealand in the south; they lie in the world's largest ocean, which occupies a third of the earth's surface. These islands range in size from the small atolls formed by coral reefs to the large volcanic islands of Hawaii, Vanuatu, the Solomon Islands, and the world's second largest island, New Guinea. The peoples of Oceania are culturally divided into three major groups: Polynesians, Micronesians, and Melanesians.

Polynesia, meaning "many islands," is comprised of 450,000 islanders in ten island groups: Hawaii, Tuvalu, Tokelau, Wallis and Futuna, Western Samoa, American Samoa, Tonga, Niue, Cook Islands, and French Polynesia. The Maori of New Zealand are also culturally and linguistically Polynesians. Because Polynesia is culturally and linguistically the most homogeneous region in the Pacific, Christianity spread rather rapidly through the region, and many Polynesians became an effective missionary force within Polynesia.

Micronesia, meaning "small islands" (an estimated 2,500 islands with just over a thousand square miles), is comprised of 300,000 people on four archipelagoes (Mariana Islands, Marshall Islands, Caroline Islands [Federated States of Micronesia and Belau] and Gilbert Islands [Kiribati]), and two isolated islands (Nauru and Banaba). Micronesia is culturally and linguistically more diverse than Polynesia, but appears relatively homogeneous in contrast to the tremendous diversity of Melanesia.

Melanesia, meaning "black islands," is the term coined by the French navigator Dumont d'Urville in 1832 to describe those parts of the Pacific inhabited by people with dark skin. Today there are over four million Melanesians scattered over hundreds of islands, encompassing four independent island nations (Papua New Guinea, Solomon Islands, Vanuatu, and Fiji), a colony of France (New Caledonia), and a

Province of Indonesia (Irian Jaya). Not only is Melanesia the most heterogeneous region in Oceania, it is also one of the most culturally and linguistically diverse areas of the entire world. For example, over 1,250 of the world's 6,280 languages are spoken in this relatively small geographic region. This diversity contributed to a much slower and far more difficult spread of Christianity than either Micronesia or Polynesia experienced (cf. Whiteman 1982)

The Spread of the Church

The spread of Christianity in Oceania is a story that spans over 150 years, beginning with the London Missionary Society in Tahiti in 1797 and ending in the Highlands of Papua New Guinea and the interior of Irian Jaya in the 1950s and 1960s. Although it is not possible in this chapter to provide a detailed discussion of mission history in the Pacific islands,[2] it is nevertheless important to have a general understanding of how the church has spread, because islanders are still influenced today by the way the gospel was first introduced into their societies. For example, in some Melanesian churches today one can see Polynesian influences, the result of Polynesian missionaries who brought their culture along with the gospel to Melanesia (Latukefu 1978). Moreover, the tradition or denomination that the first missionaries brought to an island or region is frequently the dominant church in that area today. To anticipate the mission challenges of the twenty-first century in Oceania, we need an understanding of the last century's beginnings in mission.

The general pattern for the spread of Christianity was from the Polynesian islands of Tahiti and Honolulu in the east to Melanesia in the west and Micronesia in the north. The way in which Pacific Islanders adopted the new faith was greatly influenced by the social structure and leadership patterns of their societies. For example, in Polynesia

2. The major histories for the whole Pacific are Garrett (1982a), Gunson (1978) for Protestant missions, and Wiltgen (1979) for Roman Catholic missions. Forman (1982) has written the definitive twentieth-century history of the church in Oceania. Other histories dealing with specific missions include Laracy (1976) for Catholic missions in the Solomon Islands; Hilliard (1978) for the Anglican Melanesian Mission; Wetherell (1977) on the Anglican church in Papua New Guinea; Wagner and Reiner (1986) for the Lutheran Church in Papua New Guinea; and Williams (1972) and Threlfall (1975) for the United Church in Papua New Guinea and the Solomon Islands. Thornley (1979) has written on the Methodist Church in Fiji; Latukefu (1974) on the Wesleyan Methodists in Tonga; David and Leona Crawford (1967) on Protestant missions; and Hezel (1970, 1978) on Catholic missions in Micronesia.

where a hierarchical social structure and chief ruler prevailed, most people embraced the new faith in large group movements once their leader converted (cf. Tippett 1971; Boutilier 1985). Examples of this were the conversion of Pomare II of Tahiti in 1815, Queen Kaahumanu in Hawaii following missionary contact in 1820, and Taufa'ahau, known as King George Tupou I, of Tonga in 1830. The pattern was similar among the Polynesian Maori in New Zealand. Once a chief embraced the new faith, his people followed. Although Fiji is more Melanesian than Polynesian, it has a chiefly tradition from Tongan influence. Thus, when Ratu Cakobau of Bau converted in 1854, it was the beginning of a significant Christian movement among Fijians.

In Melanesia the diversity of languages and the nonhierarchical structure of societies worked against any large movements of people into the church. The spread of Christianity was far slower and more difficult, but even here, as in Micronesia, the decision to embrace the newly introduced faith was made in the context of a group — a family, extended family, clan, village, etc. Individual conversion, in the pattern that is so familiar to us in the West, was alien to Pacific Islanders. Individuals certainly made personal decisions, but they did so as members of a group. This pattern of conversion has of course had profound implications for the church's role in communal life. It is one of the reasons why today the church is frequently part and parcel of Pacific societies, the center of village life throughout the region.

The first permanent Christian mission in the Pacific was established by Spanish Jesuits in 1668 coming from the Philippines to Guam in what are now called the Mariana Islands of Micronesia. Today the Mariana Islanders are predominantly Catholic. Spanish influence in the Pacific waned after the seventeenth century, as did Catholic missions, which did not spread much beyond the Marianas until more than 150 years later.

It was in 1797 that the Protestant missionary effort got under way. The newly founded London Missionary Society (LMS) sent as its first missionaries a group of thirty mostly middle-class artisans aboard the mission ship *Duff*. After a seven month voyage, the missionaries arrived in Tahiti in March 1797, believing that the best way to convert the Tahitians to Christianity was by first introducing them to English culture (Wilson 1799). The mission was unsuccessful in its early years, but the turning point came with the conversion of the Tahitian chief Pomare II in 1815. From Tahiti, the LMS expanded to the Cook Islands in 1821, and from there to Samoa in 1830. A couple of generations later the LMS sent Samoan and Cook Islander missionaries to the Loyalty Islands and southern Papua in Melanesia (Crocombe and Crocombe 1982).

Meanwhile, to the north in Hawaii, fourteen congregational missionaries from the Boston-based American Board of Commissioners for Foreign Missions (ABCFM) began work in 1820. They sailed into a religious vacuum created by the Hawaiians' recent destruction of much of their own traditional religious system with its heavy emphasis on taboo. The Hawaiian Missionary Society was established in 1851 and played an important role in the spread of Protestant Christianity in Micronesia. Within a generation of the mission's beginning, an independent Hawaiian church was founded (1852).

The British Wesleyan Methodist Missionary Society entered the scene in Tonga, officially in 1826, and from there to Fiji in 1835. The British were aided significantly by Tongan missionaries. And with the conversion of Fijian chiefs, notably Ratu Cakobau in 1854, the Wesleyan church grew to the point that by 1875 Fijian evangelists were volunteering as missionaries to New Britain in the Bismarck Archipelago off the coast of New Guinea. In the following years hundreds of Fijian Methodists would become missionaries in Melanesia.

Christianity continued its western expansion into Melanesia, but missionaries encountered quite a different reception here than they had often received in Polynesia. It is important to note also that they were preceded by European traders, whalers, bêche-de-mer fishermen and sandalwood cutters, importing firearms, liquor, tobacco, and trade goods. A first disastrous attempt to introduce Christianity into Melanesia was made on the island of Erromanga in Vanuatu (New Hebrides) by the legendary LMS missionary John Williams in 1839. As he stepped ashore at Dillon's Bay he was clubbed to death and eaten, ending a flamboyant twenty-one-year missionary career at the age of forty-three (Gutch 1974). In the next nine years the LMS sent Cook Islanders and Samoans as missionaries to the various islands of Vanuatu, where they faced many hardships including their deadly encounter with malaria.

In 1848 with the help of the LMS the Presbyterians came to Vanuatu in the person of John Geddie and his wife Charlotte from Nova Scotia, settling on the island of Aneityum. One of his trademarks was establishing an indigenous leadership as quickly as possible for the Presbyterian church. Unfortunately, this perspective did not become the philosophy of the mission nor that of his missionary colleagues. By 1860 there had been a good response to his ministry, but a measles epidemic, brought to the islands by sandalwood traders, killed nearly a third of the population on Aneityum and brought devastation to other islands. This scene and these kinds of setbacks would become all too frequent in Melanesia, but from this slow and difficult beginning the Presbyterian church grew, and is today the dominant church in Vanuatu.

Anglican Christianity promoted by the Melanesian Mission began in the northern islands of Vanuatu and the Solomon Islands in 1849 with the itinerant Bishop George Augustus Selwyn from New Zealand cruising among the Melanesian islands. His goal was to recruit young men, remove them from their islands for conversion and training, and then send them back as evangelists to their own people. The method met with limited success, but slowly a Christian presence was made. The Melanesian Mission had some outstanding missionaries, including John Coleridge Patteson, a gifted linguist who spoke twenty-four Melanesian languages and always believed that his mission task was to introduce Melanesians to Christ, not to make them Englishmen (Gutch 1971). The Melanesian Mission became the independent Church of Melanesia in 1975, and today it is the dominant church in the Solomon Islands and northern Vanuatu (Whiteman 1983). The founding and present Prime Minister of Vanuatu, Fr. Walter Lini, is an ordained Anglican priest in the Church of Melanesia.

The spread of Christianity became more difficult and complex as it moved eastward across the Pacific to New Guinea. The island was partitioned by colonial interests in the nineteenth century, dividing it between the Dutch claim on the western end in 1828, and the British and the German to the southeastern and northeastern portions respectively in 1884.

Protestant work in New Guinea began with the arrival of the LMS in 1871 in Papua. The mission relied on veteran missionaries such as the flamboyant James Chalmers who had Polynesian experience (Langmore 1974) and a host of island missionaries whose influence is felt to this day.

Other mission work commenced in New Guinea with the Australian Methodists in New Britain in 1875. George Brown and a large contingent of Fijians led the way. Fifteen years later, on invitation from the new Governor of Papua, William MacGregor, the Methodists began work in the Papuan Islands region, establishing the Methodist mission on the island of Dobu in 1891. It was a strategic placement because the Dobuans were active in the Kula ring that connected a circuit of islands in trade, paving the way for the gospel to travel from one island to another. William Bromilow, a veteran missionary from Fiji, headed the mission, assisted by a handful of fellow European missionaries and a contingent of twenty-two Pacific Islander missionaries, most of whom were Fijians but some of whom were Tongans and Samoans (Bromilow 1929).

The Anglicans entered British New Guinea in 1891, beginning at Dogura in Bartle Bay among Wedau-speaking Papuans. Anglican Christianity grew slowly in New Guinea (Wetherell 1977). The French Catholic Missionaries of the Sacred Heart (MSC) began work in two locations: first on New Britain in 1882 at Matupit on the Gazelle Peninsula and, in 1885, on Yule Island off the Papuan coast among the Oro people (Delbos 1985). Other Catholic work began in 1896 with the Divine Word Missionaries (SVD) at Alexishafen in the Madang area of German New Guinea (Huber 1988).

In the same year German Lutherans ventured forth at Finschhafen on the Huon Peninsula, but after thirteen frustrating years only two schoolboys had been baptized as the first converts. In that same year 1899, Christian Keysser came to New Guinea from Bavaria and worked among the Kate people from his station at Sattleberg. Keysser pioneered a missiologically insightful, but controversial, approach to conversion, whereby people were encouraged to convert to Christianity not as isolated individuals against the social and cultural tide of their tribe or clan, but as members of a social group, coming to faith as a clan or village with their social structure intact. His insights, published in 1929 (English translation 1980), predate J. Waskom Pickett's (1933) and Donald McGavran's (1955) arguments in favor of people movements as the best way for the church to grow. Following the Keysser method, and using hundreds of Melanesian evangelists as missionaries into the interior, the church here has grown into one with a membership of about 600,000 today (Fugmann 1986; Wagner and Reiner 1986).

In 1968 the Methodist and LMS traditions merged to form the United Church in Papua New Guinea and the Solomon Islands. Together with the Anglicans, Lutherans, and Roman Catholics, these four churches comprise eighty-five percent of the Christians in Papua New Guinea, who make up ninety-seven percent of the population.

Following World War II with the opening of the New Guinea Highlands, a proliferation of conservative evangelical and fundamentalist missions arrived to usher in a new spirit of sectarianism. In fact, today Papua New Guinea has one of the highest ratios of Christian missionaries to population in the entire world. In Irian Jaya the pattern is similar to that of the New Guinea Highlands, with conservative evangelical and fundamentalist missions dominating the interior, and the Dutch Reformed Church and Catholics prevailing in the coastal areas.

In discussing the spread of the church across Oceania over a period of 150 years, it would be easy to conclude that the dominant players have been European missionaries. It is true that the high profile personalities of people like Hiram Bingham, John Williams, George Brown, James Chalmers, John Paton, and the like are well known because their stories were published widely. But the dominant role, if not the most public one, has been played by islander missionaries, whether it was Polynesian missionaries in Melanesia, or Melanesians from one island going to Melanesians in another (cf. Crocombe and Crocombe 1982; Latukefu 1978; and Tippett 1977). Their full story has yet to be told.

Pacific Christianity Today —
Challenges for the Twenty-First Century

Looking at Christianity in the Pacific today, it is useful to see how it is organized institutionally in churches, but it is even more valuable to consider it phenomenologically and discover what it means to the Islanders who call themselves Christians. How do they understand and practice their faith? An abundance of literature is available to help us understand the "map" of Christianity in Oceania, but very little of it gives us insights into the Islanders' perceptions and practices of their faith (cf. Barker 1985, 1990; Boutilier et al. 1978: part 4; Hogbin 1939; Read 1952; Tippett 1967; Whiteman 1983). This later field of inquiry, however, will help us anticipate the missionary needs and agenda in Oceania for the twenty-first century.

In this section we will address three areas that will help us understand the present and anticipate future concerns for the church in Oceania: (1) Ecumenical Cooperation and Sectarian Strife, (2) Nominal Christian Faith and New Religious Movements, and (3) Contextualization: Traditional and Modern.

Ecumenical Cooperation and Sectarian Strife

A map of Christianity in the Pacific today is remarkably similar to the way Christianity was first brought to the islands. For example, where Catholic missionaries first landed and established a church one will frequently find only a Catholic worshiping community today, such as on Wallis and Futuna. This pattern of today's churches reflecting yesterday's missions is in part a legacy of the comity agreements made in the nineteenth century between Protestant missions. Yet it also reflects the church's integration into the social fabric of village life. Allegiance to Christianity is far more of a communal experience than an individual-

114

istic one for Pacific Islanders. This does not mean that individuals do not experience profound personal faith; it means that they experience it as members of a group instead of as individuals at variance with their society. This form of Folk Christianity, or what Christian Keysser called *"Volkskirche" — a people* church — is a dominant characteristic throughout the Pacific Islands.

Despite this close relationship between church and cultural identity there is nevertheless increased ecumenical cooperation between churches. Although Christianity was first planted by competing missions, one of the most remarkable features of the church in the Pacific is the way denominational differences have diminished in importance for today's Pacific Islanders. What John Garrett observes about Kiribati is characteristic of most of the Pacific Islands:

> In Kiribati, in Micronesia as a whole, the coming of Christianity has helped to exorcise the haunting presence of the feared local spirits, the *anti*. Ill will between fellow-Christians, generated by competing missions, has had to wait longer to be dispelled; but the missionaries of the past would be amazed to see how fast the tares they sowed with the wheat are withering away, to give promise of a better harvest as a new breath blows among Christians — the reconciling Spirit of Christ. (1982b:49)

This reconciliation is found in cooperation between churches at a formal level in such organizations as the Melanesian Council of Churches in Papua New Guinea founded in 1965, the Evangelical Alliance of the South Pacific Islands (1964), and the Melanesian Association of Theological Schools (1969). National church councils were also established in Fiji, Vanuatu, the Solomon Islands, Samoa, and Tonga; and in 1961, at a conference at Malua, Samoa, plans were laid for Pacific-wide ecumenical cooperation in the form of the Pacific Conference of Churches (PCC), officially inaugurated in 1966. In 1973 The Conference of Roman Catholic Bishops of the Pacific Islands joined the PCC (cf. Afeaki et al. 1983; Forman 1986).

But not all is ecumenical bliss in the peaceful Pacific Islands. Following World War II many smaller fundamentalist and sectarian groups began entering the Pacific and wooing people away from their earlier church affiliation. Forman observes that:

> For many years a small number of long-established Christian denominations have made up the Christianity of Oceania. But now, with

115

easier travel and rapid social change everywhere, new missions, mostly of Pentecostal and conservative evangelical groups, are coming in and formerly marginal groups are showing new strength, challenging the hold of the long-established churches. A new wave of Christianity is trying to supplant the old. (1990:29)

In a region already characterized by cultural and linguistic diversity, this plethora of Christian denominations and sects is creating a situation requiring creative, Christ-like responses from the churches.

Nominal Faith and New Religious Movements

Today churches across the Pacific are facing the "fallout" of apparent missionary success. Christianity has been accepted in one society after another to the point where in many places it has been present for more than three or four generations. The initial dynamism of first generation Christians is fading, and in many villages the church has become more of a social organization than a source of spiritual vitality. Consequently, the churches are confronted with a growing nominalism in many places. In writing of his experience in Melanesia, Michael Maeliau in the Solomon Islands notes that:

> . . . many areas of Melanesia are seeing a decline of interest in church attendance and activities. Religious activities seem to have become mere formalities, to have lost their vitality and excitement. According to various traditional religions, any god who fails to communicate directly with its worshippers is either dead or has transferred to other realms. Such a god deserves little else than a memorial, just to remind its worshippers that there used to be such-and-such a god, or just in case the god decides to return at a later date. (1987:119)

What Maeliau describes of his experience in Melanesia could easily be found across the Pacific. For many Islanders Christianity has lost its power. For others it has not met their most pressing needs and so they turn to other sources. For most, unlike their traditional religion, which was integrated into all of life, Christianity has become far more compartmentalized and constricted to a Sunday-only activity (cf. Whiteman 1984).

This state of affairs has lead to a spiritual vacuum to which revivals and other religious movements are now responding, especially in Melanesia. An example is the Solomon Islands revival that began on

116

Malaita in the South Sea Evangelical Church in the early 1970s, but spread to other parts of the Solomons, to Vanuatu, and even to the New Guinea Highlands. Today there are what Islanders call "Holy Spirit Movements" in the Catholic and Lutheran churches, and classic Pentecostal, neo-Pentecostal, or charismatic movements and revivals are all found in recent developments in Melanesia (cf. Flannery 1983-1984). In discussing these movements in Melanesia, John Barr notes:

> Perhaps I could evaluate the joy that unexpectedness and surprise might generate within the bounds of the Holy Spirit movements. It is overwhelmingly clear to many participants that the Holy Spirit is theirs in a truly indigenous sense. The coming of the Holy Spirit marks the end of 'foreign' Christianity and a chance to encounter faith in spontaneous, experiential manner with 'power' — to encounter spiritual realms with confidence and authority. It is also clear to many that the Holy Spirit has opened a way to a dynamic reworking of faith and a re-organizing of the Christian community with emphases on healing, the reconciling of relationships and the empowering of the laity (and particularly women). (1983:vii)

Religious movements like these always bring with them the challenge of discernment of spirits and the problems of abuse and excess, but in areas where the church has become "cold," this kind of supernatural experience is an attractive antidote to nominal Christianity. Many Pacific Islanders are attracted to it, even to the point of leaving long-established churches if they believe that their only hope for a meaningful "salvation" is outside their church.

In addition to religious movements whose goal is renewal within the church, there are many other movements, frequently called "cargo cults," which, while often appearing bizarre to outsiders, are, in the words of John Strelan (1977), a "search for salvation." They are driven by an underlying worldview theme of cargoism, which is alive and well and is, in my mind, one of the most urgent areas for the church to understand and respond to in ways that are pastorally appropriate (cf. Flannery 1983-1984; Steinbauer 1979).

Contextualization: Traditional and Modern

In the same way that colonialism in the Pacific finally gave way to many independent nations, primarily in the 1970s and 1980s, most of the missions that brought Christianity to the Pacific have now evolved into

117

independent churches. This does not mean, however, that these churches are financially independent; most are not. It also does not mean that they are automatically indigenous just because they are now independent. In fact, most of them have a long way to go before they become truly indigenous churches (cf. Whiteman 1983:323ff.). Efforts are being made to indigenize worship (cf. Garrett and Mavor 1973; Hagesi 1972; O'Brien 1980; and Suri 1976) and to begin theologizing in more culturally specific and appropriate ways. This has been evidenced by the founding of the *Melanesian Journal of Theology* in 1985, and recent collections of essays that point to some promising theological reflections by Pacific Islanders (cf. Knight 1977; May 1985; and Trompf 1987).

Contextualization in the Pacific is in its early stages of development, but there is every reason to believe that significant strides will be made in this area. Such efforts will renew the life of the church, which in many places is languishing after several generations of Christianity. One of the main challenges for mission in the twenty-first century will be to empower Pacific Island Christians to engage the gospel with the deepest levels of their culture. Out of this encounter will emerge theologies that are relevant and worship that is meaningful but also faithful. Some of the issues in these "deeper areas" that must not go unaddressed include ancestors and other spirits, magic and sorcery, taboo, causes of sickness, healing, power, meaning of dreams, the relationship of traditional healers and priests to Christian ministries, reconciliation and payback, mediation, and a theology of land.[3]

Unless Christianity becomes truly indigenous and contextualized within the changing cultures of the Pacific, it runs the risk of quickly being perceived as irrelevant and powerless. But not only must the church face the issues of relating the gospel to the deeper levels of Islander worldviews influenced by past traditions, it must also be prepared to face the challenges of modernization and the impact this has made on Pacific communities. Of special concern are alcohol abuse, identity for youth, unemployment, urbanization, tribal fighting in some regions, and even such broad regional concerns as a nuclear-free Pacific and the negative impact of tourism (cf. Schwarz 1985).

3. Many of these issues have been addressed in some very creative workshops on Christianity and culture in the Solomon Islands, Vanuatu, Tonga, Kiribati, and Papua New Guinea facilitated by Dr. Cliff Wright. The reports of these workshops are available from him at: 4 Fairy Street, Ivanhoe, Victoria 3079, Australia. See Donald McGregor's *The Fish and the Cross* (1982) for an excellent example of engaging the deeper questions of cultural identity with the claims of the gospel and the challenge of the kingdom of God.

The church's challenge to relate to traditional culture and contemporary concerns is articulated by Gernot Fugmann when he notes that:

> Now most of those fathers in faith have died but their commitment
> to witness has become a heritage and a challenge for all those in
> leadership positions today.
> More than ever this is necessary today as the old is rapidly passing
> away, the traditional unity is disintegrating and new identities are
> being forged. For many young people it is by no means sufficient any
> more to be born and baptized into the belief of their fathers. Instead,
> the old faith, the faith of the fathers needs a new religious inspiration;
> an inspiration which redeems the growing loss of identity, gives
> meaning in the midst of confusion, and direction where the horizons
> of hope have become obscure. (1986:274)

Summary and Conclusion

Christianity has indeed been successfully established in the Pacific,
perhaps more successfully than anywhere else in the world. Still one
wonders if its penetration to the deepest level of Islanders' worldviews
has been as successful. The challenge for the twenty-first century in the
Pacific will be to strive for greater Christian unity amidst increasing
sectarian forces and to promote ongoing contextualization by coming
to grips with both deeply rooted traditional beliefs and with the increasing secularizing power of encroaching modernity. In conclusion,
anthropologist John Barker provides us with an excellent summary of
Christianity in Oceania:

> While Pacific Christianity in its local manifestations continues to
> reflect and nurture the diverse cultural traditions of small-scale island
> communities, as a global religion it has also brought the world to
> Pacific islanders and encouraged their entry onto the world stage.
> (1990:21)

For Further Reading

Afeaki, Emiliana, Ron Crocombe, and John McClaren, eds.
  1983   *Religious Cooperation in the Pacific Islands*. Suva, Fiji: Univer-
            sity of the South Pacific.

Barker, John
1985   "Maisin Christianity: An Ethnography of the Contemporary
            Religion of a Seaboard Melanesian People." Unpublished
            Ph.D. diss., University of British Columbia.
————, ed.
1990   *Christianity in Oceania: Ethnographic Perspectives.* ASAO Mono-
            graph No. 12. Lanham, MD: University Press of America.
Barr, John
1984   "Foreword." In *Religious Movements in Melanesia Today (2).*
            Edited by Wendy Flannery. Goroka, Papua New Guinea: The
            Melanesian Institute, pp. v-viii.
Boutilier, James, Daniel Hughes, and Sharon Tiffany, eds.
1978   *Mission, Church, and Sect in Oceania.* ASAO Monograph No.
            6. Lanham, MD: University Press of America.
1985   "We Fear Not the Ultimate Triumph: Factors Effecting the
            Conversion Phase of Nineteenth-Century Missionary En-
            terprises." In *Missions and Missionaries in the Pacific.* Edited
            by Char Miller. New York: The Edwin Mellen Press, pp.
            13-63.
Bromilow, William E.
1929   *Twenty Years Among Primitive Papuans.* London: The Epworth
            Press.
Crawford, David, and Leona Crawford
1967   *Missionary Adventures in the South Pacific.* Rutland, VT:
            Charles E. Tuttle Company.
Crocombe, Ron, and Marjorie Crocombe, eds.
1982   *Polynesian Missions in Melanesia: From Samoa, Cook Islands
            and Tonga to Papua New Guinea and New Caledonia.* Suva,
            Fiji: Institute of Pacific Studies, University of the South
            Pacific.
Delbos, Georges
1985   *The Mustard Seed: From a French Mission to a Papuan Church,
            1885-1985.* Port Moresby: Institute of Papua New Guinea
            Studies.
Flannery, Wendy, ed.
1983-1984 *Religious Movements in Melanesia Today,* 3 vols. Point Series
            Nos. 2-4. Goroka, Papua New Guinea: The Melanesian Insti-
            tute.
Forman, Charles W.
1982   *The Island Churches of the South Pacific: Emergence in the Twen-
            tieth Century.* Maryknoll, NY: Orbis Books.

1986   *The Voice of Many Waters: The Story of the Life and Ministry of the Pacific Conference of Churches in the Last 25 Years.* Suva, Fiji: Lotu Pacifika Productions.

1990   "Some Next Steps in the Study of Pacific Island Christianity." In *Christianity in Oceania: Ethnographic Perspectives.* Edited by John Barker. ASAO Monograph No. 6. Lanham, MD: University Press of America, pp. 25-31.

Fugmann, Gernot, ed.

1986   *The Birth of an Indigenous Church.* Point Series No. 10. Goroka, Papua New Guinea: The Melanesian Institute.

Garrett, John

1982a   *To Live Among the Stars: Christian Origins in Oceania.* Geneva: World Council of Churches.

1982b   *A Way in the Sea: Aspects of Pacific Christian History with Reference to Australia.* Melbourne, Australia: Spectrum Publications.

———, and John Mavor

1973   *Worship the Pacific Way.* Suva, Fiji: Lotu Pacifika Productions.

Gunson, Niel

1978   *Messengers of Grace: Evangelical Missionaries in the South Seas 1797-1860.* Melbourne, Australia: Oxford University Press.

Gutch, John

1971   *Martyr of the Islands: The Life and Death of John Coleridge Patteson.* London: Hodder & Stoughton.

1974   *Beyond the Reefs: The Life of John Williams, Missionary.* London: Macdonald.

Hagesi, Robert

1972   "Towards Localization of Anglican Worship in the Solomon Islands." B.D. thesis, Pacific Theological College, Suva, Fiji.

Hezel, Francis X.

1970   "Catholic Missions in the Caroline and Marshall Islands: A Survey of Historical Materials." *Journal of Pacific History* 5:213-27.

1978   "Indigenization as a Missionary Goal in the Caroline and Marshall Islands." In *Mission, Church and Sect in Oceania.* Edited by James A. Boutilier, Daniel T. Hughes, and Sharon W. Tiffany. ASAO Monograph No. 6. Lanham, MD: University Press of America, pp. 251-73.

Hilliard, David

1978   *God's Gentlemen: A History of the Melanesian Mission, 1849-1942.* St. Lucia, Queensland: University of Queensland Press.

Hogbin, H. Ian
1939   *Experiments in Civilization: The Effects of European Culture on a Native Community of the Solomon Islands.* London: Routledge and Kegan Paul.

Huber, Mary Taylor
1988   *The Bishops' Progress: A Historical Ethnography of Catholic Missionary Experience on the Sepik Frontier.* Washington, DC: Smithsonian Institution Press.

Kaldor, Peter, and Sue Kaldor, et al.
1988   *Where the River Flows: Sharing the Gospel in Contemporary Australia.* Homebush West, Australia: Lander Books, Anzea Publishers.

Keysser, Christian
1980   *A People Reborn.* Translated by Alfred Allin and John Kuder. Pasadena, CA: William Carey Library.

Knight, James, ed.
1977   *Christ in Melanesia: Exploring Theological Issues.* Goroka, Papua New Guinea: The Melanesian Institute.

Langmore, Diane
1974   *Tamate — a King: James Chalmers in New Guinea 1877-1901.* Melbourne, Australia: Melbourne University Press.

Laracy, Hugh
1976   *Marist and Melanesians: A History of Catholic Missions in the Solomon Islands.* Canberra: Australian National University Press.

Latukefu, Sione
1974   *Church and State in Tonga: The Wesleyan Methodist Missionaries and Political Development, 1822-1874.* Canberra: Australian National University Press.
1978   "The Impact of South Sea Islands Missionaries on Melanesia." In *Mission, Church, and Sect in Oceania.* Edited by James Boutilier, Daniel Hughes, and Sharon Tiffany. ASAO Monograph No. 6. Lanham, MD: University Press of America, pp. 91-108.

Maeliau, Michael
1987   "Searching for a Melanesian Way of Worship." In *The Gospel Is Not Western: Black Theologies from the Southwest Pacific.* Edited by G. W. Trompf. Maryknoll, NY: Orbis Books, pp. 119-27.

May, John D'Arcy, ed.
1985   *Living Theology in Melanesia: A Reader.* Point Series No. 8. Goroka, Papua New Guinea: The Melanesian Institute.

McGavran, Donald
1955   *The Bridges of God: A Study in the Strategy of Missions.* London: ⟋ World Dominion Press.
McGregor, Donald E.
1982   *The Fish and the Cross.* Point Series No. 1. Goroka, Papua New Guinea: The Melanesian Institute.
Nichol, Christopher, and James Veitch, eds.
1983   *Religion in New Zealand.* Wellington, New Zealand: Christopher Nichol.
O'Brien, Helen, ed.
1980   *Christian Worship and Melanesia.* Point No. 1. Goroka, Papua New Guinea: The Melanesian Institute.
Pickett, J. Waskom
1933   *Christian Mass Movements in India.* Lucknow, India: Lucknow Publishing House.
Read, K. E.
1952   "Missionary Activities and Social Change in the Central Highlands of Papua and New Guinea." *South Pacific* 6:229-38.
Schwarz, Brian, ed.
1985   *An Introduction to Ministry in Melanesia.* Point Series No. 7. Goroka, Papua New Guinea: The Melanesian Institute.
Steinbauer, Fredrich
1979   *Melanesian Cargo Cults: New Salvation Movements in the South Pacific.* St. Lucia, Australia: University of Queensland Press.
Smith, John
1989   *Advance Australia Where? A Lack of Meaning in a Land of Plenty.* Homebush West, Australia: Anzea Publishers.
Strelan, John G.
1977   *Search for Salvation: Studies in the History and Theology of Cargo Cults.* Adelaide, Australia: Lutheran Publishing House.
Suri, Ellison
1976   ·"Music in Pacific Island Worship with Special Reference to the Anglican Church in Lau Malaita Solomon Islands." B.D. thesis, Pacific Theological College, Suva, Fiji.
Thornley, Andrew W.
1979   "Fijian Methodism, 1874-1945: The Emergence of a National Church." Unpublished Ph.D. diss., Australian National University.
Threlfall, Neville
1975   *One Hundred Years in the Islands: The Methodist/United Church*

in the New Guinea Islands Region, 1875-1975. Rabaul, Papua New Guinea: Toksave Buk.

Tippett, Alan R.
1967   *Solomon Islands Christianity: A Study in Growth and Obstruction.* London: Lutterworth Press.
1971   *People Movements in Southern Polynesia: Studies in the Dynamics of Church-planting and Growth in Tahiti, New Zealand, Tonga, and Samoa.* Chicago: Moody Press.
1977   *The Deep Sea Canoe: The Story of Third World Missionaries in the South Pacific.* Pasadena, CA: William Carey Library.

Trompf, G. W., ed.
1987   *The Gospel Is Not Western: Black Theologies from the Southwest Pacific.* Maryknoll, NY: Orbis Books.

Wagner, Herwig, and Herman Reiner, eds.
1986   *The Lutheran Church in Papua New Guinea: The First Hundred Years 1886-1986.* Adelaide, Australia: Lutheran Publishing House.

Wetherell, David
1977   *Reluctant Mission: The Anglican Church in Papua New Guinea, 1891-1942.* St. Lucia, Queensland, Australia: University of Queensland Press.

Whiteman, Darrell L.
1982   "Melanesia: Islands of Diversity." *Response,* May, pp. 7-9, 32-33.
1983   *Melanesians and Missionaries.* Pasadena, CA: William Carey Library.
1984   "Melanesian Religions: An Overview." In *An Introduction to Melanesian Religions: A Handbook for Church Workers.* Edited by Ennio Mantovani. Goroka, Papua New Guinea: The Melanesian Institute, pp. 87-121.

Williams, Ronald G.
1972   *The United Church in Papua, New Guinea, and the Solomon Islands: The Story of the Development of an indigenous Church on the Occasion of the Centenary of the L.M.S. in Papua, 1872-1972.* Rabaul, Papua New Guinea: Trinity Press.

Wilson, James
1799   *A Missionary Voyage to the Southern Pacific Ocean, Performed in the Years 1796, 1797, 1798.* London: T. Chapman.

Wiltgen, Ralph M.
1979   *The Founding of the Roman Catholic Church in Oceania 1825 to 1850.* Canberra: Australian National University Press.

Latin America

Samuel Escobar

As we look at Latin America from the perspective of Christian mission we are confronted with some amazing and contradictory facts. By the end of this century half of the Roman Catholics of the world will be living in Latin America, and missiologists point out that they will have a special missionary responsibility in the evangelization of the world. On the other hand, Belgian missionary specialist Franz Damen, an advisor to the Catholic Bishops of Bolivia, reports that "Every hour in Latin America an average of 400 Catholics move to membership in Protestant sects which today represent an eighth, that is 12% of the population of the continent, but in countries like Puerto Rico and Guatemala, they constitute nothing less than 25 or even 30% of the population" (Damen 1987:45). Five centuries of evangelization in Latin America were commemorated in 1992. And from the missionary force going out of North America, both Catholic and Protestant, the largest contingent of missionaries are still being sent to Latin America, more than to any other region of the world.

A Contradictory Missionary Situation

As the twentieth century comes to an end, Catholics and Protestants alike are confronted by a continent where life can only be described

Samuel Escobar, Professor of Missions at Eastern Baptist Theological Seminary in Philadelphia, Pennsylvania, served previously as regional secretary for Latin America of the International Fellowship of Evangelical Students.

with a vocabulary of superlatives: wild urban accumulation, desperate migration, skyrocketing inflation, monstrous foreign debt, dramatic emergence of marginal sectors, unprecedented ideological confusion, unbelievable misery, and the cold callous indifference of the ruling classes of a supposedly Christian population. If what Paul the Apostle says is true, that "the whole creation has been groaning as in the pains of childbirth" (Rom. 8:22), these groans take a somber acuteness in the context of Latin America. At the same time, however, the name of Jesus is being proclaimed loudly and clearly in crowded streets of the mega-lopolis as well as in remote villages, and simple people as well as sophisticated intellectuals are ready to risk their lives for what they consider the demands of a faith in Jesus Christ as their Lord. Some churches decline in numbers and influence, but other churches grow. Scripture is being translated into hundreds of dialects. Among the hundreds of thousands of Latin Americans that go to other parts of the world through voluntary or forced exile, there is a small but significant number of evangelicals who are taking their enthusiastic faith and spreading it "as they go." The missionary situation in Latin America is filled with contrasts.

Remembering five centuries of Christian presence on the continent, since the arrival of Christopher Columbus on an island in the Caribbean in 1492, has become a matter of controversy. As Emilio Castro describes it, "From a European perspective a Te Deum could be called for: from the perspective of the oppressed people of the Americas, the survivors of the original inhabitants of those countries, it will be the occasion for a Requiem" (Castro 1990:147). In any case, we are confronted with a set of searching questions about mission in this part of the world, especially because of the puzzling missionary situation in which Latin America finds itself today. On the one hand, both Protestant and Catholic sources now have movements committed to mobilizing Latin American resources, especially personnel, for Christian mission in other parts of the world in the coming century. On the other hand, Latin America presently receives proportionately more missionaries by both Catholics and Protestants from other continents than do other parts of the world. Should Latin America still be considered a *mission field* where human, technical, and financial resources are poured in by the churches of North America and Europe for missionary purposes? Since the last century and for a wide variety of reasons this question has been a matter of debate in missionary circles everywhere, and it is still being debated. However, nowadays in Latin America itself the question is now being formulated in a different way. With its five hundred years of Christian presence, shouldn't Latin America be considered rather as a *mission base,* from which missionaries go as messengers of Jesus Christ to plant Christianity in other continents of the world?

Latin America as a Mission Field

In the Jerusalem meeting of the International Missionary Council in 1928, John A. Mackay established the legitimacy of a Protestant missionary presence in Latin America on the basis of his own twelve years of experience among youth, intellectuals, and students in that continent. He dismissed the idea that evangelical missionaries were "religious buccaneers devoting their lives to ecclesiastical piracy" and described the spiritual condition of the continent as follows: "My work lay among the great unchurched masses of the South American continent. . . . The great majority of men in South America have repudiated all religion" (Mackay 1928:121). Almost forty years later José Míguez Bonino, a well-known Argentinean theologian, explained that "Latin America was never 'Christian' in the sense that Europe or even North America can be said to be so. What took place here was a colossal transplantation — the basic ecclesiastical structures, disciplines and ministries were brought wholesale from Spain and were expected to function as a Christian order: a tremendous form without substance" (Míguez Bonino 1964:168). And for Protestantism this mission field has proved very fertile, especially in recent decades. The 170 thousand Protestants of 1916 have grown to become an estimated forty-eight million in 1990. A Catholic journalist says that "If current growth rates continue, Latin America will have an evangelical majority in the early 21st century. Actually in terms of church participation 'practicing' evangelicals may already outnumber 'observant' Catholics" (McCoy 1989:2).

Among evangelical missionaries there has been a tendency to consider Latin America as a territory in need of basic evangelization, a field for pioneer missionary experiences where the New Testament model could be applied almost literally. In their most enthusiastic moments they have expressed their hope that something unseen before could happen here, using the New Testament days as a point of reference. In 1916 Brazilian Protestant leader Erasmo Braga wrote that "[the] lesson from history allows us to hope that under the impact of a simple but sincere gospel message, such as that preached by the Apostles in ancient Rome, there will also come for Latin America an end to paganism" (Braga 1916:195). This vision was echoed almost sixty years later by Reformed missiologist Roger Greenway, writing about an urban missionary strategy for Latin America: "If revitalized churches whose leaders have been trained in church growth oriented schools can be turned loose in the burgeoning cities, then a multiplication of churches will occur such as the world has not seen since the first century" (Greenway 1973:236). This attitude and this dream are not uncommon among the 12,000 Protestant foreign missionaries working in Latin America today, and the predominant evangelical missiology has yet to articulate a coherent understanding of the uniqueness of this mission field.

In a recent volume about the contemporary scene, evangelical missiologist William D. Taylor states that "Latin America offers a world of unreached peoples." Like other observers of the massive population shift from rural to urban, he suggests that "the cities must be given the first place for evangelism, church planting and leadership training." Taking Mexico City as an example of the urban challenge to mission, he states the need for "sensitive and cooperative missionary help that is willing to enter into partnership relationships with existing Mexican churches instead of starting an uncounted flock of new denominations" (Taylor and Núñez 1989:177). The other segments of population that Taylor considers "unreached peoples" in Latin America include untouchable upper classes and economic elites; slum populations locked into hopeless poverty; university students and faculty; military in their enclaves; labor-union officials; the world of the media; and the tribal communities that require missionaries with language and cross-cultural training. To the question "Is there room for the North American or European missionary in Latin America?" Taylor's answer is clear and eloquent: "Yes, of course. *But* he or she must be a missionary who comes devoid of even latent paternalism, one ready to learn from Latin ministry patterns, one who has talents and training but is also humble, one who will learn the language with the highest proficiency possible, and one who will understand and come to love the history and cultural mosaic that makes Latin America what it truly is and can become by God's grace" (Taylor-Núñez 1989:178).

Mission as a Promising Investment

The awakening of Latin American Roman Catholics to the missionary situation of their continent took place only after the Second World War.

Starting in 1955 with a meeting of bishops from all the continent in Rio de Janeiro, the Latin American Episcopal Council (CELAM) was formed. One of its first actions was to issue a call for foreign missionaries to come and help a church that felt threatened by the growth of Protestantism and Marxism among the masses (Escobar 1987a:36). Roman Catholic missionary efforts from Europe and North America to Latin America were presented as a necessary investment that would allow later mobilization of a Latin American missionary force to other parts of the world. That was the perception of Pope Pius XII when he wrote in 1955: "We are confident that the benefits now received will later be rendered back a thousandfold. There will come the day when Latin America will be able to give back to the entire Church of Christ all that it has received." These words were quoted in a famous speech that Mgr. Agostino Casaroli addressed to the Major Religious Superiors of the Catholic Church in North America in August 1961 (Costello 1979:276). On behalf of the Pontifical Commission for Latin America he was requesting of his audience that every religious province of the Roman Catholic Church aim to send a tenth of their religious priests, brothers, and sisters as missionaries to Latin America. At that point the "tithe" suggested by the Commission would have meant twenty thousand missionaries! The ideal was never achieved, but it certainly generated enthusiasm, to the point that even today nearly half of the United States' Catholic missionary force goes to Latin America.

Catholic missionaries from North America and Europe were very influential in awakening the social conscience of the Roman Catholic Church that fostered the movement of Liberation theologies. Though this development has not been adequately studied by specialists (Cleary 1985:10), it can be traced back clearly, taking as milestones the CELAM meetings of Medellín (1968) and Puebla (1979) (Escobar 1987). Foreign missionaries were equally influential in the development of a missiological awareness, the course of which has been carefully studied by Juan Gorsky in his analysis of the theological orientations of the Missions Department of CELAM between 1966 and 1979 (Gorski 1985). It was the acknowledgment of a critical situation that opened the door to a call for foreign missionary help in 1955. In the following years a critical self-evaluation slowly and even reluctantly uncovered a problematic reality: important segments of the Latin American population need basic evangelization. There is here a genuine "mission field," though missiologists like Segundo Galilea refuse to use that terminology (Galilea 1981:16). However, he quotes a missiological document of 1979 that describes the condition of ethnic and cultural groups of "approximately 100 million people (especially indigenous and Afro-Americans) whose situation demands a first evangelization; a sub-continent of un-evangelized people" (Galilea 1981:24).

During the Nineteenth Assembly of CELAM in 1983 Pope John Paul II proposed a "New Evangelization" for Latin America. The concept was developed and clarified later on at CELAM 1990. A distinction was made between "re-evangelization," which would have meant an acceptance that the first evangelization in the sixteenth century had failed, and a "New Evangelization" that is "new in its fervor, its methods, and its expression," but presupposes that the first evangelization was successful in spite of its shortcomings. As the bishops said at Puebla, "Despite the defects and the sins that are always present, the faith of the church has set its seal on the soul of Latin America. It has left its marks on Latin America's essential historical identity, becoming the continent's cultural matrix out of which new peoples have arisen" (Puebla 445). Using categories of Vatican II and the document *Evangelii Nuntiandi* of Pope Paul VI, the concept of "evangelization of cultures" has been developed. The future Catholic missionary task in Latin America, writes Aubry, will concentrate on the "ancient cultures" (indigenous and Afro-American peoples), "changing cultures" (masses of migrants to the great cities), and "new cultures" (peoples affected by the impact of modernization) (CELAM 1990:76-80).

Inquiring into the kind of missionaries necessary today, North American Catholic observers have evaluated the experience of mission during the critical days of the sixties when "a new mission approach began to emerge, radically new. . . . The missioners who remained began to learn instead of to teach, to serve instead of to lead" (Costello 1979:5). A veteran of twenty years of work in Nicaragua put it this way: "Unless a person wants to 'put on the mind of Christ', he'd do better not to enter Latin American work. . . . Christ came as one of the oppressed with a message of life for the oppressors. We, the church today, tend to come as the oppressors to the oppressed telling them *we* have a message of life — and they say, 'Oh, yeah? Show us!' " (Costello 1979:41). An American missionary who serves in Peru has used his christological perspective of Matthew 25:31-46 to describe the experience of "the recognition of the face of Christ in the faces of the Latin American woman, campesino, or laborer," a recognition that "grows out of the concrete day-to-day experience of those who have pitched their tents among the poor . . . not those who occasionally visit the world of the poor as would a county agricultural extension worker, but to those who dwell among the poor" (Judd 1987:7).

130

Mission beyond Latin America

Among the vigorous and lively evangelical churches that have developed in Latin America there has been a growing willingness to assume responsibilities for Christian mission beyond the continent. Denominations such as the Baptists, Methodists, and Assemblies of God in countries such as Brazil and Argentina have been sending missionaries to other Latin American nations, Africa, and Europe for more than forty years. Also, as in other moments of history, young people have become the pioneers for a new stage in missionary advance. In July 1976 five hundred university students and graduates from all over Latin America gathered in the First Latin American Missionary Congress at the University of Paraná in Curitiba, Brazil. They gathered to affirm the commitment of a generation to missionary work in Latin America and overseas. The "Curitiba Covenant" that this congress issued is a short missiological statement patterned after the spirit of the Lausanne Covenant of 1974 (ABU 1978). This covenant affirms the acceptance of the missionary history of evangelicals in Latin America; God's initiative through Jesus Christ in history; the missionary vocation of the church; and the new missionary situation in the world. It concludes with the missionary commitment of a generation: "As in the past the call of Jesus Christ and his mission was a call to cross geographical frontiers, today the Lord is calling us to cross the frontiers of inequality, injustice and ideological idolatry. We are called to carry the presence of Jesus Christ proclaiming his redemptive gospel, serving the world and thus transforming it through his love, patient in the hope of the new creation that he will bring to reality, and for which we groan" (ABU 1978:125).

Eleven years later in November 1987, another continental gathering called "Ibero American Missionary Congress" (COMIBAM) attracted 3,100 delegates and observers, evidence of a growing missionary conviction among Latin American evangelicals that could be summarized in a phrase repeatedly used in the congress: "Latin America declares itself to be a mission force." COMIBAM had the intention of being more a process than an event, geared to heighten the awareness of the churches, the sharing of information, and the formation of missionary structures (COMIBAM 1987). The meeting expressed a great amount of enthusiasm for the missionary task. Yet it failed to grapple with basic concepts in the understanding of mission including both the blatant reality of poverty that surrounded the very place where delegates met, and the structures of mission at a time of crisis for traditional Latin American structures. Probably because of the North American model on which the conference was patterned, its observers missed a note of realism that a Brazilian summarized with the question "How can we Latin Americans avoid the same mistakes committed by Western Missions?" (Ford 1988).

The Catholic bishops in Puebla also projected their sight to mission at a global level. "Finally the time has come for Latin America to intensify works of mutual service between local churches and to extend them beyond their own frontiers *ad gentes*. True, we ourselves are in need of missionaries; but we must give from our own poverty" (Puebla 368). This phrase, "to give from our own poverty," has become the motto of the Department of Missions of the Bishops Conference (DEMIS-CELAM) and the basis for a missionary program and promotion that has continued to grow since 1979. According to information circulated during the Missionary Congress of Bogotá in 1987 (COMLA 3), there were at that time two thousand Latin American Catholics serving as missionaries in other parts of the world, and thirty more were commissioned at that meeting (Pacher-Ballán 1987:24). The great concern in COMLA 4 (Lima, February 1991) was that though 42 percent of the Catholics of the world live in Latin America, less than 2 percent of the total Catholic missionary force in the world comes from that continent (COMLA 4:267). What would these missionaries have to offer in other parts of the world? According to the bishops, "our Churches have something original and important to offer all: their sense of salvation and liberation, the richness of their people's religiosity, the experience of the CEBs (Base Christian Communities), their flourishing diversity of ministries, and their hope and joy rooted in faith" (Puebla 368).

Missiological Questions for the Future

In a continent where life is tense with the pressures of social change and the drama of historical processes in conflict, the practice of Christian mission does not allow much time for reflection. However, in recent years a missiological agenda has been developing and some of its themes have entered the missiological dialogue at a global scale. We will introduce briefly some of the questions that express better the Latin American experience of mission.

"Mission in the 1990s needs to concentrate on spreading the actual knowledge of the story of Jesus of Nazareth," writes Emilio Castro, reminding us of the words of the hymn "Tell me the old, old story," a favorite of Latin American evangelicals in the past. Castro believes that the proclamation of Jesus Christ is fundamental for mission, "because finally it is the only contribution we have to offer to modernity — a mirror, a point of reference, a yardstick, a life, Jesus Christ; but difficult, because this very life has been made the object of manipulation and reductionism, of soap operas, of commercial deformations. In the jungle of competitive offerings, of miracle solutions to all human problems, a finger pointing clearly to Jesus, the Lamb of God, is the best service we can render today" (Castro 1990:146).

From the Latin American scenario has come also the most articulate evangelical criticism of the managerial missiology that stresses verbal proclamation and numerical growth of church affiliation as the main component of Christian mission, and that is reluctant to criticize the imperialistic nature of its ideological assumptions. Against the easy triumphalism of statistics, and the tyranny of data control, the success of Protestant advance in Latin America has been interpreted by asking tough questions about its transformational dynamism in society and its contribution to justice in social relations (Costas 1974; Escobar and Driver 1978). The basis for this questioning has been a clear commitment to the enterprise of mission and evangelism, but also a conscious search to carry on that enterprise according to biblical standards (Padilla 1985). Thus a new contextual theology calling for the "integrity" of mission is developing; it tries to integrate evangelical zeal with holistic passion. Emilio Núñez from Guatemala has expressed it clearly: "To fulfill her mission the church has to live out the Gospel in the power of the Holy Spirit. The world has *to listen* to the Gospel, but it has also *to see* it in action in the lives of those who profess to be Christians. The church is called to be the community in which the signs of the Kingdom of God are present — the signs of love, joy, peace, justice, peace and the power in the Holy Spirit" (Taylor and Núñez 1989:373).

Valdir Steuernagel, a Brazilian missiologist who has studied the theological developments within the Lausanne movement, calls our attention to what he considers a useless debate within evangelicalism, the struggle about the "primacy" of evangelism. Steuernagel expresses the Latin American insistence on a holistic and biblical approach when he states, "Evangelism is not only central, but also essential to the life of the Church. Of this fact the Church must be constantly reminded. If there is no evangelism there is disobedience. If there is no evangelism every hope will disappear from the human community and the sign of death will proclaim victory. However, even if evangelism is so central let us not think of it apart from the whole mission of the church that challenges us to take the whole Gospel of the whole person to the whole world" (Steuernagel 1990:16).

The colossal migration process that has turned Latin American cities into urban nightmares has brought to light new segments of the population that were previously hidden in the distant rural areas but have now invaded the streets of capitals like Lima, Mexico City, Guatemala, São Paulo, Caracas, and Bogotá. The expansion of popular Protestantism in the form of Pentecostal churches among these emerging masses has become a surprising phenomenon. David Martin, a well-known sociologist of religion, has come to the conclusion that the paradigm that can be used to study and interpret this reality is the Wesleyan movement of the eighteenth and nineteenth centuries (Martin 1989). Here we can see a redemptive evangelistic spiritual experience and the social dynamism it provokes.

Measured by the standards of academic Marxism, this growth was considered negative, because it would not mobilize social forces into a Marxist-style revolution. But measured by the standards of a missiology that takes seriously New Testament theology and church history, such growth becomes a phenomenon of tremendous missiological significance. The expansive power of these popular forms of Protestantism comes from their ability to mobilize laypeople, to adopt truly contextual forms of worship, congregational life, and pastoral practices. For the masses in transition these churches are providing not only a haven or refuge in the more limited sense but the only available way to find social acceptance, achieve human dignity, and survive the impact of anomic forces at work in the big cities.

Because Pentecostal communities emphasize the ministry of the Holy Spirit and the spiritual conflict involved in mission, their presence and style pose the question of how spiritual realities are understood today. With the background of several years of missionary life in Brazil and missiological research at the doctoral level, Neuza Itioka has posed the question in very clear terms: "Certainly one of the most important issues worldwide missions must face in the 1990s is how to confront the destructive supernatural evil forces that oppose the missionary enterprise. For too long the Western church has tended toward an intellectual expression of its faith, failing to face realistically the supernatural manifestations it must confront" (Itioka 1990:8). Other missionaries in the Third World have recently written about this issue, among them Daniel Fountain, a medical doctor in Zaire (Fountain 1989), and Viv Grigg, a church planter in the slums of Manila (Grigg 1984). Like them, Itioka sees a close connection between spiritual oppression and the social conditions of poverty and exploitation. Her missiological proposal is a forceful challenge: "The rational intellectual approach we have used for so long brings only new information, a new way of thinking. What we need to reach people who coexist daily with the supernatural is the powerful presence of the risen Christ. He is the missionary and evangelist par excellence. Without his intimate involvement we have no mission and there will not be transformation in the lives of people" (Itioka 1990:9).

Each one of these proposals can provoke fiery theological and missiological debates. Once the cloud of dust from theological skirmishes is cleared, we believe that what Latin America can contribute to missiological formulations is the development of missionary models free from the imperialistic tones and styles that have marked the missionary enterprise in its European and North American phase. As the Constantinian missionary cycle that developed into the Crusades comes to an end, and new missionary vigor and passion stems from a church of the poor in a poor continent, new avenues of mission may be opened for the missionary challenges of the Third Millennium.

For Further Reading

ABU
    1978   *Jesus Cristo: Senhorio, Propósito, Missão.* São Paulo, Brazil: ABU Editora.

Braga, Erasmo
    1916   *Panamericanismo: Aspecto Religioso.* New York: Sociedade de Preparo Missionario.

Castro, Emilio
    1990   "Mission in the 1990s." *International Bulletin of Missionary Research* 14 (4):146-49.

CELAM
    1990   *Nueva Evangelización. Génesis y Líneas de un Proyecto Misionero.* Bogotá, Colombia: Consejo Episcopal Latinoamericano.

Cleary, Edward L.
    1985   *Crisis and Change. The Church in Latin America Today.* Maryknoll, NY: Orbis Books.

COMIBAM
    1987   *Reto Iberoamericano COMIBAM '87.* Guatemala City, Guatemala: Comibam.

COMLA 3
    1988   *América, llegó tu hora de ser Evangelizadora.* Bogotá, Colombia: Consejo Episcopal Latinoamericano.

COMLA 4
1991   *Memorias del COMLA 4*. Lima, Peru: Obras Misionales Ponti-
            ficias.
Costas, Orlando E.
1974   *The Church and Its Mission: A Shattering Critique from the Third
            World*. Wheaton, IL: Tyndale House.
1989   *Mission to Latin America*. Grand Rapids, MI: Wm. B. Eerd-
            mans Publishing Company.
Costello, Gerald M.
1979   *Mission to Latin America*. Maryknoll, NY: Orbis Books.
Damen, Franz
1987   "Las sectas: ¿avalancha o desafío?" *Cuarto Intermedio*, 3
            Mayo, pp. 45-63.
Escobar, Samuel
1987   *La Fe Evangélica y las Teologías de la Liberación*. El Paso, TX:
            Casa Bautista de Publicaciones.
1987a   "Mission and Renewal in Latin American Catholicism." *Mis-
            siology* 15 (2):33-46.
Escobar, Samuel, and John Driver
1978   *Christian Mission and Social Justice*. Scottdale, PA: Herald Press.
Ford, Donald
1987   *COMIBAM '87 First Iberoamerican Missionary Congress*. Lon-
            don: Evangelical Union of South America.
Fountain, Daniel E.
1989   *Health, the Bible and the Church*. Wheaton, IL: BGC Mono-
            graph.
Galilea, Segundo
1981   *La Responsabilidad Misionera de América Latina*. Bogotá,
            Colombia: Ediciones Paulinas.
Goodpasture, H. McKennie
1989   *Cross and Sword*. Maryknoll, NY: Orbis Books.
Gorski, P. Juan F., M.M.
1985   "El Desarrollo Histórico de la Misionología en América La-
            tina." Unpublished Ph.D. diss., La Paz.
Greenway, Roger
1973   *An Urban Strategy for Latin America*. Grand Rapids, MI: Baker
            Book House.
Grigg, Viv
1984   *Companion to the Poor*. Sutherland, NSW, Australia: Albatross
            Books.

Itioka, Neuza
1990   "Mission in the 1990s." *International Bulletin of Missionary Research* 14 (1):7-10.

Judd, Steven
1987   "The Seamy Side of Charity Revisited: American Catholic Contributions to Renewal in the Latin American Church." *Missiology* 15 (2):3-14.

Lernoux, Penny
1989   *People of God.* New York: Viking Press.

Mackay, John A.
1928   "The Power of Evangelism." In *Addresses and Other Records. Report of the Jerusalem Meeting of the International Missionary Council.* London: Oxford University Press, Vol. 8, pp. 121-25.

Martin, David
1989   *Tongues of Fire: the Explosion of Protestantism in Latin America.* Oxford: Basil and Blackwell.

McCoy, John
1989   "Robbing Peter to Pay Paul. The Evangelical Tide." *Latinamerica Press* 21 (24), June 22, 1989.

Míguez Bonino, José
1964   "Latin America." In *The Prospects of Christianity throughout the World.* Edited by M. Searle Bates and Wilhelm Pauck. New York: Charles Scribner's Sons, pp. 166-82.

Pacher, Gianni, and Romeo Ballán
1987   "América Latina: continente de la esperanza misionera." *Misión Sin Fronteras* 89 (Sept. 1987):18-25.

Padilla, C. René
1985   *Mission between the Times.* Grand Rapids, MI: Wm. B. Eerdmans Publishing Company.

Puebla Document
1979   Official translation in John Eagleson and Philip Scharper, *Puebla and Beyond.* Maryknoll, NY: Orbis Books, 1980. The document has been quoted by its paragraph numbers.

Spykman, Gordon, ed.
1988   *Let My People Live.* Grand Rapids, MI: Wm. B. Eerdmans Publishing Company.

Steuernagel, Valdir R.
1990   "Social Concern and Evangelization. Our Journey Since Lausanne I." *Transformation* 7 (1):12-16.

Stoll, David
  1990   *Is Latin America Turning Protestant?* Berkeley, CA: University
            of California Press.
Taylor, William D., and Emilio A. Núñez
  1989   *Crisis in Latin America.* Chicago: Moody Press.

/

Northeast Asia

Yoshinobu Kumazawa

The general tendency of Christian mission in the twentieth century can be summarized by the phrase "the dewesternization of Christianity." According to David B. Barrett's *World Christian Encyclopedia*, in 1900 the Christians in the less developed regions of the world were only fifteen percent of the total number of Christians, while those in the more developed regions were eighty-five percent. By 1985, Christians in less developed regions had grown to 47.6 percent, and by the year 2000 they are predicted to be 56.6 percent of the total (1982:4).

What does this mean for mission? It means that the less developed nations that were long treated as mission lands are such no longer. Instead, they are now sending out missionaries to other parts of the world, including the Western world. The Western world has rapidly become a mission land itself.

In his "Annual Statistical Table on Global Mission: 1989," in the *International Bulletin of Missionary Research,* Barrett makes this remarkable comment: "Before 1980 most Western Christians regarded the Far East as hostile to the Christian faith. . . . Today there is in place in East Asia a massive Christian colossus of 80 million Christians, mostly Chinese, Korean, and Japanese" (1989:20). Within two years, Barrett increased this estimate to 88,810,300 (1991:25). Compared with his estimate of 16,149,600 Christians in that region in 1980 (in his *World Christian Encyclopedia,* 1982), the number of Christians increased five and a

---

Yoshinobu Kumazawa is Professor of Theology at Tokyo Union Theological Seminary, and coeditor of *Christianity in Japan, 1971-90* (1991).

half times in one decade. He forecasts a Christian population of 128,000,000 for the region by 2000, which would be an almost eightfold increase in two decades. The mission of God is moving ahead in East Asia as the twenty-first century approaches.

China

China's Christian communities mark the arrivals of the Nestorian Alopen in 635, the Franciscan John of Montecorvino in 1294, the Jesuit Matteo Ricci in 1582, and the Protestant Robert Morrison in 1807. Britt E. Towery, Jr., gives a Protestant periodization by describing the years of beginnings from 1807 to 1949, the years of new beginnings from 1950 to 1960, the years of the locust (the Cultural Revolution) from 1966 to 1976, and the years of renewal from 1979 to the present (Towery 1987). Towery recalls a poster that was put up during the Cultural Revolution at the entrance of the former YMCA building in Beijing that was typical of the frenzy of those days. It read: "There is no God; there is no Spirit; there is no Jesus; there is no Mary; there is no Joseph. How can adults believe in these things? . . . Priests live in luxury and . . . like Islam and Catholicism, Protestantism is a reactionary feudal ideology, the opium of the people, with foreign origins and contacts. . . . We are atheists; we believe only in Mao Zedong. We call on all people to burn Bibles, destroy images and disperse religious associations" (Towery 1987). Churches were closed for worship and were used for everything from factories and storehouses to local headquarters of the Red Guards.

After the death of Chairman Mao in 1976 and the subsequent changes of governmental leadership, restrictions began to be lifted from religious organizations of all kinds, and from 1979 church buildings began to be returned to their worshiping communities. To give but one example, the Muen Church in Shanghai was reopened in 1979 after it had been closed for thirteen years. When the present writer visited that church in the summer of 1990, over four thousand people were attending the three Sunday services; the church building had been beautifully renovated and was in full use by its congregation.

According to officially recognized statistics of 1988, there were 6,375 churches in China, 2,683 of them newly established since 1980. There were also 20,602 meeting points, of which 15,855 had some contact with the China Christian Council. In 1990 Chinese Christians estimated that there were over five million Protestants — seven times as many as the 700,000 in 1949 — and over four million Catholics. (These

140

estimates are considerably lower than those of Barrett, quoted previously.) To meet the urgent needs of theological education for the clergy, the Protestants have one national seminary and thirteen provincial seminaries. The Catholics have two national seminaries and six provincial seminaries. Since it opened in 1987, the Amity Publishing Company has printed over two million Bibles, and other publications for the churches.

China's 1982 constitution contains a guarantee of freedom of religion, a great improvement over the 1954 and 1975 constitutions, both of which gave atheists the right to propagate their beliefs, a right religious groups did not share. China's Protestants continue to follow their heritage of the "three-self" principle: self-governing, self-supporting, and self-propagating (Shenk 1990). Because Christians have shared in the sufferings of their fellow citizens since 1949, the Chinese public has become more aware that Christianity is not a Western religion, but is deeply rooted among the Chinese people. There are tensions among Protestants between those who cooperate with the China Christian Council and those who continue to meet primarily in house churches, apart from the Council's supervision. Catholics have their tensions between those who are related to the Catholic Patriotic Association, which has no official ties with the papacy, and the traditional Catholics who affirm papal ties. While it is too early to foresee how these tensions might be resolved, they will indeed play a role in how the churches face the challenges of the twenty-first century.

The demonstrations in Tienanmen Square for democratization in the spring of 1989 evoked widespread support among Chinese Christians. Bishop K. H. Ting of the China Christian Council on May 23 issued a public statement praising the patriotism of the hunger strikers. After the June 1, 1989, suppression of the Tienanmen Square protests, Bishop K. H. Ting and his colleague Han Wenzao of the Amity Foundation wrote Amity colleagues in Hong Kong: "We are with our people in this time of suffering and uncertainty. . . . We firmly believe God's justice and people's democracy will prevail" (McLean 1989:543). The ultimate effects of the political situation in China on its Christian community are too difficult to predict, but it may be assumed that Christians will play an increasingly significant role in the life of their nation in the twenty-first century.

Hong Kong is a British crown colony that will be returned to China in 1997, with some provisions for local autonomy. In the mid-1980s, 800,400 Christians were reported in Hong Kong, including 357,200 Catholics, 358,350 Protestants and Anglicans, and 84,850 others

141

(Barrett 1982:361). The Tienanmen Square repressions evoked wide-spread protests in Hong Kong, and stirred fears among Christians that their lot would be far more difficult after 1997. The main Christian groups have put plans in place, however, to ensure the continuity of the Christian community in Hong Kong into the next century.

Taiwan's future is more uncertain, for after Tienanmen Square any easy rapprochement between Beijing and the mainland and Taiwanese groups on the island seems more distant than ever. In the mid-1980s, Taiwan had 470,400 Catholics, 491,540 Protestants and Anglicans, and 326,200 others, for a total of 1,288,140 Christians (Barrett 1982:235). Among the Protestant groups, the Presbyterian Church in Taiwan has the largest membership and has been active in seeking self-determination for the people of Taiwan. There has been remarkable growth among the Christians of Taiwan, undimmed by continuing problems with the island's governing authorities. As in the case of Hong Kong, the Christian community in Taiwan has members with considerable commercial and technological skills, as well as wide international contacts. This should insure its continued vitality whatever the political developments.

Korea

By almost any measurement, the growth of Christianity in Korea in the last century is one of the most amazing stories of our time. Korea's Catholics date their history from 1784, while the first Protestant missionaries arrived in 1884. There were periods of remarkable growth during the years of Japan's occupation of the country (1905-1945). Indeed, Christianity in Korea has grown significantly since the end of the Second World War in 1945, with the division of the country into North Korea, with ties to the USSR and China, and South Korea, allied with the United States. The Korean War between the northern and southern halves of the country and their respective supporters (1950-53) ended in an armistice, but large groups of Christians and other refugees fled to the South, where they swelled the already expanding Christian population. By the mid-1980s South Korea had 1,460,300 Catholics, 4,508,800 Protestants and Anglicans, and 5,440,700 other Christians, for a total of 11,409,800, or 30.5 percent of the total population (Barrett 1982:441).

The strength of South Korea's Christians is not to be found in numbers alone but also in persistent commitment to the faith despite numerous adversities. A network of Protestant and Catholic schools and universities and the involvement of Christians in social issues of all kinds are other signs of strength. The Presbyterian churches, which comprise the largest group of Protestants in South Korea, have generally adhered to the "three-self" principle that China's Protestants have embraced since 1949. The difference, however, is that the "three-self" principle was brought to Korea in 1890 by a missionary from China, and was soon put into practice in Korea to an extent virtually unknown among other Protestant missions until a much later date. This "three-self" principle, together with other factors of Korean society that became intertwined with the Japanese occupation of the country, led to the Korean Protestant churches having a predominantly conservative outlook. That is still the case today.

Since the Korean War, small groups of progressive Protestants have found themselves in opposition to the periodic repressive tactics of South Korean government leaders and have developed a *Minjung* (oppressed people) theology. Numbers of Korean Catholics have joined progressive Protestants in criticizing government repression, leading to frequent arrests and imprisonments of Christian leaders. But the majority of Protestants have stressed strategies of church growth. Because of this they have penetrated Korean society both in the rural areas where they have been traditionally strong, and in the burgeoning urban areas.

Large numbers of Koreans have emigrated to the United States, Europe, South America, and Southern Asia, and active Christian churches have sprung up among these communities also. South Korean Christians have established a number of mission-sending organizations, and have sent missionaries to serve not only Koreans abroad but other groups of people as well. South Korean Christians, along with other members of younger Christian communities in the Two-Thirds World, have taken important initiatives for Christian world mission.

It is tragic that North Korea, once the major center of Korean Protestantism, has seen its Christian community dwindle drastically under the communist government of President Kim Il-Sung, which has been in control since shortly after 1945 (Clark 1971:233-36; Rhodes and Campbell 1964:209-10). Despite his personal ties with Christians from his boyhood, Kim Il-Sung and others in his regime looked upon the Christians with deep suspicion because of their long-standing ties with Americans and their post-1945 sympathies with the South Korean government of President Syngman Rhee, which included many Christians in its leadership, from the president on down. After initial efforts to control Christian activities, the North Korean government embarked on a series of measures against the Christian churches, leading to tens of thousands of North Korean Christians and others fleeing to South Korea (Sawa 1978:12-27). With the outbreak of the Korean War, Christians in North Korea were seen as probable subversives, and this led to further repressive measures and additional thousands of refugees fleeing south. By 1972, in a public sense, the Christian community of North Korea was virtually extinct, although a few thousand people continued to hold the faith secretly. By the mid-1980s, there were estimated to be 161,900 Protestants in North Korea, virtually all of them in the category of "crypto-Christians" (Barrett 1982:439).

The situation began to change somewhat from about 1985. Although the South Korean government took strenuous efforts to prevent any private contacts between its citizens and North Korea, connections with Christians in North Korea began to be made by Christians in Western countries, many of whom were of Korean ancestry. By 1986, the World Council of Churches was able to sponsor an international conference on the problem of unity in the Korean peninsula that was held in Glion, Switzerland. And here Christians from both North and South Korea were able to meet after a long interruption. Other contacts were arranged in subsequent years, particularly by Christian groups in Japan, West Germany, and the United States. Despite severe punishment meted out by the South Korean government on its Protestant and Catholic citizens who have traveled to North Korea, contacts continue to multiply. The collapse of communist regimes in East Europe and the long-delayed reunification of the two Germanys in 1989-90 brought hope to Korean Christians that the reunification of their country might not be too far off. The implications of such a reunification for Korean mission in the twenty-first century are indeed far-reaching and momentous.

Japan

In contrast to the outstanding Christian growth in both China and South Korea, the minimal growth of Christianity in Japan makes it an exception in Northeast Asia.

In a widely questioned tabulation, Barrett reported that in Japan in the mid-1980s there were 3,526,400 Christians. This was made up of 748,000 Catholics, 1,160,000 Protestants and Anglicans, and 1,618,000 others, of whom ninety-six percent were in the categories of Japanese *secret Kiai*

"indigenous Christians, marginal Protestants, and crypto-Christians" (Barrett 1982:419). *The Christian Yearbook, 1990,* the most widely used reference work among Japanese Christians, on the other hand, reported in 1990 that there were 435,826 Catholics and 638,850 Protestants, a total Christian population of 1,074,616 (Christian Newspaper Publishing Company 1990). Such a sum actually represents a decrease of 23,432 from that source's 1989 statistics. This would mean that Christians are about 0.9 percent of the country's total population.

The discrepancy between the reported adherents of Japanese Christian groups and the large number of sympathizers and crypto-Christians may be accounted for in part by the number of people who express sympathy for Christianity without being formally related to the Christian community. This is reflected in reports of large numbers of Bibles sold by the Japan Bible Society and other Protestant and Catholic publishing companies (cf. Drummond 1971:242-43). The number of Bibles and Bible portions sold in Japan jumped from almost none in 1945 to one million the following year, and at the height of the religious boom in 1951 had reached three million. Then, for several years, interest in Christianity subsided, and so did the sales of Bibles; but annual sales climbed back to over eight million in 1970, and remain today in the range between seven and nine million. In other words, among the Japanese there are far more Bible readers than there are church attenders. Mission in Japan toward the next century needs to bring these Bible readers into the churches by providing a credible interpretation of what the Bible has to say to the Japanese people today. The situation is not unlike that of the Ethiopian official who asked Philip, "How can I understand unless someone explains it to me?" (Acts 8:31, TEV).

Japan has achieved very high economic, technological, and material levels of success in the post-1945 period. There are signs, however, that even though most Japanese are surrounded with abundance they are not satisfied. The proportion of those over sixty-five is gradually increasing, and is predicted to be twenty-five percent of the total population by 2022. There may be yet another "religious boom" in Japan in the twenty-first century as elderly Japanese revive their quest for meaning. Most will turn to Buddhism, but some to the Christian faith.

The political and social situations that have developed in Northeast Asia in recent years have been very serious. Despite the collapse of communist regimes in Eastern Europe and the changes taking place in the former USSR, the communist regimes in China and North Korea have largely maintained control of their nations. The South Korean government has made some modifications, and because of the country's economic development, it has been able to dampen the influence of its critics. In Japan, the major problem that must be faced is the emperor system. Although the emperor supposedly renounced his divine status in 1946, and Article 21 of the Japanese Constitution of 1947 has guaranteed religious freedom to all citizens, the emperor system continues to pose problems for Japanese citizens, particularly in the Christian community (Phillips 1981:25, 42, 46, 239, 279). After Emperor Hirohito's death in January 1989, ceremonies were held during his funeral that compromised the constitutional separation of religion and state. Further problems arose with the Enthronement Rites of Emperor Akihito in November 1990. Many Japanese Christians and others fear that the emperor system may continue to undermine not only religious freedom but other kinds of freedoms that the Japanese have enjoyed in the period since 1945.

With such difficulties in Northeast Asia, cooperation between Christians in this area is increasingly necessary for mission in the years ahead. Even though small in numbers, Japanese Christians have provided opportunities for Christians from North and South Korea to meet in Japan, and additional measures might be taken in the future. Similar encounters might be arranged for Christians from mainland China and Taiwan. At the same time, Christians and others in China, Korea, and Southeast Asia who suffered from Japan's imperial policies during the Second World War might help Japanese Christians prevent the reinstatement of the emperor system in Japan itself. In these and in many other ways, Christians in Northeast Asia may be able to help each other as they move toward the next century of Christian mission.

For Further Reading

Barrett, David B.
  1982   *World Christian Encyclopedia.* Nairobi: Oxford University Press.
  1989   "Annual Statistical Table on Global Mission: 1989." *International Bulletin of Missionary Research (IBMR)* 13:20-21.
  1990   "Annual Statistical Table . . . 1990." *IBMR* 14:26-27.
  1991   "Annual Statistical Table . . . 1991." *IBMR* 15:24-25.
Brown, G. Thompson
  1986   *Christians in the People's Republic of China.* Revised edition. Atlanta: John Knox Press.

146

Christian Newspaper Publishing Company (Kirisuto Shimbunsha)
1990   *The Christian Yearbook, 1990* (in Japanese, *Kirisutokyo Nenkan, 1990*). Tokyo: Kirisuto Shimbunsha.

Clark, Allen D.
1971   *A History of the Church in Korea.* Seoul: Christian Literature Society of Korea.

Drummond, Richard H.
1971   *A History of Christianity in Japan.* Grand Rapids, MI: Wm. B. Eerdmans Publishing Company.

Kumazawa, Yoshinobu, and D. L. Swain
1991   *Christianity in Japan, 1970-91.* Tokyo: Kyo Bun Kwan.

MacInnis, Donald E.
1989   *Religion in China Today: Policy and Practice.* Maryknoll, NY: Orbis Books.

McLean, Cynthia K.
1989   "China Update." *China Notes* 27, Summer 1989, pp. 542-43.

Phillips, James M.
1981   *From the Rising of the Sun: Christians and Society in Contemporary Japan.* Maryknoll, NY: Orbis Books.

Rhodes, Harry A., and Archibald Campbell
1964   *History of the Korea Mission, Presbyterian Church in the USA,* Vol. 3. New York: United Presbyterian Church.

Sawa, Masahiko
1978   *North Korean Religious Policies and Christianity* (in Japanese, *Kita-Chosen no Shukyo Seisaku to Kirisutokyo*). Tokyo: Privately printed.
1991   *Unaccomplished History of Christianity in Korea* (in Japanese, *Mikan Chosen Kirisutokyoshi*). Tokyo: Privately printed.

Shenk, Wilbert
1990   "The Origins and Evolution of the Three-Selfs in Relation to China." *IBMR* 14 (Jan.): 28-34.

Towery, Britt E., Jr.
1987   *The Churches of China* (second edition, revised).

147

Europe a sequel essay

Peter Kuzmic

"Our problem is, therefore, how to get in touch again
with the masses of the 'unfaithful faithful'." in action the

Prof. Regin Prenter, Denmark

"The life and death question for Europe is, then,
whether it can rediscover its own specific mission."

Dr. W. A. Visser 't Hooft

From *Corpus Christianum* to a New Europe

There was a time when "Europe" and "Christendom" were almost synonymous terms. The symbiosis of the two is summed up in H. Belloc's epigram, "The faith is Europe, and Europe is the faith" (Will

---

Dr. Peter Kuzmic is cofounder and director of the Evangelical Theological Seminary in Osijek, Yugoslavia. Since 1986 he has served as chairman of the Theological Commission of the World Evangelical Fellowship. He is a member of the Lausanne Committee for World Evangelization and is one of the founding executives of the Council of Evangelical Christians of Yugoslavia. He has authored numerous articles and four books, including a major study of the influence of Slavic Bible translations on Slavic literature, language, and culture.

148

1981:6). A contemporary of Martin Luther, the geographer Wachelus, published in 1537 a woodcut map of Europe as "The Queen Virgin." It was to illustrate the unity and integrity of "Christian Europe" as conceived by medieval Catholic ideology. Wachelus' map shows Spain as the head of the virgin, Italy as the right arm, and Denmark the left; Germany, France, and Switzerland are the breast; Poland, Hungary, "Illyricum," Albania, Greece, Lithuania, Romania, Bulgaria, and others are all identified on the virgin's illustrious gown.

Already at that time, however, the transition from the monolithic religious "Christendom" to the secular "Europe" was in progress. Though the rise of Islam initially strengthened the idea of Christendom, the fifteenth-century Ottoman Islamic push westward almost broke it when some Christian powers, for selfish reasons, aligned with the enemy against other Christian nations. When Erasmus made his appeal for the crusade against the Turks, he did not appeal to the members of Christendom, but, noticeably, to "the nations of Europe." The Reformation and the following developments only speeded up the process of transition. In the seventeenth and eighteenth centuries science came into its own and the secular state established itself. In the nineteenth and twentieth centuries the industrial revolution and the birth of Marxist socialism completed the process of the disintegration of *Corpus Christianum*. The post-Enlightenment culture became a major European "missionary problem" (Newbigin 1986).

The European map today is in a state of political and economic, as well as cultural and religious flux. This chapter is written at a time of rapid changes and an intensive search for a "new Europe." Presently Europe lives in the intensive period "between 1989 and 1992," the year 1989 marking the beginning of the wholesale collapse of communism and 1992 the beginning of a "United States of Europe," initially a West European economic and political integration. The European Community's (EC) move toward a closer union has been recently accelerated in response to dramatic events in Eastern Europe. The demand for change in the East European countries has been promoted and strengthened by the political freedoms and economic success of Western Europe, which have acted as a magnet drawing the East toward the West.

Today Europe seems to be fully alive and bursting with visions, programs, and activities that make it again "the most important theater of contemporary world events" (Burstein 1991:11). Western Europe is in the process of dismantling its frontiers and gearing itself for new economic growth, energetically engaged in overcoming the two interrelated diseases of the early 1980s — "Eurosclerosis" and "Europessimism." For a while these often lamented twin ills threatened to make Europe a largely unimportant, uninteresting, and conceivably even an irrelevant continent. Europe was for a while playing only a minor and increasingly diminishing role in the global geopolitical game. The constant complaints that Europe is an "economic giant and a political pygmy" and "merely the chessboard over which American and Soviet masters made their strategic moves" (Burstein 1991:37) became somewhat obsolete when the oil-shocked 1970s and their alarming growth of unemployment resulted in economic collapse along with political impotence.

Where did the new will and vision come from? Are there analogies to be drawn and lessons to be learned in a somewhat similarly discouraging religious situation in Europe? Many diagnose the European churches as suffering from similar conditions of "sclerosis" (stagnation) and "pessimism" (loss of will and power to stem the tide of decline).

The turning point in the transition from the "old" to the "new Europe" was an almost "spiritual" event. Jacques Delors, the incoming president of the European Community's executive commission, acted as a visionary prophet when in December 1984 he summoned other commissioners to Royaumont Abbey (outside Paris) for a crucial contemplative retreat. Delors analyzed the crisis of Europe and the failed dream of a new, united Europe with precision, brutal frankness, and vision. He warned his fellow commissioners that if Europe did not recognize its *kairos*-time (this author's expression) and failed to seize the historic moment, it could anticipate a twenty-first century in which it would be little more than a "museum to be visited by American and Japanese tourists who like our cuisine and culture."

"Europe's choice is between survival and decline" was the challenge of Delors as he called the EC to undertake a "solemn commitment" to work toward a strategic plan for recovery (Burstein 1991:36). The facts of a structural crisis had to be faced squarely and basic structures remade so as to become an efficient servant of the new Europe. Lessons were to be learned from others — even from ideological opponents! — especially in the area of removing government barriers for free trade. A willingness to forget and forgive the animosities of the past (see the amazing "metanoia" from Franco-German enmity to Franco-German amity!) was also required in order to pave the way for a more viable future.

Does this brief survey contain any lessons or discernible seeds for changing the European spiritual climate? While the European church relies on the centuries of Christian history and benefits from the in-

150

herited traditions and institutions, its future should not become a hostage of its glorious past. Neither should the present lack of spiritual vitality, denominational divisions, religious indifference, and other "Christian ills" allow the church to reconcile itself to a status quo position and thus incapacitate itself for its God-given mission in and on behalf of the new and spiritually revitalized Europe.

The Spiritual Crisis of Europe

A North American evangelical missiologist in his introduction to a popular and largely pessimistic assessment of Europe's Christianity writes: "Europe appears to be a continent on the verge of moral collapse. Decades of anemic Christianity and humanistic philosophies have eaten the spiritual interior of this continent and Europe now stands at crossroads. Can it be saved?" (Henley 1978:9). This sounds very similar to the question, "Can the West be converted?" asked by Lesslie Newbigin, an author known for his perceptive analysis of the post-Enlightenment Western culture as a specific missionary challenge (Newbigin 1987:2). A European missiologist begins his survey "The Church in Europe" with the sentence: "There is a general agreement that the Church in Europe is in a poor state of health." He collaborates this diagnosis with, among other things, the statistical statement that "some 1.8 million people in Europe leave the Church each year" (Cotterell 1989:37).

The late Bishop Stephen Neill, writing at the time when he was a professor of ecumenics and missions at the University of Hamburg, was equally pessimistic: "Church attendance in Europe is everywhere declining; the lack of ordained ministers is grave in every country whether Roman Catholic or Protestant. The secularization of life proceeds apace. We seem to be watching a steady diminution of the spiritual capital of Europe, the disappearance of the old synthesis of religion and culture, and a desiccation of the human spirit, as a result of which men not merely are not religious, but can see no reason why they should concern themselves beyond the world of the senses" (1964). In 1970 (April 2), *Time* magazine reported the progressive paralysis of European religious life and the advance of "a secular-minded culture that suggests eclipse rather than the presence of God" (cf. Detzler 1979). Addressing the West European Consultation on Evangelism in 1977, W. A. Visser 't Hooft pointed out that "European culture has become a debate between three forces: Christianity, scientific rationalism and neo-pagan vitalism"

151

(1977:355). For a long time the impression was created that scientific rationalism was victorious. However, recent decades with the negative results of technocratic civilization, nuclear threat, and ecological devastation have changed the picture and given rise to a growth of a new irrationalism, Europe's neo-paganism. Visser 't Hooft seems to agree with Carl Gustav Jung who claimed that the Christian message has neither reached nor transformed the soul of the European person and that Christianity in Europe is like a cathedral built on the foundation of a pagan temple. His conclusion: "Now there is surely need for evangelism, revival and renewal. There are millions of lapsed Christians who need to hear anew what the Gospel has to offer them. But there are today in Europe even more millions who are not adequately described as lapsed Christians, because they have in fact turned to another religion" (Visser 't Hooft 1977:350).

The real status and strength of the Christian faith in Europe today cannot be ascertained by review of its historical role nor by present-day statistics of church membership. Europe is far less "Christian" than its history, religious institutions, and statistical figures seem to indicate. There is now a growing realization among churches in Western Europe that a baptized person or a person who pays church taxes is not necessarily a Christian. Nominal Christians among the Protestants in central and northern Europe, among the Catholics in France and southern Europe, as well as among the Orthodox in southeastern Europe and the former USSR are increasingly seen, not only by evangelical mission activists from North America but in many cases by their own concerned bishops, as "unreached people groups" in need of evangelism. In that very context, the questions about the role of baptism in the appropriation of salvation and about the assurance of salvation are increasingly pushing themselves on the agenda of theological debates and ecclesiastical practices.

Any discussion of the future of the Christian mission in Europe must take into account a growing indifference to anything religious such as is found in no other continent in the world. Bishop Hanns Lilje (at the time the presiding bishop of Germany's Lutherans and president of the European Council of Churches) in his *Christianity in a Divided Europe* distinguishes between three types of atheism: *atheismus militans* (militant atheism, especially of the communist type associated with Eastern Europe), *atheismus subtilis sive philosophicus* (subtle or philosophical atheism of the rationalistic intellectuals), and *atheismus practicus* (practical atheism). The last term is borrowed from the well-known biblical scholar Johann Albrecht Bengel, who in his famous commentary

152

Gnomon Novi Testamenti points out that the rich man in the Lord's parable (Luke 16:19-31) was not condemned for wrong belief or heresy but because he lived by a certain *atheismus practicus* ignoring God and eternity. Lilje is convinced that though this formula is more than two hundred years old, it is "an excellent description of the most difficult, spiritual phenomenon in the Western world today. For it suggests what it says: not an explicit antitheistic theory but the actual and practiced disregard of God. Here is not apostasy but weakness, not an open revolt, but the silent paganization" (1965:32-33). This is a biblical picture of modern Europe that seems to see no need for God or any theistic concepts. This widespread phenomenon is in agreement with the attitude expressed in Jean-Paul Sartre's philosophy: "What man needs is to find himself again and to understand that nothing can save him from himself, not even a valid proof of the existence of God" (Sartre 1956:311). Whether God exists or not does not matter any longer, for it seems to make no difference to the average European, who may be a culturally conditioned nominal Christian but is actually a practicing atheist. By this European majority God is completely disregarded and the Christian church largely ignored.

For most of the West European Christians faith does not make much difference in life. Sunday is not a day of worship (as it still seems to be in North America) but only a welcome break between two working weeks. The process of secularization was the breeding ground of Christian nominalism, which was in turn followed by a marked shift from nominal Christianity to varying degrees of pragmatic atheism throughout Europe. As a result the church is now largely disregarded and seems to have no significant influence on individuals, families, or public life. "Despite the various degrees of influence presiding in different countries, at no point can it be said that Christian conviction — divorced from political pretension — is giving decisive direction to the trends of events in Europe" (Herman 1953:198). There is a general lack of clarity over what Christianity stands for and widespread ignorance of the most basic facts and values of Christian faith.

The workshop "Nominalism Today" at the 1989 Lausanne Congress on World Evangelization in Manila estimated that at least one billion, or seventy-five to eighty percent, of professing Christians are nominal. The conclusion was that this is "the largest religious group in need of evangelization today" (Douglas 1990:446). The workshop divided the nominal Christians into four categories: "ethnic-religious identity" nominal, the second generation nominal, the ritualistic nominal, and the syncretistic nominal. The Catholic, Protestant, and Or-

153

thodox churches in Europe are in themselves a complex mission field in which all four types of nominals exist and should become priority concern for intentional and comprehensive programs of evangelization. Awakening the religiously indifferent and those who have found false security in a superficially sacramentalistic, cultural and/or nationalistic, and yet only nominal Christianity is a very complex challenge. Evangelism in Europe must also take into account large numbers of those who have been "disappointed by Christianity or have remained at a level of a merely psychological piety or legal morality" (Weber 1979:78).

In 1978, the Lutheran World Federation sponsored a Regional Consultation (for North America, the Nordic countries of Europe, and Germany) on mission and evangelism. The consultation was a significant step beyond the traditional understanding of mission as something the churches and missionary organizations in Europe and North America, which are relatively rich in qualified personnel and financial resources, do, considering the poorer countries of the southern hemisphere in the Third World as their sole mission fields. It concluded, as did other recent gatherings, that "mission is indivisible" and began grappling seriously with the thesis that "mission begins on our doorstep. And for the superficially large churches it is precisely here that there is a vital need for mission" (Lutheran World Federation 1979:vi). The West European churches need to take a hard look at themselves and face the realities of their spiritual crisis in order to realize that they themselves have become a mission field. "Folk and state churches are conscious of the paradox of their empty churches on the one hand, and their solid church institutions, on the other; the evidence of secularization; religious frustration; materialism with all its ramifications in western societies; the invasion of new religions and pseudo-religions . . ." (ibid.). These realities are descriptive not only of the more secularized Protestant West European countries but also of their Catholic counterparts, as evident from the recent Vatican encyclicals and repeated calls of Pope John II for "re-evangelization" of Europe.

The Challenges of a New Eastern Europe

Whatever is written about the future of Eastern Europe at this time must be written in pencil. All across Eastern Europe and in the Soviet Union monumental changes are taking place at breathtaking speed and in most dramatic and unpredictable ways. The impact of *glasnost* and *perestroika* has put into reverse process the revolutionary events of 1917 and the post–World War II European developments. The massive collapse of communism in Eastern Europe at the end of 1989 and in the former Soviet Union in August 1991 have removed from the European scene the most impressive competitor to Christian faith and its most powerful opponent.

It is a well-known fact that wherever communists came to power their long-term goal was not only a classless but also a religionless society. Christian faith was viewed as a superstitious, obscurantist, obsolete, pre-scientific, and thus totally irrelevant way of thinking. Christian institutions were treated as a reactionary remnant of the old order and a hindrance to the progress of the new society and full human liberation of their citizens. Since communists had monopoly on both power (which they have abused) and truth (which they have distorted), they developed comprehensive strategies and powerful instruments for the eventual elimination of religion. This included restrictive legislation, total atheization of educational institutions and media, control of selection and activity of church leadership, and so on. The policies and methods have differed from country to country and in different periods even within the same countries, depending on what was politically expedient. Generalizations are impossible, for Eastern Europe has never been monolithic in its treatment of religion. Its religious complexity has been shaped by national, cultural, and religious histories of different nations and international relationships and considerations. At best, however, Christian faith was barely tolerated and Christians marginalized and discriminated against as "second class citizens," and at worst, they were brutally persecuted. In Albania, for example, all visible expressions of religion were in 1967 totally eradicated as that small country prided itself on becoming the "first atheistic state in the world." The story of Christian persecution under Stalin in the Soviet Union and during the Khrushchev era is well known (Hill 1991:69ff.) and does not need to be retold.

With the collapse of communism a new spirit of hope has filled widened horizons. Today we are witnesses of the historical fact that titles Michael Bourdeaux's latest book, *The Gospel's Triumph over Communism* (1991). Though the dramatic changes contain many elements of unpredictability, the followers of Christ all across Eastern Europe are aware that this is the work of the Lord of history who has seen their suffering and longing for freedom, answered their prayers, and provided them with a special *kairos* period to call their nations back to God and to the spiritual foundations for a free and truly "new society."

155

The general euphoria of East Europeans with a newly found free-dom is, however, very quickly giving place to a sober encounter with realities threatening a free, peaceful, and prosperous future society. Eastern Europe is presently going through a very difficult political transition, moving away from the one-party totalitarian regimes toward some kind of multiparty parliamentary democracy. Mistakes are being made as the ABCs of democracy are learned, and new democratic institutions and traditions have yet to be established. The transition is equally painful economically as Eastern Europe moves away from the centrally planned "command" economy toward some kind of a viable free-market economy. Economic recovery will be slow as the huge bureaucratic apparatuses are dismantled, many state-subsidized facto-ries closed (potentially causing massive social unrest and thus bringing instability to the society), and the mindset of the people changed. Re-education for the formerly stifled creativity and initiative, so important for the free-market economy, may take considerable time. Social unrest, the disillusionment of the impoverished masses, and the general men-tality of dependence may create environments conducive to new dic-tatorships or at least tempting politicians to control the economy in ways similar to those of the communist period.

The major problem for the Christian church and its mission may be the temptation to return to a quasi-Constantinian model of church-state cooperation. In the process of replacing communist ideology with nationalistic ideologies, there is an intense and valid rediscovery of national-religious identity. The churches are given the rightful recogni-tion for having historically preserved the sense of nationhood, lan-guage, and culture, especially in the Balkans under the centuries of Islamic Ottoman-Turkish imposition. They are also rightfully credited for their opposition to the communist system and for keeping alive certain endangered national and spiritual values. On the negative side, however, the discernible shifts "from totalitarianism to tribalism" (is-suing in inter-ethnic conflicts and wars) and "from rights to roots" threaten the democratic processes in most of the East European coun-tries. They also present a dangerous resurgence of new national-religious totalitarianisms. National churches, especially Orthodox in several republics of the former Soviet Union, Romania, Bulgaria, and Serbia and Catholic in Poland, Hungary and Croatia, reassert their monopolistic claims on religious life and activity in their nations. In these countries, belonging to the national church is becoming less a question of theological persuasion and allegiance to Christ and more a question of patriotism and bona fide citizenship.

Protestantism in general is looked upon with great suspicion as that radical movement which in the past divided Christendom and which in the present, as a modernized, Western faith and thus a foreign intrusion, in its various fragmented forms threatens the national and religious identity and unity of the people. Democratically and ecumenically illiterate clergy and militant fanatics among laity are frequently opposed to Protestant evangelicals as disruptive sectarians involved in dangerous proselytizing and unpatriotic activities. Violent clashes, legal and illegal discrimination, and cultural marginalization are not excluded. It is not inconceivable that some leaders of religious minorities (evangelical and other) could become the new "dissidents" of the post-communist era in Eastern Europe.

The New Europe: What Is to Be Done?

The necessary shortness of this chapter and the vastness and complexity of the subject treated do not allow for a comprehensive analysis and proposal for the Christian mission in the new Europe. The religious situation in Europe is a peculiarly complex one and generalizations are hardly possible since the situations and status of the churches differ from country to country and there are significant variations between different parts of the same countries. Christian institutions play a prominent part in some countries, while in others they are virtually ignored. The following proposals are in no way exhaustive and need to be both expanded and further elaborated if the gospel is to make a significant impact in post-Christian Western and post-communist Eastern Europe.

First, the church must *reclaim the historical reliability and truthfulness of the Christian gospel.* The spiritual crisis of Europe is also an intellectual crisis, a crisis of truth that is at the very center of the "modern eclipse of God." In our age of relativity, atheism, agnosticism, and denial of all absolutes, when the very truth of any truth is under suspicion, the validity of the gospel truth is either outrightly denied or largely ignored. All across Europe the proclamation of the gospel must become once again a communication of the foundational facts of Christian faith as revealed in the Holy Scriptures and centered in the life, teaching, death, and resurrection of Jesus Christ. By this gospel you are saved, "that Christ died for our sins, according to the Scriptures, that he was buried, that he was raised on the third day according to the Scriptures, and that he appeared" (I Cor. 15:2-5). The faithful, brave, and creative proclamation of the gospel must be grounded in this universally valid truth,

157

for only upon truth can trust be built. Or as Stephen Neill puts it in *Call to Mission*, "The only reason for being a Christian is the overpowering conviction that the Christian faith is true" (Neill 1970:10). Whether it is in the context of a Western relativity of all religions or in the encounter with the Marxist-type "scientific atheism," it is necessary to remember William Temple's dictum: "The Gospel is true for all, if it is true at all" (Temple 1937:82). This gospel must be unashamedly proclaimed all across the lands of Europe not only as the truth about God and our own lost condition apart from Christ, but also as "the power of God for salvation for everyone who believes" (Rom. 1:16).

Second, we must *renew the credibility of the Christian witness*. Missions and evangelism are not primarily a question of methodology, money, management, and numbers but rather a question of authenticity, credibility, and spiritual power. For a significant impact of the Christian gospel in Europe, both West and East, the question of world evangelization, *How shall they hear?* can be rightly answered only after we have answered, *What shall they see?* Biblical logic demands that *being* precede *doing*. Newbigin is right when he concludes *Foolishness to the Greeks* with the chapter "The Call to the Church" and focuses on the question, "What must we be?" (1986:124ff.). In Eastern Europe we have learned that Marxist criticism of religion is not always wrong, for Christian religion has a long and heavy historical ballast that presents a serious hindrance for the re-evangelization of our continent. The rise and spread of both Western and Marxist atheism seems to be proportionally related to the shrinking credibility of the Christian church. In going out to evangelize in Yugoslavia, I frequently tell our seminary students that our main task may be simply to "wash the face of Jesus," for it has been dirtied and distorted by both the compromises of institutional Christianity through the centuries and the antagonistic propaganda of atheistic communism in recent decades. The mission and the message of the Christian church have no credibility apart from their visibility as expressed in the quality of new life, mature and responsible relationships in the believing community, and a loving concern and sacrificial service on behalf of the needy in society. Renewing the credibility of Christian witness goes hand in hand with the recovery of the whole gospel, which implies a joyful celebration of God's gift of salvation and continuous openness to the Holy Spirit to authenticate supernaturally the Word of God. As I have stated elsewhere, "The whole Gospel covers proclamation of truth and exhibition of love, manifestation of power and integrity of life. In the task of world evangelization, it will also require less competition and more cooperation, less self-sufficiency and more self-

158

denial, less ambition to lead and more willingness to serve, less of a drive to dominate and more of the desire to develop" (Kuzmic 1990:201).

Third, one of the central and most urgent tasks for both Western and Eastern European churches is to *recover a practical missionary ecclesiology, the missionary character of the believing community* (Newbigin 1989). European churches have to recognize that faith is not automatically inherited from generation to generation and that the main task of the church is not its institutional and mechanistically sacramental self-perpetuation. The church's mission in the world should not be reduced to isolated political statements and good deeds as if the church were just a religio-social agency. Neither should the ministry of the clergy be reduced to the servicing of baptisms, weddings, and funerals. The churches need to be internally renewed by the Holy Spirit, in order to become recognizable as "the spontaneous overflow of a community of praise . . . the radiance of a supernatural reality . . . a place of joy, of praise, of surprises, and of laughter — a place where there is a foretaste of the endless surprises of heaven" (Newbigin 1986:149). This will also require, as Newbigin puts it, "the energetic fostering of a declericalised lay theology" (1986:142), the rediscovery of the priesthood of all believers along with the discovery of the gifts of the Holy Spirit and the related idea of Christian stewardship. The recognition that the congregation is the proper agent for missionary and evangelistic activities and that the task should not be relegated to outside agencies, specialized ministries, and zealous evangelistically minded individuals is an imperative. The post-Reformation institutional divorce between church and mission that made the voluntary groups rather than the churches responsible for mission has to be overcome by new theological and structural developments. In conjunction with this, one of the crucial questions to be studied is "Are parish and congregational structures in Europe sufficiently flexible to be missionary congregations?" (Senft 1979:96).

Fourth, the recovery of historical reliability and truthfulness has to be accompanied by an effort to *renew the intelligibility and relevance of the Christian faith* for contemporary secularized and religiously indifferent Europeans. The gospel of Jesus Christ "is not something that man made up," for it was received by "revelation from Jesus Christ" (Gal. 1:11-12). This is why the New Testament never uses the word "gospel" in the plural. It is important to recognize, however, that Jesus and other New Testament evangelists portray considerable flexibility and creative freedom in adapting, translating, and communicating the gospel in different political and cultural settings. While the basic content of the message is always recognizable and unchanging, the presentations are never the same. There are no pre-packaged, universally applicable formulations of the gospel given for either indoctrination or as if there was some magic power in the language itself. The missionary vocation of the church is to build bridges across the wide gap between the ancient world of the true and powerful biblical story and the biblically illiterate of the modern secularized technological age. Helmut Thielicke, that rare example of a German theologian who was also an effective preacher and creative communicator, reminds us that "the Gospel must be preached afresh and told in new ways to every generation, since every generation has its own unique questions. This is why the Gospel must be constantly forwarded to a new address, because the recipient is repeatedly changing his place of residence" (1970:10). The potential recipients of the gospel in Europe, both East and West, have been "changing their address" ideologically, philosophically, and culturally in this century more frequently and drastically than in any other area of the world. The radical ideologically inspired secularization in Eastern Europe and the similar cultural developments in the pluralist and materialistic West European countries have produced new generations of biblically illiterate Europeans. The message of the cross and salvation have very little meaning for the relativistic and pluralist consumer-oriented Western societies, and even less significance for those who grew up in a system which denied that Jesus ever existed and "scientifically" argued that any belief in God and spiritual realities is superstition. The Soviet government, for example, only a few years ago claimed that one of the successes of its educational system and atheistic propaganda is evident in the fact that around ninety percent of its young people ages sixteen to nineteen adhere to atheism as their worldview. Though these figures need to be relativized and conclusions qualified, they remain indicative of a major missionary challenge in the new Europe.

The missionary outreach to these spiritually impoverished and disoriented generations will require an ability to understand their beliefs and prejudices and to translate the gospel into their thought categories with intelligence, clarity, and relevance. In this process of incarnating the gospel in the new European culture, the pitfalls of some of the Western Protestant "apostles of modernity" must be avoided. For in their almost neurotic anxiety about the relevance of Christianity they have frequently amputated rather than adapted the biblical message and thus rendered it powerless. "This-worldliness" with its concern for relevance and modernity at the expense of transcendence (a liberal

Protestant and to a lesser extent a modern Catholic temptation) must be avoided. Equally the total theological and communicative rigidity and overpious "other-worldliness" in the name of historical faithfulness (the temptation of the Eastern Orthodox and evangelical fundamentalists) are not the way ahead for the Christian mission in contemporary Europe. Both betray the gospel of Jesus Christ. The first, in its attempt to make it more attractive and palatable to secularized minds, renders it powerless. And the second renders it meaningless in its refusal to dialogue with the world and inability to translate contextually the message of salvation to its secularized contemporaries.

Fifth, in spite of the relative failures of the twentieth-century ecumenical dreams and efforts, *the quest for Christian unity remains an imperative* in the light of both biblical and contemporary missionary requirements. Churches need to continue to ask themselves the painful question: "How can a sinful and divided church announce to the world the gospel of salvation and reconciliation?" The mainstream Christian churches in Western Europe, but especially in Eastern Europe with the recent political openness and the "attractiveness" of that "mission field," will increasingly face competition with new groups and denominations, both indigenous and imported. The uncoordinated and at times culturally and religiously ill-prepared and insensitive missionary activities from North America will create confusion, unnecessary duplication, and growth of new denominations and independent groups with various theological emphases, ecclesiological models, and missionary practices. Sects and cults will also flourish, taking full advantage of the spiritual void, political freedom, and the abysmal ignorance of the basic tenets of Christian faith by so many Europeans. In light of the cultural and ecclesiastical history of East European nations, the creation of a competitive free religious market will not be without pain and conflict. If the questions of biblical unity, cooperation, mutual trust, and integrity — all under the biblical umbrella of the lordship of Jesus Christ — are not properly addressed, this process will become counterproductive and result in discrediting the message and the mission of the church at the time of its greatest opportunity and need.

For Further Reading

Bourdeaux, Michael
  1991   *The Gospel's Triumph over Communism*. Minneapolis: Bethany
             House Publishers.

Burstein, David
1991   *Euroquake: Europe's Explosive Economic Challenge. Will the World Change?* New York: Simon and Schuster.

Cotterell, Peter
1989   "The Church in Europe." *Evangelical Review of Theology* 13 (1):37-47.

Detzler, Wayne A.
1979   *The Changing Church in Europe.* Grand Rapids, MI: Zondervan Publishing House.

Douglas, J. D., ed.
1990   *Proclaim Christ Until He Comes.* Minneapolis: World Wide Publications.

Herman, Stewart Winfield
1953   *Report from Christian Europe.* New York: Friendship Press.

Henley, Wallace
1978   *Europe at the Crossroads: A Reporter Looks at Europe's Spiritual Crisis.* Westchester, IL: Good News Publishers.

Hill, Kent R.
1991   *The Soviet Union on the Brink: An Inside Look at Christianity and Glasnost.* Portland, OR: Multnomah Press.
1991   *Turbulent Times for the Soviet Church: The Inside Story.* Portland, OR: Multnomah Press.

Kuzmic, Peter
1980   "Evangelical Witness in Eastern Europe." In *Serving Our Generations: Evangelical Strategies for the Eighties.* Edited by Waldron Scott. Colorado Springs: World Evangelical Fellowship, pp. 77-85.
1990   "How to Teach the Truth of the Gospel." In *Proclaim Christ Until He Comes.* Edited by J. D. Douglas. Minneapolis: World Wide Publications, pp. 197-203.

Lausanne Committee for World Evangelization
1981   *Thailand Report: Christian Witness to Nominal Christians among Roman Catholics.* Wheaton, IL: Lausanne Committee for World Evangelization.
1982   *Thailand Report: Christian Witness to Nominal Christians among Protestants.* Wheaton, IL: Lausanne Committee for World Evangelization.
1983   *Thailand Report: Christian Witness to Nominal Christians among Orthodox.* Wheaton, IL: Lausanne Committee for World Evangelization.

Lilje, Hanns
    1965   *Christianity in a Divided Europe*. Philadelphia: Fortress Press.
Lutheran World Federation
    1979   "Foreword." In *Mission and Evangelism, Report of a Regional Consultation, Loccum, 1978* 4:vi.
Neill, Stephen Charles
    1970   *Call to Mission*. Philadelphia: Fortress Press.
Newbigin, Lesslie
    1986   *Foolishness to the Greeks*. Grand Rapids: Wm. B. Eerdmans Publishing Company.
    1987   "Can the West Be Converted?" *International Bulletin of Missionary Research* 11 (1):2-7.
    1989   *The Gospel in a Pluralist Society*. Grand Rapids, MI: Wm. B. Eerdmans Publishing Company.
Sartre, Jean-Paul
    1956   "Existentialism." In *Existentialism from Dostoyevsky to Sartre*. Edited by Walter Kaufmann. New York: Meridian Books, pp. 311ff.
Senft, Kenneth C. (Chairman), and Ernst Bauerochse (Secretary)
    1979   "Working Group IB: Frontiers of Mission." In *Mission and Evangelism, Report of a Regional Consultation, Loccum, 1978* 4:96.
Temple, William
    1937   *Basic Convictions*. London: Hamish Hamilton.
Thielicke, Helmut
    1970   *How Modern Should Theology Be?* London: Fontana.
Visser 't Hooft, W. A.
    1979   "Evangelism Among Europe's Neo-pagans." *International Review of Mission* 66 (264):349-57.
Weber, Gerhard
    1979   "Home Mission: Where Do We Stand? Where Do We Go?" In *Mission and Evangelism, Report of a Regional Consultation, Loccum, 1978* 4:72-88.
Will, James E.
    1981   *Must Walls Divide?* New York: Friendship Press.

The Middle East

Norman A. Horner

The first mission agency in North America, the American Board of Commissioners for Foreign Missions (ABCFM), sent Pliny Fisk and Levi Parsons to Asia Minor and Syria-Lebanon in 1819. What did these Protestant forebears in mission know about the Middle East so early in the nineteenth century? Slow travel by sailing vessels and the lack of any rapid communication such as today's radio and television limited their knowledge, to be sure. But they did know that the Middle East was essentially different from any other mission field. It was unlike the "heathendom" of sub-Sahara Africa or East Asia. It was instead the birthplace of Christianity itself, and living remnants of that early Christianity were still there despite the predominance of Islam throughout the region for many centuries.

Mission to the Middle East in Historical Perspective

Three separate and distinct missionary movements have taken place in the Middle East through the centuries:

Norman A. Horner is now retired in Louisville, Kentucky. He served as a Presbyterian missionary in Cameroun, West Africa (1939-49), as Professor of Mission and Evangelism at Louisville Presbyterian Theological Seminary (1950-68), as a Presbyterian fraternal worker in the Middle East (1969-76), and as associate director of the Overseas Ministries Study Center (1976-82).

The mission of the ancient Eastern churches began in the apostolic
era, and churches established in apostolic times have continued there
in one form or another ever since. These churches claim specific apostolic founders: James in Jerusalem, Peter and Paul in Antioch (as well
as Rome), Thomas in Babylonia (and as far as India), Mark in Alexan-
dria, Barnabas in Cyprus, and so forth.

In the early centuries these Eastern churches were large and strong
throughout much of the region. They also maintained a vigorous missionary enterprise within the Middle East and beyond it far into East
Asia. But they were overwhelmed by the Islamic conquest beginning
in the seventh century. Under Muslim rule they progressively lost both
political power and missionary zeal. These ancient Eastern churches
then retreated into the isolation of a minority people, second-class
citizens at best, and it was in that weakened condition that early Catholic and Protestant missionaries found them.

Roman Catholic missionaries were in the Middle East from the
time of the Crusades. Efforts to establish their Latin-rite structures were
only moderately successful; Latin-rite dioceses were organized that
continue into the present. But from the sixteenth to the early nineteenth
centuries, Roman Catholic initiatives resulted in the emergence of
several Eastern-rite Catholic churches. This strategy permitted affiliation with Rome by churches with patriarchs (supreme bishops) of their
own. Such churches retain the ancient liturgies in the traditional languages of their Orthodox Church origins, a married parish clergy, and
an essentially Eastern lifestyle. Each of them enjoys considerable autonomy, but they are all nevertheless ultimately responsible to Rome.
Meanwhile Western Catholic missionaries continue to serve throughout
the area in parishes, schools, hospitals, agricultural projects, welfare,
and so forth.

The Protestant mission dates to the early part of the nineteenth
century, as indicated above. Protestants believed that Christians of the
ancient Orthodox churches in the Middle East were best able to evangelize the Muslim majority, but only if they could be awakened from
the millet mentality to which they had been reduced under centuries
of Ottoman rule. Hence the early Protestant missionaries were in-
structed by the American Board of Commissioners for Foreign Mission
(ABCFM) to work *within* the Eastern churches rather than to establish
Protestant congregations in separation from them.

The determination of early missionaries to follow this mandate
was expressed by William Goodell, an ABCFM missionary who took
residence in Constantinople in 1831:

We tell them [Christians in the Gregorian and Greek churches], "You have sects enough among you already, and we have no desire of setting up a new one, or of pulling down your churches or drawing away members from them in order to build up our own." (Strong 1910:92)

A similar policy governed the original ABCFM missions throughout the region from Constantinople (now Istanbul) eastward through Persia (now Iran). Justin Perkins, American pioneer missionary in Persia, recorded the instructions given him by Rufus Anderson, the Board's Foreign Secretary, at Perkins' commissioning service on September 8, 1833:

Your main object will be to enable the Nestorian Church, through the grace of God, to exert a commanding influence in the spiritual regeneration of Asia. . . . You will remember the antiquity of this branch of the Church of Antioch, and how extensively its doctrines were once diffused. . . . Your first duty among the Nestorians will be to cultivate an intimate acquaintance with their religious opinions and sentiments. . . . A primary object which you will have in view will be to convince the people that you have come among them with no design to take away their religious privileges nor to subject them to any foreign ecclesiastical power. (Perkins 1843:29-32)

Nevertheless, the missionaries soon came into conflict with the hierarchies of the traditional churches throughout the region. Probably there was misunderstanding and fault on both sides. The old churches had become in some respects decadent and corrupt. For their part, the nonliturgical Protestant missionaries misinterpreted the veneration of icons and other Eastern Christian practices as "idolatrous." But, in this writer's judgment, a major cause of conflict was that the missionaries had never been invited by the host churches. The missionaries also seemed unaware of the extent to which the traditional churches were incapacitated by their status as a subject people. Whether "awakened" or not, it was impossible for them to engage in overt evangelistic activities among the Muslim majority. In any case, the early ABCFM missionaries soon found it impossible to work harmoniously in accordance with their original mandate. Protestant churches as such were established. These have prospered to some extent, especially in Egypt. Many missionaries who subsequently came into the area from other denominations and countries were less reluctant to draw members away from the old churches. Perhaps the major tragedy is that in the

increasingly divided Christianity of the Middle East, each church came
to know less and less about the real life of the others.

Anglican missionaries have been characteristically more deferen-
tial toward the Orthodox churches than have their Protestant and Catholic counterparts. Anglican work in the Middle East must be credited
to pioneers of the Church Missionary Society (CMS). Some of these
went to Malta in 1815 to print Bibles for use in Turkey and the Arab
Levant. There were also CMS missionaries in Egypt from the early 1820s
until they were obliged to leave temporarily in 1840. In 1841 an Anglican bishopric was first established in Jerusalem. Since then, through
the efforts of the CMS and the Church Mission to the Jews (now called
the Church Ministry Among the Jews), small Anglican churches composed very largely of former Muslims and Jews have emerged in
various countries of the region.

The Present Turmoil

Much of the Middle East is currently in the throes of political and
religious turmoil. This is not a new experience to people for whom the
massive destruction of armies and bitter religious discord throughout
the centuries is a vivid part of their corporate memories. But in some
respects today's conflicts are more divisive and widespread than ever
before in history.

The current turmoil is a political and social struggle, not a religious
war. Muslims are not characteristically hostile to Christians as such.
Christian communities have long survived as protected minorities in the
Middle East, some of them having fled the persecution even of fellow
Christians in the West. As a recent writer notes: ". . . because the Qur'an
recognizes Christianity as essentially a legitimate faith-community,
Christianity has survived in the Muslim world in a variety of forms
which the West could not tolerate" (Ayoub 1989:25). USSٰ.

Muslim toleration of Christian minorities in their midst does not
extend, however, to missionary evangelism. They regard that as unac-
ceptable proselytism. In the Muslim mind, Christian missionaries are
not legitimate witnesses of religious faith but agents of colonialism.
Citing a book by Omar Farrukh, *Evangelization and Colonialism in Arab
Lands* (Beirut 1982), Ayoub writes:

> Missionary work has a long history of cooperation with colonialism,
> with which it enjoyed a symbiotic relationship. . . . Farrukh regards

missionary work as of greater harm to our countries than colonialism, because colonialism penetrated into our lands only under the cover of missionary activity. . . . The motives behind missionary activity are not, in the eyes of Omar Farrukh, in the least religious. This is because, he argues, western society is itself atheistic. . . . Then, quoting the words of a Lebanese Arab Christian, he continues, "America, which worships gold, iron, and petrol, has nonetheless covered half the earth with missionaries, claiming to call others to a spiritual life and religious peace." Likewise, he argues, France is a secular state at home, yet abroad it protects missionaries. The Jesuits, who have been expelled from France as enemies, are its reliable agents and friends in its colonies. (Ayoub 1989:35)

The hostility of Muslims toward Christian missionaries has reached new proportions in recent years, largely a result of political turmoil throughout the region. In the Arab East (the Arabic-speaking Fertile Crescent from Egypt northward and eastward through Iraq) where a majority of the Middle East's Christians now live, no date in modern history is more crucial than 1948. In that year Israel became a sovereign state with military power and territorial ambitions. This began a chain of events that revived ancient antagonisms and introduced new rivalries among Christians as well as Muslims.

Anti-missionary sentiment among the non-Christian majority is hardly surprising. It is a familiar enough phenomenon in other parts of the world as well. But in the Middle East the antipathy toward Western missions is shared to some extent by Christians of the traditional Eastern churches. They regard both Protestant and Catholic missions as engaged in sheep stealing rather than evangelization, citing the fact that most of the churches founded by those missions have drawn their membership largely from the ancient churches and not from Islam. We still have to convince some Orthodox bishops that

. . . the modern missionary contribution to this situation is much oversimplified if it is presented in terms of an American or British Protestantism which has never cared about the great Orthodox tradition and has been content to proselytize from the Eastern churches. Even behind some of the present-day situations which superficially lend themselves to this representation, there is a record of early attempts to serve with rather than against the Eastern churches in a task which was seen to be pre-eminently their own. (Goodall 1958:7)

Intra-Christian proselytism is today rejected in principle by all major Protestant and Anglican churches in the Middle East. Yet it continues in a variety of sectarian groups that see other churches of all kinds as fields for their particular harvest. Orthodox church leaders do not always distinguish between ecumenical and sectarian forms of Protestantism. On all sides there is a clear need for better understanding of the difference between proper evangelism and proselytism.

Guidelines for the Future

The role of Western Christian missionaries, both Roman Catholic and Protestant, has never been more problematic in the Middle East than it is today. Some governments in the region have become increasingly restrictive. Elsewhere, notably in Lebanon, continuing warfare and political chaos make the residence of any foreigners all but impossible at present. Yet such limitations do not in any way signal the end of mission. There are signs of encouragement as we approach the twenty-first century.

Christians in the Middle East are slowly growing in numbers, despite the fact that massive emigrations have considerably eroded their strength in some parts of the region during the last forty years especially. Not all such emigrations have taken people overseas. Many of them have merely resulted in a redistribution within the region itself, bringing greater numbers and vitality to other parts of the same area. This, along with natural increase and the relative stability of the Christian population in many of the countries, accounts for numerical growth of Christians in the region as a whole. This is not to suggest that we can expect mass movements into Christian faith anywhere in the Middle East. Conditions in this heartland of Islam have never been conducive to that. Christians are likely to remain a small part of the total population and will continue to be politically powerless. Yet the fact that their numbers are growing, however slowly, is cause for rejoicing.

Possibilities for ecumenical cooperation are greater now than at any other time in history. In 1974 the almost solidly Protestant and Anglican Near East Council of Churches (NECC) was dissolved to form a much wider association, the Middle East Council of Churches (MECC). From that date the much larger Orthodox churches have joined with Protestant and Anglican bodies in joint efforts of various kinds. The Catholic churches are not yet an organic part of the MECC,

169

but they participate regularly in many of the Council's activities. Most significantly, the Catholic seminaries have become key members of the Council's association of theological schools.

This relative stability of the Middle East's Christian communities and the new possibilities for ecumenical cooperation help to determine the directions mission should now take.

Evangelistic mission will depend increasingly on the churches in the area rather than on overseas agencies and personnel. This has been said of the worldwide missionary enterprise so often as to have become platitudinous, but it is nowhere more relevant than in the Middle East. Churches that feel their minority status so keenly are the very communities that most need to develop a sense of proprietorship in the missionary task. For the past decade and a half that has been especially hard to achieve. Continuous warfare in some countries of the region has reduced church activities to the parish level, frustrating all efforts at wider associations or joint planning. One hopes that the waning years of the present century will bring real peace to that troubled part of the world. But whether or not that occurs, the local churches and they alone can provide the kind of Christian witness that matters most to their wider milieu.

The Christian communities of the Middle East must participate more heartily in the social and political development of their respective countries. In some of those countries the majority of Christians belong to ethnic minorities. These Christians cannot and should not forsake their historic languages and lifestyle, but efforts to maintain particular integrities must not lead them to ghetto-like isolations. They also have a responsibility to transcend their minority mentality and actively participate in worthy goals of the larger society. In other countries most Christians share the language and culture of the non-Christian majority but still remain on the sidelines of great social developments around them. Among the strong voices now urging Arab Christians to a wider participation is that of Melkite Archbishop Neophytos Edelby in Aleppo, Syria. Edelby is probably the most widely respected and influential Christian leader in his city. Through writings and television appearances he has repeatedly called upon his fellow Christians throughout the region to demonstrate their Arab identity by joining with others, irrespective of religious affiliation, in whatever promotes the welfare of their nations as a whole. Unless and until that happens, Christians in the Middle East will remain marginalized and will be regarded by the Muslim majority as essentially foreign communities.

Western mission effort in the Middle East in the twenty-first century will begin with massive programs of welfare and reconstruction. Lebanon is currently in ruins. Iran and Iraq have been badly crippled by long and senseless warfare. Cyprus has been divided into two mutually hostile nations on one small island.

Recovery and restoration throughout the area is certainly not the sole responsibility of Western missions. But Western-funded efforts such as those coordinated by the MECC and by the Lutheran Contact and Resource Center in Beirut throughout the worst of the war years will be needed for years to come. The most persuasive evangelism to Muslims may still be the willingness of Christians to serve their physical needs. Missionaries, rather than governments, are best able to provide the necessary personal involvement.

Christian mission in the Middle East now demands a stronger focus on the non-Christian majority of the population. Western missions during the last century and a half have rendered enormous service through church-related colleges and universities, primary and secondary schools, hospitals and sanitaria, orphanages, welfare projects, and homes for the aged. Most of these have always served Muslims as well as Christians. But evangelization in the traditional sense of that word has been less successful. Evangelism has never been easy anywhere in the Muslim world, and it is certainly no easier today. Yet the future of mission demands an ongoing search for ways to share Christian faith more effectively with the avowedly non-Christian masses, rather than to be content with gaining church membership at the expense of other churches — or even with making already professing Christians more devout.

For Further Reading

Ayoub, Mahmoud M.
    1989   "Roots of Muslim-Christian Conflict." *The Muslim World* 79:25-45.
Betts, Robert B.
    1978   *Christians in the Arab East.* Atlanta: John Knox Press.
Dehqani-Tafti, Hassan
    1981   *The Hard Awakening.* New York: The Seabury Press.
Goodall, Norman
    1958   "Some Reflections on the Near and Middle East." *International Review of Missions* 47:5-10.

Horner, Norman A.

1978   "Ecumenical Roadblocks in the Middle East." *Worldmission* 29:11-17.

1984   "The Future of Christian Mission in Lebanon." *International Bulletin of Missionary Research* 8:146-49.

1989   *A Guide to Christian Churches in the Middle East.* Elkhart, IN: Mission Focus Publications.

Perkins, Justin

1843   *Residence of Eight Years in Persia.* Andover, MA: Allen, Morrill, and Wardwell.

Strong, William E.

1910   *The Story of the American Board: An Account of the First Hundred Years of the American Board of Commissioners for Foreign Missions.* Boston: The Pilgrim Press.

Foundational Disciplines
of Mission

Reflections on Biblical Models of Mission

David J. Bosch

The Need for a "Biblical Theology of Mission"

There can be little doubt that what has traditionally been referred to as the "biblical foundations of mission" will be as important in the twenty-first century as it has been in the past. In fact, if we want the missionary enterprise to be authentic and our reflections on mission to be relevant, we will have to pay even more serious attention to this branch of missiology than we used to do.

At least since the days of William Carey, two centuries ago, Protestant missionary advocates have argued that they were defending and propagating an enterprise that had its roots in Scripture. And indeed, much trouble was taken to find biblical authorization for the missionary enterprise. Unfortunately, this was frequently done by gleaning so-called "missionary texts" from the Bible to undergird the contemporary missionary enterprise. As far as the Old Testament was concerned, one accepted, even if only implicitly, that it was "particularistic" and therefore hardly usable to support mission. If, however, we looked carefully

---

David J. Bosch (1929-92) was professor of missiology at the University of South Africa in Pretoria from 1972. He served as a missionary in the Transkei (1957-71). Bosch was general secretary of the Southern African Missiological Society from 1968 and editor of its journal *Missionalia* from 1973. His books in English include *A Spirituality of the Road* (1980), *Witness to the World* (1980), and his major work on missiology, *Transforming Mission* (1991).

among the rocks and rubble, we would detect small nuggets of pure "missionary" gold — stories of pagans like Ruth and Naaman who accepted the faith of Israel, "universalistic" expressions scattered throughout the Psalms and Second Isaiah, stories like Jonah's, a prophet of the God of Israel, who was sent as a missionary to Nineveh, and so on. Sometimes the "mine" would not readily yield such clearly identifiable gold nuggets. Then we would have to smelt the biblical ore, as it were, in order to extract our "missionary" gold from it.

The New Testament, of course, yielded its gold far more promptly. And yet advocates of mission tended to approach even the New Testament as a mine from which they might extract isolated missionary texts. This is, for instance, what Carey did in respect of the so-called Great Commission at the end of Matthew's Gospel (28:18-20). He isolated these verses from the rest of the Gospel, viewed them as a *verbatim* command of the risen Lord, and built his case for a worldwide mission in his own day on the argument that, if the promise of Jesus' presence (Matt. 28:20) remained valid, his *commission* (28:19) retained validity too.

Behind this entire approach lay the assumption that one already knew what "mission" was and now only had to prove that it was mandated by Scripture. And, of course, in the modern era mission meant (and by and large still means) the geographical movement from a Christian locality to a pagan locality for the purpose of winning converts and planting churches in that area. Please note that I am not — at least not at this stage — saying that mission does *not* mean this. What I do say is that, in looking for a biblical foundation for mission, missionary advocates as a matter of course took it for granted that it was *the enterprise they knew and were engaged in* that had to be justified biblically.

It may, in this respect, be salutary to remind ourselves that the very term "mission," used in the sense just outlined, is of fairly recent origin. It was introduced by the Jesuits in the sixteenth century to depict the ministry of those members of the society sent to distant places in order to reconvert Protestants or to convert pagans — the latter particularly in those territories recently colonized by the nations of "Christian" Europe. The origins of the term "mission" thus were intimately bound up with the colonial expansion of the West. Like colonization, it implied traveling to distant countries and "subjugating" pagans to the one and only true religion.

I do not draw attention to these origins of the concept "mission" out of a desire to participate in mission- and missionary-bashing, so popular a pastime in some circles today. Indeed, I am convinced that

176

the missionaries were, by and large, a breed fundamentally different from their colonizing compatriots. Nevertheless, the socio-historical context in which they found themselves could not but influence their theology, mission work, and day-to-day conduct. They carried the odor of the colonial enterprise with them — much the way the stale smell of cigarette smoke clings to the clothes of a non-smoker coming out of a room full of smokers.

In spite of these exacerbating circumstances the terms "mission" and "missionary" can boast a respectable biblical pedigree. "Mission" means "sending," the idea expressed by the verbs *pempein* and *apostellein*, which together occur 206 times in the New Testament. The "missionary," that is, the one sent, is an *apostolos* (79 times), and the apostle's task or "mission" is *apostolē* (four times) (cf. Legrand 1990:xiv). This, however, suggests that if we wish to reflect on "biblical foundations for mission," our point of departure should not be the contemporary enterprise we seek to justify, but the biblical sense of what being sent into the world signifies. It also means that, however important single biblical texts may (seem to) be, the validity of mission should not be deduced from isolated sayings but from the thrust of the central message of Scripture. In other words, either mission — properly understood — lies at the heart of the biblical message or it is so peripheral to that message that we need not be overly concerned with it.

Fortunately, in more recent decades scholars have indeed begun to read the entire Bible missiologically. Even before the 1910 International Missionary Conference at Edinburgh, Martin Kähler suggested that mission was "the mother of theology" or of the New Testament: it was because of their involvement in mission that the early Christians began to theologize ([1908] 1971:190). More recently, Martin Hengel said essentially the same: the history and the theology of early Christianity were, primarily, "mission history" and "mission theology" (1983:53). Moreover, writes Heinrich Kasting, "Mission was, in the early stages, . . . a fundamental expression of the life of the church. The beginnings of a missionary theology are therefore also the beginnings of Christian theology as such" (1967:127). Ben Meyer concurs: "Christianity had never been more itself, more consistent with Jesus and more evidently en route to its own future, than in the launching of the world mission" (1986:206). And Donald Senior (1984) talks about mission as the "vantage point" for New Testament investigation. Rudolf Pesch (1976:61) describes the Gospel of Mark as a *Missionsbuch;* and much the same could be said of the other three Gospels and of the letters of Paul (cf. Bosch 1991:56-178; Legrand 1990:107-45; Senior 1984:71-81).

The advantage of reading the New Testament missiologically (I will return to the Old Testament) is that, instead of reflecting on isolated "missionary texts," we may look at them as a whole. And we may recognize that one of the main reasons for the existence of this body of literature is the missionary self-understanding and involvement of the people who gave birth to it.

The examples mentioned thus far are mostly from Protestant sources. Traditionally, the "biblical foundations of mission" received rather scant attention from Roman Catholics. In his 927-page handbook on missiology, Thomas Ohm (1962), for instance, refers only in passing to the biblical foundation of mission. Scripture indeed plays a role in his discussion of the rootedness of mission in God's, Jesus', and the church's "general salvific will" (cf. Ohm 1962:217-59), but all of this has merely an indirect bearing on the biblical *foundation* of mission. Still, in recent decades it has been Catholics rather than Protestants who are working to uncover the roots of mission in the Bible. In 1981, for instance, a number of German-speaking Roman Catholic New Testament scholars gathered in Würzburg to reflect on the "theology of mission in the New Testament." These outstanding papers were edited by Karl Kertelge and published the following year (Kertelge 1982). In 1983 two biblical scholars from Catholic Theological Union in Chicago, Donald Senior and Carroll Stuhlmueller, published *The Biblical Foundations for Mission*, still the best study in the entire field. And in 1990 the English translation of Lucien Legrand's biblical theology of mission, first published in French in 1988, came out. One might even say that, by and large, Catholic biblical scholars are currently taking the missionary dimensions of Scripture more seriously than their Protestant counterparts. Even so, there are Protestant biblical scholars who are doing superb work in this respect; for instance, Ferdinand Hahn, Martin Hengel, and Ben F. Meyer.

Uncovering the "biblical foundations of mission" is, however — as Nicholas Lash (1985) has rightly pointed out — not a relay race in which the biblical scholar, after having identified the "original meaning" of the text, hands over the "baton" to the missiologist who now has to "apply" it. What is necessary, rather, is for biblical scholars and missiologists to reflect *together* on this matter. It is this conviction that lies behind the decision of the International Association for Mission Studies (IAMS), in 1976, to launch a project called BISAM — an acronym for "Biblical Studies and Missiology." In spite of having had some ups and downs, the project is still on track and should remain on the agenda of IAMS; as a matter of fact, it is my firm conviction that it should also be on the agenda of the various societies for biblical stud-ies.[1] We shall, after all, never reach the point where we will have established once and for all the "biblical foundations for mission."

Against this general background we may now proceed to draw the contours of a "biblical theology of mission." Such a project seeks answers (which of necessity will have to be preliminary and related to specific contexts) to three basic questions (cf. Spindler 1988:139-40):

1. *Why mission?* Here we attempt to reflect, from the perspective of the witness of the Judeo-Christian Scriptures, on the fundamental charter of mission. Robert Schreiter (1982) refers to this as reflecting on "the Bible *for* mission." We are exploring the conviction that the church is sent *because* Jesus was sent, in terms of the words of the Johannine Jesus: "As the Father has sent me, so send I you" (John 20:21).

2. *How mission?* Here we examine the conviction that the church is sent as Jesus was sent. I refer once again to John 20:21: "*As* the Father has sent me, *so* send I you." There is an intimate relationship between the sending of Jesus and the sending of the church. I shall return to this theme in more detail.

3. *What is mission?* Here we explore what Schreiter (1982) refers to as "the Bible *in* mission." What is the content of our missionary involvement in the world? In reflecting on this it is important to realize that being faithful to the biblical models of mission does not mean copying them in minute detail. Neither did Jesus' disciples and the early church simply imitate Jesus. Rather, as Stanton puts it, "the early Chris-tian communities handled the traditions about the life and teaching of Jesus . . . with creative but responsible freedom. Traditions were re-tained carefully, but they were also modified to meet new circum-stances" (1985:72). Hugo Echegaray makes a similar point: Jesus has not left us a rigid model for action; rather, he "inspired his disciples to prolong the logic of his own action in a creative way amid the new and different historical circumstances in which the community would have to proclaim the gospel. . ." (1984:xv-xvi). In our missionary involve-ment today we must do the same.

In light of the exposition above it should be clear that it would not do to build a biblical theology of mission on isolated proof-texts.

1. Sadly, very little of this collaboration is evident at the moment. I mention one example: Some time ago the Department of Old Testament at my university invited the Department of Missiology for a seminar discussion on the question what missiologists expect of Old Testament studies. However, as I pointed out to my Old Testament col-leagues, it never occurred to them to ask, "What do Old Testament scholars expect of missiology?"!

This is not to suggest that what we might refer to as the classical missionary texts are of no value for our quest. It does mean, however, that we should view them within their contexts and attempt to extrapolate our theology of mission from there. Hence in this chapter I will identify *four cardinal missionary motifs in Scripture* and discuss some of the classical missionary texts within the framework of these.

Compassion

A fundamental missionary motif in both the Old and the New Testament is that of God's compassion. God refuses to bypass humankind: he sends prophets, messengers, even his Son into the world. This divine compassion manifests itself already in the election of Israel. Israel had no claim to God's attention and yet God took compassion on Israel. Nowhere is this illustrated more dramatically than in Ezekiel 16:4-7a:

> . . . on the day you were born your navel cord was not cut, nor were you washed with water to cleanse you, nor rubbed with salt, nor wrapped in cloths. No eye pitied you, to do any of these things for you out of compassion for you; but you were thrown out in the open field, for you were abhorred on the day you were born. I passed by you, and saw you flailing about in your blood. As you lay in your blood, I said to you, "Live!"

This is indeed one of the most powerful "mission statements" in the whole Bible, since it depicts God as the One who has compassion on the lost and the marginalized. This is also why the Exodus event ("I am the Lord your God, who brought you out of the land of Egypt, out of the house of slavery" — Exod. 20:2) became the cornerstone of Israel's confession of faith: God took compassion on a band of slaves in Egypt and saved them. "Father of orphans and protector of widows is God in his holy habitation. God gives the desolate a home to live in . . ." (Ps. 68:5-6).

In several periods of its history Israel understood its election either as an expression of favoritism or, especially in later Judaism, as something that it had *deserved* (it was sometimes even suggested that Yahweh *needed* Israel; without Israel he would have been a God without worshipers!). This does not, however, eclipse the fundamental conviction that Israel's election was unmerited and an expression of God's gratuitousness. In fact, precisely this is the point of the book of Jonah. We tend to view it in modern terms, as a story about a missionary who was sent to proclaim God's word to a pagan nation. It is nothing of the sort, however, since Jonah was not sent to preach a message of salvation but to announce judgment on Nineveh. The thrust of the story lies elsewhere. It ridicules the narrow ethnocentrism of Jonah (and Israel!), who "allowed" God to work only within Israel (cf. Verkuyl 1978:97) and sulked about God treating those outside the covenant the same way he treats those inside (ibid. 99; Legrand 1990:24-25). It is a story about God's *compassion*, which knows no boundaries and which, ironically, forms the basis of Jonah's complaint against God (4:2):

> O Lord! Is not this what I said while I was still in my own country? That is why I fled to Tarshish at the beginning; for I knew that you are a gracious God and merciful, slow to anger, and abounding in steadfast love, and ready to relent from punishing!

Jonah is the only "missionary" I know of who fervently hoped that his listeners would not heed his message! But God does not allow his compassion to be subverted. So the story of Jonah is a call to Israel to be converted to a compassion comparable to that of Yahweh.

It is, however, in the person and ministry of Jesus of Nazareth that the missionary dimensions of God's boundless compassion are expressed in an unequaled way. For instance, it is striking to note the way in which the people on whom Jesus has compassion are depicted; they are called the poor, the blind, the crippled, the leprous, the hungry, those who weep, the sick, the little ones, the widows, the captives, those who are weary and carrying heavy burdens, and the like (cf. Nolan 1976:21).

As God has compassion on Israel and others, and as Jesus overthrows the codes of society in boundless compassion on the marginalized, so we too are called to show compassion. This is a fundamental thrust of the biblical picture of mission. Those who have experienced divine compassion are moved by the plight of others, whether or not their plight is "spiritual" or "material." When Jesus looks at the crowds, "harassed and helpless, like sheep without a shepherd" (Matt. 9:36), he is moved to compassion. His followers, too, should be compassionate; so he says to his disciples, "The harvest is plentiful, but the laborers are few; therefore ask the Lord of the harvest to send out laborers into his harvest" (9:37-38). The commission, ". . . teaching them to obey everything that I have commanded you" (28:19) thus includes compassion with those who suffer. To a significant extent it was because of

Jesus' boundless compassion that the early church saw in him "the primal missionary" (cf. Hengel 1983:63). A faith in which compassion occupies so central a position is indeed missionary.

Martyria (2)

Out of compassion flows passion — in the original sense of the word, which means suffering and martyrdom. Mission is not a triumphalist enterprise. It is by definition done in weakness. *me une u sunat*

We already see this in the Old Testament. The mightier Israel became, the less its existence revealed a missionary dimension: the nations moved into the background and remained at a distance. Conversely, the more Israel was stripped of earthly power and glory, the more the prophets recognized a missionary dimension to its life. Second Isaiah is a case in point. It reflects a period in Israel's history when Israel was, politically speaking, completely insignificant. And yet precisely these chapters represent a high point in Old Testament missionary thinking. In the case of the Servant of the Lord, being God's witness not only implies preaching but also silent suffering for the sake of others. Isaiah 53 thus reveals both the highest and the deepest dimensions of mission in the Old Testament: through his suffering many would find salvation. Small wonder that, since the beginning of the Christian movement, the Suffering Servant of Isaiah 53 was regarded as archetypal of Jesus of Nazareth: "the Son of Man came not to be served but to serve, and to give his life a ransom for many" (Mark 10:45). His mission was one of self-emptying (cf. Neely 1989).

What is true of the Master's mission is true of the disciples' also. After Paul's conversion the risen Lord says to Ananias, "I myself will show him how much he must suffer for the sake of my name" (Acts 9:16). And indeed, wherever Paul proclaims the gospel, opposition arises: in Pisidian Antioch, in Iconium, in Corinth, and finally in Rome. Nowhere is this more apparent than in Paul's second letter to the Corinthians (cf. Bosch 1979). Paul is not a "peddler of the gospel" (II Cor. 2:17) like the "super-apostles," who define mission in the categories of triumphalism. Rather, he is a captive who glories in weakness (12:9). In fact, weakness, affliction, and suffering are key concepts in this letter in which Paul defends his ministry. Suffering and affliction are *normal* experiences in the apostle's life, but for those who can only think in success categories they remain a *skandalon*, a stumbling block. The difference between the Pauline mission and that of his opponents in Corinth lies in the cross — not only Christ's, but also the missionary's. So we read in Colossians 1:24, ". . . in my flesh I am completing what is lacking in Christ's afflictions for the sake of his body, that is, the church." To the Corinthians Paul writes, "For while we live, we are always being given up to death for Jesus' sake, so that the life of Jesus may be made visible in our mortal flesh. So death is at work in us, but life in you" (II Cor. 4:11-12). It is Paul the *missionary* who says, "I carry the marks of Jesus branded on my body" (Gal. 6:17).

In Greek, a witness is a *martys*. Almost imperceptibly, however, the noun *martys* acquired an added meaning in the early church, that of "martyr," of the one who seals his witness (*martyria*) with suffering, even death. In Acts 22:20 Paul refers to the blood of Christ's "witness," Stephen. We could, however, also translate *martys* here as "martyr," for this is what Stephen became, because of his witness, his mission. William Frazier is correct when he says that Luke's writings, in particular, have a significance far beyond the first-century church. Referring to the Roman Catholic ritual that usually crowns the sending ceremony of missionary communities, where the new missionaries are equipped with cross or crucifix, he adds (Frazier 1987:46),

> Somewhere beneath the layers of meaning that have attached themselves to this practice from the days of Francis Xavier to our own is the simple truth enunciated by Justin and Tertullian: the way faithful Christians die is the most contagious aspect of what being a Christian means. The missionary cross or crucifix is no mere ornament depicting Christianity in general. Rather, it is a vigorous commentary on what gives the gospel its universal appeal. Those who receive it possess not only a symbol of their mission but a handbook on how to carry it out.

N.-P. Moritzen (quoted in Triebel 1988:9) expresses the same conviction: "It belongs to the essence (of the Christian faith) that it needs the weak witness, the powerless representative of the message. The people who are to be won and saved should, as it were, always have the possibility of crucifying the witness of the gospel." Hans von Campenhausen (1974:71) underscores this notion: "Martyrdom and mission — so experience teaches us — belong together. Martyrdom is especially at home on the mission field." This is also the thrust of Tertullian's famous statement, at the end of the second century: *Semen est sanguis Christianorum* — freely translated: "The blood of the martyrs is the seed of the church" (see further Triebel 1988).

God's Mission

Inherent in the biblical understanding of mission is the conviction that the real author and sustainer of mission is God. This is particularly clear in the witness of the Old Testament. The Servant of the Lord in Second Isaiah, for instance, is a missionary figure, but by no means a prototype of the modern missionary who travels great distances to proclaim the gospel. The "proclamation" is not the spoken word but rather the events concerning the Servant. He is brought into court to witness in a lawsuit between Yahweh and the nations. He is, however, an extraordinary and, yes, a useless witness, for he can neither talk nor see (Isa. 42:18-20; 48:8-13)! Evidently the message of this dumb and blind witness does not consist in verbal preaching; rather, by his mere existence and experiences he is a witness for Yahweh. "Mission" is what God is doing *to* and *through* the Servant, not what the Servant does.

In other words, mission has two specific characteristics. It is a divine activity — God manifesting his glory in the sight of the nations by saving his people. It is an activity addressed primarily to the people of Israel, and to other nations only through them (cf. Legrand 1990:20). Through Israel, God is busy with the nations. The emphasis is on what God does. This does not imply that Israel is excluded or passive. It is a perversion to suggest that if God is the primary "agent" of mission, people are inactive, or vice versa. That would be to argue that God's activity is the enemy of human freedom, that the more one emphasizes God's actions the less one can emphasize ours. Rather, the opposite is true: the more we recognize mission as God's work, the more we ourselves become involved in it. This is what Paul means when he says, "I worked harder than any of [the other apostles] — though it was not I, but the grace of God that is with me" (I Cor. 15:10). If, however, we separate God's work from human activity, we soon land ourselves in one of two untenable positions: if we overemphasize the first, we become fatalists; if we stress only the second, we become fanatics and arrogant zealots.

In the early church, so it would seem, many Greek-speaking Jewish Christians appreciated this creative tension. They got involved in mission without viewing it as something they did in their own power. In the story Luke tells us in the book of Acts, mission is first and foremost the work of God; to be more precise, for Luke it is accomplished by the Spirit. Under no circumstances does this, however, exclude human mediation, and Luke recounts the unreserved commitment of many Christians to mission (cf. Legrand 1990:105-6; Bosch

184

1991:113-17). The same applies to the way Paul interpreted mission. Primarily, it is the *gospel* that is the power of God for everyone's salvation (Rom. 1:16). And yet, Paul does not allow himself a moment's rest as he traverses the Roman Empire, preaches ceaselessly, and establishes churches.

Many Aramaic-speaking Christians, by contrast, could not bring themselves to an active missionary involvement. They believed that the salvation of the Gentiles would take place by means of an eschatological pilgrimage of the nations to Jerusalem, as depicted in the Old Testament. God alone would bring them in, in his own time, and to attempt to precipitate their coming was blasphemy and human arrogance. Throughout the history of the church various Christian groups, because of a perverted understanding of predestination, would adopt a similar attitude: If God wished the heathen to be saved he would see to it himself! All of this, however, flows from a distorted interpretation of the biblical model of mission.

Others have tended to the opposite extreme. They were inclined to make the "success" of mission almost completely dependent upon their own zeal and hard work. Perhaps this is, in part, what lies behind the tendency — particularly in Protestant circles — to interpret the Matthean version of the Great Commission (Matt. 28:18-20) primarily as a *command* and, with that, to overemphasize the auxiliary verb "go" (Greek: *poreuthentes*). As I have argued elsewhere, this is based on a faulty exegesis (Bosch 1983:219-20, 229-30; cf. also Legrand 1990:78-79). It is also, however, the product of a deficient theology: in semi-Pelagian manner, we tend to prioritize human intervention and relegate the power of God to secondary status. This happens particularly where the Great Commission is, for all intents and purposes, limited to verses 19 and 20a, that is, where we ignore the fact that the commission proper *follows on* the statement of authority given to Christ in verse 18 and *is dependent upon* the promise, in verse 20b, of the abiding presence of him who is the real missionary (Legrand 1990:81).

History

The religion of Israel is a *historical* religion: God has a history with people and takes them into a new future. For the people of Israel faith could never be a matter of embracing or acquiescing to the status quo. God is "the God who *acts*" (cf. Wright 1952). The religions of Israel's neighbors, by contrast, were *nature* religions, caught up in the cycle of the seasons, where winter and summer follow each other in an eternal battle for supremacy. In Israel's faith the emphasis was on *salvation*, in the religions of its neighbors it was on *blessing*. Still, the God of Israel — the God who saves — is also the God who blesses, but in such a way that his blessing *flows from* his salvific (or historical) activities. This, too, has tremendous significance for our reflections on the biblical foundation of mission. We might even say that only a historical religion can be truly missionary. History means that nothing needs to remain unchanged. The Bible does not contain eternal, immutable truths — that would be Platonism. Neither is God an immutable God; the miracle of the story of Israel (and of the church) is that, again and again, God changes his mind and decides *not* to punish people as he intended to do!

History is, by nature, specific and concrete, or it is not history. God does not elect humankind in general or in the abstract; God elects a specific people. At first glance, the theme of election seems to run counter to that of universal mission (Legrand 1990:8). In reality, however, election is for service — more particularly: for the sake of the nations. When Abraham, the father of the people of Israel, is called from Ur of the Chaldeans to go to the land of Canaan, the purpose of his calling is not just that God intends to make his name great, but also that he may be a blessing; indeed, that in him all the families of the earth shall be blessed (Gen. 12:1-3). Yahweh breaks the cycle of the eternal return and journeys with Israel into the future, for the sake of the nations. Israel, Jerusalem, and the temple remain at the center, however. The Lord of the universe has, as it were, a concrete, specific, historical address — in the famous words of Blaise Pascal: He is not the God of the philosophers or the scholars, but of Abraham, Isaac, and Jacob.

The same historical specificity characterizes the New Testament. It is not true that, when we move from the Old Testament to the New, we suddenly move from the historical, mundane, and material to the eternal, celestial, and spiritual (*contra* Ohm 1962:247). Salvation in the New Testament also is from the Jews (John 4:22). Jesus is born a Jew, at a specific locality and within a particular socio-historical and political context. During his earthly ministry he is subject to human and historical constraints and limits his ministry almost completely to the people of Israel. It is from within Israel's experience that Jesus opens new horizons. This is confirmed in the Gospel stories, particularly in the Gospel of Luke, the only Gentile author of a New Testament book. The temple is, for Luke, more than an edifice; it is the center from which the word radiates forth to the ends of the earth (Legrand 1990:88, 97).

So we shall not understand Jesus' ministry nor be able to reflect on it missiologically if we sever it from its historical moorings and simply universalize and spiritualize it.

The historical dimension of the faith also implies that things did not end with the life and ministry of the earthly Jesus. With his death on the cross and, even more particularly, his resurrection, a new era was inaugurated, an era with tremendous implications for mission. It is certainly no accident that all four Gospels link the beginning of the worldwide mission of the church explicitly with the resurrection. It is abundantly evident that the Easter experience determined the early Christian community's self-understanding and identity. This experience is both the springboard of mission and the main content of the missionary message: it is the risen Christ that is proclaimed by the early church. And intimately related to the resurrection, almost part of the Easter event itself, is the gift of the Spirit, which is likewise integrally linked to mission. It was Easter that gave those first Christians certainty, but it was Pentecost that gave them boldness; only through the power of the Spirit did they become witnesses (Acts 1:8). Easter is also the dawn of the end time. This introduces a fervent eschatological note to the church's mission. It looks forward to a real, historical *eschaton*. At the same time it knows that the end is not only still pending: it has already come. The church engages in mission on the basis of the already present eschaton and through its mission reaches out to the end that is still to come in fullness. Of that end the resurrection of Jesus is the "first fruits" (I Cor. 15:20, 23), "first installment," "pledge," or "guarantee" (II Cor. 1:22; 5:5; Eph. 1:14).

The four biblical "missionary motifs" discussed above are, of course, all intrinsically interrelated and interdependent. The God who has *compassion* on the stranger, the widow, the orphan, and the poor in Israel is also the God who turns human categories upside down: he uses the weak, the suffering, and those of no consequence as his *witnesses (martyres)* in the world. Ultimately, however, mission remains God's *mission, missio Dei*, since he retains the initiative, creates *history*, and guides it toward its fulfillment.

Mission in Biblical Perspective

Only now are we in a position to reflect on some of those passages that have traditionally been invoked in support of mission. Three observations may be made at this point.

First, it is impossible to infer missionary principles or models in a direct manner from isolated texts or passages. This would be to disregard the fundamentally historical and contextual nature of Scripture. There are no simplistic or obvious moves from the Bible to contemporary missional practice (cf. Brueggemann 1982:408). Second, and linked to the above, we may never utilize biblical sayings to undergird, in a one-to-one manner, the specific missionary projects in which we are involved. We would then be using those sayings not as texts, but as pretexts (cf. Schreiter 1982:431). Third, at no stage — not even in the first stages of the missionary involvement of the early church — was there a uniform view of mission. The Bible, Old and New Testament, reveals a variety of mission types. We may also not range the various forms of mission "along a linear evolutive trajectory that would begin with the Old Testament and finally come to the New" (Legrand 1990:151).

Why would this be so? Basically, because of the four motifs outlined above: by its very nature, *compassion* takes concrete forms according to specific circumstances; *witness* depends on the situation in which one finds oneself; *God's actions in mission* are manifested in the contexts in which people live; *history* is, by nature, always contingent and never simply a rerun of what has been. And since the Christian faith is inherently *incarnational*, in the sense of God taking a concrete human form in a specific social context, the Christian mission — if it wishes to be incarnational — also has to be specific and contextual. In our reflections on the missionary dimensions of the biblical message, we must therefore be willing to be challenged by the rich variety of the biblical accounts. This variety corresponds to the diversity of what we actually see in mission today.

No two situations are exactly the same. Mission in Asia with its rich and ancient religious traditions will be very different from mission in Latin America, or in secularized Europe, or in those countries where for decades Marxism has been the official creed, or in Africa where people live in face-to-face communities. We will therefore — to cite Echegaray again — have to allow ourselves to be inspired by Jesus and the first missionaries to prolong the logic of their ministry in a creative way amid new and very different circumstances (1984:xv-xvi).

Studying the Scriptures in this spirit, we may indeed be enabled to draw on biblical sayings to validate but also to challenge, critique, and transform our missionary models and projects. We may, by all means, draw on the Great Commission, but we should do so in a way that does not violate the text's intentions. We will note, for instance, that each of our four Gospels contains its own version of the Com-

mission.② All Gospels are unanimous that it is the resurrection of Jesus
that generates mission. Put differently, mission is "the gospel confirmed
and universalized by the power of the Resurrection" (Legrand 1990:73).
The four Gospels do this in different ways. *Matthew,* for instance, views
mission as ministry done in the consciousness of the universal authority
of Jesus and of his abiding presence (28:18-20). Mission is, primarily,
making disciples, that is, turning others into what the disciples themselves are: those who practice justice-love and emulate "the works of
Jesus" (Matt. 11:2) (cf. Bosch 1991:56-83). In his Great Commission, *Luke*
(24:46-49) understands mission as: fulfillment of scriptural promises;
becoming possible only after the death and resurrection of the Messiah
of Israel; proclaiming the message of repentance and forgiveness; intended for all nations; beginning from Jerusalem; carried out by "witnesses"; and accomplished in the power of the Spirit (cf. Bosch 1991:84-
122; Senior and Stuhlmueller 1983:260-69). And *John's* version of the
Commission (20:21) underscores the intimate relationship between
Jesus' mission and that of his disciples: they have to emulate him. The
Commission follows directly after he has shown them his hands and
his side (20:20); this undeniably suggests that, as I have argued above,
mission will take place in the context of suffering and opposition.

Each evangelist thus reports the Great Commission from within
the context of that evangelist's particular orientation. The variations in
the commissions reflect a variety of missionary experiences. This does
not suggest arbitrariness, however, since the elements that the four
Gospels share in their "definitions" of mission far outweigh those about
which they differ. The mission of the church has continuity with that
of the historical Jesus. For at least Matthew and Luke (and, of course,
Paul) the church remains dependent on and committed to Israel. At the
same time, all New Testament authors agree that the key to entering
God's reign cannot be ethnic origin but faith in God through Jesus
Christ. "Where faith appears, the Reign is present" (Legrand 1990:61).

The mission of the church, then, has all the dimensions and scope
of Jesus' own ministry and may never be reduced to church planting
and the saving of souls. It consists in proclaiming and teaching, but
also in healing and liberating, in compassion for the poor and the

---

2. Of course, the longer ending of Mark's Gospel (16:9-20), where the Markan Great
Commission appears (16:15-16), is not found in the best manuscripts and is regarded as
inauthentic. Still, as more and more scholars are now recognizing, at least the two verses
containing the Commission have a more Markan stamp than the rest and probably belong
to the original but now lost ending of Mark (cf. also Legrand 1990:75 and 173, n. 7, where
additional references are given).

downtrodden. The mission of the church, as the mission of Jesus, involves being sent into the world — to love, to serve, to preach, to teach, to heal, to save, to free. ⁊ℓ *ʃʰₑₙʃ ˡₒₙₙₑᵢₙ ᵧ ℓℓ*.

These reflections bring us in close proximity to another Lukan passage that has, for good reasons, been dubbed the _real_ Great Commission of the third Gospel: Luke 4:16-21. Indeed, within the overall structure of Luke, these verses are at least as important as the more explicit Great Commission in 24:46-49. The words Jesus quotes from Isaiah (Luke 4:18-19) are set within the context of the dramatic story of Jesus' first public ministry in his hometown, Nazareth, and they introduce at least three crucial Lukan missionary motifs: the centrality of the poor and other marginalized and oppressed people in Jesus' (and the church's) ministry; overcoming vengeance by forgiveness and peace; and moving beyond the confines of Israel, first to the Samaritans and then to the Gentiles (Bosch 1991:89-113). These motifs constitute a charter also for the church-in-mission today.

As the mission of the first apostles was, essentially, the resumption of the mission of Jesus, our mission is the continuation of theirs. Mission certainly involves human mediations, but always in total dependence on the initiative of God, particularly his initiative in the Christ-event. Mission is first and foremost the God who comes, in Jesus Christ (Legrand 1990:152).[3] The gospel is the power of God for salvation (Rom. 1:16), and this power is more basic than the activities of the missionaries (Legrand 1990:127). And yet, that power seeks to manifest itself in our missionary ministry. This is never performed in unbroken continuity with the biblical witness; it remains, always, an altogether ambivalent and flawed enterprise. Still we may, with due humility, look back on the witness of Jesus and our first forebears in the faith and seek to emulate them.

For Further Reading

Bosch, David J.
    1979   *A Spirituality of the Road.* Scottdale, PA: Herald Press.
    1983   "The Structure of Mission: An Exposition of Matthew 28:16-20." In *Exploring Church Growth.* Edited by Wilbert R. Shenk. Grand Rapids, MI: Wm. B. Eerdmans Publishing Company, pp. 218-48.

3. Cf. the original title of Legrand's book: *Le Dieu qui vient* (= the God who is coming) (Paris: Desclée, 1988).

1991   *Transforming Mission: Paradigm Changes in Theology of Mission.* Maryknoll, NY: Orbis Books.

Brueggemann, Walter
1982   "The Bible and Mission: Some Interdisciplinary Implications for Teaching." *Missiology* 10:397-411.

Echegaray, Hugo
1984   *The Practice of Jesus.* Maryknoll, NY: Orbis Books.

Frazier, William, MM
1987   "Where Mission Begins: A Foundational Probe." *Maryknoll Formation Journal* (Summer), pp. 13-52.

Hengel, Martin
1983   "The Origins of the Christian Mission." In *Between Jesus and Paul: Studies in the Earliest History of Christianity.* London: SCM Press, pp. 48-64, 166-79.

Kähler, Martin
1971   *Schriften zur Christologie und Mission.* Munich: Christian Kaiser Verlag.

Kasting, Heinrich
1969   *Die Anfänge der urchristlichen Mission.* Munich: Christian Kaiser Verlag.

Kertelge, Karl, ed.
1982   *Mission im Neuen Testament.* Freiburg i. B.: Herder & Herder.

Lash, Nicholas
1985   "What Might Martyrdom Mean?" *Ex Auditu* 1:14-24.

Legrand, Lucien
1990   *Unity and Plurality: Mission in the Bible.* Maryknoll, NY: Orbis Books.

Meyer, Ben F.
1986   *The Early Christians: Their World Mission and Self-Discovery.* Wilmington, DE: Michael Glazier.

Neely, Alan
1989   "Mission as Kenosis: Implications for our Times." *The Princeton Seminary Bulletin* 10:202-23.

Nolan, Albert
1976   *Jesus before Christianity.* Cape Town, South Africa: David Philip.

Ohm, Thomas
1962   *Machet zu Jüngern alle Völker: Theorie der Mission.* Freiburg: Erich Wevel Verlag.

Pesch, Rudolf
1976   *Das Markusevangelium.* Freiburg i. B.: Herder & Herder.

Schreiter, Robert J.
1982   "The Bible and Mission: A Response to Walter Brueggemann
            and Weverly Gaventa." *Missiology* 10:427-34.
Senior, Donald, and Carroll Stuhlmueller
1983   *The Biblical Foundations for Mission.* Maryknoll, NY: Orbis
            Books.
Senior, Donald
1984   "The Struggle to be Universal: Mission as Vantage Point for
            New Testament Investigation." *The Catholic Biblical Quarterly*
            46:63-81.
Spindler, Marc
1988   "Bijbelse fundering en oriëntatie van zending." In *Oecu-
            menische inleiding in de Missiologie.* Edited by A. Camps, L. A.
            Hoedemaker, M. R. Spindler, and F. J. Verstraelen. Kampen:
            Kok, pp. 137-54.
Stanton, Graham N.
1985   "Interpreting the New Testament Today." *Ex Auditu* 1:63-73.
Triebel, Johannes
1988   "Leiden als Thema der Missionstheologie." *Jahrbuch Mission*
            20:1-20.
Verkuyl, J.
1978   *Contemporary Missiology: An Introduction.* Grand Rapids, MI:
            Wm. B. Eerdmans Publishing Company.
Von Campenhausen, Hans
1974   "Das Martyrium in der Mission." In *Kirchengeschichte als Mis-
            sionsgeschichte. Bd. I: Die Alte Kirche.* Edited by H. Frohnes
            and U. W. Knorr. Munich: Christian Kaiser, pp. 71-85.
Wright, G. Ernest
1952   *God Who Acts: Biblical Theology as Recital.* London: SCM Press.

Mission Theology

James A. Scherer

The "theology of mission" as here understood is that special concern within the wider, more generic or inclusive study of mission theology which deals with the justification or validity of the Christian world mission. It is directed at the very nature and existence of the church's missionary apostolate, and renders the unique service of defending the Christian mission against its adversaries and establishing it on a firm and reliable foundation. Other chapters in this section relate to the theological issues of contextualization, indigenization, dialogue, and the response to other living faiths. This essay will focus on the past condition and probable future status of the theology of mission within the ecumenical movement.

Nearly three decades ago Gerald Anderson, in a pioneering book dealing with the theology of mission among twentieth-century Protestants, prophetically observed that

> the underlying principles and theological presuppositions for the Christian mission have been called into question and Christians are challenged to rethink the motives, message, methods and goals of their mission. . . . The fundamental task, therefore, of the missionary enterprise today is to clarify the nature and meaning of its being. (Anderson 1961:3-4)

James A. Scherer is Professor of World Mission and Church History, Lutheran School of Theology, Chicago. Formerly a Lutheran missionary in China and Japan, he is the author of *Gospel, Church & Kingdom: Comparative Studies in World Mission Theology* (1987).

This theological clarification was necessary, he added, both to make the gospel mission more effective and to give Christians a deeper understanding of their missionary task in the world. Anderson compared the deepening crisis of a church attempting to do mission with a deficient theological basis to a person descending the spiral staircase of a seven-story building, briefly pausing at the landing on each floor to take his bearings. The six landings were roughly analogous to world mission conferences held between Edinburgh 1910 and Ghana 1957/8. They posed these questions to the Christian community in its missionary obedience: "How missions?" (1910), "Wherefore missions?" (1928), "Whence missions?" (1938), "Whither missions?" (1948), "Why missions?" (1952), and finally the most radical question, "What is the Christian mission?" (1957/8).

Anderson believed that before the final two questions could be answered — "why missions?" and "what is the Christian mission?" — the traveler would find it necessary to descend even further into the basement of the building — down to its very *foundations,* in fact — for a valid understanding of the church's missionary basis (Anderson 1961:5-7). His own proposal called for reformulating the theology of mission "from the view of *radical trinitarian theocentrism*" (ibid. 15). Anderson's views reflected a growing ecumenical consensus regarding major changes needed in order to ground the theology of mission and the mission enterprise itself on a sounder basis. Between 1950 and 1952, in preparation for the 1952 International Missionary Council (IMC) Willingen meeting, an eminent panel of North American theologians and missiologists struggled to clarify the biblical and theological basis of mission, along with related matters such as missionary vocation, task, and policy. The heading of the landmark report of Commission I to the Willingen meeting, "Why Missions?" reflected the intensity of the Commission's task. The North American report advocated a thoroughgoing trinitarian approach that understood mission as "the sensitive and total response of the church to what the triune God has done and is doing in the world" (Anderson 1988:109). Thereby a shift toward a trinitarian but still Christocentric understanding of the church's mission as grounded in the total mission of God *(missio Dei)* was underway.

The IMC Willingen Meeting (1952) adopted a statement on "The Missionary Calling of the Church" that described the *church* as a body sent by God "to carry out his work to the ends of the earth, to all nations, and to the end of time." Willingen located the *source* of the missionary movement in the triune God, and connected mission ontologically with the very *existence* of the church:

There is no participation in Christ without participation in His mission to the world. That by which the Church receives its existence is that by which it is also given its world-mission. (IMC 1952:2-3)

However, Willingen stopped short of working out the full implications of a trinitarian basis for mission. It was unable to adopt a consentaneous statement on the relationship between mission and eschatology, and between the church's missionary obligation and the kingdom of God (IMC 1953:245). The result was that while Willingen represented a major advance over previous statements, it ended up deferring deeper theological issues for later consideration. A German observer, Wilhelm Andersen, commented on the results of Willingen:

> A theological redefinition of the basis of the Christian missionary enterprise cannot be worked out within the limits of the phrase 'the missionary obligation of the Church' . . . we must dig deeper; we must trace the originating impulse in faith in the triune God; from that standpoint alone can we see the missionary enterprise synoptically in its relationship to the Kingdom of God and in its relationship to the world. (Andersen 1955:10)

Crumbling of Old Foundations

These brief references are symptomatic of the deep anxiety felt in the post–World War II Western missionary movement to discover, or recover, the lost foundation for the church's missionary obligation. What had caused the old foundations to crumble? The period immediately following World War II, corresponding in Kraemer's apt phrase to "the end of western colonialism and the collapse of western Christendom," marked the end of an "age of innocence" as far as the Western missionary enterprise was concerned (Kraemer 1960:195). An era that had relied heavily on the Great Commission for an answer to "Why missions?" and to the "three-self church" formula of Henry Venn and Rufus Anderson for a self-evident explanation of the missionary goal, was by 1950 coming to an end. The late Prof. Walter Freytag's classical statement at the Ghana IMC meeting epitomized the dilemma facing the mission enterprise:

> Then missions had problems, but *they were not a problem themselves.*
> (IMC 1958:138; emphasis added)

195

[handwritten: UP USA is still in the dilema '.so messinari now are social workers]

Freytag meant, of course, that while many of the instruments of the old mission enterprise remained intact, its theological foundations had crumbled. This prompted the IMC in the days prior to its integration into the WCC at New Delhi (1961) to commission several fundamental studies on the nature of the church's mission. These studies viewed "missions" not as a passing historical phenomenon but as an enduring commission from God. One of them was Johannes Blauw's *The Missionary Nature of the Church*, a valuable survey of the biblical theology of mission (Blauw 1962). Another was D. T. Niles' study volume *Upon The Earth*, which sought to clarify the relation between the "mission of God" and the mission task of the church in all six continents (Niles 1962).

The deepening pessimism about the future of the world mission enterprise was sparked by many factors, both negative and positive. Atheistic ideology had extended its influence into Eastern Europe, and the cold war was mounting in intensity. A communist revolutionary government had triumphed in China, expelling Western missionaries and cutting off church ties abroad. Newly independent Third World nations, hoping to curtail the legacy of colonialism, were redefining the terms for the local church's mission and frequently barring or limiting access for foreign missionaries. Meanwhile, militant and fanatical nationalist movements, inspired by the recovery of an ancient but suppressed religious heritage, were engaging in anti-missionary propaganda, sometimes seeking to end conversions to Christianity.

In the Third World, missions shared in the discrediting of colonialism, and for a time the two appeared virtually indistinguishable. In the Western world, meanwhile, many Christians skeptically dismissed mission work as a passing symbol of a bygone imperial age, now happily replaced by a more sophisticated ecumenical era. Many Western Christians, identifying evangelization with proselytism, simply concluded that the right to communicate the gospel to people of other nations and cultures had been forfeited, and that the duty to do so had been an historical aberration. The Western missionary became a kind of cultural bigot and "anti-hero," a villain in the global movement for inter-religious peace and understanding. A new theology of mission would have to overcome and transcend these negative theological biases and cultural prejudices, a theology able to transcend this host of negative cultural vibrations.

On the positive side, new churches were emerging in Asia, Africa, and Latin America and claiming their own selfhood and cultural independence. These churches were becoming active participants in the life

196 *[handwritten: has ecumenish w/ wn .mg. replaced missin ?]*

of the World Council of Churches and in regional ecumenical bodies. Their emergence deeply affected the character of the global ecumenical agenda, particularly with regard to contextual theology, local cultural identity, interreligious relations, and advocacy of social and economic justice. Growing both in numbers and self-confidence, Third World churches were able with astonishing speed to disassociate "mission" from its Western colonial monopoly and privilege and to reclaim it as part of their own spiritual birthright. As the axis of Christian community began shifting southward, an explosive growth in numbers of Third World Christians began to be translated into a fresh and vibrant missionary outpouring from Asia, Africa, and Latin America. The late D. T. Niles and others took steps to involve theologians and church leaders from the Third World in discussions toward developing a truly six-continent-based theology of mission (Niles 1962). The results of this widened theological horizon were later seen in the growing list of volumes on mission theology produced by Third World authors, and in the agendas of WCC-CWME Mission and Evangelism Conferences held at Bangkok (1972-73), Melbourne (1980), and San Antonio (1989).

As the ecumenical world looked forward to the integration of the former International Missionary Council into the World Council of Churches at the New Delhi Assembly (1961) — an ideal marriage between the global movements for mission and for unity — an interim replacement for the Edinburgh 1910 church-centered concept of the missionary task came into view. The older view of mission as the "road from church to church" — essentially church planting and extension overseas — gave way to a view of mission as the work of the triune God entrusted to the church in each place by Jesus Christ. In a brilliant position paper written for the IMC, *One Body/One Gospel/One World*, Lesslie Newbigin seemed to be pointing beyond Willingen to a more inclusively ecumenical view of mission as the task of the church in all six continents (Newbigin 1958). Newbigin declared the church's mission to be none other than the mission of Christ himself and the apostles. The mission concerns the ends of the earth and the end of the world. The home base of mission is everywhere, and every local group of Christians is called to participate — in partnership with other churches — in the mission task both at home and at the ends of the earth. The particularity of mission in the ecumenical age consisted not so much in the crossing of geographical frontiers as in *crossing the frontier between faith in Christ as Lord and unbelief*. A missionary, said Newbigin, is anyone "sent to make Christ known and obeyed as Lord among those who do not so know and obey Him," whether the journey be long or short.

197

The Ecumenical Missionary Paradigm

This new view had the merit of freeing the mission of the church from a Western-based captivity so that it could recognize the universal character of the church's missionary calling. It also provided strong theological and practical support for the integration of the missionary movement into the life of the churches. In effect it replaced an outmoded parochial and Western church-centered view with a global and ecumenical but still ecclesiastical model. But it failed to address the issues left unsolved at Willingen: the relation between mission and eschatology, and between the missionary church and God's kingdom. By making so strong a case for church-mission integration, it could be argued, the new IMC/WCC ecumenical missionary paradigm made the solution of the unsolved issues of Willingen that much more difficult.

To put the matter more succinctly, is the church-mission *oikoumene* represented by the New Delhi act of integration the true eschatological and biblical *oikoumene* anticipated in the New Testament Scriptures, or only a modest interim arrangement for inter-church witness and cooperation on a global basis? Does a theology of mission rooted in trinitarian theology, grounded in the missionary initiative of the Father who sent the incarnate, crucified, and risen Christ in the power of the Spirit, not allow and even require us to expect a more ultimate expression of the promised transformation of God's creation — "a new heaven and a new earth" (Rev. 21:1; Isa. 65:17) — than merely a renewed and reformed ecclesial ecumenical movement? The weakness of "ecumenical" mission when defined as "the whole task of the whole Church to bring the (whole) Gospel to the whole world" — an interpretation recently adopted and virtually canonized by Lausanne II at Manila (1989) — is its lack of a dynamic eschatological vision. In both its conciliar and evangelical forms, it stops short of depicting a biblical fulfillment for the mission of God. An ecumenical theology of mission that lacks a compelling eschatological component is in danger of becoming stagnant and bankrupt.

Rebuilding the Foundations

The thesis of this essay is that the theology of mission both within and outside the ecumenical movement, that is, the inquiry into the "why" and "what" of mission in Gerald Anderson's seven-story building analogy, needs to be reconstructed in a way that brings together "mis-

198

sion in unity" with preparation for and expectation of the eschatological kingdom of God. The primary issues for a renewed theology of mission are still those identified earlier by Roger Bassham: (1) theological basis; (2) church-mission relations; (3) evangelism and social action; (4) Christianity and other faiths; and (5) mission and unity (Bassham 1979:8-9). Today's burning issues — social justice in mission, and witness to (or dialogue with) people of other faiths and ideologies — are heatedly discussed, but often as single issues unrelated to or separate from the overarching purpose of the mission of God. Yet none of these issues — including mission and unity and church-mission relationships — can be properly grasped apart from the unitary vision that is imparted by the Christian community's faithful longing for the return of Christ, the divine *parousia*, the new creation through the Spirit. Recent WCC-CWME conferences were right in recognizing the validity and urgency of such missionary themes as "Your Kingdom Come!" (Melbourne 1980) and "Your Will Be Done! Mission in Christ's Way" (San Antonio 1989). However, they did not go far enough toward developing the implications of these powerful eschatological themes for the actual practice of ecumenical mission. To take eschatology seriously is to allow present mission structures and practices to become relativized for the sake of the kingdom of God. It is to place all plans and resources at the disposal of God's own mission, following "in Christ's way" through the power of the Spirit.

We can do no more than sketch the outlines for an ecumenical reconstruction of the theology of mission. Many of the building blocks and raw materials already exist in the extraordinary theological work done in the decade of the fifties: the reports of the North American Task Force on the theology of mission in preparation for Willingen; the Willingen Meeting reports and major addresses, particularly those on eschatology; the WCC (Rolle 1951) Central Committee Statement on "The Calling of the Church to Mission and to Unity"; the Lund (1952) Faith and Order Conference Reports on "Christ and His Church," and others. In this connection the penetrating work of a single scholar, Prof. J. C. Hoekendijk, must be reconsidered.

It was Hoekendijk who protested the "denominationalizing" of mission and the "ecclesiasticizing" of the ecumenical movement. He passionately advocated a "worldly" alternative view to the concept of a churchly *oikoumene:*

> The church is only the church to the extent that she lets herself be used as a part of God's dealings with the oikoumene. For this reason

199

she can only be "ecumenical," i.e. oriented toward the oikoumene —
the whole world. (Hoekendijk 1964:40) . . . the church can only really
be the church if she is a sign and prophetic witness of the approaching
Kingdom. In her *existence* she will establish the sign of the redemption
of God's Kingdom: communion, righteousness, unity, etc. The church
cannot be more than a sign. She points away from herself to the
Kingdom; she lets herself be used for and through the Kingdom in
the oikoumene. (Hoekendijk 1964:43)

Hoekendijk's worldly eschatological understanding of the "apostolate" and his reductionist view of the church as a "function of the
apostolate" will predictably come into conflict with the developed ec-
clesiologies of the Faith and Order Commission, but the risk must be
taken.

There exists, finally, another incredibly rich but insufficiently mined
resource for reconstructing an ecumenical theology of mission: the 1954
Evanston Second WCC Assembly Report on "Christ — The Hope of the
World" (WCC 1954:430-65). Nowhere else do the main themes of ecumenical theology, integrated into a clear eschatological perspective, come
together with such polish and precision: Christ our hope, the kingdom
that now is and is to come, the church as God's pilgrim people, the
mission, unity, and renewal of the church, Christian hope, and the meaning of history in our time and world. Even today the document can be
read as a brilliant biblical commentary on the church's mission in 1992,
taking into account the collapse of false hopes and looking toward God's
purpose for the world in the twenty-first century. Its integrity stands as a
testimony to the solid biblical and theological work that underlies it, as
well as to the contributions of eminent theologians and scholars, despite
the fact that it was never intended as a statement on the theology of
mission. Let us close with a moving passage:

It is thus of the very nature of the Church that it has a mission to
the whole world. That mission is our participation in the work of
God which takes place between the coming of Jesus Christ to inaugu-
rate God's Kingdom on earth, and His coming again in glory to bring
that Kingdom to its consummation. . . . For He whose coming we
expect is also He who is already present. Our work until His coming
again is but the result of our share in the work which He is doing all
the time and everywhere. The Church's mission is thus the most
important thing that is happening in history. (World Council of
Churches 1954:442)

For Further Reading

Andersen, Wilhelm
1955   *Towards a Theology of Mission.* I.M.C. Research Pamphlet No.
           2. London: SCM Press.
Anderson, Gerald H.
1961   *The Theology of the Christian Mission.* Edited and with an
           Introduction by G. H. Anderson. New York, Toronto, and
           London: McGraw-Hill Book Company.
1971   "Theology of Mission." In *Concise Dictionary of the Christian
           World Mission.* Edited by S. Neill, G. H. Anderson, and J. Good-
           win. Nashville and New York: Abingdon Press, pp. 594-95.
1988   "American Protestants in Pursuit of Mission." *International
           Bulletin of Missionary Research* 12 (July):98-109.
Bassham, Rodger C.
1979   *Mission Theology: 1948-1975. Years of Worldwide Creative Ten-
           sion: Ecumenical, Evangelical and Roman Catholic.* Pasadena,
           CA: William Carey Library.
Bevans, Stephen B., and James A. Scherer, eds.
1992   *New Directions in Mission and Evangelism 1: Basic Statements,
           1974-91.* Maryknoll, NY: Orbis Books.
Blauw, Johannes
1962   *The Missionary Nature of the Church: A Survey of the Biblical
           Theology of Mission.* London: Lutterworth Press.
Bosch, David J.
1980   *Witness to the World: The Christian Mission in Theological Per-
           spective.* London: Marshall, Morgan & Scott.
Gensichen, Hans-Werner
1971   *Glaube für die Welt: Theologische Aspekte der Mission.* Güterslo-
           her Verlagshaus: Gerd Mohn.
Hoekendijk, Johannes Christian
1964   *The Church Inside Out.* Edited by L. A. Hoedemaker and Pie-
           ter Tijmes, translated by I. C. Rottenberg. Philadelphia: West-
           minster Press.
International Missionary Council (IMC)
1952   *The Missionary Obligation of the Church.* New York and Lon-
           don: International Missionary Council.
1953   *Missions Under the Cross: Addresses and Statements of the 1952
           Willingen Meeting.* Edited by Norman Goodall. New York:
           Friendship Press.
1958   *The Ghana Assembly of the International Missionary Council.*
           Edited by R. K. Orchard. London: Edinburgh House Press.

Kraemer, Hendrik
1960   "The Missionary Implications of the End of Western Colonialism and the Collapse of Western Christendom." In *History's Lessons for Tomorrow's Mission.* Geneva: World's Student Christian Federation.

Mueller, Karl
1987   *Mission Theology: An Introduction.* Studia Instituti Missiologici Societatis Verbi Divini No. 39. Steyler Verlag: Wort und Werk.

Newbigin, J. E. Lesslie
1958   *One Body, One Gospel, One World: The Christian Mission Today.* London and New York: International Missionary Council.
1978   *The Open Secret: Sketches for a Missionary Theology.* Grand Rapids, MI: Wm. B. Eerdmans Publishing Company.

Niles, Daniel T.
1962   *Upon the Earth: The Mission of God and the Missionary Enterprise of the Churches.* London: Lutterworth Press.

Scherer, James A.
1971   "Missions in Theological Education." In *The Future of the Christian World Mission.* Edited by W. J. Danker and Wi Jo Kang. Grand Rapids, MI: Wm. B. Eerdmans Publishing Company, pp. 143-53.
1987a   *Gospel, Church and Kingdom: Studies in World Mission Theology.* Minneapolis: Augsburg.
1987b   "Missiology as a Discipline and What It Includes." *Missiology* 14 (1987):507-22.

Senior, Donald, and Carroll Stuhlmueller
1983   *The Biblical Foundations for Mission.* Maryknoll, NY: Orbis Books.

Verkuyl, Johannes
1987   *Contemporary Missiology: An Introduction.* Edited and translated by Dale Cooper. Grand Rapids, MI: Wm. B. Eerdmans Publishing Company.

Vicedom, Georg F.
1965   *The Mission of God: An Introduction to a Theology of Mission.* Translated by A. A. Thiele and D. Higendorf from the German original, *Missio Dei* (1957). St. Louis, MO: Concordia Publishing House.

World Council of Churches
1954   "Report of the Advisory Commission on the Main Theme of the Second Assembly: Christ — the Hope of the World." *Ecumenical Review* 6 (July):430-65.

Spiritual Formation for Mission

Barbara Hendricks, M.M., and
Thomas E. Clarke, S.J.

Planning the future of Christian mission with respect to spiritual formation is light-years away from market analysis, recording of financial
trends, explorations of demographic shifts, and the like. In the face of
admittedly massive obstacles, ecclesiastical as well as secular, spiritual
formation is an exercise of neither optimism nor pessimism. It is rather
an expression of hope, rooted in eschatological faith, and it views all
specific historical futures as participations in the Absolute Future that
is God. It cannot consist in value-free analysis, for it is committed to
the promotion of God's reign within and beyond history. At once sober,
realistic, and nonutopian, it yet dares to dream of a better future within
history, energized by that search for God which is the heart of spirituality. This essay is an expression of the spiritual hope that drives every
dream of mission in the twenty-first century.

Our essay will be developed in three parts. We will first set forth
some basic assumptions regarding the principal terms and what we
consider to be the horizon or basic option for mission in coming decades.

Barbara Hendricks, M.M., is co-director of the Maryknoll Mission Institute,
Maryknoll, New York. She served as a Maryknoll missioner in Peru and
Bolivia in the 1950s, 1960s, and the 1980s, and was President of the Maryknoll Sisters Congregation from 1970 to 1978. Thomas E. Clarke, S.J., is a
staff member of Christ the King Retreat House in Syracuse, New York. He
was Professor of Systematic Theology at Woodstock College and a Research
Fellow at Woodstock Theological Center, Washington, DC, and has written
several books about Christian spirituality.

We will then offer a core reflection on several key aspects of this basic option. Finally, in the light of the core reflection, we will briefly list some of the foreseen implications touching spiritual formation for mission.

Some Assumptions

"Spirituality"

Historically and presently, the term "spirituality" is far from being a universal favorite among Christian denominations (Raitt 1987; Sudbrack 1975; Schneiders 1989). Its choice by editors of this volume indicates its growing appeal in ever wider missionary circles. But the term continues to be most favored in Roman Catholic and Anglican milieux. Lutherans and others have preferred to speak of piety, and the languages of discipline, worship, and devotion are indeed legitimate alternatives that point to specific dimensions of what we here describe as spirituality.

Unfortunately, past dichotomizing of soul and body (or spirit and flesh) has often given the term "spiritual" a false or unwelcome connotation. This does not, however, outweigh its value. We understand spirituality here in a theological sense, as the relationship, in lived experience and reflective understanding (practice and theory), between the human spirit, individual and communal, and the divine spirit or whatever is conceived within a specific tradition, East or West, as ultimate in human and cosmic life. Spirituality is distinctively Christian when this relationship is conceived as mediated through the one Mediator, Jesus Christ, and when the divine spirit is understood as the Holy Spirit, poured forth by Father and Son into the heart of each believer, the church, the whole of humankind, and the whole of creation.

"Formation"

Too often the language of religious and spiritual formation tends to become bland and abstract. In contrast, mission bearers in the twenty-first century from technologically developed countries such as the United States must in their spiritual formation counteract the powerful cultural *deformation* affecting potential future missionaries. When this is done, then formation is understood in continuity with the biblical, and specifically the Pauline, themes of *reformation*, *conformation*, and *transformation* (e.g., Rom. 8:29; 12:2; II Cor. 3:18; Phil. 3:21; see Col. 3:10). Given the pervasive contexts of consumerism, individualism, racism, sexism, militarism, and the like, formation in coming decades will be realized not as a tranquil unfolding of human potential but rather as costly discipleship and profound cultural *conversion*, both creational and redemptional in character, which prepares the missioner for impasse, conflict, and virtual martyrdom (Conn 1986; Happel and Walter 1986; Wallis 1981).

Where might formation as conversion and transformation take place? Here again the radicalness of our situation tends to explode traditional assumptions. It seems clear that the central locus for such formation must be, not a school or training center separated from the actual missionary encounter, but the daily scenes in which mission is actually exercised. This does not exclude the importance of formal programs of formation, in the home country or abroad, academic or not, preparatory or experienced in the course of an ongoing commitment to mission. But all such programs need to take their shape and character from their relationship to the primary locus of formation, namely a lived insertion into the community and culture of the people to whom one is sent.

Who Is Being Formed for What?

Formerly, formation for mission was seen as the special education of a healthy middle-class or lower-middle-class North American or European Christian for proper religious ministry in some overseas culture where the gospel had not been effectively proclaimed or the church not fully rooted. Formation for the twenty-first century will reflect some of the radical new ways of understanding church, mission, and evangelization. Among new paradigms of mission, one speaks of "reverse mission" and of the "ebb and flow" of evangelizing currents between the First and Third Worlds (Dussel 1987).

Within such paradigms, who are the evangelizers and who are the evangelized, and how does spiritual formation touch all who are involved in the process? New paradigms have emerged also with respect to the relationship of missionary evangelization to social, economic, political, and cultural dimensions of life, and with respect to the place of non-Christian religions in God's plan of salvation (Snyder and Runyon 1987). Given the present wide diversity of theological views regarding both of these questions, the need for dialogue among Christians themselves will continue to be a major constituent of spiritual formation. It is not conflicting doctrinal or pastoral viewpoints but the refusal or neglect of dialogue with fellow Christians of different persuasions that represents the scandal that hinders missionary evangelization. We will not here explore the implications of any one current view for spiritual formation. We must also regrettably leave aside discussion of the impact on spiritual formation of the women's movement and the ecological movement, both of which can be expected to penetrate deeply into formation programs. We limit ourselves to dealing with spiritual formation of Christians from the United States, whatever their situation within their respective churches.

The Horizon or Basic Option of Christian Mission Today

Historically, the many Christian spiritualities have each made a kind of basic option, responsive to the signs of the times, regarding the root metaphors, symbols, motifs, and paradigms through which they were to energize the Spirit-life of Christians (Sudbrack 1975; McGinn and Meyendorff 1985; Raitt 1987; Jones, Wainwright, and Yarnold 1986). Examples of such basic options might be: the Johannine motif of life and light; the Pauline dramatization of the sin-grace struggle; the Benedictine theme of *ora et labora;* Teresa of Avila's mansions, and John of the Cross' journey of ascent in the dark night of faith. It is also possible to write the history of distinctively missionary spiritualities, more eloquently lived than verbally formulated, in such heroic figures as Ignatius of Antioch, Boniface, Augustine, Cyril and Methodius, Patrick and Columba, and such later evangelizers as Francis Xavier, Theophane Venard, James Anthony Walsh, and, on the Protestant side, John Wesley, Hudson Taylor, William Carey, David Livingstone, Toyohiko Kagawa, V. S. Azariah, and E. Stanley Jones.

Such a history quite clearly discloses the centrality of the motif of the *martyrion,* the witness unto death on behalf of the gospel. Spiritual formation in mission, let it be said in passing, while responsive to contemporary events, will always need to be animated by stories of missionary endeavors of the past two millennia. Each of these stories represents a "dangerous memory," grounding an embattled hope for the future in the unnostalgic remembrance of the past (Metz 1972:88-118).

But we now need to ask: Is it possible to discern today a similar "sign of the times" that might ground such a choice of basic horizon for missionary formation? From the experience of many missionaries in the Third World in the second half of the twentieth century, we are convinced that *the cry of the poor* constitutes such a divinely given sign, so that spiritual formation for mission in the twenty-first century needs to actualize a basic option for the poor as the heart of its endeavor.

Integral to such a concept of spiritual formation is the fundamental assumption of "the hermeneutical privilege of the poor," that is, the active presence within the poor of the divine power of salvation for all, rich as well as poor (Hellwig 1983).

A Core Reflection

Evangelization, understood with Paul VI as involving the total life, witness, and ministry of the church, implies inculturation, so that mission today is increasingly understood as essentially transcultural (Paul VI 1976). United States missionaries of the twenty-first century will carry a gospel that, for better and for worse, has become inculturated within a home culture that we should neither unduly disparage nor uncritically canonize. And they will carry it to different cultures within which the gospel has been — again for better and for worse — differently inculturated, and in which other belief systems, religious and secular, have found cultural insertion, often far more expressive of the people's meaning and values than is the Christian presence. Any sound spiritual formation for mission must foster in missionaries attitudes and habits that are congruous with this basic axiom of evangelization as inculturation.

Within such a context of integral evangelization as inculturation, the preferential option for the poor and a recognition of the evangelizing power of the poor are to take flesh in the spiritual formation process. Not only is poverty a socio-economic reality that, like wealth, involves important cultural antecedents and consequences, it is even possible to locate the core of poverty, from a gospel standpoint, in dehumanizing cultural disparagement (Clarke 1988). When the heart of Christian mission is seen as the bringing of good news to the poor — the good news being notice of their preferential choice and empowerment by God in Jesus Christ and the Spirit — the primary focus of evangelization as inculturation then becomes the penetration of the culture of the poor with the leaven of the gospel, or perhaps more correctly, the disclosure and naming of the hidden power of the Spirit already at work in the poor for the healing of the nations.

Not only are there massive differences between First and Third World cultures, but the missionary born and bred within the American culture is typically deformed by consumerism, individualism, elitism, and the like. Hence, a truly evangelizing inculturation within the culture inhabited by the poor, if it is to be truly a basic option for the poor, requires a profound conversion. The challenge to such conversion is usually most stark in the initial stages of missionary life, but it remains a lifetime imperative.

A primary requisite for such conversion is surely a lived commitment to mutuality in the evangelizing process. The ramifications of mutuality are extensive, touching not only the attitudes of individuals, but the structures and policies of the formation process. Some formation, for example, will occur when First World natives make it their missionary role to receive missionaries from the Third World within an "ebb and flow" or "reverse mission" process. Paolo Freire's "pedagogy of the oppressed," a method created to transform literacy efforts into instruments of social analysis and effective social change, provides both experience and axioms, such as the contrast between "banking" and mutuality attitudes on the part of teachers. Such axioms are more comprehensively applicable to spiritual formation processes (Freire 1972).

A realization of the evangelizing power of the poor brings the learning missioner beyond mutuality to an acknowledgment of the missioner's own need to be enriched through the voices and lives of the poor. It is not fanciful to envisage the poor as God's agents for the spiritual conversion of missionaries. From the standpoint of spiritual formation and spiritual growth, we cannot exaggerate either the challenge or the fruitfulness of total conversion inherent in the transcultural encounter of "rich" and "poor."

Another pregnant metaphor for the spiritual formation process is John Dunne's image, deepened over a period of two decades, of "passing over" (Dunne 1972, 1982; Nilson 1987). The missioner, while remaining faithful to the gospel meanings and values learned within the home context, must still be willing to risk journeying fully into the basic standpoint of another people in another culture. The grace of such a passage, which shares in the death-resurrection character of the paschal mystery, is an enlightenment and enrichment of one's own basic standpoint that could not otherwise be gained. "We can gain insight into our own lives only if we are willing to pass over into the lives of others, for it is only in the moment of passing over into other lives that one has a glimpse of what full enlightenment would be" (Hendricks 1982:15). Hence, "the authentic missioner is one who has the experience of passing over to other lives and discovering always some basis in his or her own life for understanding others . . . one who comes back to him/herself with the insight that the same creative power seems to be at work in time as humankind goes from prehistory to history, as world religions arise, and as humankind in our present time goes from history to world history" (ibid.:67).

208

When this passing over is understood in the context of the option for the poor of other lands, it involves insertion into the culture of the poor not only as this is shaped by social, economic, and political forces, but also and more challengingly as it is defined by the religious traditions, Christian or not, that have provided the symbolic systems, meanings, and values out of which life, death, and resurrection are interpreted and actualized. In other words, missionary conversion or evangelization (inculturation) as a process of spiritual formation includes the risk of passing over into "popular religiosity," the beliefs, devotions, and rituals through which the poor seek and find stamina and relief in recourse to the hidden power of God in history (Pieris 1988). Such a passing over is made all the more difficult by the fact that it not only permits but requires fidelity to the gospel as understood by missioners and their Christian communities. No relativizing of faith in Jesus Christ is allowable, and yet some contingent cultural expressions of that faith in the homeland may need to be relinquished if the conversion — the passing over and return — is to be accomplished.

Such an encounter with the religious culture of the poor has the potential to mediate deep spiritual transformation in the missioner. "What began as an outward journey has become an inner journey to a deeper and more authentic self" (Hendricks 1982:72). Coming to *know* the poor in their lived experience of suffering and powerlessness, and at the same time in the richness derived from their popular religiosity and faith in God, the missioner willing to relinquish and pass over will discover, perhaps in anguish, his or her own poverty before God, but also the unfathomable riches of Christ bestowed only on the poor in spirit.

Thus at the core of a mission spirituality, the faithful missioner is asked to realize the paschal mystery in the missioner's own flesh within the conflictual but mutually enriching encounter of diverse cultures. The alchemy worked by the Spirit, employing especially the hidden power of the poor in history, transforms human striving and human suffering into the gold of a holiness that is at once personal and social, contemplative and apostolic.

Some Specifics of Spiritual Formation

There is space to do little more than name, without extended comment, some implications of the core reflection for the concrete process of spiritual formation.

First, from the wide variety of *psychological resources* available for spiritual formation, we list three particularly valuable ones:

1. The insights and models of developmental psychology, especially as these have been integrated into the perspectives of morality, faith, and spirituality (Erikson 1982; Fowler 1981; Gilligan 1982; Conn 1986)
2. The self-understanding gained through the spiritual use of Jungian personality types as codified by Isabel Briggs Myers (Grant et al. 1983)
3. Adler's analysis of culture shock as a transitional experience (Adler 1975; Hendricks 1982:69-73).

Yet these and similar resources, however valid and useful in themselves, bear within them, at least in their concrete application, some of the hidden assumptions of the United States culture in which they originated. Hence in using such resources missioners must employ a certain degree of "ideological suspicion," being prepared for "passing over" into the culture of the poor. Further, the resources themselves are capable of being both challenged and enriched by the actual experience of overseas mission.

Second, spiritual formation will contain the element of *initiation into varieties of prayer experiences.* Prayer is here understood as comprising not only various solitary exercises but group and liturgical prayer. In all three of these areas the centrality of praying the Scriptures is manifest. The exigencies of passing over into the culture of the poor, as we have described it above, would seem to call for an accent on contemplative forms of prayer, which foster the posture of letting go required by such an encounter. Here both Christian and non-Christian traditions (e.g., Buddhist, Hindu, Islamic, and African religions) are in fact being made available for fostering contemplative depth in missioners and others (de Mello 1978; Griffiths 1983; Johnston 1981, 1986; Pieris 1988b). There is room both in formal programs and throughout a lifetime of missionary insertion for special contemplative times and spaces apart. But if, as we have said, the primary locus of spiritual formation is the actual inculturation within the culture of the poor overseas, spiritual formation needs to develop in missioners an habitual facility in "finding God in all things," particularly through the Christian discernment of spirits, here understood as Spirit-directed apostolic decision (Clarke 1979; Libanio 1982; Spohn 1983). One of the principal resources being retrieved in our own day with a view to guiding such discernment is the

210

tradition of spiritual direction, in which a mentor or companion or even a small group accompanies the missioner searching for divine guidance in the choices by which life is shaped (Barry and Connolly 1982; Edwards 1980; Fischer 1988; Jones 1982; Kelsey 1983; Leech 1977).

Third, the very heart of spiritual formation for mission consists in *an authentic experience of basic community* at home and abroad, realizing the vision of global church as a network of local ecclesial communities (Barreiro 1982; Marins 1983; Boff 1986; Barbé 1987). The basic community is the central realization at once of evangelization, inculturation, and passing over into the culture of the poor, and the spiritual center of the personal and communal quest for God. The indispensable carrier of basic community is a congruous method of pastoral-theological reflection. Such a process, which has been variously structured by such groups as the Maryknoll community and the Center of Concern, employs a holistic model that integrates lived Christian experience, social and cultural analysis, theological reflection, and spiritual/pastoral decision. It is inherently spiritual in character, and its primary intrinsic fruit is the ongoing spiritual conversion of individual members and the community as such (Holland and Henriot 1983; Hug 1983).

Although the liberation of Eastern Europe from Stalinist oppression is an encouraging sign of the times, impasse, conflict, and even violence promise to characterize mission in the twenty-first century no less than in the twentieth. Hence spiritual formation for mission needs to be conceived as *an internship in nonviolence*, where the prospective missioner learns to deal with impasse, cultural despair, and the subtle forms of worldliness that can seduce missioners no less than other Christians (Fitzgerald 1984; Macy 1983; Miller 1964; Douglass 1983). The question here is not merely of helpful techniques for conflict resolution but of the naming of spiritual formation as discipleship to the nonviolent Jesus. Learning to relate to God, to oneself, to other persons, and to society, with both the tender compassion and the firm justice inherent in the gospel, is a whole way of life whose paradigm is the story of Jesus, Lamb of God and Lion of Judah, Servant of Yahweh who does not break the crushed reed or quench the wavering flame, but who will not waver or be crushed until true justice is established on the earth (Isa. 42:3-4).

The faithful missioner, in the measure of God's grace received, will both bring to and draw from the conflictual encounter with the embattled culture of the poor the spirit of the nonviolent Jesus. Our Lord prepared his disciples for contradiction, even persecution. Our age has once again become an age of martyrs and confessors. The term

211

"spiritual formation," in appearance so soft, in fact identifies a tough process of evangelization, inculturation, conversion, and preferential option for the poor, bravely undertaken in the power of the name of Jesus toward the coming of God's reign.

For Further Reading

Adler, Peter S.
1975   "The Transitional Experience: An Alternative View of Culture." *Journal of Humanistic Psychology* 15 (4):13-23.
Bakole Wa, Lunga
1984   *Paths of Liberation: A Third World Spirituality.* Maryknoll, NY: Orbis Books.
Balasuriya, Tisa
1984   *Planetary Theology.* Maryknoll, NY: Orbis Books.
Barbé, Dominique
1987   *Grace and Power: Based Communities and Nonviolence in Brazil.* Maryknoll, NY: Orbis Books.
Barreiro, Alvaro
1982   *Basic Ecclesial Communities: The Evangelization of the Poor.* Maryknoll, NY: Orbis Books.
Barry, William A., and William J. Connolly
1982   *The Practice of Spiritual Direction.* New York: Seabury Press.
Boff, Leonardo
1981   *God's Witnesses in the Heart of the World.* Chicago: Claretian Center for Resources in Spirituality.
1986   *Ecclesiogenesis: The Base Communities Reinvent the Church.* Maryknoll, NY: Orbis Books.
Bosch, David J.
1979   *A Spirituality of the Road.* Scottdale, PA: Herald Press.
Braaten, Carl E.
1977   *The Flaming Center: A Theology of the Christian Mission.* Philadelphia, PA: Fortress Press.
Brown, Robert McAfee
1988   *Spirituality and Liberation: Overcoming the Great Fallacy.* Philadelphia, PA: Fortress Press.
Clarke, Thomas E.
1979   "Public Policy and Christian Discernment." In *Personal Values in Public Policy.* Edited by John C. Haughey. New York: Paulist Press, pp. 212-31.

1988   "Option for the Poor: A Reflection." *America* 158 (4):95-99.

Conn, Walter
1986   *Christian Conversion: A Developmental Interpretation of Autonomy and Surrender.* New York: Paulist Press.

De Mello, Anthony
1978   *Sadhana, A Way to God: Christian Exercises in Eastern Form.* St. Louis, MO: The Institute of Jesuit Sources.

Dorr, Donal
1984   *Spirituality and Justice.* Dublin, Ireland: Gill and Macmillan.

Douglass, James
1983   *Lightning East to West: Jesus, Gandhi, and the Nuclear Age.* New York: Crossroad.

Dunne, John S.
1972   *The Way of All the Earth.* New York: Macmillan Publishing Company.
1982   *The Church of the Poor Devil.* New York: Macmillan Publishing Company.

Dussel, Enrique
1987   "The Ebb and Flow of the Gospel: When the Evangelized Poor Become Evangelizers." *International Review of Mission* 76 (301):48-56.

Edwards, Tilden
1980   *Spiritual Friend: Reclaiming the Gift of Spiritual Direction.* New York: Paulist Press.

Erikson, Erik
1950   *Childhood and Society.* New York: W. W. Norton.
1968   *Identity, Youth, and Crisis.* New York: W. W. Norton.
1982   *The Life Cycle Completed: A Review.* New York: W. W. Norton.

Ferrari, Gabriele
1989   "Mission Challenge in the Nineties." *Sedos* 89 (Feb.):60-71.

Fischer, Kathleen
1988   *Women at the Well: Feminist Perspectives on Spiritual Direction.* New York: Paulist Press.

Fitzgerald, Constance
1984   "Impasse and Dark Night." In *Living with Apocalypse, Spiritual Resources for Social Compassion.* Edited by Tilden Edwards. San Francisco: Harper & Row.

Fowler, James W.
1981   *Stages of Faith: The Psychology of Human Development and the Quest for Meaning.* San Francisco: Harper & Row.

Freire, Paolo
1972   *Pedagogy of the Oppressed.* New York: Herder & Herder.
1973   *Education for Critical Consciousness.* New York: Seabury Press.
Galilea, Segundo
1984   *The Beatitudes: To Evangelize as Jesus Did.* Maryknoll, NY:
            Orbis Books.
Gilligan, Carol
1982   *In a Different Voice: Psychological Theory and Women's Develop-
            ment.* Cambridge, MA: Harvard University Press.
Grant, W. Harold, Magdala Thompson, and Thomas E. Clarke
1983   *From Image to Likeness: A Jungian Path in the Gospel Journey.*
            New York: Paulist Press.
Griffiths, Bede
1983   *The Cosmic Revelation: The Hindu Way to God.* Springfield, IL:
            Templegate Publishers.
Gutiérrez, Gustavo
1984   *We Drink from Our Own Wells: The Spiritual Journey of a People.*
            Maryknoll, NY: Orbis Books.
Happel, Stephan, and James J. Walter
1986   *Conversion and Discipleship: A Christian Foundation for Ethics
            and Doctrine.* Philadelphia: Fortress Press.
Hellwig, Monika K.
1983   "Good News to the Poor: Do They Understand It Better?" In
            *Tracing the Spirit: Communities, Social Action, and Theological
            Reflection.* Edited by James E. Hug. New York: Paulist Press,
            pp. 122-48.
Hendricks, Barbara
1982   "The Exigencies of Global Mission in the Context of Latin
            America Today." Unpublished paper submitted to the faculty
            of the Catholic Theological Union at Chicago.
1989   "Mission in the 1990s." *International Bulletin of Missionary
            Research.* 13 (4):146-49.
Holland, Joseph, and Peter Henriot
1983   *Social Analysis: Linking Faith and Justice.* Maryknoll, NY: Orbis
            Books.
Hug, James E.
1983   *Tracing the Spirit: Communities, Social Action, and Theological
            Reflection.* New York: Paulist Press.
Johnston, William
1981   *Christian Zen: A Way of Meditation.* San Francisco: Harper &
            Row.

1986   *Still Point: Reflections on Zen and Christian Meditation.* New
            York: Fordham University Press.

Jones, Alan W.
1982   *Exploring Spiritual Direction: An Essay on Christian Friendship.*
            New York: Seabury Press.

Jones, Cheslyn, Geoffery Wainwright, and Edward Yarnold
1986   *The Study of Spirituality.* London: S.P.C.K.

Kelsey, Morton
1983   *Companions on the Inner Way: The Art of Spiritual Guidance.*
            New York: Crossroad Publishing Company.

Leech, Kenneth
1977   *Soul Friend: A Study of Spirituality.* London: Sheldon Press.
1981   *The Social God.* London: Sheldon Press.

Libanio, J. B.
1982   *Spiritual Discernment and Politics: Guidelines for Religious Com-
            munities.* Maryknoll, NY: Orbis Books.

Macy, Joanna
1983   *Despair and Personal Power in the Nuclear Age.* Philadelphia:
            New Society Publishers.

Marins, José, et al.
1983   *Basic Ecclesial Communities: The Stand of Third World Bishops.*
            Quezon City, the Philippines: Claretian Publications.

May, Gerald G.
1982   *Care of Mind, Care of Spirit: Psychiatric Dimensions of Spiritual
            Direction.* San Francisco: Harper & Row.

McGinn, Bernard, and John Meyendorff, eds.
1985   "Christian Spirituality: Origins to the Twelfth Century." In
            *World Spirituality: An Encyclopedic History of the Religious
            Quest,* Vol. 16. New York: Crossroad Publishing Company.

de Mello, Anthony — see De Mello, Anthony
Metz, Johannes
1972   "The Future in the Memory of Suffering." In *New Questions
            on God.* Concilium 76. Edited by Johannes Metz. New York:
            Herder & Herder.

Miller, William Robert
1964   *Nonviolence: A Christian Interpretation.* New York: Association
            Press.

Neal, Maria Augusta
1977   *A Socio-Theology of Letting Go: The Role of the First World
            Church Facing Third World Peoples.* New York: Paulist Press.

215

Nilson, Jon
1987   "Doing Theology by Heart: John S. Dunne's Theological
         Method." *Theological Studies* 48 (Mar.):65-86.
Paul VI, Pope
1976   *On Evangelization in the Modern World.* Washington, DC:
         United States Catholic Conference.
Pieris, Aloysius
1988a   *An Asian Theology of Liberation.* Maryknoll, NY: Orbis Books.
1988b   *Love Meets Wisdom: A Christian Experience of Buddhism.* Mary-
         knoll, NY: Orbis Books.
Raguin, Yves
1973   *I Am Sending You: Spirituality of the Missioner.* Manila, the
         Philippines: East Asian Pastoral Institute.
Raitt, Jill
1987   "Saints and Sinners: Roman Catholic and Protestant Spiri-
         tuality in the Sixteenth Century." In *Christian Spirituality,
         High Middle Ages and Reformation.* Edited by Jill Raitt et al.
         (World Spirituality: An Encyclopedic History of the Reli-
         gious Quest, Vol. 17). New York: Crossroad Publishing Com-
         pany, pp. 454-63.
Reilly, Michael Collins
1978   *Spirituality for Mission.* Maryknoll, NY: Orbis Books.
Schneiders, Sandra M.
1989   "Spirituality in the Academy." *Theological Studies* 50 (4):676-97.
Senior, Donald, and Carroll Stuhlmueller
1983   *The Biblical Foundations for Mission.* Maryknoll, NY: Orbis
         Books.
Shorter, Aylward
1978   *African Christian Spirituality.* Maryknoll, NY: Orbis Books.
Snyder, Howard A., and Daniel V. Runyon
Jan. 1987 "Ten Major Trends Facing the Church." *International Bulletin
           of Missionary Research* 11 (Apr.):67-70.
Sobrino, Jon
1988   *Spirituality of Liberation: Toward Political Holiness.* Maryknoll,
         NY: Orbis Books.
Spohn, William C.
1983   "The Reasoning Heart: An American Approach to Christian
         Discernment." *Theological Studies* 44 (Mar.):30-52.
Sudbrack, Josef, et al.
1975   "Spirituality." In *Sacramentum Mundi.* Edited by Karl Rahner
         et al. New York: Herder & Herder, Vol. 5, pp. 147-67.

Ulanov, Ann, and Barry Ulanov
   1982   *Primary Speech: A Psychology of Prayer.* Atlanta: John Knox
               Press.
Wallis, Jim
   1981   *The Call to Conversion.* New York: Harper & Row.

Mission Strategies

Wilbert R. Shenk

Strategy in Mission Studies

Strategy is one of the important themes in mission studies.[1] It focuses on how mission has been carried out and the numerous attempts to form plans for world evangelization (Barrett and Reapsome 1988).

Ambivalence toward Strategy

A certain ambivalence has characterized discussion of strategy in mission studies. Two reasons for this ambivalence come immediately to mind. First, the term "strategy" derives from the Greek *strategos* or "general." The general of an army is the one who forms a comprehensive plan for winning a military objective. This involves the art and science of assembling all necessary resources — political, economic, psychological, and military — to form a strategy. Once a plan is adopted, it is assumed that what remains to be done is to execute this strategy by rigorously following this predetermined plan. In a military campaign the "other" is an enemy who is to be forcibly subdued

---

1. Special thanks to colleagues Roelf S. Kuitse and David A. Shank for reading a first draft of this essay and offering important suggestions.

Wilbert R. Shenk is Associate Professor of Mission at Associated Mennonite Biblical Seminaries in Elkhart, Indiana, and a consultant to the Gospel and Our Culture Programme in Birmingham, England. He was formerly Vice President for Overseas Ministries for the Mennonite Board of Missions.

218

through whatever means are available. Neither the goal nor the means employed in a military operation are appropriate to Christian mission. Second, the very term suggests calculation: a careful weighing of alternatives, searching for the most efficient means based on empirical data. How does such a stance relate to the work of the Holy Spirit? If missionary obedience involves discerning and following God's will, then a healthy tentativeness ought to mark our most carefully laid plans. The history of missions contains many surprises which remind us that, at best, we "know in part" only.

While much has been written over the past two centuries about mission strategy, one is hard pressed to point to biblical and theological explications of strategy (but see David A. Shank 1973; C. P. Wagner 1971:15-47). The failure to provide such theological guidance must be reckoned a serious default.

Strategy Culturally and Historically Conditioned

A strategy always reflects the culture and historical moment in which it is formulated. Just as the way a people wage war is shaped by their culture — in particular their values, worldview, and technology — strategy becomes a projection of the culture of the strategist. Modern mission strategy has been molded by two outstanding features of Western culture.

First, mission strategy has been informed by the philosophy of pragmatism and a concomitant confidence in technique. One of the hallmarks of Western culture for the past four hundred years has been the "scientific method." This powerful methodology has influenced how we in the West study and think. We have been schooled to believe that all phenomena can be investigated by rigorous application of the critical tools of scientific analysis. Such investigation has been carried out in order to expand human knowledge but also for the purpose of gaining control and effecting a solution. We applaud such an approach to problem solving when we are concerned to conquer a dread disease. But not all areas of human experience can be reduced to empirically verifiable categories. Social scientists have been warning Western culture of what it is paying for an uncritical acceptance of the scientific method; the price is the profound alienation found in modern society. In the words of Theodore Roszak, "While the art and literature of our time tell us with ever more desperation that the disease from which our age is dying is that of alienation, the sciences in their relentless pursuit of objectivity raise alienation to its apotheosis as our only means

219

of achieving a valid relationship to reality." Uncritical confidence in the scientific method has led us to believe that whatever is amiss in human affairs can be reduced to a manageable problem, and a problem is there to be solved. This reductionism not only distorts reality but, in the phrase of John V. Taylor, produces "fantasies of omnipotence."[2]

In the second place, the Western approach to strategy has emerged out of a linear view of history, particularly its faith in evolutionary progress. This view of history is now under attack precisely in the West where it has long been regnant (Trompf 1979)[3] The conviction that progress is inevitable and open-ended is now popularly perceived to be misguided in light of the major wars fought in this century at the initiative of peoples who are heirs of the Enlightenment. The continuing threat of military confrontation in many parts of the world and the way our burgeoning technology menaces the ecosystem daily remind us that progress is ambiguous.

Biblical Perspective

Here we can do no more than sketch God's strategy, which follows from the *missio Dei*, as found in the Scriptures. Genesis 1–3 forms a prolegomenon to the rest of Scripture by tying together creation, mission, and redemption. Several themes stand out: God is the subject; the whole of creation is an expression of God's grace and is, therefore, "good." Man and woman are created in God's image and appointed to share in leadership of God's creation. The coming of sin into the world does not alter God's intention for humankind and the created world. God is committed to redeeming the world from its bondage to sin. Even though humankind was expelled from Eden, God gave to the human couple a mission (De Ridder 1983:173-75). The *missio Dei* is moved forward through the prophetic promise of a Messiah. The New Testament reports and interprets the Christ-event as the fulfillment of the messianic promise (Matt. 3:2-3; Luke 2:22-32; 3:4ff.; 4:1-19; John 3:16).

God's strategy may be summarized in terms of three stages:

2. For a preliminary probing of the American penchant for technology see A. F. Walls (1990).

3. Every vision of history can produce distortions and lead to disillusionment. The linear view is no exception. When it loses direction, it forfeits its goal. The biblical vision is linear, with history moving toward culmination in the kingdom of God.

(1) The election and sending of Abraham so that "by you all the families of the earth shall bless themselves" (Gen. 12:3), along with the covenant binding Israel to be the instrument of salvation for the nations. (2) The sending of Jesus Christ (John 1:14) the divinely appointed Messiah, who continues the strategy of *pars pro toto*. (3) The sending of the church as an extension of the mission of Jesus Christ (John 17:18; 20:21). Each "sending" is from a position of vulnerability and weakness in obedience to God's call to bring healing and salvation to all peoples (cf. Deut. 15:15; 16:12; 24:18; 26:5; Phil. 2:5-8; John 17:18).

Several further observations may be made about the messianic strategy as seen in the self-understanding of Jesus and the apostles. Jesus insisted that he "was sent only to the lost sheep of the house of Israel" (Matt. 15:24; 10:5ff.) in spite of the fact that his total mission was to the entire world. In line with this the apostles Paul and Barnabas preached first to the Jews and then to the Gentiles (Acts 13:46-47). As Paul and others moved out in cross-cultural witness, they followed the Jewish Diaspora, and this took them to the urban commercial centers throughout the Mediterranean basin. The Diaspora thus was used by the Spirit for the *missio Dei*.

Theological Framework

The biblical materials suggest a fivefold theological framework for thinking strategically.

Missio Dei: The Source

Mission — the *missio Dei* — has its source in the nature and purpose of God. God the creator is none other than God the redeemer. God's saving purpose can be traced through the calling of Abraham and his descendants into covenant relationship for the blessing of the nations. This saving purpose is expressed supremely in the sending of God the Son to be the Savior of the world. God's saving strategy stands over all history (Vicedom 1965; Berkhof 1966) and points to the goal, the kingdom of God. Certain statements of the *missio Dei* have been indispensable in sustaining faith in God's purposes and hope for the consummation. Isaiah projected this vision — "For the earth shall be full of the knowledge of the Lord as the waters cover the sea" (11:9) and there will be "new heavens and a new earth" (65:17; cf. II Pet. 3:13). John's Revelation depicts the outcome of God's redemptive program

— shalóm — in which the unity the peoples of the world could not achieve is now realized through God's gracious provision in Jesus Christ (5:9-10 and 7:9-11). The picture is filled out in 21:1-7. These vision statements have both present and future dimensions. The Christ-event demonstrates and fulfills the *missio Dei*.

Jesus Christ: The Embodiment

The Old Testament introduces the notion that God's redemptive strategy is tied to the coming of the Messiah (Isa. 11:1-9; 42:1-4, 53; 61:1-3). The Synoptic Gospels emphasize the continuity between Old and New Testaments — that which was promised is now being fulfilled (Luke 4:16-19). When the incarnate God enters the human scene, it is as a baby (John 1:14), signifying both identification and vulnerability. Jesus inaugurates his public ministry by proclaiming the reign of God (Matt. 4:17; Mark 1:15) and embodies that reign, demonstrating its power and interpreting its meaning for the lives of his listeners. That embodiment projected a new way of being. He came as one who serves and who was self-emptying (Phil. 2:5-8), but his was a transforming presence. "From his ministry emerged a new people from and in the midst of all nations," observes David Shank. "Through that strategy of persuasion through his suffering Servant, God created a like-minded people who are servant to all peoples for their blessing and salvation. The strategy of Christian mission is nothing more — nor less — than participation in carrying out God's own strategy. Its shape is that of a cross" (Shank 1973). The risen Christ commissions that "like-minded people" to continue the mission of redemption in his name (Matt. 28:18-20; John 20:19-22). They will take their strategic clues from their Messiah leader. The coming of the Messiah leads to crisis and calls for decision. Stephen represented to the religious leaders the Christ-figure. This they rejected and, consequently, martyred Stephen (Acts 6:1–8:1). Later Paul would interpret his own *metanoia* in light of that martyr witness to Jesus Christ (Acts 22:17-21).

Holy Spirit: The Power

Building on the work of Roland Allen, Harry R. Boer in *Pentecost and Missions* (1961) demonstrated how central the Holy Spirit is to mission. The Spirit is the primary agent of the mission of the Messiah. Missionary obedience is first of all an act of submission to the leadership of the Holy Spirit. Strategic thinking ought to begin and end with the prayer

"Your will be done." Within this ambit there is ample space for the hard thinking involved in strategy-making, but it will be held in check by the awareness that the Holy Spirit is sovereign. Because mission is the will of God, the Holy Spirit is the driving force in mission. It is the primary purpose of the Spirit that the messianic reign be actualized. In our strategizing we can depend on the Spirit to slough off that which is unworthy of Christ.

Church: The Instrument

At each stage the sending is for the purpose of bringing blessing to the nations. In his life and ministry Jesus Christ has modeled all that it means to embody the life of God. It results in a new community that is characterized by shalom and a passion to extend life to the nations across lines of race, class, sex, and nationality. Thus the church continually draws on that model for its own ministry. That which does not build the new community must be rejected. Actions that produce alienation or bondage are contrary to the gospel. *who took X's way serious*

Throughout history, mission has been fulfilled by those communities for whom the Christ-event was normative: monastic orders, Anabaptists, Moravian Brethren, Pietist ecclesiola in ecclesia, Wesleyans, and Pentecostals. In these groups the Holy Spirit found openness to the reordering of congregational life for mission. It is in these groups that the priesthood of all believers began to be recovered together with the range of Spirit-given charisms.

I don't see th Presbyterian et among them, but will it be me a note w hist?

Cultures: The Context

Strategic thinking that is consistent with the other elements of this framework will respect the varied contexts of mission. All cultures can be the means through which a people hear the gospel "in their own tongue." The Apostle Paul insisted that he was prepared to "become all things to all people" in order that they might hear the gospel. Strategic thinking based on master plans far removed from a particular context must be treated with great suspicion. Vincent Donovan's attempt to reach the Masai by abandoning the conventional missions system in favor of a strategy attuned to Masai culture points us in the right direction (Donovan 1978). Other examples can be found in the history of missions where missionaries rejected "cultural diffusion" in favor of finding ways to "translate the message" into the language and culture of a people (Sanneh 1989).

223

Strategy in Early Christian History

Absence of Early Christian Strategizing

Primitive Christianity has been the scene of fresh and creative scholarly investigation in recent years. That the early church grew and extended itself on a surprising scale is a matter of agreement. But scholars remain divided as to the causes of this growth. What can be said is that there was no grand strategy and no central command (Kreider 1990). In a perhaps too categorical statement, Robin Lane Fox insists that "we cannot name a single active Christian missionary between St. Paul and the age of Constantine" (Lane Fox 1986:282). Yet the faith spread — by sheer force of its inner logic and dynamic. It had captured the loyalty-to-the-death of the rank and file, and it was they who were the vanguard of evangelization. The early Christians believed themselves to be the community of the Holy Spirit in which gifts of ministry were given for missionary witness.

As already noted, the New Testament gives us no basis for speaking of strategy in conventional terms. The Great Commission defines how the church is to understand itself in relation to the world: the church is to be a sign of God's reign and a witness to the world of the full scope of God's redemptive purpose in history. Yet it does not instruct the church concerning strategy and tactics for fulfilling this mandate.

Implicit Ecclesial Strategy

In addition to the overarching theological strategy noted above, there is an implicit ecclesial strategy found in Acts 11:19-26 and 13:1-3. The first passage is remarkable for the fact that it can report that "a great number" and "a large company" had "turned to the Lord," but there is no honor roll informing us of the leaders who masterminded this remarkable result. In response to the martyrdom of Stephen and the ensuing persecution of the church in Jerusalem, believers had scattered to places like Antioch, imbued with passion to tell the news about Jesus Christ. This result appears to have been growth from the grass roots by a process of cell division. The Holy Spirit inspired these disciples to tell family, friends, and neighbors of their faith so that the church grew.

Acts 13:1-3 introduces a contrasting pattern. The Holy Spirit instructs the Antiochene church to "set apart" two leaders who will lead the church in cross-cultural mission. Paul subsequently describes his apostolic calling as being directed to "the Gentiles" (Acts 15:12) in order "to bring about the obedience of faith . . . among all the nations" (Rom. 1:5).

224

These strategies arise out of a pneumatically empowered ecclesiology. The two patterns are complementary; neither is complete without the other. In the recorded history of the church the second claims the bulk of attention — focused as it is on a select group of heroic figures undertaking daring expeditions and crossing geographical and cultural barriers. But there are periods in the history of the church when the spread of the faith depended entirely on the unsung faithfulness of ordinary folk doing what the first believers at Antioch had done. Even in periods such as the nineteenth century when commitment to cross-cultural mission was renewed and missionaries went "to the ends of the earth," much of the work on the ground was done by local evangelists, catechists, and laypeople speaking and acting the gospel.

Emergence of New Understanding

By the fourth century A.D. the position of the church in society had undergone important changes. It had been transformed from a marginalized and persecuted minority into the religion favored by the state. With this had come a new understanding of the nature of the church. Instead of taking the incarnation and the cross as the model for strategizing, the church now looked to the political-military realm. And the nature of mission changed accordingly. It was as though the church took the Holy Spirit captive. The effects of this shift are well illustrated by the way Charlemagne went about conquering and Christianizing the peoples of Europe, drawing his inspiration from Augustine's *De Civitate Dei* (Latourette 1953:355 and 1970 II:102ff.). The forced conversion of the peoples of Europe posed no difficulties for Charlemagne and other so-called Christian rulers. Their strategy was dictated by the military model. This model continued to exert pervasive influence on strategic thinking in Christendom.[4]

The Quest for Strategy in Modern Missions

William Carey and Rufus Anderson

Modern missions have been driven by the quest for effective strategies. The operative concept is adumbrated in the title of William Carey's

---

4. Richard V. Pierard has analyzed how contemporary evangelical mission strategy draws freely on military metaphors (1990).

manifesto, *An Enquiry Into the Obligation of Christians, To Use Means for the Conversion of the Heathens,* published in 1792. Carey sought to press on the Christian public their duty to marshall the resources necessary to fulfill "the Commission given by our Lord." He did this, in part, by working out an empirical basis for prosecuting the task and then proposing such practical steps as the founding of missionary societies.

A generation later in 1837 Rufus Anderson, secretary of the American Board of Commissioners for Foreign Missions (ABCFM), preached a sermon, "The Time for the World's Conversion Come" (Beaver 1967: 59-70). Anderson advanced a threefold argument as to why this was now "the fullness of the time" of the Holy Spirit as viewed in the epochs of biblical prophecy. He asserted that only now was the way open for the "universal propagation of the gospel" in terms of three propositions. (1) Although Christians in previous epochs were faithful in their witness, they lacked the necessary knowledge and means to evangelize all nations. (2) Only now, insisted Anderson, were the "evangelical churches of Christendom" organized "with a view to the conversion of the world." (3) Not until the nineteenth century, argued Anderson, did the churches have "a commanding system of missions abroad, designed expressly for the conversion of the world." Lurking behind Anderson's argument are important cultural assumptions.

Between the publication of Carey's *Enquiry* in 1792 and Anderson's sermon in 1837, several proposals had already been made for comprehensive world evangelization, including two schemes by missionaries of Anderson's own ABCFM in 1818 and 1836. Missionaries Gordon Hall and Samuel Newell working in India's Bombay area proposed in 1818 that the world be evangelized by the sending of thirty thousand Protestant missionaries from the West to the rest of the world within the next twenty-one years to be supported with gifts averaging four dollars per Protestant and Anglican communicant. In 1837 the ABCFM passed a resolution at its annual meeting — echoing the 1836 appeal from its Sandwich Islands missionaries — proposing a worldwide evangelization effort.

The Role of Missionary Conferences

During the first several decades of the modern missions movement strategy was formulated largely by missionary societies within their own sphere of work. The main vehicle for sharing with other agencies and their missionaries was the missions magazines most societies published.

In 1854 an important new instrument for developing mission strategy was introduced. That year the famed Scottish missionary to India, Alexander Duff, visited North America and made a triumphal procession to several regions of the United States and Canada. His visit culminated in the convening of the Union Missionary Convention in New York City, November 4-5, 1854. Duff dominated the proceedings, which were organized around eight topics (Union Missionary Convention 1854; Ecumenical Missionary Conference 1900:19-23). This first effort was modest when compared to later efforts, but it was a model for future gatherings. The first question was: "To what extent are we authorized by the Word of God to expect the conversion of the world to Christ?" A second group of questions dealt with strategy. The third centered on issues of cultivating support for missions in the congregations.

In the following years missionary conferences became a standard part of the missions system. These consisted of several kinds: (1) national gatherings, such as the Union Missionary Convention, of mission boards, their staffs, pastors, and missions supporters; (2) major field conferences convened by a board with its missionary staff (as Rufus Anderson and A. C. Thompson did in India and Ceylon, 1854-56); (3) ecumenical and international conferences such as that held in London in 1888 and, most recently, Lausanne II in Manila in 1989; (4) a conference of all missions working in a particular country such as those held in China in 1877, 1906, and 1926.

Comparing the proceedings of these early conferences with those of a century later, one notes the similarity in pattern. To be sure, preparation for conferences becomes more elaborate and the use of statistical surveys and data increases in sophistication. The 1974 Lausanne Congress gave high priority to strategizing world evangelization. Probably the most significant conceptual contribution to missionary strategy in the twentieth century is the notion of "hidden" or "unreached" people groups introduced at the Lausanne Congress and since promoted worldwide (Winter 1984:17-60). But not all observers have been comfortable with the Lausanne emphasis and ethos. Charles E. Van Engen, in evaluating the congress, noted that "the mood seemed to be one of pragmatism: 'anything goes — if it works.' The fact that World Vision's highly technological MARC Center was a major consultant to the congress was a signal that the evangelicals were moving into hi-tech culture" (Van Engen 1990:222). To be sure, not all conferences over these years have had the same balance, but strategy has been a central concern.

227

"Toward the Year 2000"

As was true a century ago, the approaching end of the twentieth century, which also coincides with the end of another millennium since Jesus Christ, has given rise to an outpouring of proposals for world evangelization at the rate of one new plan per week. Some of these plans draw their inspiration from special views of biblical prophecy while others trumpet the triumphalist spirit of the High Imperial period a century ago. Still other plans are based on the traditional concern of missionary agencies to continue evangelizing the world.

According to David Barrett and James Reapsome, however, the effort is "in a mess" (Barrett and Reapsome 1988:65). Surveying the whole of Christian history Barrett and Reapsome identify 788 separate plans that have been produced since the time of Jesus. They insist: "We have not obeyed the Commission in the past; we are not obeying it in the present; we are not, on present trends, likely to obey it in the future; we are nowhere near target for fulfilling it by A.D. 2000" (ibid.). In spite of such strictures, plans and proposals continue to be spawned. Two themes predominate: (1) we are in a "countdown," and (2) the world can be evangelized by the end of this century. Neither notion can be supported from Scripture. Barrett and Reapsome react ambivalently toward what they call "a global evangelization movement." On the one hand, they are critical of many of these plans, both past and present; but they believe it is possible to produce a global strategy, including a centrally monitored "master global plan," which would enable "fulfilling the Great Commission by the year 2000" (ibid. 64).

Countervailing Currents

There have long been countervailing views with regard to strategy of mission. One of the most vigorous critics of the missions system during the past century was Roland Allen. Allen was the gadfly of missions, and his criticisms were not welcomed by the mainstream. But his influence has been felt widely because of the way the fledgling Pentecostal missions movement adopted key Allen ideas. Allen took aim at modern missions for being overly institutionalized. He jibed at missions for being preoccupied with "activities" while lacking "manifestations of the Spirit." Always at the heart of Allen's concern was the impact the system had ultimately on the new church. "The spiritual force, the

Holy Ghost," wrote Allen, "will be manifested to the people of any country to which we go when they see that Spirit ministered by us manifested in the spontaneous activity of their own countrymen", (Allen 1960:112). He judged the modern missions system to be a blunt) instrument.

The father of German missiology, Gustav Warneck, was also well known for his criticism of what he considered the misguided Anglo-American preoccupation with closely calculated plans and slogans. He called the SVM slogan, "The Evangelization of the World in this Generation," dangerous. "The mission command bids us 'go' into all the world, not 'fly,'" declared Warneck to the Ecumenical Missionary Conference in 1900. He referred sarcastically to the watchword as the "catchword" and rejected all attempts to "specify a time within which the evangelization of the world is to be completed" (Ecumenical Conference 1900:I:290).

A particularly interesting critic of conventional views of mission strategy was J. H. Oldham. He occupied a central role in the World Missionary Conference at Edinburgh in 1910, was founding editor of the *International Review of Missions* in 1912, and a close associate of figures like John R. Mott, one of the greatest mission strategists in the modern period. Although he does not acknowledge any indebtedness to Roland Allen, Oldham makes some of the same points. In *The World and the Gospel*, Oldham argues, "It has often been taken for granted that the aim of foreign missions is to preach the Gospel to the whole world. The bringing of the Gospel within the reach of all mankind is the goal towards which the Church must continually strive with all its might. But it is not the immediate aim of foreign missions, because it is something which foreign missions can never accomplish" (Oldham 1916:139). In words that combine elements of Warneck and Allen, Oldham said, "The life of the spirit cannot be measured or described in terms of arithmetic." He emphasized the importance of both the Spirit and the local church in furthering world evangelization without devaluing the role of the missionary. "The aim, then, of foreign missionary work is to plant the Church of Christ in every part of the non-Christian world as a means to its evangelization," Oldham insisted (ibid. 141).

In a wide-ranging analysis of how North American Protestants have created mission strategy in the twentieth century, Robert T. Coote faults the present generation of strategists for being guided more by "management by objectives" than the Holy Spirit and devising grandiose plans that are bound to fail. He objects to those who presume to know precisely the mind and timetable of God. Coote's counsels of caution and humility are timely (Coote 1986).

The Strategic Challenge

In 1961 Joseph T. Bayly wrote *The Gospel Blimp*, a satire on overweening confidence in technology as a means of evangelization. The church in the West is tempted by technique — the ultimate manifestation of modernity. The temptation is to view technique as itself gospel. Strategy as technique is thus confused with the message. It is of urgent necessity that mission strategy and method be subjected to theological critique.

First, more than we may admit, our culture is dominated by the "rationality" of the scientific method. This is powerful, but it is also the source of alienation. The missionary who is surrounded with sophisticated technological apparatus can be formidable vis-à-vis people who live in poverty. Mission strategy becomes an extension of that powerful system in a way contrary to the vulnerability of the cross. Second, the final years of the 1980s were full of surprises. The breakdown of totalitarian systems caught many off guard. There is growing evidence that the Christian faith is most vital, both in quantity and quality, in those countries and regions where martyrdom has been visited on the church. Conversely, the faith has been coopted by culture and has become flaccid in those parts of the world where there has been maximum freedom and affluence.

Strategic thinking that is theologically informed and critiqued will keep in view the fivefold framework presented above: the *missio Dei* as the source; Jesus Christ who embodied fully God's intention in mission; the Holy Spirit who is the source of power; the church as God's instrument in mission; and human culture as the medium through which all communication of the gospel must be made. Two pitfalls must be avoided if our strategizing is to be faithful to the gospel. First, we are being urged to make one or another emphasis the key to strategy: option for the poor, dialogue, pluralism, evangelism, development. Each one contains an important dimension but is itself only partial. Only when these dimensions are placed within the strategy of the Messiah outlined above can they be saved from distortion. Second, when we uncritically appropriate strategies from sociopolitical models around us, we risk denaturing the gospel by choosing means inconsistent with the goal of mission. The Christ-event holds ever before us the cross as the fundamental strategy by which all other strategies must be judged.

230

What Then Shall We Say about Mission Strategy?

In the world the Christian mission is subject both to the divine imperative and the sociohistorical forces that give it context. As we approach the end of the twentieth century, that context is again undergoing fundamental shifts. The bipolar world of the past forty-five years has disintegrated with the collapse of the old structures of much of the Soviet bloc. At the same time new centers of economic and political influence have emerged, with still others in the making. In terms of the Christian church, for more than a decade we have been reflecting on the fact that its center of gravity — measured in membership — has shifted from the West to the rest of the world. However, the church in the West continues to control the bulk of financial and institutional resources.

It would be foolhardy to try to predict the direction Christian mission will go in the next generation. We can, however, make several observations as to the terms and conditions with which we will be working. (1) The ideal relationship for the world Christian community is one of interdependence with a recognized system for shared decision-making and resource allocation. Until that is resolved there will continue to be tensions and resource imbalances. (2) The churches in Africa, Asia, and Latin America presently demonstrate greater vitality and growing missionary commitment, but they tend to be resource poor. This suggests that the ecclesial — rather than the cross-cultural — strategy will predominate over the next couple of decades. (3) The experience of the suffering church since World War I holds important insights concerning the role of the Holy Spirit in the mission of the church and a missionary ecclesiology. Gleaning such insights is foundational to a theologically informed missiology.

For Further Reading

Allen, Roland
    1960   *The Ministry of the Spirit: Selected Writings of Roland Allen.*
            Grand Rapids, MI: Wm. B. Eerdmans Publishing Company.
Barrett, David B., ed.
    1982   *World Christian Encyclopedia.* Nairobi: Oxford University
            Press.
Barrett, David B., and James W. Reapsome
    1988   *Seven Hundred Plans to Evangelize the World: The Rise of a Global*
            Evangelization Movement. Birmingham, AL: New Hope.

Beaver, R. Pierce, ed.

1967   *To Advance the Gospel: Selections from the Writings of Rufus Anderson.* Grand Rapids, MI: Wm. B. Eerdmans Publishing Company.

1970   "The History of Mission Strategy." *Southwestern Journal of Theology* 12 (2) (Spring):7-28.

Berkhof, Hendrikus

1966   *Christ the Meaning of History.* Richmond, VA: John Knox Press.

Boer, Harry R.

1961   *Pentecost and Missions.* Grand Rapids, MI: Wm. B. Eerdmans Publishing Company.

Conference on Missions (Liverpool)

1860   London: James Nisbet.

Coote, Robert T.

1986   "Taking Aim on 2000 A.D." In *Mission Handbook.* Edited by Samuel Wilson and John Siewert. Monrovia, CA: MARC, pp. 35-80.

Dayton, Edward R., and David A. Fraser

1980   *Planning Strategies for World Evangelization.* Grand Rapids, MI: Wm. B. Eerdmans Publishing Company.

Dayton, Edward R., and Samuel Wilson, eds.

1982   *Unreached Peoples '82 — Focus on Urban Peoples.* Elgin, IL: David C. Cook Publishing Company.

1983   *Unreached Peoples '83 — The Refugees Among Us.* Monrovia, CA: MARC.

1984   *Unreached Peoples '84 — The Future of World Evangelization.* Monrovia, CA: MARC.

De Ridder, Richard R.

1983   "The Old Testament Roots of Mission." In *Exploring Church Growth.* Edited by Wilbert R. Shenk. Grand Rapids, MI: Wm. B. Eerdmans Publishing Company, pp. 171-80.

Donovan, Vincent J.

1978   *Christianity Rediscovered: An Epistle from the Masai.* Notre Dame, IN: Fides/Claretian.

Ecumenical Missionary Conference

1900   New York: Religious Tract Society. 2 vols.

Kreider, Alan

1990   "The Growth of the Early Church: Reflections on Recent Literature." *Mission Focus* 18 (Sept.):3.

Lane Fox, Robin

1986   *Pagans and Christians.* New York: Alfred A. Knopf.

Latourette, Kenneth Scott
1953   *A History of Christianity.* New York: Harper & Brothers.
1970   *A History of the Expansion of Christianity.* Grand Rapids, MI: The Zondervan Corporation, Vol. 2.

Neill, Stephen C.
1970   "Strategy for Missions." In *Concise Dictionary of the Christian World Mission.* Edited by Stephen C. Neill, et al. London: United Society for Christian Literature/Lutterworth Press.

Oldham, J. H.
1916   *The World and the Gospel.* London: United Council for Missionary Education.

Pierard, Richard V.
1990   "Pax Americana and the Evangelical Missionary Advance." In *Earthen Vessels: American Evangelical Missions, 1880-1980.* Edited by Joel A. Carpenter and Wilbert R. Shenk. Grand Rapids, MI: Wm. B. Eerdmans Publishing Company, pp. 155-79.

Sanneh, Lamin
1989   *Translating the Message: The Missionary Impact on Culture.* Maryknoll, NY: Orbis Books.

Shank, David A.
1973   "The Shape of Mission Strategy." *Mission Focus* 1 (3):1-7 (republished in *Mission Focus: Current Issues.* Edited by Wilbert R. Shenk. Scottdale, PA: Herald Press, 1980, 118-28).

Trompf, G. W.
1979   "The Future of Macro-Historical Ideas." *Soundings* 62 (1):70-89.

Union Missionary Convention
1854   *Proceedings of the Union Missionary Convention held in New York, May 4-5, 1854. Together with the address of the Rev. Dr. Duff.* New York: Taylor and Hogg.

Van Engen, Charles E.
1990   "A Broadening Vision: Forty Years of Evangelical Theology of Mission." In *Earthen Vessels: American Evangelical Missions, 1880-1980.* Edited by Joel A. Carpenter and Wilbert R. Shenk. Grand Rapids, MI: Wm. B. Eerdmans Publishing Company, pp. 203-32.

Vicedom, George F.
1965   *The Mission of God.* St. Louis, MO: Concordia Press.

Wagner, C. Peter
1971   *Frontiers in Missionary Strategy.* Chicago: Moody Press.

Wagner, C. Peter, and Edward R. Dayton, eds.

1979   *Unreached Peoples '79 — The Challenge of the Church's Unfinished Business.* Elgin, IL: David C. Cook Publishing Company.

1980   *Unreached Peoples '80 — The Challenge of the Church's Unfinished Business.* Elgin, IL: David C. Cook Publishing Company.

1981   *Unreached Peoples '81 — The Challenge of the Church's Unfinished Business.* Elgin, IL: David C. Cook Publishing Company.

Walls, A. F.

1990   "The American Dimension in the History of the Missionary Movement." In *Earthen Vessels: American Evangelical Missions, 1880-1980.* Edited by Joel A. Carpenter and Wilbert R. Shenk. Grand Rapids, MI: Wm. B. Eerdmans Publishing Company.

Winter, Ralph D.

1984   "Unreached Peoples: The Development of a Concept" and "Unreached Peoples: What Are They and Where Are They?" In *Reaching the Unreached — the Old-New Challenge.* Edited by Harvie M. Conn. Phillipsburg, NJ: Presbyterian and Reformed Publishing Company, pp. 17-60.

Contextualization in Mission

Donald R. Jacobs

Nairobi, Sunday morning. Contextualization of the gospel in progress!
Business-suited parishioners gather at the marvelous cathedral. Up the
street comes an animated little string of robed enthusiasts of the African
Church of the Holy Spirit, moving to their outdoor place of worship
where they beat their drums, worship, and hopefully heal the sick.
Within earshot the Legion of Mary, an offshoot of the Roman Catholic
Church, is about to say the Mass, in Latin. New forms and expressions
of the Christian faith are appearing as regularly, and as predictably, as
the harvests.

Churches on all continents are now struggling with the age-old
question: How does the gospel of Jesus Christ relate to the cultures of
mankind? Our starting point is Jesus Christ himself.

The Gospel in a Hostile Spiritual World

Jesus Christ laid out the problem in its stark dimensions. He recognized the rule of Satan over societies and the willful disobedience of
our race. It was into this hostile milieu that Jesus came, God in human
flesh. Rejected, he confided to his disciples, "If the world hates you,

---

Donald R. Jacobs is Executive Director of the Mennonite Christian Leadership Foundation near Lancaster, Pennsylvania. He served as a Mennonite
missionary in Tanzania and Kenya (1953-73), and then was Director of
Overseas Ministries of the Eastern Mennonite Board of Missions.

keep in mind that it hated me first. If you belonged to the world, it would love you as its own. As it is, you do not belong to the world, but I have chosen you out of the world. That is why the world hates you" (John 15:18-19, NIV). Every believing community, he insisted, lives its life of faith in an essentially unfriendly environment because Christians are players in the cosmic spiritual battle in which the forces of evil are intent on drawing people away from God. This spiritual conflict undergirds every act, thought, and teaching of Jesus Christ and the apostles.

The Gospel in Human Cultures

But the gospel also enters living, dynamic cultures. The question is: Are human cultures friends or enemies of Christianity? The answer is both. As the recipient of natural revelation no society is bereft of divine grace. This is evidenced in the fact that in all cultures many themes, values, institutions, and behavioral patterns are consistent with the revelation of the will of God as found in the Scriptures. Likewise it is evident that all cultures contain some elements that are not at all in harmony with the gospel. It matters little whether one lives in a culture that prides itself on being "Christian" or in a culture newly introduced to Jesus Christ. The gospel is and always will be an intrusion into our cultures; it is an ever new sociological innovation. Visser 't Hooft declared that even in the West, the major themes are contrary to those of the gospel (Visser 't Hooft 1963).

Even though cultures are imperfect and often hostile, they are the contexts in which Jesus Christ meets people by grace. Lamin Sanneh reminds us that the gospel moved out of the language spoken by Jesus and his disciples into the arena of Greek. And everywhere that the gospel has been taken since then, enthusiastic evangelists have assumed that any culture can be host to Jesus Christ. A marked difference between Christian and Muslim expansion is that Christians believed the language of the people could fully express and respond to the gospel. Muslims insisted upon retaining the Qur'an in Arabic. In contrast the entire Bible now appears in over 260 languages. As Jesus Christ lived his life within the confines of a cultural context, so can the gospel find a home in any human culture in the world. This might be called the incarnational mode of contextualization.

Culture and Gospel

What is the relationship between the revealed gospel and human cultures? This was the question posed by H. Richard Niebuhr, in his classic *Christ and Culture* (1951). Is Christ *against* culture, *of* it, *above* it, or is he in a *paradoxical relationship to* culture? Does Jesus *transform* culture? This question had been posed before; but in the post-war setting in which Niebuhr wrote, the issue became dramatically clear. His concerns were not missiological because he was addressing the problems of the West; but missiologists have found his work helpful.

Modern Western missions coincided with the expansion of Western colonialism. Mission societies felt obliged to pursue a dual mandate, an evangelizing one and a "civilizing" one. The interests of missions and colonizers blended on the "civilizing" point. At that time the West was making major advances in medicine, technology, education, industry, and agricultural production. Those who were concerned with the civilizing effects of mission pressed for the introduction of programs that were unapologetically "Western," such as formal education, medical programs both to prevent and to cure illness, improved agricultural techniques, industrial programs, structures for administering the new churches, and the like. The worldview undergirding these Western programs was usually in conflict with major facets of the local worldview. But that did not seem to concern the eager exporters of Western culture.

The "dual mandate" motif, when applied to local churches, meant that new Christians were expected to abandon their cultures and their worldviews. Becoming Christian was synonymous with becoming Western.

Within the newly believing communities this was a welcome solution. By moving into the Western/Christian subculture that surrounded mission activities, they could consolidate their new faith in Jesus Christ. This gave them time to sort out how they should relate to their cultures. Furthermore, by participating in the "mission culture" believers found a new status and a power that they did not have before. The fact that they were abandoned by their cultures was offset by the security they felt in their new subcultures.

The creation of subcultures as a first stage in establishing a movement is consistent with social theory. It is also true that in later stages those communities usually develop a modus operandi with the dominant culture. That normally occurs when it is no longer to their advantage to participate in an "alienated" subculture.

Many of the more discerning missionaries and mission societies had basic misgivings about the emergence of a Christianity that was so closely connected culturally to the West. In Korea, for example, in the 1890s, John L. Nevius was instrumental in helping the church be truly Korean. He encouraged Christians, even leaders, to remain in their occupation so that they could serve their churches without charge. The structure of the church was to be just enough for the local congregation to carry, and only evangelists working away from home were to receive remuneration, and that only if the church could afford it. He also taught that the people should build their own churches according to native custom (Kane 1971).

Indigenization and Contextualization

It was Henry Venn and Rufus Anderson, in the last century, who unfurled this theme and established the "three-self" goals that have served as the guiding principles of those determined to indigenize the gospel in local cultures. These pioneer missiologists insisted that unless the new churches were truly indigenous they would not survive. Modern missiologists are bothered by the deficiencies in the three-self proposition. Paul Hiebert noted that another "self" should have been "self-theologizing" (Hiebert 1985:195-96), and Alan Tippett lists six (Tippett 1987:378-81). Nevertheless, all agree that if proper indigenizing principles are applied, the church should be a viable, relevant, prophetic force in its culture. This guiding principle has served the expansion of the church of Jesus Christ very well. Its most glaring weakness became evident, however, when churches attained the three-self goal yet persisted as foreign institutions. Surely an indigenous church must reflect the sociological context in which it lives. In order to broaden the concept, we have begun to use the term "contextualization"; it embraces the dynamics of social change processes within cultures.

Almost all missionaries of that early era embraced the concept of indigenization. It was not a divisive term. Contextualization, however, has become another matter. The conciliar movement picked up the idea of contextualization and ran with it, largely because it fit into the theological streams then flowing, particularly the Hegelian dialectic that insisted that only where theory meets context, in the praxis, can truth be known. Additionally, the new process theology welcomed the idea of contextualization because it promised ongoing discoveries in theological reflection. Evangelical missiologists, however, shied away from

238

using the term "contextualization" because they perceived that those of a more liberal persuasion were using it in almost exclusively socio-political terms. Furthermore, they felt that if context set the stage for mission, then the Bible must fit into that rather than the other way around.

The Theological Education Fund of the WCC issued its *Ministry in Context* in 1972. It states:

> It [contextualization] means all that is implied in the familiar term "indigenization" and yet seeks to press beyond. Contextualization has to do with how we assess the peculiarity of third world contexts. Indigenization tends to be used in the sense of responding to the Gospel in terms of a traditional culture. Contextualization, while not ignoring this, takes into account the process of secularity, technology, and the struggle for human justice, which characterizes the historical moment of nations in the Third World.

Bruce Fleming traces the development of the contextualizing stances of evangelicals and those of a more liberal bent in his important work *Contextualization of Theology* (Fleming 1980). He is very unhappy with the TEF formulation. He writes, "Contextualization as defined by them [TEF] implies that *context* in some way becomes part of the *content* of the Word" (Fleming 1980:66). Fleming calls the work of the TEF "political theology." He echoed the anxiety of many evangelicals. They felt uneasy about a theology that placed Bible and context on the same level. For them the Scripture is unapologetically prior to context and indeed something "other."

Having said that, all agree that contextualization, or as Fleming puts it, "context-indigenizing of theology" (Fleming 1980:74) must be done if the church is to be truly the salt and light that Jesus Christ meant it to be. It is unfortunate that the term "contextualization" should have become a bone of contention because it has taken our eyes off the task of developing local theologies. After all, the current contextualization debate is in reality a debate about biblical hermeneutics and soteriology, both legitimate issues. There is no reason why we cannot refurbish the word and employ it in both evangelism and in the life and ministry of the church.

Cross-cultural evangelists or missionaries employ all of their wit and resources to present Jesus Christ to the hearers or observers so that they get a non-distorted picture of who he is and what he can be for them. In a way, this is the first step in contextualization because it has to do with translation, functional substitutes, and all of the other concepts that missionaries are now taught. But even at their best, cross-cultural evangelists have not been noted for their ability truly to contextualize the gospel. Yet as long as people witness to Jesus Christ in cultures not their own they must do their best.

Contextualization and the Theologizing Community

Contextualization is best done by local churches. When missionaries try to do the contextualizing they often miss the mark. In my own missionary career I recall how insistent some of us missionaries were that the local people write their own hymns with local tunes and that they, as a matter of urgency, should employ traditional drumming in their worship services. These seemed to be self-evident improvements. Local hymnody did come — like a storm — but twenty years later, in its time.

Marc Spindler observed, "When Western theologians have given voice to their expectation of an Africanizing or indigenizing of theology, they have met with very marked reserve on the part of the indigenous theologians. Their expectation is considered to be both an incitement to heresy and an insufferable sign of paternalism" (quoted in Von Allmen 1975).

Authentic contextualization is the responsibility of the local believing community. They set the agenda, and they must discern the times. Missionaries at their best should simply be loving encouragers. Often the best contextualizing happens when there is no missionary presence at all such as in China from 1949 until the present.

Von Allmen asserts, "No true 'indigenization or contextualization' can take place because foreigners, the 'missionaries,' suggest it; on the contrary, true indigenization takes place only because the 'indigenous' church has itself become truly missionary, with or without the blessing of the 'missionaries'" (Von Allmen 1975:39).

All Christian communities do not do their theology in the same way. In the West, it seems, we do not believe that a theological idea is truly expressed until it is written, footnotes and all, by a qualified theologian. Yet the development of theology in many of the churches of the world, certainly those in East Africa, is done first and foremost through structures: storytelling, art forms, rituals, symbols, and by emphasizing meaningful themes. On a recent trip to the area in Tanzania where I had the privilege of serving as bishop in the 1960s I found that great changes had taken place. In the few days that I was there I heard dozens of songs that I had never heard before. Instead of concentrating their religious worship in a two-hour block on Sunday morning they now delight in lengthy services, many hours long. And healing has now become a common theme in preaching and testimony. In my days we hardly dared to speak of witchcraft and traditional healings; now the Christians are battling with these forces in the open and with great effectiveness. A study of their new hymnody would reveal the directions their theology is taking, as would their preaching and testimonies.

This church is doing its theology, but not by theses nailed to the door or theological tracts as in the days of the Reformation. They are "living" their theology. They are singing it, praying it, preaching it, and expressing it in love to neighbors by praying for the sick and spiritually troubled. John Mbiti observed, "African Christians put their faith first into practice; afterwards only a few of them care to deal with the theoretical theology of faith" (Mbiti 1986:230).

The basic tool for contextualizing is the Bible in a translation that is authentic and clear. John Mbiti asserts, "The Bible in the local language becomes the most directly influential single factor in shaping the life of the church in Africa" (Mbiti 1986:28). The Bible becomes central to all of life as the hermeneutical community, the believers, apply the Good News to daily living. Under the leadership of the Holy Spirit they are gifted to discern, to make decisions, to bind and loose, in their cultural situation.

Yet they cannot do this as though theirs is the first church in the world. Each community must be open to the learnings of the church throughout history and at the present time. This will help churches to guard against syncretisms that dilute the gospel. Contextualization can lead to breaking of bondage such as in the early Ephesian church, but unwise contextualization can lead to bondage as in the case of Constantinian Christianity.

I have observed that churches that are honestly seeking to contextualize the gospel embrace four basic assumptions.

1. *A contextualized church is a church in which the basic needs of believers are met in Jesus Christ.* Every culture has many "names" that promise life, prosperity, fulfillment, security, and hope. Christ-loving believers hear the voice of their Good Shepherd and turn away from all of the other voices (John 10). All theologies should be an illumination of who Jesus Christ of Nazareth is. The Bible is the revealed deposit of truth, and Jesus Christ is the very center of that revelation. "If you see me," he insisted, "you have seen the Father" (John 14:7).

241

As social change occurs, new "hopes" appear that often lure Christians to abandon their sole loyalty to Christ in favor of some lesser "name." For that reason contextual theologizing goes on continually in all cultures.

2. *A contextualized church is a witnessing body.* It employs forms, rituals, and behavior that are so relevant and immediate that their unbelieving neighbors receive an authentic and winsome presentation, through word and deed, of who Jesus Christ is. Every generation is responsible to update its expression of faith so that the gospel as lived in daily life does not send a garbled message to unbelievers. The church will so witness to people that whether they receive or reject Christ, they will know precisely who he is.

3. *The believing community will affirm those aspects of the culture which please Jesus Christ.* As noted earlier, all cultures have beautiful aspects that bespeak God's grace. These will be affirmed and encouraged. Christians will incorporate them into their own communal and personal life and will seek to strengthen those aspects in the culture. Christians will also receive innovations from other cultures that are Christ-honoring and that will benefit their own culture.

4. *The believing community will identify and confront those aspects of culture which are detrimental and not consistent with the gospel of Jesus Christ.* They will not impose their will on the culture, but they will rid themselves of all anti-Christlike aspects of it and will encourage their non-believing neighbors to do the same. They will expose the evils of exploitation, witchcraft, blind nationalism, graft and corruption, corporate and personal greed, the occult, and the worship of all "other names."

Contextualization is never an excuse for accommodating the gospel to culture. Visser 't Hooft observed, "In the history of the Church we find more examples of over-indigenization than of under-indigenization. The Christian message has been often uncritically adapted to the national cultures so that its true distinctiveness became lost in the process. . . . In fact there are few of the older Christian nations which have not at one time or another produced curious syncretisms of Christian and national cultural concepts" (Visser 't Hooft 1967:6).

If these are the goals of contextualized theologizing, as I believe they are, then all churches and indeed all Christians wherever they are in the world — East, West, North, or South — must seriously ask how their relationship with their culture is consistent with the clear revelation of God in Jesus Christ. Sometimes I think that the newer churches in the world are more radically contextualized than their more culture-bound fellows.

A truly contextualized gospel, by word and deed, will have the same impact today that it had when it was first lived and expressed by the disciples and apostles of Jesus Christ. It is this gospel that turns a city upside down. It is this gospel that heals and comforts. Jesus explained that his presence will act as a sword to divide peoples, but he also promised that those who would believe in him would become sons and daughters in the kingdom. The gospel, authentically lived in any culture today, will have the same effect.

For Further Reading

Bosch, David J.
    1980   *Witness to the World: The Christian Mission in Theological Perspective.* Atlanta: John Knox Press.
Conn, Harvie M.
    1984   *Eternal Word and Changing Worlds.* Grand Rapids, MI: The Zondervan Corporation.
Fleming, Bruce C. E.
    1980   *Contextualization of Theology.* Pasadena, CA: William Carey Library.
Hall, Edward T.
    1976   *Beyond Culture.* Garden City, NY: Anchor Books.
Healey, Joseph G.
    1981   *A Fifth Gospel.* Maryknoll, NY: Orbis Books.
Hesselgrave, David J., and Edward Rommen
    1989   *Contextualization.* Grand Rapids, MI: Baker Book House.
Hiebert, Paul G.
    1985   *Anthropological Insights for Missionaries.* Grand Rapids, MI: Baker Book House.
Kane, Herbert
    1971   *A Global View of Christian Missions.* Grand Rapids, MI: Baker Book House.
Koyama, Kosuke
    1974   *Waterbuffalo Theology.* Maryknoll, NY: Orbis Books.
Kraft, Charles
    1974   *Christianity in Culture.* Maryknoll, NY: Orbis Books.
Mbiti, John S.
    1986   *Bible and Theology in African Christianity.* Nairobi: Oxford University Press.

Meeks, Wayne A.
   1983   *The First Urban Christians: The Social World of the Apostle Paul.*
               New Haven, CT: Yale University Press.
Nida, Eugene A.
   1960   *Message and Mission.* New York: Harper & Row.
Niebuhr, H. Richard
   1951   *Christ and Culture.* New York: Harper & Row.
Sanneh, Lamin
   1983   *West African Christianity: The Religious Impact.* Maryknoll, NY:
               Orbis Books.
   1989   *Translating the Message: The Missionary Impact on Culture.*
               Maryknoll, NY: Orbis Books.
Stott, John, and Robert T. Coote, eds.
   1979   *Gospel and Culture.* Pasadena, CA: William Carey Library.
Theological Education Fund
   1972   *Ministry in Context.* London: New Life Press.
Tippett, Alan R.
   1987   *Introduction to Missiology.* Pasadena, CA: William Carey Li-
               brary.
Visser 't Hooft, W. A.
   1963   *No Other Name.* Philadelphia: Westminster Press.
   1967   "Accommodation — True or False." *South East Asia Journal
               of Theology.*
Von Allmen, Daniel
   1975   "The Birth of Theology: Contextualization as the dynamic
               element in the formation of New Testament Theology." *In-
               ternational Review of Mission* 64 (253):37-52.

Forming Indigenous Theologies

Tite Tiénou

The twenty-first century will mark the beginning of the third millennium of the existence of the Christian faith. The world of Christianity's third millennium will be significantly different from the one in which the modern missionary movement was born. The difference will be more clearly perceived in two areas: the global nature of the Christian faith and the recognition of the fact of cultural and religious pluralism. This double reality will no doubt influence the theory and practice of Christian mission in the twenty-first century, particularly in regard to contextualization, dialogue with other faiths, and the development of indigenous theologies.

The present essay explores issues related to the forming of indigenous theologies. Its basic argumentation rests on the assumption that rooting the gospel will continue to be one of the major challenges of mission in the next century. Indeed, many people have observed that the emphasis of mission will shift from "communicating the Gospel to those who have never heard" to "deepening and nourishing the faith of those who have accepted Christ" (Ikenga-Metuh 1989:12; see also Bosch 1991:420-57).

Tite Tiénou, a citizen of Burkina Faso, is Professor of Theology and Missiology at Alliance Theological Seminary, Nyack, New York. He has been appointed president and dean of the Evangelical Seminary of the Christian Alliance in Abidjan, Ivory Coast.

One should not think, however, that "deepening and nourishing the faith" of existing Christians is an end in itself. Rather, the continuous nourishment of the faith is one of the keys to enlisting Christians in the cause of God's mission. It is in this context that forming indigenous theologies, that is, developing theologies that are at once Christian and meaningful to the many varied audiences within Christianity, occupies a strategic place in mission.

Since the purpose of this essay is to introduce the topic of forming indigenous theologies, I will present my ideas within three general rubrics. In the first instance I will briefly deal with the question of vocabulary: given the numerous expressions utilized in missiological literature, what term best describes the process of producing theologies locally? Second, I will explore some of the major issues involved in forming indigenous theologies. And, third, I will conclude by proposing a three-dimensional methodology for developing relevant indigenous theologies.

A Variety of Expressions with the Same Meaning?

Developments in the twentieth century have taught us important lessons regarding the relationship between Christian theology, history, and indigenous cultures and religions. Specifically we have learned that all Christian theologies are products of their social, historical, and cultural environments. J. S. Ukpong even claims that "it is only in our century that we have become sufficiently aware that all forms of Christian expression are tied up with the cultural context from which they originate" (1987:168). But, is there a term that best describes the process that leads to the birth of local cultural forms of Christian expression?

Various terms have been used over the years in missiological literature. Perhaps the most common are adaptation, indigenization, contextualization, inculturation, and incarnation. They all wrestle with the same basic issue, namely the fact that Christianity never exists in a cultural and historical vacuum. That being the case, the goal of Christian witness should be to make the gospel take root in diverse cultural soils. Hence the call to adapt, indigenize, contextualize, inculturate, or incarnate the Christian faith.

Adaptation and indigenization only relate to the forming of indigenous theologies in a tangential way. Historically, adaptation "implied a selection of certain rites and customs, purifying them and in-

246

serting them within Christian rituals where there was any apparent similarity" (Waliggo 1986:11). Likewise, indigenization is probably more "useful at the concrete level like the area of liturgical music and vestments" (Ukpong 1987:166). Consequently the search for a term conveying "the reformulation of Christian life and doctrine into the very thought-patterns of each people" (Waliggo 1986:12) continued and, in many ways, still continues today.

Contextualization seems to be more closely related to indigenization, especially among Protestants. According to Richard J. Mouw, "contextualization, like its close kin indigenization, is a theme that is emphasized by people who want to draw sympathetic attention to the ways in which the Gospel is received and interpreted in diverse cultural situations" (1987:190). Yet, the promoters of the term "contextualization" saw a distinction between indigenization and contextualization.

The term "contextualization" entered missiological literature in 1972 through the report of the Third Mandate of the Theological Education Fund (the mandate covered the years 1970-1977). At that time, Shoki Coe was director of the Theological Education Fund, an agency sponsored by the World Council of Churches and administered under the auspices of the Commission on World Mission and Evangelism. According to Coe, indigenization is a static concept since it "tends to be used in the sense of responding to the Gospel in terms of traditional culture" whereas contextualization is "more dynamic . . . open to change and . . . future-oriented" (1976:20, 21).

The word "contextualization" was therefore chosen with the specific purpose of conveying the idea that theology can never be permanently developed. Everywhere and in every culture Christians must be engaged in an ongoing process of relating the gospel to cultures that are constantly changing. As long as the world endures, this process continues. For many people contextualization, not indigenization, is the term that best describes this never-ending process.

Inculturation and incarnation are more akin to contextualization than they are to indigenization, As John Mary Waliggo explains) inculturation "is the continuous endeavour to make Christianity truly 'feel at home' in the cultures of each people" (1986:12).

The title of the present essay, "Forming Indigenous Theologies," takes into account the various aspects stressed by all the terms reviewed above. Christian theology can only be current if it is being constantly reformulated. This reformulation, however, does not happen in a vacuum. It must be solidly anchored in a specific human culture.

Issues Related to the Formation of Indigenous Theologies

Accepting the necessity of reformulating theology for the multiplicity of human cultures is important to the task of forming indigenous theologies. But it is only the first step. Christians convinced that this is the direction to take must still deal with many difficult issues before their vision can become reality.

The first major issue has to do with difference. Humans either celebrate, tolerate, or attempt to suppress difference. In our day and age we are increasingly realizing that "the first freedom is the right to be different without incurring penalty or exclusion" (Ki-Zerbo 1989:11). Around the world we see people demanding access to this "first freedom." This demand will probably grow into a larger movement in the twenty-first century. That is why "global theology has to assume difference as a central category" (Schreiter 1989:18).

How does one, in practice, take difference seriously? Have we not, in society as well as in the church, devised ways of avoiding difference? Robert J. Schreiter points out five dynamics through which we negate difference. According to him we either homogenize people who are different from us, or we colonize them, demonize them, romanticize them, or pluralize them (1989:19). In homogenization difference is obliterated by pointing to similarity. In colonization difference is explained as inferiority. Consequently the inferior person or group will cease to be different when they are raised to our level. In demonization difference is an evil to be eradicated, while in romanticization the person who is different is viewed as either exotic or superior. Pluralization celebrates difference for difference's sake.

Since authentic Christian indigenous theologies cannot be developed without taking difference seriously, we must consciously avoid any of the above five dynamics. Yet Christians should not elaborate their theologies solely on the basis of antithesis or difference. We take difference seriously, then, when we allow other viewpoints to challenge us and, perhaps, reshape our own theology (Schreiter 1989:19). Mutual enrichment and mutual correction are therefore the positive results that come out of the acceptance of difference.

Accepting difference raises the second important issue related to the formation of indigenous theologies, namely the polycentric nature of Christianity. If we believe that Christians from other cultures can enrich our faith or help us correct our mistakes, we are in effect saying that Christianity is not permanently wedded to any human culture. Put another way, the acceptance of difference means that the Christian faith can be at home in any culture. Consequently Christianity has as many centers as the number of cultures of its adherents. This polycentric nature of Christianity may, in the eyes of some people, rob theology of the stability traditionally associated with it. Nevertheless returning to a Christianity with only one cultural center is now an impossibility.

The third important issue in forming indigenous theologies is the role of grass-roots Christians in the production of such theologies. This is especially crucial if we believe that "the primary agent of inculturation is the living faith community, not the evangelizer" (Arbuckle 1986:518). How to get the faith community, the so-called grass-roots Christians, to be effective participants in theological decision-making still remains a challenge for the professional theologian today, and perhaps tomorrow (see Hoefer 1981 and Kalilombe 1985).

The fourth critical issue is the matter of maintaining balance between universality, truth, and error when indigenous theologies are being formed. Christians certainly have the right to self-theologizing. One may even rejoice at the birth of many indigenous Christian theologies. But, as Schreiter reminds us, "localization and contextualization in themselves do not guarantee a greater truth" (1989:15). In that sense, indigenous theologies do not escape responsibility for seeking the truth.

A Three-Dimensional Method for Forming Indigenous Theologies

Theology is vital to the ongoing life of the church. In fact, according to Tshibangu, "Church life cannot exist without active theology" (1987:7). So far it has been argued that forming indigenous theologies is the way of providing churches with active theologies. But what method should one employ in order to produce such theologies?

One must begin by ascertaining the essential factors involved in the formation of indigenous theologies. There seems to be general agreement that these factors are basically three: the church, culture, and Scripture (see Schreiter 1985:1-21). No authentic Christian indigenous theology can be developed without serious grappling with all three. Theology, after all, is the result of the interaction of Christians with Scripture and with their culture.

Logically, the three-dimensional method for forming indigenous theologies begins with an analysis of the church, then proceeds to the investigation of culture, and concludes with interpreting Scripture. In practice, and even ideally, all three must be done simultaneously.

Forming indigenous theologies begins with an analysis of the church because churches are now established in virtually all nation-states of our globe. It is therefore impossible to theologize from scratch. That is true even in places where Christians represent a small and fragmented minority of the population. It is imperative, then, that one understand the life and thought of the church before one rushes to prescribe theological remedies.

The church must be analyzed through a multidisciplinary approach, using the expertise of as many people as possible. Anthropology, sociology, history, and even political science can reveal aspects of church life that have specific bearing on theology.

The second step in this three-dimensional method is an investigation of the culture in which the church members live and move. Particular care must be taken so as to avoid studying archaic culture. Conversely, contemporary culture is not an independent ahistorical entity. That is why culture must be investigated diachronically (through time) as well as synchronically (at a specific point in time). Again disciplines such as anthropology, sociology, history, religious studies, and linguistics are useful in investigating culture very broadly.

Third, Scripture must be interpreted so that it "speaks" to the church in its cultural context. Beside the traditional tools for interpreting Scripture such as exegesis, one needs input from philosophical hermeneutics and worldview studies.

The success of the three-dimensional method depends on cooperation between people with expertise in a variety of disciplines. In that sense the method suggests that forming indigenous theologies is a task for whole Christian communities.

Events in this century, particularly in Christian mission, have taught us to accept diversity as a fact in the affairs of the human race. Imperfect though it may be, this multiethnic, multicultural, and multireligious world is one of the irreversible realities of our time. In light of this, the challenge of Christian mission in the twenty-first century is as basic as it is urgent: how can the Christian movement become genuinely multicultural and yet remain truly universal? Forming indigenous theologies is one of the ways of facing the challenge.

References Cited

Arbuckle, G. A.
1986   "Inculturation Not Adaptation: Time to Change Ter-
         minology." *Worship* 60 (1):511-20.
Bosch, D. J.
1991   *Transforming Mission.* Maryknoll, NY: Orbis Books.
Coe, S.
1976   "Contextualizing Theology." In *Mission Trends No. 3.* Edited
         by G. H. Anderson and T. F. Stransky. New York: Paulist
         Press and Grand Rapids, MI: Wm. B. Eerdmans Publishing
         Company.
Hoefer, H.
1981   "Local Village Theology in India." *Catalyst* 2 (2):121-30.
Ikenga-Metuh, E.
1989   "Contextualization: A Missiological Imperative for the
         Church in Africa in the Third Millennium." *Mission Studies*
         12:3-16.
Kalilombe, P.
1985   "Doing Theology at the Grassroots: A Challenge for Pro-
         fessional Theologians." *African Ecclesial Review* 27:225-37.
Ki-Zerbo, J.
1989   "L'ère des slogans est révolue." *Jeune Afrique* 1484:11.
Mouw, R. J.
1987   "Christian Theology and Cultural Plurality." *The Scottish Bul-
         letin of Evangelical Theology* 5 (2):185-96.
Schreiter, R. J.
1985   *Constructing Local Theologies.* Maryknoll, NY: Orbis Books.
1989   "Teaching Theology from an Intercultural Perspective." *Theo-
         logical Education* 26 (1):13-34.
Tshibangu, T.
1987   *La théologie africaine.* Kinshasa: Editions Saint Paul/Afrique.
Ukpong, J.
1987   "What is Contextualization?" *Neue Zeitschrift für Missionswis-
         senschaft* 43 (3):161-68.
Waliggo, J. M.
1986   "Making a Church that is Truly African." In *Inculturation: Its
         Meaning and Urgency.* Edited by J. M. Waliggo et al., Kam-
         pala: St. Paul Publications/Africa.

For Further Reading

Most publications listed in the references above contain good bibliographies. Perhaps the most extensive bibliography on the topic of forming indigenous theologies is found at the end of D. Bosch's *Transforming Mission* (1991). I suggest the following short list as a beginning guide.

Costa, R. O., ed.
1988   *One Faith, Many Cultures.* Cambridge, MA: Boston Theological Institute, and Maryknoll, NY: Orbis Books.
Deddens, K.
1989   "Contextualization in Mission." *Reflection* 2 (4-5):3-11.
Drummond, R. H.
1985   *Toward a New Age in Christian Theology.* Maryknoll, NY: Orbis Books.
Fabella, V., and S. Torres, eds.
1985   *Doing Theology in a Divided World.* Maryknoll, NY: Orbis Books. (All the books edited by Fabella and Torres in conjunction with conferences of the Ecumenical Association of Third World Theologians are worth reading.)
Frostin, P.
1985   "The Hermeneutics of the Poor — The Epistemological 'Break' in Third World Theologies." *Studia Theologica* 39:127-50.
Gilliland, D. S., ed.
1989   *The Word Among Us.* Dallas, TX: Word Publishing.
Hesselgrave, D. J., and E. Rommen
1989   *Contextualization.* Grand Rapids, MI: Baker Book House.
Hiebert, P. G.
1985   *Anthropological Insights for Missionaries.* Grand Rapids, MI: Baker Book House.
Hollenweger, W. J.
1986   "Intercultural Theology." *Theology Today* 43 (1):28-35.
Kraft, C. H.
1979   *Christianity in Culture.* Maryknoll, NY: Orbis Books.
Schreiter, R. J.
1989   "Faith and Cultures: Challenges to a World Faith." *Theological Studies* 50:744-60.
Walls, A. F.
1983   "The Gospel as the Prisoner and Liberator of Culture." *Evangelical Review of Theology* 7 (2):219-33.

Popular Religions

Paul G. Hiebert

In a controversial book, Robert Ellwood (1989) argues that world religions such as Christianity, Hinduism, Buddhism, and Islam begin as high religions with clear universal visions and power to transform cultures, and gradually fade into folk religions focusing on immediate human needs and desires. Ellwood's thesis runs counter to the earlier theory that universal religions evolved from folk animism and are displaced eventually by science.

Neither theory, in fact, takes into account the continuing spread of high religions, on the one hand, and the persistence of folk religions in all human societies, on the other. Throughout the world, high religions coexist with folk religions. Folk Islam continues alongside orthodox Islam (Woodberry 1989), folk Hinduism beside philosophical Hinduism (Hiebert 1983), and folk Christianity with formal Christianity. The relationships between high and low religions are complex and often full of tensions, but neither has displaced the other. Nor have they been replaced by science.

For the most part, missiology has focused on the relationship of Christianity to other high religions and neglected the whole field of folk religions. As professionally trained leaders, missionaries have addressed their peers, the professional, theologically trained leaders in

---

Paul G. Hiebert teaches mission anthropology at Trinity Evangelical Divinity School, Deerfield, Illinois. He served as a Mennonite missionary in India (1960-65), and on the faculty of Fuller Theological Seminary in Pasadena, California. He is the author of *Anthropological Insights for Missionaries* (1985).

other religions, even though their missionary work was carried on primarily among the common folk. They assumed that village Muslims were orthodox Muslims, and that Hindus knew the doctrines of their faith. Mission was often seen as a confrontation between great religious systems.

The fact is that much of the religion of folk Muslims, Hindus, and Buddhists center around everyday issues dealing with crises such as droughts and barrenness, healing, success, guidance, and accounting for the misfortunes they experience. Moreover, the church around the world is discovering that these same issues persist among Christian converts. Many young churches today are facing the problems of witchcraft, spirits, ancestors, magic, sorcery, evil eye, healing, exorcisms, divination, and the like. In fact, these are problems for Hindu, Muslim, and Buddhist religious leaders as well as for missionaries and church leaders.

There is a growing awareness among mission leaders that these issues arising out of folk religions will be central in missiology in the twenty-first century. The issues can be divided roughly into two areas: those dealing with old folk religious practices, and those relating to the new church structures that are emerging around the world at the folk level. Before we examine these, we need to define what we mean by folk religions and examine their relationships to formal high religions.

High Religions and Folk Religions

By "high" religion we mean the beliefs and practices associated with the great religions, such as Christianity, Islam, Hinduism, and Buddhism. These deal with the cosmic questions facing humankind regarding ultimate origins, the meaning and end of this world, of humankind, and of individual persons. They claim to be universally true for all humans. The caretakers of these visions are religious specialists who, for the most part, are literate. They interpret the sacred texts and debate orthodoxy.

Around these leaders are the central institutions of the religion: the great churches and temples that symbolize the movement; the seminaries where young leaders are trained; the bureaucratic organizations that control the movement; and the service organizations such as presses, schools, hospitals, and welfare agencies. Robert Redfield and Milton Singer (1954) refer to this core of a high religion as its "great tradition."

High religions also have their "little traditions," the local gatherings of lay followers who live their lives out in the world and have little knowledge of or time for the theological debates of the great tradition. High religion provides them with a sense of the cosmic story and their place in it.

But high religions often leave unanswered the questions of everyday life. How can one prevent calamities such as drought and plagues? Why was it that *my* child died so suddenly? How can we guarantee success in crops or business? People know they need to care for their bodies to be healthy, and to plant and tend their fields to get crops. But when their folk sciences fail, what do they do? If their high religion provides no answers, they generally turn to animistic practices — to spiritism, witchcraft, and magic. For example, regarding raising crops, Malinowski writes,

> Magic is undoubtedly regarded by natives as absolutely indispensable to the welfare of the gardens. . . . [The native] knows as well as you do that there are natural conditions and causes, and by his observations he knows also that he is able to control these natural forces by mental and physical effort. . . . On the other hand there is the domain of the unaccountable and adverse influences, as well as the great unearned increment of fortunate coincidence. The first conditions are coped with by knowledge and work, the second by magic. (1955:28-29)

Folk religion is an ad hoc mix of the local expressions of high religions and animism (see Figure 1, p. 256). It is a set of loosely related practices, often mutually contradictory, used not to present a coherent view of reality, but to produce immediate results. It provides various courses of action for those facing immediate problems such as drought, plagues, bad fortune, and sudden deaths; for those seeking success in love, farming, business, and school; and for those wanting guidance in making important decisions.

Clifford Geertz's analogy is useful here (1985). He compares folk religion to the inner part of an old city, with its narrow, winding streets, dark corners, and many little shops where there is often little apparent order, yet much is going on. People of many kinds crowd the lanes and fill the cafes with raucous laughter and animated gossip. High religion, on the other hand, is like the suburbs surrounding the inner city with their neatly-laid-out streets and spacious houses arranged in precise order. Here life is more sedate and peaceful, and sometimes those living here venture into the inner city for its excitement and color.

255

Figure 1.   The Nature of Folk Religion

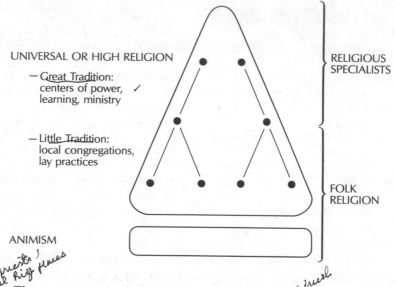

UNIVERSAL OR HIGH RELIGION

— Great Tradition:
centers of power,
learning, ministry

— Little Tradition:
local congregations,
lay practices

ANIMISM

RELIGIOUS
SPECIALISTS

FOLK
RELIGION

There are tensions between specialists in high religions and practitioners of folk religions. In Hinduism Brahmin priests despise the low
caste shamans who perform blood sacrifices to village and nature spirits. In Islam the *mullas* reject the *fakirs* with their folk practices. Similarly,
in Christianity pastors condemn magicians and witch doctors. The
conflict, in part, arises out of the different nature and functions of high
and folk religions (see Table 1, p. 257).

High and folk religion represent poles on a continuum, not distinct
categories. Analysis of them is further complicated by the fact that many
folk religious movements become established and begin to develop
their own institutions. In the process they develop religious specialists,
formal beliefs, and institutions, and through this process of institutionalization they become high religions.

With this framework of analysis, let us look at issues related to
folk religion that are crucial in missions in the twenty-first century.

Unfinished Business in Missions

In the nineteenth and early twentieth centuries many missionaries accepted unwittingly an evolutionary view of religion. In tribal societies

Table 1. A Comparison of High and Folk Religions

HIGH RELIGION	FOLK RELIGION
Ultimate reality: looks at things from a cosmic perspective.	Immediate realities: looks at things from a personal perspective.
Universalistic: believed to apply to all people.	Particularistic: applies to our specific group or selves.
Doctrinaire: concerned with truth and morality, with formal rationality and with internal logical consistencies.	Pragmatic: concerned with power and with solving immediate problems. Not logically consistent. Little formal rationalization.
Exclusive: claims full allegiance of the believer.	Inclusive: uses many mutually contradictory systems simultaneously.
Key Questions: ultimate origin, purpose, and end of this universe, our people, and myself.	Key Questions: meaning of a death for the living, how to avoid disasters, how to succeed, how to find guidance for daily decisions.

they condemned religious practices such as witchcraft, magic, ancestor veneration, and spiritism as "superstitions." Many assumed that these practices would simply die out as people became Christians and adopted modern science. Others believed that the church should forcibly stamp them out. For example, Dietrich Westermann, in his Duff Lectures of 1935 (published as *Africa and Christianity*, 1937), said,

> However anxious a missionary may be to appreciate and retain indigenous social and moral values, in the case of religion he has to be ruthless. . . . he has to admit and even to emphasize that the religion he teaches is opposed to the existing one and the one has to cede to the other. (1937:2)

The Edinburgh World Missionary Conference of 1910 concluded that Africa's traditional religions contained "no preparation for Christianity" (World Missionary Conference 1910, Report of Commission IV, p. 24).

Tribals did become Christians in the millions. The superiority of the Christian teachings and the power of Western technology were self-evident to many. But tribal beliefs and practices did not die, nor were they stamped out. They simply went underground. Christian weddings in the church were followed by traditional weddings in the bush. Children continued to wear amulets, but hidden under their clothes.

257

The picture was different in peasant societies. There Hinduism, Buddhism, Islam, and Shinto coexisted with various folk religions. Missionaries were aware that Christianity stood in direct confrontation with the high philosophical religions, so they studied them and consciously undertook the apologetic task. Few, however, studied the folk practices of the villages. Most assumed that these "superstitions" would fade, or could be stamped out by legalistic means. Latourette expressed this opinion when he wrote (1975:328), "A 'primitive' religion yields more readily to a 'high' religion than does a 'high' religion to another 'high' religion."

There are notable exceptions to this lack of interest in the religious practices of the common people rather than of the elite. In South India missionaries such as Elmore (1925) and Whitehead (1921) did pioneer work on village religion. In Africa Junod (1962) gave us in-depth analyses of tribal religions. In the Muslim world, Macdonald (1912) and Zwemer (1920, 1939) wrote definitive works on folk Islam.

In part, the missionaries in peasant societies were successful. Hindus, Buddhists, and Muslims became Christians and left their temples, shrines, and mosques. But the old folk religious practices continued, generally in secret for fear of missionary rebuke. Farmers continued to protect their crops from the evil eye by placing pots covered with spots in the field. Patients came to mission hospitals, but stopped on the way to visit the magician, astrologer, and diviner.

It is clear today that folk religious beliefs and practices remain an unfinished agenda in the lives of young churches around the world. Christian converts found in the gospel the way of ultimate salvation, but the church often had few answers to their immediate questions about sickness, witchcraft, spirits, guidance, and success. So they returned to their old ways for answers to these questions, even as they went to church for forgiveness and fellowship with God. When the missionaries and church leaders condemned them for doing so, they simply continued in secret.

Issues related to folk religion are surfacing in young churches around the world. Witchcraft, sorcery, spirits, ancestors, magic, drums, dances, and traditional life-cycle rites are once again living issues that church leaders must confront. The debate surrounding these issues has been heated.

Nowhere is this more true than in Africa. In the Catholic Church this is seen in the Vatican's response to Bishop Milingo (1984), and in the writings of Aylward Shorter (1985). In Protestantism, Mulumba (1988) and others have wrestled with the problem. Kwame Bediako, in his analysis of the roots of African theology, goes so far as to say (1989: 59),

> There is probably no issue more crucial than the need to under-
> stand this heightened interest in the African pre-Christian religious
> tradition if Africa's theologians are to be interpreted correctly and
> their achievement duly recognized. What is the explanation for the
> extraordinary fact that the very religious traditions that were previ-
> ously deemed to be of scant theological significance should now come
> to occupy "the very centre of the academic stage"?

Regarding African theologians, Andrew Walls observes (1981:49),

> Each . . . was trained in theology on a Western model, but each has
> moved into an area for which no Western syllabus prepared him, for
> each has been forced to study and lecture on African traditional
> religions — and each has found himself writing on it.

The same picture is emerging elsewhere around the world. In
Latin America, despite two centuries of Christian presence, the central
struggle of the church today is with Umbanda, Candomblé, Xango, and
other types of spiritism. In India, P. Luke and J. Carmen (1968) trace
the impact of folk religious practices on village churches.

Issues raised by folk religions are not only the unfinished business
of missions, they are also increasingly the concern of the Western
church. Despite a centuries-long battle against witchcraft and paganism, the church in North America today faces the revival of neopa-
ganism and the emergence of new folk religions loosely referred to as
the New Age (Groothuis 1986). Like folk religions elsewhere, these are
concerned primarily with the existential problems of everyday life.

Responding to traditional folk religions has never been a simple
task in the history of the church. Despite the papacy's continuing opposition, witchcraft, magic, sorcery, and other folk religious practices
persisted for more than a thousand years in the European church. In
some ways the Reformation was as much a reaction to the inroads of
pagan folk religious practices into Christianity, such as the selling of
amulets and merits, as it was to the theological teachings of the Roman
church. The same picture is true in Latin America where the coexistence
of orthodox Catholicism with syncretistic folk practices has under-
mined the power of the church.

What should the churches' response be to these folk practices?

They will not simply die out, nor can we stamp them out by law and discipline. On the other hand, we cannot accept them uncritically in the church. To do so leads to Christo-paganism (Nida 1961).

The church must consciously deal with folk religious beliefs and practices, using the process of critical contextualization (cf. Hiebert 1987). First, it must study the beliefs and practices without rejecting them outright in order to understand them and the questions they answer. Then the church must test them in the light of biblical teaching. Some practices will be kept, some rejected, some reinterpreted, and new ones created to express new Christian beliefs. Finally, those that are accepted must be integrated as meaningful practices into the life of the church.

One model of this critical response to traditional religious practices is the way God dealt with them in the Old Testament. Many, such as idolatry, human sacrifice, magic, divination, and necromancy, were strictly prohibited. Others, such as altars, the offering of sacrifices, washing of the body, bowing in prayer, numerous birth, wedding, and funeral customs, and words such as *El* (God), *chatta'ah* (sin), and *ga'al* (to redeem) were given new meanings in the context of new teachings and rituals.

The same model is found in the response of Jesus and the early church to the folk religious practices of that day. Jesus used saliva and laid hands on people, but he condemned magical approaches to power and refused to perform signs and wonders as ends in themselves (Matt. 12:38-39; Luke 23:8-9; John 6:14-15). Peter used handkerchiefs, but cursed Simon for wanting to use religious power for personal ends (Acts 8:9-24).

In both models it is clear that God neither rejected nor accepted old practices uncritically. He offered something that transcended the old categories altogether, and served to judge them. The gospel relativizes all religious practices, for they must be judged by it.

It is not our purpose here to predetermine the outcome of these debates arising out of the church's confrontation with traditional folk religions. The very process by which churches seek to understand God's voice in their specific religiocultural contexts is essential to their growth in discernment and maturation in faith. Rather, our purpose here is to note that these issues remain an unfinished business in the life of the church around the world that will require its immediate attention in the twenty-first century, and that this process of reevaluating the church's response to traditional religions has already begun in many places. Moreover, our purpose is to note the great potential in the life of the church for dealing with these issues, since it will help the church speak again to the common folk. There is also, however, a great danger of new forms of syncretism. Throughout history, the church has suffered as much from syncretism at the level of folk religion as from heresy at the level of high religion.

Discerning New Church Structures

Another set of issues related to folk religion that will play a central role in the missiology of the twenty-first century has to do with the structures of the church. By the end of this century sixty percent of the church will be in the non-Western world, and most of this sixty percent will be among the poor who cannot afford paid ministers and large institutions. For the most part, missionaries in the past have brought the professional models of ministry they knew in the West. Today young churches are struggling with these models and looking for other models that enable the church to survive and multiply among the poor and oppressed.

The question is not new to the church. As Yoder points out (1987), Christianity began as a movement among the common people. The early church had no professional religious elite that ruled over an obedient laity. Every Christian was to be a priest, not only theologically, but also in the organizational life of the church. Every member had a gift (*charisma*), which she or he was to use for the good of the congregation, and all gifts were to be valued in the church (I Cor. 12 and Rom. 12). Francisco Lepargneur of São Paulo notes (Hollenweger 1968:167),

> . . . according to St. Paul the supernatural quality is not the criterion which distinguishes the charismatic. . . . Rather Paul subsumes under the term charisma such ordinary things as almsgiving, exercising leadership, teaching (Rom. 12:6-8), marriage or celibacy (1 Cor. 7:7).

In short, the early church was more folk than professional in its organization.

Yoder (1987) points out that the early church soon abandoned the idea of universal ministry in favor of a professional leadership set apart from the laity. The result was the establishment of a clerical monarchy. The process was complete after Constantine when Christianity was wedded to the Roman state, and church leaders became part of the government. Since then the churches, Eastern Orthodox, Roman Catholic, and Protestant alike, have built their organizations of professional clergy who are separate from the laity.

This hierarchical model of church organization is being challenged today on the frontiers where the church is growing rapidly. In many parts of the world it is simply impossible, numerically and economically, to train enough professional leaders to meet the needs of the exploding church. Moreover, much of the young church cannot afford elaborate organizational structures. Consequently, new forms of church organization have emerged to meet the needs of this rapid growth.

One such form appeared earlier in the congregationalism of the early Baptists, Anabaptists, Disciples, Methodists, and Pentecostals. For example, the lay Methodist circuit riders and Baptist "farmer-preachers" of the American mission frontier provided much of the leadership that was reserved for the professional clergy of other churches. Similarly, the early Pentecostals built their churches with a minimum of professionalization. Lay leaders grew in the use of their gifts, and lay men and women went out to begin new churches. Consequently, their expansion was not strangled by the lack of professionally trained leaders on whom many other missions and churches depended.

A second form of "folk church" to emerge has been the "independent churches." These have emerged in Africa, India, and other parts of the world. Whereas mission churches have been heavily dependent upon expatriate missionaries and highly trained nationals, the independent churches have relied, for the most part, on lay, uneducated leaders. The flexibility such leadership gives them to identify with the local culture and to address the issues of folk religion such as witchcraft, spirit possession, ancestor veneration, and magic, has facilitated rapid growth on the frontiers of the independent churches.

A third form of laity-based church has emerged in the Catholic Church in the form of "base communities." A generation ago sociologically informed church leaders in Central and South America realized that the existing structures could never provide enough priests, trained and ordained, to meet the needs of the church. New structures were needed to minister to the masses and the poor. Consequently, the leaders created the role of "delegates of the Word," modestly trained and formally authorized teachers of basic Christian knowledge. For the most part these base leaders were able by cultural affinities to communicate with their poor peers better than a fully "qualified" expatriate priest ever could. At first they gave catechetical instruction. Later the *delegados de la Palabra* led in meetings for prayer, Bible study, consciousness-raising, and community development. The result was simple Christian communities that sprang up in such places as rural Brazil and in the mountainous countrysides of Central America.

Parallel to this, those working among the parishes of the urban poor realized that there would never be enough priests to go around. The bishops began to authorize the organization of neighborhood lay groups, meeting with a priest to read the Scriptures and lead prayers, to organize around community needs, and to develop the skills of community process and leadership. Yoder notes (1987:98),

> Leadership roles are freed to evolve ad hoc in the power of the Spirit, accrediting already recognized natural giftedness, discerning through the leaders' effectiveness in facilitating consensual decision processes, regardless of sex (at least at the *barrio* level), or formal education.

Out of these two movements have emerged what have come to be called "base ecclesial communities." In recent years these have sprung up in great numbers throughout Latin America, and in parts of Africa and India (Cook 1985).

Similar, in some ways, to the base communities are the many Bible study groups and house churches springing up in many parts of the world.

Are these various forms of "folk churches" a restoration of the New Testament church pattern? The answer is yes and no. In one sense they represent returns to the more flexible, laity-based structures of the early church. Some argue that this is a form of primitivism that characterizes most movements at their birth, and that it is peripheral to the concerns of the gospel. Yoder responds (1987:87),

> When the entire outline of the Epistle to the Hebrews centers around the end of the priesthood, when in 1 Corinthians 12 to 14 the central theme is the multiplicity of gifts in the church, and when in Ephesians 4 this unity in multiplicity is in fact referred to as "the perfection of Christ," it would seem obvious that the apostolic interpretation of the meaning of multiplicity of ministries forbids our treating the matter as merely a temporarily fitting solution to a pragmatic question of optimum social management.

Yet each of these attempts has failed to capture fully the biblical vision of the church. The Baptist, Anabaptist, Pentecostal, and other congregational movements have, over time, institutionalized their

263

structures and reinstated a professional clergy. The independent churches range from thoroughly Christian to neoprimal in their theologies (Turner 1981), and many have strong "father" or "chief" leaders rather than a multiplicity of leaders. The base communities are not permitted by the Catholic Church to administer the sacraments, and so are incomplete in their churchly functions.

Nevertheless, these new forms, born out of the missionary outreach of the church, give us some idea of what much of the church of the twenty-first century might look like. Given the rapid changes taking place in the world, that church will need to be flexible. Given the growing persecution of Christianity in some lands, that church will need to survive underground with a minimum of structures. Given the fact that many of the churches will be in the Two-Thirds world among the poor, those churches will need to survive and evangelize without large budgets and complex institutions.

Missions have always challenged the *status quo* of the church, and forced it to ask new questions and seek new forms. In the twenty-first century, many of the questions and forms the church will face relate to God's work among the common people, particularly those in the young churches planted by the missionary movement of the nineteenth and twentieth centuries. The outcome may be the reinvention of the church (Schlabach 1989), the emergence of new syncretistic forms of Christianity, or both.

For Further Reading

Bediako, Kwame
  1989   "The Roots of African Theology." *International Bulletin of Missionary Research* 13 (2):58-65.
Cook, Guillermo
  1985   *The Expectation of the Poor: Latin American Base Ecclesial Communities in Protestant Perspective.* Maryknoll, NY: Orbis Books.
Ellwood, Robert
  1989   *The History and Future of Faith.* New York: Crossroad Publishing Company.
Elmore, W. T.
  1925   *Dravidian God in Modern Hinduism: A Study of Local and Village Deities of South Africa.* Madras, India: Christian Literature Society.

Geertz, Clifford
1985   *Local Knowledge: Further Essays in Interpretive Anthropology.*
        New York: Basic Books.
Groothuis, Douglas R.
1986   *Unmasking the New Age.* Downers Grove, IL: InterVarsity
        Press.
Hiebert, Paul G.
1983   "Folk Religion in Andhra Pradesh: Some Missiological Im-
        plications." In *The Gospel among Our Hindu Neighbors.* Edited
        by Vinay Samuel and Chris Sugden. Bangalore: The Asso-
        ciation for Evangelical Theological Education in India.
1987   "Critical Contextualization." *International Bulletin of Mission-
        ary Research* 11 (3):104-12.
Hollenweger, Walter
1968   "Evangelism and Brazilian Pentecostals." *Ecumenical Review*
        20:163-70.
Junod, Henri Alexandre
1962   *The Life of a South African Tribe: Mental Life.* Vol. II. New Hyde
        Park, NY: University Books. First edition 1912, second edi-
        tion 1927.
Latourette, Kenneth Scott
1975   *A History of Christianity.* Vol. I. New York: Harper & Row.
Luke, P., and John B. Carmen
1968   *Village Christians and Hindu Culture.* London: Lutterworth Press.
Macdonald, D. B.
1909   *The Religious Attitude and Life in Islam.* Chicago: University
        of Chicago Press.
Malinowski, Bronislaw
1955   *Magic, Science and Religion.* Garden City, NY: Doubleday.
Milingo, E.
1984   *The World in Between: Christian Healing and the Struggle for
        Spiritual Survival.* London: C. Hurst and Company.
Mulumba, Mukundi
1988   "Witchcraft among the Kasaian People: A Phenomenological
        Approach, Challenge and Response." Unpublished Ph.D.
        diss. School of World Mission, Fuller Theological Seminary.
Nida, Eugene A.
1961   "Christo-Paganism." *Practical Anthropology* 8:1-15.
Redfield, Robert, and Milton Singer
1954   "The Cultural Role of Cities." *Economic Development and Cul-
        tural Change* 3:53-73.

Schlabach, Gerald
1989   "Mission Strategy and the Reinvention of the Church in Latin
           America." *Mission Focus* 17 (1):5-8.
Shorter, Aylward
1985   *Jesus and the Witchdoctor: An Approach to Healing and Whole-
           ness.* Maryknoll, NY: Orbis Books.
Turner, Harold W.
1981   "Religious Movements in Primal [or Tribal] Societies." *Mis-
           sion Focus* 9 (3):45-55.
Walls, Andrew F.
1981   "The Gospel as the Prisoner and Liberator of Culture." *Faith
           and Thought* 108 (1-2):39-52. (Reprinted in *Missionalia* 10
           [3]:93-105.)
Westermann, Dietrich
1937   *Africa and Christianity* (Duff Lectures, 1935). London: Oxford
           University Press.
Whitehead, H.
1921   *The Village Gods of South India.* Calcutta: Association Press.
Woodberry, J. Dudley, ed.
1989   *Muslims and Christians on the Emmaus Road.* Monrovia, CA:
           MARC.
World Missionary Conference 1910, Report of Commission IV.
1910   *The Missionary Message in Relation to Non-Christian Religions.*
           Edinburgh and London: Oliphant, Anderson and Ferrier.
Yoder, John Howard
1987   *The Fullness of Christ: Paul's Revolutionary Vision of Universal
           Ministry.* Elgin, IL: Brethren Press.
Zwemer, Samuel M.
1920   *The Influence of Animism on Islam.* New York: Macmillan Pub-
           lishing Company.
1939   *Studies in Popular Islam.* New York: Macmillan Publishing
           Company.

IV. Special Challenges in Mission

The Teaching of Missions

Alan Neely

How anomalous to be writing about the teaching of mission in the next
century when less than fifteen years ago professors of mission were
openly questioning the future of their discipline. The call for a moratorium was widespread, major sending agencies in the West were cutting back their overseas personnel, established chairs of mission in
many schools were going unfilled, and courses in mission were being
phased out or the titles changed to make them more palatable to a
generation sensitized to Western imperialism and colonialism. These
were not necessarily unwholesome or menacing developments given
the monumental changes in the world, but, looking back, it is evident
the results were not uniformly beneficial. Lessening the emphasis on
the traditional doing of mission accompanied by the marked retrench-
ment in missionary personnel led many grass-roots members of mainline denominations to question whether their leaders were still committed to mission. No single development can or should be identified
as the cause for the dramatic downturn in membership and support in
the mainline churches that began in the 1960s, but surely one contributing factor was the growing feeling of many that their church had ceased
to be involved in the Christian mission to the world. The truth of
Brunner's oft-quoted aphorism, "The church exists by mission, just as

---

Alan Neely was for thirteen years a Baptist missionary in Colombia, South
America. Since that time he was professor of missiology at Southeastern
Baptist Theological Seminary and is now Henry Luce Professor of Ecumen-
ics and Mission at Princeton Theological Seminary.

fire exists by burning,[1] and Moltmann's more recent observation that "mission does not come from the church; it is from mission and in the light of mission that the church has to be understood"[2] have surely been verified during the past three decades.

All is not bleak, however, for in 1987 and 1988 the Norwegian missiologist Olav G. Myklebust conducted a survey, his second since the mid-1950s, regarding the teaching of Christian mission in contemporary theological education. In contrast to his earlier investigation, which is limited to Protestant theological schools in the West, this last study is ecumenical and includes Asian, African, and Latin American institutions offering courses in missiology, as well as those in Western Europe and North America. Myklebust's conclusion is that missiology as a discipline rather than disappearing is in reality increasingly appearing as part of theological curricula in most areas of the world.[3]

As we move into a new millennium, the question, therefore, is not: Will there be any teaching of missiology in the next century? but What factors will shape it and what will it include?

Mission as a Legitimate Academic Discipline

Though as early as the thirteenth century the indefatigable and visionary Ramon Lull proposed both to kings and popes the establishment of schools for the training of missionaries, he was too far ahead of his time. Lull's ambitious plan was never really implemented nor was his Majorca school replicated.[4] Thus until the seventeenth century, if

1. Emil Brunner, *The Word and the World* (New York: Charles Scribner's Sons, 1931), p. 108.

2. Jürgen Moltmann, *The Church in the Power of the Spirit,* trans. Margaret Kohl (New York: Harper and Row, 1977), p. 10.

3. "Missiology in Contemporary Theological Education: A Factual Survey," *Mission Studies* 12 (1989):87-107.

4. Kenneth Scott Latourette, *The Thousand Years of Uncertainty,* Vol. 2 of "The Expansion of Christianity" (New York: Harper & Brothers, 1938), p. 322; and Samuel M. Zwemer, *Raymond Lull: First Missionary to the Moslems* (New York: Funk & Wagnalls, 1902), pp. 63-72, 78-79. E. Allison Peers is less positive about Lull's missionary college. "Its life," he says, "was not a long one, and it is not known ever to have sent out any missionaries, though the natural presumption is that it did so." *Raymond Lull* (London: Society for Promoting Christian Knowledge, 1929), p. 135. Myklebust, while recognizing the significance of Lull, insists that Ramon de Penyafort, not Lull, was "the first to found missionary colleges for the study of Hebrew and Arabic. To this distinguished church leader, the founder of the Roman Catholic mission to Jews and Mohammedans, Lull was greatly indebted." Myklebust also observes that Aquinas wrote his *Summa contra Gentiles* (1261-

270

Roman Catholic missionaries studied missions at all, they did so informally or by reflecting on their own experience. The Catholic churches of East and West, nonetheless, were in the missionary business for more than a millennium before the Protestant Reformation, and almost two more centuries would pass before Protestants in any significant numbers became involved in world missions. One should remember, however, that as early as 1590 the Dutch Reformed pastor and professor Adrianus Saravia, who later migrated to England and became an Anglican and Dean of Westminster, insisted that Christ's commission to preach the gospel to every creature was a mandate to the church in every age, not merely to that of the apostles.

Though the impact of Saravia's theology was limited, it is evident in Justus von Heurn, who in 1618 appealed to his compatriots to awaken to the mission opportunity of the times and begin sending missionaries to the new Dutch colonies. Not limiting himself to admonitions, von Heurn established a seminary in Leyden in 1622 for the purpose of preparing young men to be missionaries. Though the institution was fairly short-lived, a dozen or so were trained and went as missionaries to the Dutch East Indies.[5] Saravia's influence is likewise seen in the life and work of Gisbertus Voetius, who in 1652 chose for his inaugural lectures at the University of Utrecht the theme "De plantatoribus ecclesiasticis." Voetius argued that central to the life of the church is mission, and that the Christian mission is to convert the heathen, plant the church, and bring glory to God.[6]

During the remainder of the seventeenth and throughout the eighteenth century, sporadic attempts were made to evoke the interest of Protestants in their responsibility for "the heathen," but the results were largely fruitless. Myklebust recounts in detail not only the general attitudes among Protestants in the various European lands toward mission, but, more important, the efforts of individual theologians and pastors

64) at Penyafort's request. *The Study of Missions in Theological Education* 1 (Oslo: Forlaget Land og Kirke, 1955), p. 33.

5. Kenneth Scott Latourette, *Three Centuries of Advance,* Vol. 3 of "The Expansion of Christianity" (Harper & Brothers, 1939), p. 43.

6. J. Verkuyl, *Contemporary Missiology* (Grand Rapids: Wm. B. Eerdmans, 1978), pp. 21, 183-84. Shortly thereafter, the first Puritan missions to Native Americans in the New England colonies were underway, but like earlier missionaries, the only formal preparation John Eliot had, for instance, was working with an Algonquian to learn the language, after which Eliot communicated the gospel by a system of trial and error. See Ola Elizabeth Winslow, *John Eliot, Apostle to the Indians* (Boston: Houghton Mifflin, 1968), pp. 86-110; also Martin Moore, *Memoirs of the Life and Character of Rev. John Eliot, Apostle of the N. A. Indians* (Boston: T. Bedlington, 1822), pp. 13-30.

who preached, lectured, and wrote on the subject.[7] Efforts to establish colleges of mission, however, were frustrated except for the remarkably influential University of Halle, founded in 1702 by August Hermann Francke for the purpose of "training of missionaries for India."[8] Though one can find notable exceptions, Protestants generally were as dilatory in beginning the teaching of mission as they were in becoming part of the Christian missionary effort. Other than a few isolated lectureships, almost three-quarters of the nineteenth century would pass before a chair of missions would be established and occupied in a Protestant university.[9] The number of courses, professors, and chairs of mission, however, increased dramatically in the first three decades of the twentieth century, only to be followed by the aforementioned downturn in the 1960s and 1970s.

Today, as already indicated, the study of mission appears to be enjoying some revival, but according to Myklebust's data, a course in missiology is offered as a separate and permanent part of the curriculum in less than half the institutions responding to his inquiry.[10] Moreover, in many schools in North America missions courses are not required and must compete with other options in the ever-growing smorgasbord of electives. The most encouraging fact is, as Myklebust indicates, that the study of mission in one form or another seems to be increasingly accepted as a legitimate part of theological education.

Furthermore, as the opportunities for missionaries with skills in teaching English as a second language, media production, economic development, business administration, marketing, newer forms of medicine, computers, and human services — just to mention a few — are increasing, the number of courses in mission and related subjects available to a seminary or divinity school student are also increasing. Many students of my generation recall what they describe as listless, interminable lectures they were forced to endure in the history or theology of mission classes. Some missionary colleagues profess amazement that they ever became missionaries given the negative feelings they still

7. *The Study of Missions in Theological Education* 1 (1955):41-92.
8. Ibid., p. 50.
9. Here I am referring to Alexander Duff's Chair of Evangelistic Theology established in the University of Edinburgh in 1867. The retired director of the Leipzig Mission, Karl Graul, was named to a chair of missions in the University of Erlangen in 1864, but unfortunately he died before assuming the post (ibid., p. 93). See also James A. Scherer, "Missions in Theological Education," *The Future of the Christian World Mission*, ed. William J. Danker and Wi Jo Kang (Grand Rapids: Wm. B. Eerdmans, 1971), p. 144, n. 2.
10. "Missiology in Contemporary Theological Education" (1989), pp. 98-99.

nourish about their seminary mission studies. Professors of mission nowadays are not all scintillating and innovative, nor have they abandoned altogether the lecture method, but the array of teaching techniques now utilized has been greatly enlarged and includes student-professor designed learning modules, well-produced and less polemical audio-visuals, simulation games, case studies, field trips, and the frequent use of resource persons, including students who have had firsthand mission experience.

With the wide variety of opportunities for study available to seminarians who are interested in the church's world mission or who aspire to vocational involvement in mission, one could understandably conclude that most of them take advantage of the opportunities. Some do, but in those institutions where a course in mission is not required, most do not. Moreover, even for those who elect to study mission, it is very difficult to crowd more than one or two courses into a three-year Master of Divinity program. Consequently, one can assume that most non-evangelical seminarians graduate without any directed study of the Christian mission, and many of those who later choose to serve as short-term or vocational missionaries begin their work with little or sometimes no formal preparation at the seminary level.

Sending agencies, recognizing this deficiency, seek to compensate by providing orientation training. But most of these programs are far too brief and theoretical. Lacking previously acquired knowledge or firsthand experience, newly named missionaries are too often unprepared to benefit fully from this kind of learning. Also, few orientation programs prepare missionaries for true ecumenical involvement, and pressure is there from the beginning to finish and get on to the field.

Developments Affecting the Teaching of Mission

Given the reservoir of knowledge we already have about the world and its people, about teaching and learning, about history, anthropology, the Bible, culture, world religions, theology, linguistics, and communication, together with the vastly increasing amount of new information, we should now be in a better position to prepare people for engagement in mission than at any time in the past. But just when we have more experience, knowledge, and tools, the future is more problematic and less predictable. Social, political, economic, and ideological changes in the world are occurring at a breathtaking rate. The center of the world's wealth and economic power seems to be shifting toward Asia and away from the West, especially from the United States.[11]

Meanwhile, the world's population continues to increase at a frightening pace in the economically poorer nations, environmental problems are pushing us toward natural thresholds, and though public awareness and concern are growing, the political and economic barriers to reform appear insurmountable. Rural people still migrate to the urban areas in such numbers that local water supplies, fuel sources, housing, and the capacity for waste disposal are dangerously close to overloading and breaking down the systems altogether. The cost of the infrastructure necessary to provide for the burgeoning number of urban inhabitants is astronomical and drives tax rates higher and higher, so much so that the future of the city as the economic center and a demographic magnet is very much in doubt.[12] We live in a world not only culturally, ethnically, linguistically, politically, and religiously divided, but also in a world increasingly divided economically. Living standards for approximately half the world's people are improving, while for the rest they are rapidly deteriorating. In the 1950s and 1960s, programs for economic growth promised better standards of living for virtually everyone. But since 1973, the whole picture has changed as masses of people in the Third World suffer the impact of their nations' inability to compete and their mounting and unpayable foreign debt. Country after country now devotes "the lion's share of export earnings to paying interest on external debts."[13] This is true not only for Latin American nations, but also for many countries in Africa and Asia. The most extreme example is that of the Sudan, where eighty percent of the nation's export earnings go to servicing their foreign debt.[14] Who would have predicted twenty years ago that by the end of the 1970s, the so-called "Decade of Development," many of the nations struggling to improve their economies would not be able to do so, but rather would be suffering severe declines?[15]

What do these changes and problems portend for a church on

11. Numerous data indicate this fact — e.g., fourteen of the world's twenty largest banks are in Japan; none is in the U.S. Moreover, the GNP of the U.S.A. has dropped from first in the world to sixth.

12. Early in 1990, Peter Drucker declared that we are not only "already deep into the new century, a century that is fundamentally different from the one we still assume we live in," but also "the city as we know it is obsolete." Edward Reingold, "Facing the Totally New and Dynamic," *Time* 135 (January 22, 1990):6-7.

13. Linda Starke, ed., *State of the World 1987* (New York: W. W. Norton, 1987), p. 27.

14. Ibid.

15. Ibid., pp. 27-28.

274

mission? As already implied, the opportunities to engage in mission are expanding, but they are also changing. In several countries, particularly in Asia, if visas are available at all for persons identified as missionaries, the time they are allowed to live and work in those countries is severely limited. Moreover, the kind of relationship possible between churches of one land with those of another is a relationship of cooperation and exchange, not one of unilateral sending and receiving. But these developments may prove to be insignificant in comparison with others that are beginning to unfold. What are some of the major changes that will likely affect the way the Christian mission will be done in the coming decades? The following are among the more probable.

- The movements toward "democracy" in Eastern Europe as well as in other parts of the world and the instability resulting from these struggles will occasion new openings for Christian mission, but not necessarily in traditional ways.
- The challenge to Western European and North American economic predominance by Asian countries, especially by Japan, Korea, Taiwan, Hong Kong, and Singapore, and the economic pressure on the United States resulting from the growing strength of the European Economic Community, particularly the economic and political reunification of Germany, will reveal the nature and test the limits of Christian stewardship in North American churches.
- The continual increase in costs in the sending and maintaining of North American and Western European vocational missionaries will be accompanied by a growing number of mission agencies sending missionaries from the "Two-Thirds World."[16]
- The unprecedented and increasing costs of land on which to construct church buildings in urban areas, and the need to "do church" differently from the way most of us in the West are accustomed, will demand that those involved in mission be able to think and work creatively.[17]
- The changing urban scene, diverging food and income trends, and

16. See Larry D. Pate, *From Every People* (Monrovia, CA: MARC, 1989). This handbook includes a directory, histories, and analyses of mission agencies in the Two-Thirds world, the kinds of mission in which they are engaged, and their growth rates.

17. Drucker, Alvin Toffler, and others can be of help in thinking in new ways. See, for example, Peter F. Drucker, *The New Realities* (New York: Harper & Row, 1989), and Toffler, *Previews and Premises* (New York: Morrow, 1983).

the growing awareness among the poor of the world that their suffering and marginalization are not the results of blind fate but of inequitable social, political, and economic structures, will make it necessary for missionaries to respond in ways not ordinarily addressed in traditional theological training.

· The current satisfaction and smugness of people in the West with our own political and economic systems and the apparent downfall of the communist regimes will be short-lived as the inherent inequities of capitalism become evident and are challenged anew.

· The impact of secularization and the increasing influence of non-Christian religions on Christian theology will reveal the true significance of living in an age no longer dominated by Christian values and philosophies.

· The shrinking percentage of money that will come to the churches for traditional missionary efforts and the competition for funds among church and parachurch missionary agencies will call for missioners who can work without the financial support systems long enjoyed by their predecessors.

· Until the glamour of short-term mission projects wears off and the limitations of the "fast-food" approach to mission are recognized, enlisting people for vocational mission will continue to be difficult.

· Those who serve as vocational missioners will be the core of the church's apostolate in the world. Especially for these, preparation for the missionary vocation will necessarily be a lifelong process.

· The growing consciousness of Christians in the West that they live in multifaith and multiethnic societies will mean new fields for mission involvement.

Teaching Christians to Live as Missioners in the World

When we review the history of the teaching of mission, two needs are evident: the need to awaken as well as to inform the church of ways to continue Christ's mission in the world, and, no less important, the need to prepare and support those whom the Spirit sets apart for a ministry and mission to the world. For the coming century, what kind of curriculum will best prepare believers to be part of God's mission in the world?

The basic teaching and training unit for Christian mission is not the seminary but rather the church. Two developments both enhance and threaten the church as a base for mission. One is the growing number of super churches that have the resources and generate the enthusiasm needed to involve their members directly in mission. Many of these congregations become in themselves training and sending agencies. The contribution they make is not to be denied, but oftentimes their "go-it-alone" approach deprives them of resources that could prevent them from "reinventing the wheel" and, even more seriously, from making needless mistakes, being misled and even defrauded.[18] Furthermore, few congregations are strong enough to engage in mission to the world alone. To be involved, they need some means to cooperate with other congregations in joint ventures. The super church model tends to be a hybrid.

A second development that holds both threat and promise to the local congregation as the primary mission entity is the growing number of parachurch agencies. They hold promise because they provide a multiplicity of ways in which individuals and churches can plug into a mission that challenges them. But supporting parachurch endeavors can leave the congregation even further removed from direct mission involvement, making the church not the means and source of mission but a kind of *tertium quid*.

The most formidable task facing the church in the coming century, therefore, will be discerning where God is at work, inculcating in Christian believers a theology of mission adequate for the times, preparing them to live in an increasingly secular and pluralistic world, and motivating them to engage their culture with commitment, courage, and expectancy. Those who live in the East as well as the West should study and ponder Lesslie Newbigin's penetrating question, "What must we be?"[19] His list of qualifications for effective missionary encounter represents what he regards as necessary for presenting the gospel to the West. Responses of believers in Asia, Africa, Latin America, and even

18. See the data of David Barrett, "Annual Statistical Table on Global Mission: 1986," *International Bulletin of Missionary Research* 10 (January 1986):22-23. For Barrett's data from 1987 through 1990, see ibid. 11 (January 1987):25; ibid. 12 (January 1988):17; ibid. 13 (January 1989):20-21; and ibid. 14 (January 1990):26-27. Also see the editorial "The Curses of Money on Mission to India," *Evangelical Missions Quarterly* 22 (July 1985): 294; and Rajamani Stanley, "Money for Ministry or Ministry for Money?," ibid., pp. 295-97; Roger E. Hedlund, "Evangelism or Evangelistic Tourism?," ibid., pp. 297-300; and J. P. Masih, " 'People Movement' Problems," ibid., pp. 300-302.

19. *Foolishness to the Greeks* (Grand Rapids: Wm. B. Eerdmans, 1986), pp. 124-50. See also Lesslie Newbigin, "Can the West be Converted?" *International Bulletin of Missionary Research* 11 (January 1987):2-7.

in North America will doubtless be different, but surely they will include an unshakable faith in the crucified and living Christ and a burning desire to proclaim the gospel to all people.

The second setting for the teaching of mission is the theological school. But what is the place of mission in the theological curriculum? Ted Ward is right when he says, "Every decision about curriculum reflects someone's view of the future."[20] I will forego summarizing Ward's provocative analysis and prescription except to note that he centers his discussion on the academic preparation needed by the would-be missionary, and therein addresses the multiplicity of evangelical schools that still regard the preparation of persons for vocational mission as a crucial part of their educational responsibility. Yet, as is well known, many theological schools no longer consider the preparation of students to be missionaries a needed part of theological education. In most of these schools, the numbers of women, older persons, and ethnic minorities are increasing,[21] and relatively few of these students envision themselves as missionaries. Their image of the missionary is that of the nineteenth century. What does this imply therefore for the teaching of mission?

First, it suggests the urgency of shaping theological education in such a way that students are confronted with the implications of "the church's mission to the entire inhabited world" by what is now referred to as "the globalization of theological education."[22] Obviously, such an ambitious undertaking involves curriculum questions, but more basically, it involves faculty and administrative awareness. For globalization implies new institutional relationships, innovative programming, flexibility in the use of resources, faculty and student exchanges, language requirements and alternatives (other than German and French), and continuous and rigorous evaluation. None of these things will happen, however, unless and until trustees, administrators, and faculty are committed to making their institution a vital part of God's mission to the whole world.[23]

20. "Educational Preparation of Missionaries — A Look Ahead," *Evangelical Missions Quarterly* 23 (October 1987):398.

21. Ellis L. Larsen and James M. Shropshire, "Profile of Contemporary Seminarians," *Theological Education* 24 (Spring 1988):75.

22. *Theological Education* 22 (Spring 1986):5-137. Though the discussion and models set forth are limited to North America, theological educators in other parts of the world will benefit from studying and reflecting on what is said.

23. Compare the statement on mission recently adopted by trustees and faculty of Fuller Seminary: "We aim to have an active part in the evangelization of the whole world

278

One can conceive an ideal situation in which seminarians progressively become internationally aware and determined to live out their Christian commitment as missioners in their own or in another land. If indeed students' global awareness is to some degree determined by their seminary experience, then in the globalization of theological education is there not an institutional responsibility for providing as an integral part of the curriculum academic as well as practical preparation for cross-cultural mission? If so, other than mission theology and history, what should the educational components of such a responsibility be?

Assuming also that evangelization is a, if not the, primary mission of the church, do students not need preparation in evangelization plus firsthand experience in attempting to reach the millions of "unreached peoples" with the gospel, preparation that includes knowing what peoples are unreached and how the gospel is communicated? As Ralph Winter says, "We need to know which peoples are unreached," not so much to distinguish Christians from non-Christians, and certainly not for the purpose simply of counting them, "but primarily in order to know how the Church should go about evangelizing them."[24] Knowing something about the cross-cultural communication of the gospel is now imperative not only for persons who would be missionaries in other lands, but likewise for anyone who is concerned about the welfare of people from multiple ethnic and national backgrounds who now are

---

. . . to unite the study of theology with the doing of evangelism . . . to encourage approach [sic] to evangelism which reflects Christ's incarnation . . . to support the church as it seeks renewal in theology, spirituality, and mission, [and] . . . exercise responsible partnership in the evangelical movement," with that of the Lutheran School of Theology at Chicago: "The purpose of the school is to serve God and the church by advancing the mission of the Gospel in the world through equipping men and women for the church's work of ministry . . . the school is to be a major theological center for the church, serving Lutherans and other Christians in this country and throughout the world. . . . It will foster the church's goal of becoming inclusive, giving special attention to the full participation in the seminary's own life and that of the church at large, of men and women of various colors and cultures, especially Black and Hispanic people . . . through its members the school will reach out in witness and service to the church and the world." Paul E. Pierson, "School of World Mission Fuller Theological Seminary," ibid., p. 74, and David L. Lindberg, "Lutheran School of Theology at Chicago: An Institutional Response to a Global Mission," ibid., p. 92.

24. Winter has written extensively on this subject, and to understand precisely what he means, one should be familiar with his thought and work. The complexity as well as the challenge of communicating the gospel to the unreached peoples is summarized in his essay "Unreached Peoples: What, Where, and Why?" *New Frontiers in Mission,* ed. Patrick Sookhdeo (Exeter, U.K.: Paternoster, 1987), pp. 146-59.

present, in many cases by the tens of thousands, in virtually every urban center in the world including those of Western Europe and the United States. Our multicultured societies are now so obvious that the old domestic-foreign missions distinctions have little meaning.

In the past, preparing people to utilize their skills in education, medicine, and agriculture along with evangelization came to be accepted as necessary not to gain entry into other lands, but in order to give a holistic witness. In the coming decades, however, the possibility of gaining entry into some nations and cultures will depend on whether the would-be missioner has something to offer other than his or her Christian witness. True, in some countries missionary evangelists are still requested by the national church, but this is certainly not the case everywhere. On the other hand, missioners with needed technical knowledge and experience will often gain entry into societies closed to the traditional evangelistic missionary.[25] If, therefore, the study of mission is to be made accessible to those engaging in new kinds of missions, then ways other than the standard three-year Master of Divinity program will have to be developed. If the theological schools are unwilling to do this, they will find their teaching of mission increasingly unrelated to the real needs and opportunities.

As already indicated, the teaching of mission involves more than imparting information or data. Ajith Fernando of Sri Lanka describes the qualities needed to be an effective witness in a cross-cultural context. Imperative, he insists, are humility, teachability, patience, and a "cooperation mentality."[26] Whether these can be *taught* in the classroom may be debated, but they are basic Christian attitudes, and they surely can be *learned* by students who are exposed to the right kinds of models. No less necessary, Fernando says, is the ability to de-contextualize one's theology before attempting to contextualize the gospel.[27] A knowledge of cultural anthropology can be incalculably beneficial and will be part

25. Examples are numerous, such as a U.S. pediatrician who since the end of the Vietnamese conflict has repeatedly worked for lengthy periods of time in Kampuchea. Though he is forbidden to proselytize, the government and those who work with him know that he is a Christian on mission. Because of government restrictions he has been unable to get a permanent visa, and consequently he resides with his family in an adjacent country. Much like the Methodist circuit rider of previous generations, this doctor and others like him have found a way to respond to Christ's commission.

26. "Missionaries Still Needed — But of a Special Kind," *Evangelical Missions Quarterly* 24 (Jan. 1988):19-20.

27. Fernando's example is that of asking the Sri Lankan to respond to a presentation of the gospel as evangelists often do in the West. "But in our culture," Fernando notes, "people are very polite. They have come to a Christian meeting. They are strangers; the

of any comprehensive mission curriculum. But a willingness to de-contextualize is more than an academic exercise.

Finally, a readiness to work ecumenically will determine whether new believers become disciples of Jesus Christ or denominational prose-lytes. One can celebrate those means and occasions wherein Christians manifest unity, such as councils of churches, the Lausanne movement, and regional and local ecumenical groups organized for evangelistic, political, and social action. But unless these contacts result in mutual respect and collaboration at the grass-roots level, the ecumenical relation-ships are at best superficial. Fernando offers a striking example of the need for ecumenical understanding and cooperation. In Sri Lanka, he says, there are twenty-five thousand villages, and only about two percent of these have any Christian witness whatever. But what is happening? A group of Christians goes to a village and initiates a slow and painstaking work among the fifty to sixty families (an average-size village). Finally, some of the villagers begin to respond, and as soon as this happens, another Christian group comes "to compete with the first group."[28] Note the word: *compete*. Inculcating charity among Christians for each other, and teaching cooperation and the need for unity are arduous tasks. But two millennia after Jesus prayed for unity among his disciples, to pre-sume to engage in Christian mission competitively rather than coopera-tively, to divide rather than attempt to heal the divisions and brokenness in the human community is not merely counterproductive, it is scan-dalous.[29] If the study of mission should be required, so should ecumenics.

If seminarians are to be taught to live as Christian missionaries in the contemporary world, theological education will have to be "global," evangelical, contextual, and ecumenical. This is a tall order but one well within reach. As for the basic level of the teaching of mission, the congregation, the situation will be more demanding in the coming decades than at any time since the Middle Ages. A church on mission will be required to conceptualize as well as actualize new ways of being

---

Christians are the hosts. The Christians ask them to raise their hands. They raise their hands. Christians ask them to come forward; and they come forward. Besides, why not get help from Jesus along with the other deities, they think" (ibid., p. 21). The amount being written today about contextualization is extensive, and any relevant preparation for mission must deal with this issue.

28. Ibid., p. 23.

29. Fortunately, a growing number of evangelical as well as conciliar missiologists recognize this fact. See Simon Barrington-Ward, "Packaging or Partnership: A Model for True Church Growth," in *New Frontiers in Mission*, pp. 51-52; David M. Gitari, "The Unity and Diversity of the World-wide Church," ibid., pp. 88-100; and J. P. Masih, " 'People Movement' Problems," *Evangelical Missions Quarterly* 22 (July 1985):302.

church. Direct contact with peoples of other faiths and those with no faith will require new understandings and different approaches. The church began in the first century C.E. *without* many of the advantages we have come to regard as deserved and indispensable — social and political status, extensive and ever-increasing economic resources, and real property. I am not suggesting that we will or should return to a situation comparable to that of the first century, but what I am saying is that despite remarkable technological advances, the challenges faced by the church in the next century will be no less rigorous than those faced by the church of the New Testament. Christians will be increasingly pressed to depend more on God and on each other than most of us have in the twentieth century. Without spiritual development, other kinds of development will not matter.

For Further Reading

Aagaard, Anna Marie
 1989   "Mission in the 1990s." *International Bulletin of Missionary Research* 13 (July):98-100.
Amaladoss, Michael
 1989   "Mission in the 1990s." *International Bulletin of Missionary Research* 13 (Jan.):8-10.
Drucker, Peter F.
 1989   *The New Realities.* New York: Harper & Row.
Glasser, Arthur F.
 1989   "Mission in the 1990s." *International Bulletin of Missionary Research* 13 (Jan.):2-8.
Hendricks, Barbara
 1989   "Mission in the 1990s." *International Bulletin of Missionary Research* 13 (Oct.):146-49.
Hiebert, Paul G.
 1987   "Critical Contextualization." *International Bulletin of Missionary Research* 11 (July):104-12.
Jansen, Frank K., ed.
 1989   *Target Earth.* Pasadena, CA: Global Mapping International.
Newbigin, Lesslie
 1986   *Foolishness to the Greeks.* Grand Rapids, MI: Wm. B. Eerdmans Publishing Company.
 1989   "Missions in the 1990s." *International Bulletin of Missionary Research* 13 (July): 100-102.

Padilla, C. René
  1989   "Mission in the 1990s." *International Bulletin of Missionary Research* 13 (Oct.):149-52.
Pate, Larry D.
  1989   *From Every People.* Monrovia, CA: MARC.
Sookhdeo, Patrick, ed.
  1987   *New Frontiers in Mission.* Exeter, U.K.: Paternoster Press.
Starke, Linda, ed.
  1987   *State of the World 1987.* New York: W. W. Norton. (Also available for 1988, 1989, and 1990.)
Thomas, Norman E.
  1989   "From Missions to Globalization: Teaching Missiology in North American Seminaries." *International Bulletin of Missionary Research* 13 (July):103-7.
Tutu, Desmond M.
  1990   "Missions in the 1990s." *International Bulletin of Missionary Research* 14 (Jan.):6-10.

Women in Mission

Ruth A. Tucker

What is the future for women in mission? Such a question might better be addressed by a futurologist than a historian, but maybe there are lessons and trends and role models from history that can offer us guidelines and inspiration that are available nowhere else. Indeed, if we are looking for a broad-based model for women's involvement and leadership in mission, the past provides a far better landscape than does the present.

One of the great tragedies of twentieth-century Christian mission has been the incredible brain drain resulting from the demise of the Women's Missionary Movement. Gone is the golden era of "female agencies," when women stretched their minds to find solutions to problems and worked together to develop strategies for more effective outreach. Gone are the days when female mission board leaders and female missiologists grappled with the knotty issues involved in cross-cultural evangelization and rivaled their male counterparts in name recognition.

The Women's Missionary Movement of the late nineteenth and early twentieth centuries encompassed millions of women. Indeed, it was the largest mass women's movement up to that time, surpassing in size the Woman's Christian Temperance Union. The movement was loosely connected through the Central Committee on the United Study

---

Ruth A. Tucker, Ph.D., is Visiting Professor at Trinity Evangelical Divinity School, Deerfield, Illinois. She is the author of *Daughters of the Church, First Ladies of the Parish,* and the widely used history of missions, *From Jerusalem to Irian Jaya.*

of Foreign Missions, which during a forty-year period published more
than four million mission textbooks and organized summer school
programs that attracted thousands of women and girls.

Like other missionary movements in history, the Women's Missionary Movement was born out of fervor for missions, but it was also
born out of desperation — a desperation felt most keenly by single
women called by God but rejected by men. Women had been denied
opportunity to serve through traditional mission channels. They had
served effectively as missionary wives and as fund-raisers and prayer
warriors on the home front, but they were not permitted to be missionaries in their own right.

Narcissa Prentiss is a case in point. She was a kindergarten teacher
in the 1830s from western New York state, who had been challenged
by the often-repeated story of the Nez Perce Indians pleading for someone to bring them the "Book of Life." How she longed to be that
individual, but because of her sex she was considered unfit for missionary service. Marcus Whitman faced no such obstacle. He too felt called
to bring the gospel to the Indians of the Oregon Territory. It was this
common concern that brought them together and allowed Narcissa to
become a missionary wife. Shortly after their arrival in Oregon, Marcus
began building a mission compound that soon became a way station
for land-hungry immigrants. For Narcissa, more time was consumed
serving as a hostess to weary travelers than bringing the "Book of Life"
to the Indians. In 1847, less than twelve years after her mission began,
she and Marcus and a dozen others were killed by the Indians. Had
she served as a single missionary, her ministry might have equalled
that of Kate and Sue McBeth or Jeannie Dickson, women who later
effectively preached the gospel to the Indians as missionaries in their
own right.

The rationale for denying women ministry was straightforward.
The Apostle Paul did not permit women to teach or have authority in
the church. They were to be silent. How could mission work be justified
if the Bible was not taken at face value?

But the tenacity of women *called* of God won the day, and one by
one "female agencies" emerged. Beginning in 1861, with the Woman's
Union Missionary Society, the Women's Missionary Movement
spawned forty such organizations by the turn of the century. The impact
was soon felt throughout the churches. Observing the untiring labors
and success of these women, denominational churchmen gradually
relented and opened their mission societies to single women. Eventually the women's boards merged with the denominational boards, and

the once-vibrant Women's Missionary Movement faded from the scene. It was an amazing turn of events, considering the emphatic opposition to women missionaries only decades earlier.

How could these churchmen justify such a change of heart in light of the biblical passages? Did they reexamine the texts and conclude that they had erred? No, it was a pragmatic gesture, and the Pauline passages that once were seen as barring women from ministry came to be viewed as non-binding if women's teaching and preaching were done among "natives" or if it were done in the name of "home" missions. (This reversal of Scripture application did not extend to women seeking to preach the gospel in the institutionalized church on the home front.)

Not all churchmen concurred with this rationale. There were exceptions to the rule — especially among some of the "faith mission" leaders who gained prominence in the late nineteenth century. Among them was Fredrik Franson, the founder of The Evangelical Alliance Mission (TEAM). He is known for his work entitled "Prophesying Daughters," which vigorously defended women's public ministry, asserting that "There is no prohibition in the Bible against women's public work, and we face the circumstance that the devil . . . has been able to exclude nearly two-thirds of the number of Christians from participation in the Lord's service. . . . The loss for God's cause is so great that it can hardly be described" (Franson 1897:2).

Franson's verdict — that the exclusion of women from ministry was of the devil — should not be lightly dismissed. Today the challenge of world evangelization is greater than ever before. As was true in his day, more "participation in the Lord's service" is needed, not less. Nor can we justify a double standard — one for women preaching the gospel to "natives" and one for women preaching to the American middle class. The racial imperialism of the past can no longer be tolerated in a worldwide church that is built on mutual respect and partnership.

Those who continue to perpetuate such inconsistencies are caught in a web of ethnocentrism or racism. Africans — and others — are sensitive to this. A Kenyan student at Trinity Evangelical Divinity School challenged this very practice — demanding to know why it was that American churches restricted women in leadership in this country, while at the same time they commissioned them to go to Africa and other foreign lands to serve in leadership positions there. "Was this not racism," he wondered.

This is a serious problem for the church in its worldwide mission, and missiologists and mission executives can no longer simply avoid the question. Women are in the majority of world Christianity, and their exclusion from leadership roles — be it in the "church" or in the "mission" — is a critical issue that must be addressed.

Although many mainline Protestant denominations have extended full equality to women in recent years, such is not the case with the majority of American churches, including the Roman Catholics, the Southern Baptists, the Missouri Synod Lutherans, the Presbyterian Church in America, the Christian Reformed Church, the Christian and Missionary Alliance, and the Evangelical Free Church — Franson's own denomination. In these churches and many others women are still relegated to a secondary role. Ordination and full opportunity for ministry is denied them. And even in denominations where women are officially granted equality, the reality is far less.

Some suggest that the current debate over women in ministry has arisen out of a creeping spirit of liberalism — that the Bible is no longer taken at face value in many churches and that women have been granted equality as a result of the feminist movement. Such reasoning, however, fails to penetrate the heart of the issue. The essence of church ministry is mission, and any concept of mission that is biblically based is gender neutral. No credible biblical scholar today would argue that Jesus' final challenge — the "great commission" as we know it — ought to be heeded by men only. Nor would they argue that Jesus' stirring summons in Acts 1:8 was for men only: "But you will receive power when the Holy Spirit comes on you; and you will be my witnesses in Jerusalem, and in all Judea and Samaria, and to the ends of the earth."

Still, women are denied equal opportunity in ministry. The two reasons that have most influenced the debate over the centuries have been (1) church tradition, and (2) isolated biblical passages that relate to women. With regard to the former, it is safe to say that many of the stipulations barring women from ministry today have come out of tradition that has developed since the close of the New Testament era. Indeed, many would argue that the custom of clerical ordination — the ultimate tool for excluding women from ministry — is far more a product of church tradition than of biblical precept, and they would be at a loss to find scriptural support for denying an unordained person the opportunity to serve communion or officiate baptisms.

The role of women has also been influenced through the tradition of some of the church's most celebrated theologians. Among those relegating women to a secondary role in the church have been Thomas Aquinas and Martin Luther, whose dogmas were based on personal sentiments far more than on biblical interpretation. Wrote Aquinas:

"The woman is subject to the man, on account of the weakness of her nature, both of mind and of body. . . . Woman is in subjection according to the law of nature, but a slave is not. . . . Children ought to love their father more than their mother." Luther was convinced that woman was "weaker in body and intellect" than man, and that she was "inferior to the man both in honor and dignity" (Tucker and Liefeld 1983:164, 174).

John Wesley also believed that women played a secondary role in the church, but he was willing to make exceptions in order to further the cause of Methodism. If a woman had an "extraordinary call," she did "not fall under the ordinary rules of discipline." Why? Because "the whole work of God called Methodism is an extraordinary dispensation of His providence." Wesley went on to argue that "St. Paul's ordinary rule was, 'I permit not a woman to speak in the congregation'" (John Wesley, *The Letters of the Rev. John Wesley*, 8 vols., ed. John Telford [London: Epworth, 1931], 5:227).

This Pauline admonition in I Corinthians 14:34-35, as well as the passage in I Corinthians 11 (which refers to male headship), and I Timothy 2 (which speaks of women not teaching and having authority) have been most frequently used to restrict women in ministry. All three passages are enmeshed with the cultural particularities of their day. I Corinthians 11 focuses on the issue of head coverings and hair length for both women and men — regulations that are not enforced today. I Corinthians 14:34-35 is part of a lengthy passage relating to glossolalia, a practice that likewise is not considered applicable in most churches today. I Timothy 2 speaks of appropriate conduct for Christians — lifting hands in prayer and not wearing braided hair, gold, or pearls. The problems surrounding all of these issues were particularly related to cultural phenomena encountered by the early church.

But apart from the cultural relativity inherent in these passages, it is the recent scholarly biblical exegesis that most convincingly calls for a reexamination of the restrictions on women's ministry based on these verses. Word studies on *kephale* (rendered *head* in I Cor. 11), for example, have indicated that the meaning of the word is likely *source*, rather than *authority* as it has been traditionally interpreted (Mickelsen 1986:97-110). If this is true, arguments for subjecting women on the basis of biblical headship are certainly undercut. The reference to women being silent in I Corinthians 14, if taken literally, blatantly contradicts I Corinthians 11, which speaks of women *praying* and *prophesying* with their heads covered. It is more likely that the women asking questions of their husbands were disruptive, and were thus admonished to be

288

quiet. The same admonition is made a few verses earlier in the passage addressed to people speaking in tongues without interpreters.

The passage most often cited by people who would restrict women in ministry is I Timothy 2, beginning with verse 11: "A woman should learn in quietness and full submission." Contrary to traditional interpretations, this verse is actually revolutionary in tone. The writer is saying a woman *must* learn. The verb is in the imperative. It is a command. Jewish women were not permitted to study the Torah, but here it is commanded that Christian women learn. That women were to learn in silence was not demeaning: "silence was . . . a positive attribute for rabbinic students" and "women were to be learning in the same manner as did rabbinic students" (Spencer 1985:75).

Verse 12 states, "I do not permit a woman to teach or to have authority over a man; she must be silent." The verb here is present tense, and the phrase could accurately be rendered, "I am not presently permitting a woman to teach." The word translated *or* is *oude* in the Greek, and might be better rendered "in a manner of." The verb *authentein* rendered *authority* occurs only in this instance in the New Testament. *Exousia*, the common Greek term for authority, is not used probably because a stronger term was needed — such as to domineer or to "usurp authority," as the verb is rendered in the King James Version. Thus the instructions here might better be phrased, "I am not presently permitting a woman to teach in a manner of usurping authority over a man; she must be quiet."

Verses 13 and 14 offer an explanation: "For Adam was formed first, then Eve. And Adam was not the one deceived; it was the woman who was deceived and became a sinner." It makes little sense to argue that being first in creation confers authority, especially considering the fact that the animals were created before Adam. It does make sense, however, if first formed meant first educated. Adam, according to Old Testament scholar Walter Kaiser, "had the educational and spiritual advantage of being 'formed first' (v. 13). The verb is *plasso*, 'to form, mold, shape' (presumably in spiritual education) not, 'created first' (which in Greek is *kitzo*). Paul's argument, then, is based on the 'orders of education,' not the 'orders of creation'" (Kaiser 1986:12-I).

Adam was given the instruction forbidding him to eat of the fruit before Eve was formed. She lacked instruction — presumably hearing of the restriction only through Adam. It would seem natural, then, that she could be more easily deceived. So, it would seem plausible that women here were being admonished to be properly educated before they became involved in teaching or leadership responsibilities.

289

Such a rendering of the passage allows it to harmonize with the Great Commission and the Lord's challenge in Acts 1:8, and it does not conflict with the bestowal of spiritual gifts, which are not gender based. It likewise allows harmonization with the many biblical examples of women in ministry. The Apostle Paul, despite severe cultural restrictions on women of his day, depended heavily on women in his dynamic missionary outreach. Romans 16 lists nine of them, including Phoebe, who likely traveled to Rome with the gospel (and with that epistle), and Priscilla, of whom Paul stated that "all the churches of the Gentiles" were grateful for her willingness to risk her life for the gospel (Rom. 16:3-4).

These biblical women are role models that ought to energize the church today in its mission at home and abroad. So equally are the countless women in the centuries since whose ministries have made an extraordinary mark on the church, despite the opposition they faced simply because they were women. They stand as monuments to the faith just as surely as do the men whose names embellish the pages of our history books as reformers and revivalists and missionary statesmen.

Katherine Zell is an example. She served as a Protestant pastor's wife in Strassburg during the Reformation. So involved was she in the ministry that at the time of her husband's death she felt constrained to defend her activities. "I am not usurping the office of preacher or apostle," she insisted, but she hastened to add, "I am like the dear Mary Magdalene, who with no thought of being an apostle, came to tell the disciples that she had encountered the risen Lord" (Tucker 1988:33).

Despite her defense, the criticism continued. When charged with disturbing the peace, she gave a stinging response: "Do you call this disturbing the peace that instead of spending my time in frivolous amusements I have visited the plague infested and carried out the dead? I have visited those in prison and under sentence of death. . . . I have done more than any minister in visiting those in misery. Is this disturbing the peace of the church?" (Tucker 1988:34).

She openly criticized the clergy for their persecution of other Christians. "Why do you rail at Schwenckfeld?" she demanded of a Lutheran leader. "You talk as if you would have him burned like the poor Servetus at Geneva. . . . The Anabaptists are pursued as by a hunter with dogs chasing wild boars. Yet the Anabaptists accept Christ in all the essentials as we do." Her reward for speaking the truth was harassment and imprisonment. Yet, she continued preaching until she died (Tucker 1988:32-36).

There were other women of the Reformation who courageously preached the gospel. Martin Luther lauded one of them: "The Duke of Bavaria rages above measure, killing, crushing and persecuting the gospel with all his might. That most noble woman, Argula von Stauffer, is there making a valiant fight with great spirit, boldness of speech and knowledge of Christ. . . . She alone among those monsters, carries on with firm faith. . . . She is a singular instrument of Christ" (Tucker and Liefeld 1987:186).

Among Roman Catholics, Madame Jeanne Guyon stands out as an effective itinerant missionary of her day. She was a seventeenth-century French woman who traveled from town to town preaching in private homes and in open-air meetings. One of her converts was a physician, who had turned away from the faith of his younger years. Another was a young nun who was contemplating suicide.

Another Roman Catholic French woman who made a powerful contribution to world mission was Anne Marie Javouhey, the founder of the Sisters of St. Joseph. She initially felt called to bring the gospel to Africa, but by the time of her death in 1851 she had commissioned some nine hundred nuns to serve throughout the world. Yet she did not escape continual opposition from her bishop, who felt she had overstepped her bounds as a woman.

Malla Moe, inspired by Fredrik Franson, began her missionary service in Swaziland in the late nineteenth century. She had a wide-ranging ministry and functioned as an evangelist, a teacher, a preacher, a church planter, and unofficially as a bishop. Yet, when she returned to the United States and to her homeland of Norway, she was barred from many churches. "Officials of the State church reminded her to read Paul's instruction that 'women should keep silence in the church'" (Nilsen 1956:135).

Johanna Veenstra of the Christian Reformed Church was a student volunteer at Calvin College during the heyday of the Student Volunteer Movement, and later in the 1920s and 1930s ministered very effectively in Nigeria, where she preached and trained young men to be evangelists. Though not ordained, she did the work of an ordained minister. Today her memory is revered and a women's dormitory is named for her at Calvin College — while at the same time young women who would seek to follow her example in this country are restricted at every turn.

The Roman Catholic Church is plagued with similar inconsistencies today. Despite official restrictions that prohibit women from serving as priests, the actual practice of the church is quite different. Women have circumvented the obstacles since medieval times, and they continue to do so today. Due to a shortage of priests in recent decades, nuns have often been the only resident spiritual leaders available to the laity. This is not only true in Latin America and other areas of the Third World, but it is also true in America, as Tony Campolo relates:

> Recently I spent some time with a Roman Catholic bishop who explained to me how women had been a godsend to many of the churches in his diocese which lacked priestly leadership. He explained that nuns were serving as the pastors for many of his rural congregations, although the people did not actually call them pastors. These nuns visited the sick, taught the catechism, preached the homilies, and even served Holy Communion. He explained that once a month, he or one of his auxiliary bishops would visit each of these female-led parishes, perform the mass, and sanctify the bread and wine. These "sanctified elements" would then be stored until worship time, when they would be given to communicants by the nuns. When I pointed out that these nuns did everything that priests do and therefore should be ordained, he agreed. Then he added, "Most people in these parishes would also agree, but you know how the church is." Indeed I do. (Tony Campolo, *20 Hot Potatoes Christians Are Afraid to Touch* [Waco: Word Books, 1988], 41.)

It is this inconsistency — this double standard — more than anything else that has prevented women from assuming leadership alongside men in mission today. Women continue to outnumber men in mission work, but they are as noticeably absent in the positions of missiologists and executives in most mission organizations as they are in those of theologians and ordained ministers in most churches. As long as this inequity persists and women are relegated to secondary roles, the church's mission — be it at home or abroad — will be seriously impeded.

Today as we move rapidly toward the twenty-first century, world evangelization is high on the agenda of mission organizations and denominations. Indeed, there are probably more mission strategies and plans afloat than ever before in history. High-level meetings and conferences are being convened to target priorities and map out goals. But where are the women? They are out in the trenches involved in the work, but by and large they are absent from decision-making bodies.

Women ought to be recruited for leadership positions not only because it is the right thing to do but because their input is crucial. The history of the church and its worldwide mission might have taken a very different course had women been permitted leadership roles. There might have been less theological dissension and fewer denominational divisions and there might have been more energy expended in simply sharing the love of Jesus in word and in deed. Women often bring a different perspective than do their male counterparts. They approach problems from different angles, and they respond to problems with different emotions.

The world is changing rapidly, and so must our approach to world evangelization. Questions involving global partnership, contextualization, religious pluralism, building bridges to other religions, and the sharing of wealth beg for fresh solutions. No longer can we be satisfied with utilizing the ideas and counsel of only one sex. Collaboration and teamwork between men and women is crucial to the future success of world mission. Indeed, we must insist on nothing less than equal partnership — partnership that erases all cultural, racial, and sex barriers. May we ever be reminded of the glorious hallmark of our faith, that "there is neither Jew nor Greek, slave nor free, male nor female, for you are all one in Christ Jesus" (Gal. 3:28).

For Further Reading

Beaver, R. Pierce
   1980   *American Protestant Women in World Mission: A History of the First Feminist Movement in North America.* Grand Rapids, MI: Wm. B. Eerdmans Publishing Company.

Hardesty, Nancy A.
   1984   *Women Called to Witness: Evangelical Feminism in the 19th Century.* Nashville: Abingdon Press.

Hassey, Janette
   1986   *No Time for Silence: Evangelical Women in Public Ministry Around the Turn of the Century.* Grand Rapids, MI: The Zondervan Corporation.

Hill, Patricia R.
   1985   *The World Their Household: The American Woman's Foreign Mission Movement and Cultural Transformation, 1870-1920.* Ann Arbor: University of Michigan Press.

Kaiser, Walter C., Jr.
   1986   "Shared Leadership or Male Headship." *Christianity Today,* October 3, pp. 12ff.

293

Mickelsen, Alvera, ed.
1986   *Women, Authority and the Bible.* Downers Grove, IL: InterVarsity Press.

Nilsen, Maria
1956   *Molla Moe.* Chicago: Moody Press.

Spencer, Aida
1985   *Beyond the Curse: Women Called to Ministry.* Nashville: Thomas Nelson.

Tucker, Ruth A.
1988a   *First Ladies of the Parish: Historical Portraits of Pastors' Wives.* Grand Rapids, MI: The Zondervan Corporation.
1988b   *Guardians of the Great Commission: The Story of Women in Modern Mission.* Grand Rapids, MI: The Zondervan Corporation.

Tucker, Ruth A., and Walter L. Liefeld
1987   *Daughters of the Church: Woman and Ministry from New Testament Times to the Present.* Grand Rapids, MI: The Zondervan Corporation.

Mission and
the Problem of Affluence

Very well underlined? missionary materialism? organizations.

Jonathan J. Bonk

Western missionaries around the world are increasingly laboring under
the onerous necessity of having to justify their motives, since from the
perspective of most of this world's citizenry, they do exceedingly well by
doing good.[1] Whatever one makes of relative GNP (Gross National
Product), GDP (Gross Domestic Product), or PPP (Purchasing Power Par-
ity) standards of comparison, the fact remains that most of the people in
the world would gladly trade economic positions with virtually any
Western missionary. Indeed, were it not so, it is not farfetched to wonder
whether there would be any substantial number of missionaries from the
West.

Rice Christians

Throughout the nineteenth century, it was common missionary practice
to hire "native agents" to preach the gospel. This made good sense,

---

1. Portions of this chapter appeared in the January/March 1991 issue of *Transformation*, and are here used by permission.

Jonathan J. Bonk is Professor of Mission Studies at Providence Theological
Seminary, Otterburne, Manitoba, Canada. Raised in Ethiopia by Canadian
missionary parents, he subsequently served there with SIM International
(1974-76). He is the author of four books, including *Missions and Money:
Affluence as a Western Missionary Problem* (1991).

particularly in those countries where the language and the culture were difficult or inconvenient for the Western missionary to master. "Native agents" were born and raised in the culture, understood the indigenous languages, had built up immunities and resistance to tropical diseases that devastated foreign missionaries, would automatically make their preaching and teaching culturally appropriate, didn't have the stigma of "foreigner" during times of political unrest, and could live and travel far more simply than could or would the foreign missionary. In short, it was argued, indigenous workers were many times more effective in reaching their fellow countrymen than foreign missionaries could ever hope to be.

John Livingstone Nevius (1829-1893) arrived in China in 1856 as a missionary of the American Presbyterian board. He soon became profoundly dissatisfied with abuses that he saw as an inherent and inevitable result of a system in which native agents were paid to evangelize their fellow countrymen. The problem, as Nevius observed, was that the credibility of the "paid agent" was seriously compromised, since it tended, in his words, to

> . . . excite a mercenary spirit, and to increase the number of mercenary Christians. . . . The opprobrious epithet, Rice Christians, has gained almost universal currency in the East, as expressive of the foreigners' estimate of the actual results of missionary work. (Nevius 1979:256-67)

Accordingly, Nevius formulated an alternative plan in keeping with the "three-self" principle: self-propagation, self-government, and self-support. While first put into effect by Presbyterians in Korea, the "Nevius method" came to be a hallmark of many Western cross-cultural missionary endeavors.

As a generalization applied to all Christians in China, the designation "rice Christian" was no doubt false and dangerously misleading. Nevertheless, Nevius confessed,

> . . . it is worse than useless to ignore the readiness of large classes of China men to become 'Rice Christians'. . . . The general opinion of the China man as to the motive of one of his countrymen in propagating a foreign religion, is that it is a mercenary one. When he learns that the native preacher is in fact paid by foreigners, he is confirmed in his judgment. What the motive is which actuates the foreign missionary . . . he is left to imagine. (1979:266-67)

296

Rice Missionaries

Ironically, many of those elements which Nevius and his fellow missionaries found most reprehensible in the practice of hiring native agents to "peddle the word of God for a profit" (II Cor. 2:17) appear to have become firmly embedded within the structural *modus operandi* of Western missionary societies themselves. It is not unusual, for example, for nondenominational agencies to insist that potential candidates raise the prescribed amount of support before being permitted to venture forth. Furthermore, should support for a particular missionary wane, that missionary will not be permitted to remain on the field, but must return home to garner more support. Such Western mission agencies thus operate on a blatantly "rice-missionary" principle: no money — no missionary. Curiously, missionaries with such agencies are by no means reticent in proffering their criticism of indigenous churches and missionaries attempting to operate according to similar principles.

I recently received a letter from a young married couple, as yet childless, on their way to a mission assignment in Taiwan . . . if they can garner enough support. The well-known and highly respected mission agency under whose aegis they have chosen to work has stipulated as a matter of general policy that they cannot leave North America until one hundred percent of their support has been pledged. In this instance, the support level is pegged at $3887 per month, $46,644 per year. Of course, only $18,168 of this is designated as "Personal Salary" . . . the rest being applied to housing, travel, medical and insurance plans, ministry expenses, anticipated cost-of-living increases, and home office administration. Nevertheless, this salary will ensure them a place among the affluent in a land where the average childless couple can expect to earn $3184, of which an estimated 38.2 percent will be spent on food (Jansen 1989:78-79).

The following tables (p. 298) provide some indication of the escalating support requirements of Western missionaries, on the one hand, and of the deepening poverty of peoples in those parts of the world still popularly regarded as "missionary receiving" countries, on the other.

On the basis of the data provided in these tables, a number of observations may be made. In the first place, it seems clear that successive generations of Westerners have been enculturated to uncritical redefinition of personal material "needs" in accordance with continually escalating notions of entitlement that most of the world's popula-

Table 1. Typical monthly support required for one adult:[2]

YEAR	MONTHLY SUPPORT
1906	$ 30
1926	80
1946	85
1966	150
1986	1095
1988	1345

Table 2. Typical monthly support structure for family members in 1989

Adult	$1345	(x 2 x 12 = $32,280)
Child to 5 years	403	(x 12 = 4,836)
Child 6-11 years	572	(x 12 = 6,846)
Child over 12 years	740	(x 12 = 8,880)

TOTAL SUPPORT FOR FAMILY OF FIVE = $52,880 PER YEAR

Table 3. Per Capita Income and Percent of Income spent on Food[3]

COUNTRY	$ INCOME	% SPENT ON FOOD	$ REMAINING	$ PER/WK
BANGLADESH	150	66.1	50.85	.98
BELIZE	790	55.1	354.71	6.82
CENTRAL AFRICAN REPUBLIC	210	70.5	61.95	1.19
CHAD	110	45.3	60.17	1.16
ETHIOPIA	90	57.4	38.34	.74
GUINEA	250	61.5	96.25	1.85
HAITI	360	77.9	79.56	1.53
KENYA	190	46.5	101.65	1.95
NIGER	190	50.5	94.05	1.81
TANZANIA	250	54.3	114.25	2.20
UGANDA	230	58.0	96.60	1.86

2. This information is derived from the brochure "SIM: Where your gift goes" (1989). Support covers missionary salaries, travel, medical expenses, housing, retirement, administration, etc. Funds designated for special mission-approved projects are over and above support levels, but are also tax deductible.
3. These figures are from Jansen 1989:78-79.

tion can only regard as wildly profligate. It comes as no surprise, therefore, that the support, security, technology, and organization undergirding Western missions today place missionaries among the powerful of
this world. Second, indications are that the gulf between developed and
developing countries will continue to widen (Sivard 1989:5).

It is in the context of such considerations that the awkward question suggested in the title of this essay must be asked: Might not those
agencies whose policies carefully preclude the possibility of engaging
in missionary work on anything less than ample support be said to
have enshrined as policy the "rice missionary" principle? And cannot
North American missionaries who either refuse or are not permitted to
obey their calling unless they are richly supported be called "rice missionaries"?

I am not condoning either "rice Christians" or "rice missionaries."
But surely the same standard must be applied to all. Any missionary
who would do away with the mercenary motive in new converts must
first attend to his or her own motives. No *Christian* missionary of any
race should "peddle the word of God for profit" (II Cor. 2:17, NIV).
There are occasions when it is better for a missionary to accept no
reimbursement for his work of preaching the gospel. It is never appropriate for a *Christian* missionary to make his service conditional upon
reimbursement. Removing this condition one step by pointing to the
mission agency's "full support policy" fools no one: not the poor, not
the missionary, and certainly not God.

But even more disturbing questions remain. What effect does
plenitude have upon Western missionaries as communicators and
teachers of good news to the poor? To put it more bluntly, what impact
does the material privilege of a missionary have on his or her personal
credibility, and on poverty-stricken unbelievers' perceptions of the content and relevance of the good news itself (cf. Bonk 1991)? What are the
implications of support requirements for North American missionaries
serving among peoples the nature and scale of whose poverty is inti-
mated by the figures in table 3 above?

One fact is indisputable. Our relative power economically has not
made us more effective in accomplishing our primary task. Tragically,
the Western church has never been as impotent in bringing the Good
News to those who have traditionally been most responsive to it — the
poor (Grigg 1987). Indeed, while our missionaries find plenty of worthwhile things to do all over the world, they seem to be a declining force
in the fierce spiritual battle gripping our globe. New believers and new
churches are almost inevitably a result of the efforts of much weaker

299

"native" evangelists and missionaries, whose command of material resources can only be described as negligible.

Thus, for example, each of the 462 missionaries comprising the Indian Evangelical Team serving in Northern India operates at an average monthly support level of $18. Missionaries from the Kachin Baptist Church in Burma do the work of an apostle for even less, serving six-year terms throughout that region of Burma and in Yunan Province without any financial remittance whatsoever. These missionaries, poor and lacking in training, have accomplished tremendous results, reporting 6,550 conversions as a direct result of their evangelizing in Yunan Province during the past four years. The growth and the effectiveness of financially and organizationally "weak" non-Western mission agencies and missionaries far outstrips that of their Western counterparts. Despite their deepening poverty with its concomitant weakness relative to their brothers and sisters in Western lands, even conservative projections estimate that by the year 2000 most Christian missionaries will be from the "Two-Thirds World" (Pate 1989:11-57).

If our missionaries are not faring well on the evangelistic front, their association with affluence has made them among the most effective advocates of the popular "gospel of plenty," so aggressively proclaimed and compellingly modeled by the West to all the world (Potter 1954; Kennedy 1949). Ironically, with the world's peoples now poised on the brink of the greatest mass conversion in human history, we have become aware that our Western way of life — enshrining as it does covetousness, greed, and gluttony as virtues — is spiritually sterile and probably economically doomed. That conditioning fondly referred to as "education" has successfully inculcated within us and now in the rest of the world the notion that we are *entitled* to consume this planet's resources at a rate so phenomenal as to ensure the imminent destruction of our planet.

It is now clear that the Western way of life — built upon the premise that the chief end of humankind is to bring glory to the Gross National Product — cannot be sustained for any but a tiny fraction of the globe's population. Thus, by impassioned, even hysterical, word — though not yet by example — the West now urges upon so-called "developing" nations policies of economic austerity and environmental conservation. The tragedy is that it may be too late. Recently converted to the gospel of plenty, poorer populations will not be denied their right to profligate consumption in their pursuit of the "good" life implicitly promised in Western enculturation and modeled in Western lifestyles.

300

Good News for the Poor:
The Gospel of Plenty or the Gospel of Our Lord?

The Western penchant to make missionary obedience conditional upon ample support is, it seems to me, not so much a problem of culturally sanctioned greed as it is a loss of faith in the unique ways and means whereby God has consistently accomplished his will on earth.

Current events in the Middle East remind us that whenever one kingdom attempts to displace another, there is war. The Scriptures are full of talk of war, making it clear that those who follow Christ are not only pilgrims and strangers on this earth, but that we are soldiers behind the lines in enemy territory — at great peril, engaged in a life-and-death struggle to wrest territory away from an enemy who — in the words of our Scriptures — is ruler of this dark world.

The background to this cosmic struggle between Good and Evil is outlined by St. John in Revelation 12:7-17. The church is engaged in mortal combat against an enemy who will give no quarter; no prisoners are taken; there is no neutral zone; no treaty is possible. The question that is of vital concern to every Christian missionary is this: How is victory over this terrible enemy — under whose occupation all of creation groans — to be achieved?

I will never forget being a nine-year-old witness to a brief but brutal altercation between Ethiopian troops and Somali villagers in 1954. Following an outbreak of trouble that local police were unable to control, troops took up positions on the bridge just in front of our house in Kallafo, overlooking the Wabi Shebelli. It was my ninth birthday, and my sister and I were engrossed in a treasure hunt when the shooting started. Most of the Somalis simply ran to escape the barrage; but some of them fought back with makeshift slings, fashioned out of their skirts. The fight was short, bloody, and completely one-sided. Cloth catapults were no match for machine guns. Dozens of Somalis were killed, and approximately seventy were injured. That night, we heard the sounds of hyenas and lions feeding on the remains of the wounded who had dragged themselves into the banana plantation across the river in a vain attempt to find sanctuary. The next day, my father's truck was commandeered by the army and used to carry away the bodies of dead Somalis to their mass grave in the desert some miles away from the town. The point of this illustration is, of course, the tragically pathetic inadequacy of the weapons used by the Somalis in their encounter with their gun-touting enemies.

God persistently delights in using the small, weak, foolish things

301

in accomplishing his purposes (I Cor. 1:27). A mighty nation destined to play a significant role in God's redemptive plan for mankind issues from the shriveled bodies of two geriatrics; a travesty of justice leading to the execution of a Galilean falsely accused of sedition accomplishes salvation and life for millions.

Paul, in his second letter to the Corinthians, puts it this way: "For though we live in the world, we do not wage war as the world does. The weapons we fight with are not the weapons of the world. On the contrary, they have divine power to demolish strongholds" (II Cor. 10:3-4). These most potent of Christian weapons fall naturally into three categories: the *incarnation,* the *cross,* and *weakness.*

The Incarnation

The incarnation is at the very heart of our Christian faith. "The Word became flesh and lived for a while among us" (John 1:14). Personal affluence and temporal security make it increasingly difficult for us Western Christians to regard the incarnation as a model for personal action. *For many of us who call ourselves Christians, the incarnation is merely a theologically descriptive, rather than a strategically prescriptive, event.*

The incarnation teaches us that power, speed, mobility, comprehensiveness, efficiency, and success — those elements which we in the West have in abundance — cannot be the *modus operandi* of any truly *Christian* missionary. Jesus' decision to enter the world as an illegitimate child, born to a poor family in an occupied back-eddy of the Roman Empire, was neither an accident nor a case of mistaken judgment.

The missiological lessons of the incarnation are clear: "As you have sent me into the world, I have sent [those whom you gave me] into the world," Christ prayed as he pleaded with his heavenly Father for those who, like him, were "not of this world" (John 17:16, 18). "Your attitude should be the same as that of Christ Jesus," Paul reminded believers at Philippi — whose methods for achieving personal objectives were only too natural (Phil. 2:5). At the very least, the incarnation means giving up the power, the prestige, the privilege, and the social position to which we feel naturally entitled.

Christ's mission done in Christ's way must always begin, proceed, and end with the great renunciation. There is no room for the power-generating, ego-inflating, career-building, self-protecting approach so characteristic of much that is called mission. Those who are really serious about making any headway against the enemy must return to this "foolishness" of our Lord. No matter how enlightened the techniques, how sophisticated the technology, or how numerous, how dedicated, and how well qualified the personnel, nothing but God's incarnational strategy will prevail against either "the powers of this dark world" or "the spiritual forces of evil in heavenly realms" (Eph. 6:10-18). However strange or inappropriate this weapon must seem to natural man, without it there can be no hope of victory.

The Cross

The second weapon is equally strange, and no less essential. *The cross is not merely a symbol of the atonement, but a prescription for the only way of life promised to all who would follow Jesus.* Those who would follow Jesus look forward not only to the comforting prospect of "pie in the sky in the sweet by and by," but to inconvenience, suffering, and death in the here and now. For Jesus deliberately chose to make the fellowship of the cross an integral part of what he offers each disciple (Matt. 10:38; Mark 8:31-34).

\ The cross not only gives life — it takes it. The cross not only achieves reconciliation between God and man — it divides — separating those whose kingdom is not of this world from those at home with the spirit of their particular age. For Christ's followers, the cross is not only the power of God unto salvation; it is the guarantee of misunderstanding, persecution, and suffering at the hands of those to whom it is a foolish and obnoxious stumbling block (I Cor. 1:17-18; Gal. 6:12-14). There is nothing humanly attractive, easy, secure, comfortable, convenient, strategically efficient, economical, or self-fulfilling about a personal cross!

Many, regarding themselves as Christ's disciples because they have accepted — at the superficial level — what Christ offers through the cross, are in actual fact frauds. Encountering such "believers" in Philippi, Paul tearfully acknowledged that "many live as enemies of the cross of Christ . . . [for] their mind is on earthly things." The fellowship of the cross was foreign to these church members. They were not conformed to Christ's death. "Their destiny is destruction," was Paul's sorrowful conclusion (Phil. 3:18, 19).

For such persons, the cross meant judgment. Their lives — shaped, directed, and consumed by self-gratification — were a mute but effective denial of the Christ whom they professed to represent. Horrified at the prospect of bearing the foolishly painful cross of the Lover of their souls, they surrendered to their mortal enemy. Living out their lives in pleasant, self-fulfilling ways — according to the wisdom of their particular age — they were impotent in the spiritual struggle between Good and Evil.

Likewise any contemporary ecclesiastical enterprise that does not operate according to the principles of the cross — the heavy, awkward, impeding, unappealing, death-dealing cross — may be mission, but it is not *Christian* mission. For the mission or missionary that is *Christian* in the most profound sense of the term, self-denial is not merely a periodically inconvenient necessity, but a radical strategy marking all of those who are in step with Christ.

Weakness

The third paradoxical element characterizing all truly Christian mission is weakness. Humankind has always been awed and cowed by power. Power of various kinds — military, political, social, ecclesiastical, missiological — is avidly sought and clung to in the natural course of human affairs. We Westerners are a privileged people; privileges require protecting; protection requires power — in the case of Western missions, the power of money, excellent organization, well-educated missionaries, and skillful strategies.

According to the New Testament, on the other hand, Christ's followers are neither to strive for nor to maintain personal power and privilege. All that they do is to be marked by personal vulnerability and self-giving. The missionary who truly serves his or her Head never looks for ways of gaining and wielding power and influence, but for ways of subjecting himself or herself on behalf of others.

Christmas reminds us that the power of God began with the powerlessness of a poor infant, in the presence of an assortment of peasants, shepherds, and common barnyard animals. The mortal struggle against the terrible forces of evil in our universe pitted all the violent power of which Satan is capable against the pathetic weakness of a newborn infant.

The infant survived, and grew, but came to a tragic and early end. Unable to answer charges of political insurrection brought against him by the people he came to save, he died. Unable to defend either himself or his followers, he hung — pain-racked in body and spirit, a victim of trumped up charges — on a cross between two thieves.

His mother, tearful witness to the death agonies of her beloved firstborn, must have recalled with bitter irony the joyful outpouring of hopes and expectations with which she had greeted the news that *this* child would liberate Israel (Luke 1:46-55)! How naive she had been!

304

How differently her son's life had unfolded before her: he had not brought down rulers from their thrones — they had brought him down; he had tried to lift the humble, but had been rejected by them; he had on occasion filled the hungry with good things and sent the rich empty away, but now the rich had their revenge. Her son's weakness was no match for their power.

St. Paul's testimony was similar. "It seems to me," he wrote in what is the most complete New Testament description of missionary lifestyle that we have, "that God has put us apostles on display . . . like prisoners condemned to die, at the end of the procession" (I Cor. 4:8-13). What was it that distinguished Paul as a missionary? Not his strength, but his weakness; not his honor, but his humiliation; not his healthy body, fine wardrobe, and comfortable home, but his poverty, rags, and homelessness; not the flattering accolades of the powerful, but curses, slander, and persecution at the hands of the powerful. In short, according to Paul, to be a missionary meant to become "the scum of the earth, the refuse of the world."

Like his Savior's before him, Paul's life did not have a happy ending. He did not spend his last years like a "missionary statesman," surrounded by devoted supporters and fellow veterans in a Christian retirement village somewhere in California or Florida, swapping slides and stories about the good old days! Rather, he spent his last days almost alone, in a Roman dungeon, a frail old man whose life was finally snuffed out by executioners at the behest of a powerful emperor. It is hard to imagine a weaker, more vulnerable person than this. Yet through Paul, God touched the foundation of history, and he let Paul touch it too.

Of course, we know that it was not the crucifiers, but the crucified, not the executioner, but the executed, who manifested the mighty power of God that transforms persons, nations, and the course of history!

If the Western church is really serious about doing Christ's mission in Christ's way, in making some headway against the enemy forces under whose domination all creation groans, it must return to those weapons which God has designed to defeat the enemy: the incarnation, the cross, and weakness. Missiological plans, policies, practices, and ambitions must move away from their essentially self-serving character to reflect once again the incarnation. Self-preservation must no longer serve as the bottom line governing mission principles and practices; rather, method and message alike must manifest the cross. The poor must no longer be impressed chiefly by the wealth and power of West-

Mother Theses

ern missions, but by their weakness and vulnerability. Any other path will ensure that Western Christian endeavors will continue to be of the "rice missionary" variety, and that the good news that Jesus died for our sins will continue to be obscured by the good news of plenty.

Conclusion

In these days of inflated Western material expectations, is it possible for Western mission agencies to get back to the faith principle? It remains to be seen. Can Western mission agencies abandon their "rice missionary" policies for practices more in keeping with the sacred original "Missionary Manual"? Is it possible for some missionaries from the Western churches to follow in the footsteps of Paul? "Unlike so many, we do not peddle the word of God for profit," Paul could remind the young church at Corinth (II Cor. 2:17), elsewhere elaborating, ". . . we worked night and day, laboring and toiling so that we would not be a burden to any of you. We did this, not because we do not have the right to such help, but in order to make ourselves a model for you to follow" (II Thess. 3:8-9).

What if Western mission societies were to move away from their security and benefits as preconditions for missionary service? Would there still be missionaries from the North American church? I believe there would be a few, but these would resemble those described in I Corinthians 4, scarcely recognizable by our popular definition of "missionary." There would certainly be no "rice missionaries." Only those obedient to the gifts and the compulsion of the Holy Spirit would go. The rest could stay home.

As a boy growing up in Ethiopia, I used to observe my mother at work in her clinic. Penicillin was the wonder drug, and patients coming to the clinic with infected wounds soon learned that they could expect to be cured after one or two injections of the mysterious milky fluid. But within a few months an alarming number of people with painful abscesses on that part of the human anatomy typically designated for penicillin injections began to appear at the clinic. Investigation soon uncovered a clandestine "clinic" on the other side of town. Its proprietor, having availed himself of our discarded syringes, needles, and empty vials, and by cleverly substituting milk for penicillin, was able to offer "penicillin" injections at half the cost. His tools and his techniques were reassuringly similar to those employed by my mother. The milk he was using was to the untrained eye indistinguishable from penicillin. The problem lay not in the appearance of things, but in their reality. He made the mistake of seeing only the appearance of things, and overlooked the possibility that there might be a level of reality invisible to him. As a result, not only were his patients not healed; their condition after his treatment was indescribably worse than it had been before.

Likewise, when Christian mission utilizes tools and resources that take cognizance only of the surface of things, the resultant "cure" cannot but be worse than the original ailment. Yet much of what we call mission can operate by means of the cross, weakness, and incarnation . . . those instrumentalities which alone have power against the hidden realities behind our world's evils.

As Western Christians we rightly regard the poverty of our fellow human beings as a gigantic problem about which we seem able to do very little; we have proven less willing to view our personal affluence as an even greater problem. Global poverty *is* an acute material problem, no doubt; but Western affluence is a profoundly spiritual one. Is it not at least as difficult for us members of the Western church to overcome our affluence as it is for our poverty-stricken brothers and sisters in the rest of the world to survive their poverty? Failure to counter wealth's insidious effects upon our endeavors will ensure the continued ebb of the Western churches as a kingdom force.

Unless we come to see our Western world through the eyes of Jesus and the writers of the Scriptures, we will continue to excuse the personal and collective covetousness that has made us "great." And above the locked door to the heart of the richest church the world has ever seen will be written — perhaps in glittering neon — the word "ICHABOD." Our Savior will remain on the outside. Like its first-century counterpart in Laodicea, the Christlessness and spiritual impotence of the Western church will be increasingly apparent to everyone but the church itself. Increasingly mesmerized by the deceitfulness of its own riches and by the cares of its tiny, materially secure, ego-sized world, the richest church in the world will have no good news for the poor.

Addendum

This chapter has not been written flippantly. As the son of missionaries who spent the best part of their lives in service to the people of Ethiopia, as one whose closest friends include numerous missionaries, and as one devoted to the task of sharing with the world the good news of Jesus as Savior and Lord, I write with a deep sense of personal unworthiness, for I am well aware of the deep and often sacrificial commitment to service characterizing many missionaries.

It has been my intention to speak the truth, insofar as I am able to discern it. This chapter has been an attempt to explore, however inadequately, one aspect of Western missionary life and ministry that has, for a variety of reasons, been virtually ignored in the writing and teaching of most contemporary missiologists. The conscience, someone once said, is like a sundial. The person who shines his flashlight on it in the middle of the night can get it to tell him any time he wants. But when the sun shines on the dial, it can only tell the truth. That our consciences have been infected by the highly contagious hedonism characterizing Western societies cannot be denied. It remains to be seen whether the infection is lethal.

For Further Reading

Bonk, Jonathan J.
1991   *Missions and Money: Affluence as a Western Missionary Problem.* Maryknoll, NY: Orbis Books.

Duncan, Michael
1990   *A Journey in Development.* The Bridge Series, no. 3. Victoria, Australia: World Vision of Australia.

Grigg, Viv
1984   *Companion to the Poor.* Sutherland, NSW, Australia: Albatross Books.
1987   "The Urban Poor: Prime Missionary Target." *Evangelical Review of Theology* 11 (3):261-72.

Jansen, Frank Kaleb, ed.
1989   *Target Earth.* Kailua-Kona, HA: University of the Nations, and Pasadena, CA: Global Mapping International.

Kennedy, Gail, ed.
1949   *Democracy and the Gospel of Wealth.* Boston: D. C. Heath and Company.

Nevius, John L.
1979   "Planting and Development of Missionary Churches." In *Classics of Christian Missions.* Edited by Francis M. DuBose. Nashville: Broadman Press.

O'Brien, Niall
1987   *Revolution from the Heart.* New York and Oxford: Oxford University Press.

Pate, Larry D.
1989   *From Every People: A Handbook of Two-Thirds World Missions
            With Directory/Histories/Analysis*. Monrovia, CA: MARC.
Potter, David M.
1954   *People of Plenty: Economic Abundance and the American Char-
            acter*. Chicago and London: University of Chicago Press.
Samuel, Vinay, and Chris Sugden, eds.
1983   *Evangelism and the Poor: A Third World Study Guide*. Revised
            Edition. Oxford: Oxford Centre for Mission Studies.
Schlabach, Gerald W.
1990   *And Who Is My Neighbor? Poverty, Privilege, and the Gospel of
            Christ*. Scottdale, PA, and Waterloo, Ontario: Herald Press.
Sivard, Ruth Leger, with Arlette Brauer and Milton I. Roemer
1989   *World Military and Social Expenditures 1989*. 13th ed. Wash-
            ington, DC: World Priorities.

Mission and Social Justice:
An American Dilemma

William E. Pannell

Like many North American evangelicals, I discovered God's concern
for the poor rather late in my evangelistic career. There were several
reasons for this, I suspect. For one thing, evangelists tend to read the
Scriptures selectively. Their aim is persuasion, and texts dealing with
grievous social issues do not always lend themselves to an invitation
at the end of the sermon. For another, most of us did not know any
poor people. The churches we served, while certainly not wealthy,
nevertheless did not have associations with the poor as part of their
normal course of existence. They did not define ministry or mission
in ways to include the poor. Then too, when we thought about mission,
we really meant missions, and that meant evangelistic ministry to
people overseas. As one European definition had it, evangelism is
what we do for people at home, missions is what we do when we go
overseas.

   We have become more sophisticated of late. And we have even
found references to the poor in Scripture. There are few books on the
church's mission that do not include some important references to
God's intentions toward the poor. Nevertheless, many of God's people

---

William E. Pannell is Associate Professor of Evangelism and Director of
Theological Studies for Black Pastors at Fuller Theological Seminary,
Pasadena, California. He has lectured and written widely on topics related
to evangelism and social concern.

still debate their responsibility toward the "wretched of the earth." One thing is clear, however. The integrity of the church as the people of God is at stake on this issue. This is especially true of the churches in affluent Western countries. Two realities make this clear. First, there are more poor and marginalized people than ever before, and they are not all overseas. As L. S. Stavrianos put it some years ago, "Because of the unprecedented impact of modern science and technology, people of both the developed and underdeveloped countries find themselves today in the same boat, plagued by similar problems, and confronted with the grim and very real prospect of drowning together" (Stavrianos 1981:24). Included in this boat are the growing thousands of homeless persons in the midst of America's affluence. Increasing numbers of these people are children. Poverty in the colored Two-Thirds World is the prevailing human condition.

The second factor should be even more disturbing to the Christian community in the West. There is a correlation between spirituality and poverty. Where the church is the most deprived in terms of physical supplies, she is the strongest spiritually. Conversely, where the church is the most wealthy, the church is also the weakest spiritually. Thus the foundation issue in the future is not poverty per se, but the spiritual condition of those who possess the means to alleviate such suffering if they had the will to do so. The key issues will be spirituality, theological ethics, and the relationship between evangelism and justice.

My introduction to the relationship between evangelism and social ethics occurred in the late fifties. I was an itinerant evangelist, familiar with small-town America, many fine congregations in the rural Midwest, and the blue-collar suburb of Detroit where I lived. This time I was in Cleveland where any half-awake evangelist would know that this bastion of Eastern European ethnicity screamed for ethical reflection. My lesson came from a local pastor. Vern Miller had served the Lord in the central city for years and came to his pastoral and evangelistic task from within the Mennonite tradition. I had worked with several pastors of the same background in urban ministries in all the major cities in the Midwest. But I knew almost as little about the Mennonite perspective on social ethics as I did about Cleveland.

Still, I did know that something was happening to change the balance of the Christian presence in all our major cities. Evangelicals had begun the long march to the suburbs. I watched it happen during the decade of the mid-fifties to the mid-sixties. In Detroit the exodus would be completed after the devastating riots in the summer of 1968. During the next twenty years all the major cities in the United States

311

would witness the Christian presence change complexion. The face of
Christ would be black and brown . . . and poor.

But in the early sixties the real story was not in Cleveland. It was
in a city in the South, in Montgomery, Alabama, where a young pastor
was making news in the streets. Martin Luther King, Jr., was becoming
the topic of conversation all over the nation, and many of us from the
evangelical camp were convinced that the streets were not an appropriate pulpit for a bona fide pastor. It was Pastor Miller who questioned
that assumption when it surfaced in me. He gave me a copy of King's
early book, *Stride Toward Freedom*. The argument of that piece was that
the social ethic of the church must be shaped by the love of God as it
was revealed in the life and teaching of Jesus. So far so good. But why
the streets? How do you get from love of one's enemies to civil disobedience? What was more vexing to us was the seeming absence of an
evangelistic message in those sermons, whether they were preached at
curbside or from a jail in Birmingham. There were no "altar calls," no
sawdust nestled like new mown hay beneath a canvas sky. So where
was the evangelism in this Baptist's ministry?

Evangelicalism, at least that part of it which I knew, was not
oriented toward love. We knew the words, but not the music. We had
apparently missed the element of compassion in the life of Jesus. Our
orientation had been shaped by the success of Billy Graham's ministry
during the fifties, whose premise was that in order to change society
one must first change people. To be sure, this would entail a good deal
of love as Mr. Graham himself demonstrated, but it seems clear that
the love in question was God's and that it was focused chiefly upon
the saving of the souls of humankind. It had little to do with their
bodies. We would sing about the love of God, "so rich, so pure, so
measureless and strong," but translating it into concrete expressions
escaped most of us. Furthermore, the prevailing conviction was that
preaching was the chief vehicle through which the good news of salvation was to be experienced. This is another way of admitting that we
had no idea how the theology of presence was related to the theology
of preaching. In short, we had not been willing to plumb the depths of
Christ's incarnation as the starting point for an understanding of mission in the world. The key was his humanity, but since liberals spoke
most of that, we didn't dare touch it for fear of being linked with them.
It was something of an exercise in negative self-definition.

Evangelicalism was naive about politics also. Like most Americans, we were often more American than Christian. We knew America
was the hope of the world, the last and best bulwark against com-

munism, and everyone from presidential candidates to J. Edgar Hoover was quick to remind us of it. And we might be excused our political naivete during the late fifties, and early sixties. The entire nation was recovering from a debilitating war and it was time to feel good about the country and its future. The cold war was very real, but at the least it was not a real, hot war. Besides, it was over there. What the country needed was to get back to the business of America, which, of course, was business. The country wanted cars, red and yellow ones and two-tone ones, roadmasters with round portholes on the front fenders and long black ones with fins to distinguish the upper class from the mid-dlers. And there were kids to feed and clothe, and houses to be built for all the family start-ups that spawned Levittowns all across the landscape. What the country needed, indeed demanded, was peace in order to pursue happiness.

In order to secure that peace, the country had elected an ex-war hero as its thirty-fourth president, convinced that a warrior would fight as hard to maintain the peace as he had fought to win it. President "Ike" did not disappoint. He began to roll eggs on the White House lawn again, and practiced golf shots in his "back yard." He was also in charge when the 1954 Housing Act was passed, as he was when the Highway Act of 1956 was enacted. These historic bills provided the necessary federal sanctions, backed with huge outlays of money, to make it possible for white America to pursue its version of happiness, while discrimination in the handling of these funds made it certain that black citizens would be trapped in inner cities. Those policies set in motion the movements of whites to the suburbs and the ghettoizing of people of color in the cities. The President didn't have this effect in mind in supporting these bills, but he, along with the rest of the country, was not overly concerned about black people. Yet it was in the fifties that the battle of social ethics was taking place in America, and it was being fought, and lost, in our cities.

Not many Americans had the prescience to see the future of the nation as the future of our cities. LeRone T. Bennett was one who did. Writing in a small but influential book entitled *The Negro Mood*, Bennett argued in 1964 that the issues then exploding in the cities were not about black people per se, although the treatment of black people in those centers was certainly at the core of the problem. Indeed, he asserted, black people "hold the key to the city and the future of American democracy." But at a still deeper level, "the issue was . . . not civil rights, but the city, not love, but the creation of that America that could have been and should have been and never was" (Bennett 1964:48).

313

But the voice of another American was heard even more widely, and this man became one of the most influential spokespersons of his time. He was Michael Harrington, and his book *The Other America*, on poverty in America, proved to be the flip side to the famous Kerner Report on the causes of violence among black urban people in the mid-sixties. The Kerner Report argued that racism was the root cause of those riots, and that the country was dangerously close to a divided society, one black, the other white — "separate and unequal." Harrington's book ripped apart the veil of complacency and revealed an America teeming with poor people. Hundreds of these books found their way into mayoral offices across the land, and helped shape the agenda for aspiring political candidates in key cities (Harrington 1984). It became clear that a ground swell of concern was rising across the country as Americans began to respond to the rhythmic songs of civil rights marchers and to mounting evidence that the country had defaulted on promises to its own citizens. They were heady days: a president was murdered, and the young preacher from Montgomery won the Nobel Prize for Peace. Viet Nam was coming unglued, and President Johnson was heading a national coalition of armed forces against a possible repeat of the riots that had torn the country. Later, this same president would undertake a war on one of the chief causes of those riots, poverty, and it would prove to be no more successful than the undeclared one in Southeast Asia. But at least it was on the nation's agenda.

There have been innumerable "wars" on the slums, and the energy expended to eradicate them has been impressive. They have all failed dismally. Today slums are an integral part of the urban landscape, especially in non-Western countries. As these countries become more and more urban, the percentage of slum dwellers will multiply. These people, crammed into their cardboard and tin shanties, are the poorest of the poor.

But Bennett was not talking about slum clearance, nor about shantytowns in Mexico City. He was addressing a deep malaise within the American system, a fundamental contradiction among its peoples. White people escaped the slums; few black people did. And these two destinies had little to do with native ability or performance in the workplace. The difference was a matter of simple justice.

Yet justice is not a simple matter. And in the late fifties and into the early sixties, few evangelicals give it much thought one way or another. The evangelistic task was clear and simple. When we assembled in Berlin in 1966 to address the task of the church, it was quite clear: there was One Task, even as there was One Gospel, for One World (see conference papers, *One World, One Gospel, One Task*, Minneapolis, 1966). Yet even in Berlin there were some rumblings of discontent. There was the unbrotherly conduct of some South African whites against two of their countrymen evangelists. Some of us from the United States were unhappy about the conference's lack of depth in dealing with the "world." And the issue of justice as a central motif for missiological and theological reflection was nowhere in sight.

Meanwhile back in the United States, justice was indeed the central motif in one man's sense of mission. Martin Luther King, Jr., had moved into one of Chicago's worst slums to draw attention to the oppressive housing conditions among the poor there. More than most religious leaders, King knew firsthand that people are poor because of injustice far more than because of laziness. And in Chicago, as in all the earth's exploding cities, injustice was the province of politicians and the wealthy who keep them in power. King demonstrated that one's theological and experiential starting point does make a difference in one's praxis of Christian mission. Thus from the mid-sixties to the present it is possible to argue that the stage for the shaping of mission understanding in much of the Christian world was set by the hermeneutics of two American preachers. They were both from the American South. They were both Baptists. One was black, the other white. In 1966 one of them was in Berlin arguing the case for the primacy of evangelism over social concerns; the other was in a slum tenement in Chicago demonstrating the case for justice over against the privatization of Christian experience at the hands of most of those in charge of the evangelical agenda.

The social issues, and the theological underpinnings that inform them as they were represented by these two giants of Christian mission, will continue to be high on the church's agenda. The reason is simple, if painful. The issues of the sixties have not been resolved, and have only gotten worse for the poor. Whereas the church was divided racially in the sixties, and still is, the divisions that are now being sanctified are more economic than racial in nature. Theologies of prosperity and healing have come to prevail over theologies of liberation and justice. The Western church seems to have exhausted its theological energies, bent on debating issues that could only concern the middle classes. The one exception is the debate that rages over Christology, and this is one that directly concerns all people everywhere. Yet even here, the question is still whether Christ is from uptown or from the barrio, from the West or the non-West, or much worse, whether it makes any difference at all where he's from, since for many church leaders the uniqueness of Christ is passé anyway.

But surely the mission of the church must be identical to that of Christ. The church in the twentieth century has known this. The problem seems to have been that she conceived that mission in too narrow and exclusive terms. This was true whether one looked at it from the right or the left theologically. On the issue of the poor the church may at last be approaching some sort of consensus, and this attitude seems not to be informed by politics, but by a willingness to look at the New Testament and Christ's own teaching on the reign of God among the dispossessed and the poor.

In his fine book in which he chronicles his life among the poor, Viv Grigg recalls how his understanding and practice of evangelism were transformed. It began when he noticed John the Baptist's emphasis on "economic repentance" in Luke 3. "He who has two coats, let him share with him who has none, and he who has food let him do likewise." Says Grigg, "As I spoke I was struck by the fact that I had never before spoken of economic repentance when I had been preaching the Gospel. The repentance I had spoken of had been purely in spiritual terms. From this time on my preaching would define repentance economically, spiritually, socially, and where necessary, politically. It transformed my evangelism" (Grigg 1984:79). This remark pinpoints the overwhelming challenge facing the Western church in the immediate future. Will we allow the gospel and its demands on discipleship to convert us to God's concern for the poor? Will the church repent economically and politically in order to express solidarity with the poor and the powerless? Will we allow the Spirit of God to break our captivity to the syncretism with our culture that keeps us from being light and salt? The issue is really not them, but us; not about poverty, but affluence; not about saving our lives, but losing them — all for the sake of Jesus and the gospel.

For Further Reading

Bennett, LeRone T.
    1964   *The Negro Mood.* New York: Ballantine Books.
Cosmao, Vincent
    1981   *Changing the World: An Agenda for the Churches.* Maryknoll, NY: Orbis Books.
Grigg, Viv
    1984   *Companion to the Poor.* Sutherland, NSW, Australia: Albratross Books.

Gutiérrez, Gustavo
   1984   *We Drink from Our Own Wells*. Maryknoll, NY: Orbis Books.
Harrington, Michael
   1964   *The Other America: Poverty in the United States*. New York: Macmillan Publishing Company.
Hanks, Thomas
   1983   *God So Loved the Third World*. Maryknoll, NY: Orbis Books.
Ilung, Bakole W. A.
   1984   *Paths of Liberation: A Third World Spirituality*. Maryknoll, NY: Orbis Books.
Lundin, Roger
   1985   *The Responsibility of Hermeneutics*. Grand Rapids, MI: Wm. B. Eerdmans Publishing Company.
National Conference of Catholic Bishops
   1986   *Economic Justice for All*. Washington, DC.
Scott, Waldron
   1980   *Bring Forth Justice*. Grand Rapids, MI: Wm. B. Eerdmans Publishing Company.
Stavrianos, L. S.
   1981   *Global Rift*. New York: Wm. Morrow & Company.
Washington, James, ed.
   1986   *A Testament of Hope: The Essential Writings of Martin Luther King, Jr.* New York: Harper & Row.

Urban Mission

Harvie M. Conn

Outlining a Christian mission to the city in a new century is not a new experience. One hundred years ago, in the 1890s, menacing words like "urban crisis" had begun to appear in Anglo-Saxon vocabulary. The growth of what H. G. Wells was calling "the whirlpool cities" was already frightening some.

The urban world at the end of the nineteenth century was still largely an English-speaking world. Only a little over fourteen percent of the world, 2,327,000 of its people, lived in cities (Barrett 1986:16). But in England by 1890, seventy-two percent of the population were living in districts classified as "urbanized," in the United States twenty-eight percent (Fishman 1987:10-11).

The coming century of missions was to become, in the language of Stephen Neill, "beyond question the American century" (Neill 1965:458). But for many Protestant Americans at the turn of the nineteenth century, urban changes had become causes for alarm. They saw an awesome shift in immigration patterns that was changing the religious demographics of America's cities. And in the light of those changes they looked at the urban world outside their borders.

Harvie M. Conn is Professor of Missions and Director of the Urban Missions Program, Westminster Theological Seminary, Philadelphia, PA. He served in Korea as a missionary of the Orthodox Presbyterian Church (1960-72), and is the editor and author of many books, including *Evangelism: Doing Justice and Preaching Grace* (1982), *Eternal Word and Changing Worlds* (1984), and *A Clarified Vision for Urban Mission* (1987).

Industrialization had lured Roman Catholics and Jews in large numbers from southern Europe. The stability and purpose of the American republic were seen as threatened by the perils of immigration, "Romanism," intemperance, and socialism. And all these perils were perceived as intensified in the American city.

Given these concerns, what would happen to America's responsibility for the Christianization of the world, their long felt "errand into the wilderness" (Hutcheson 1987:1-42)? Josiah Strong, Secretary of the American Home Missionary Society, may have answered that question for many in his 1885 best-seller, *Our Country*. Like many others, he saw the United States as the unique providential custodian of "civil liberty" and "spiritual Christianity." God had been "preparing in our Anglo-Saxon civilization the die with which to stamp the peoples of the earth." Now, if ever, was the time God had prepared humanity "to receive our impress." With the West filled up and the nation industrialized, we were to move out into the world to see at last the coming of Christ's kingdom.

If Strong is a good sample, the last two decades of the nineteenth century saw imperfectly and far too pessimistically the global future of mission — its problems and its promises. And both were urban. Strong may have spoken for many when he said that "the new civilization is certain to be urban; and the problem of the twentieth century will be the city" (Teaford 1986:1).

It would take time for Strong's prophecy to be fulfilled. And in the process, the shape of the urban world and the understanding of Christian mission were to change. Especially spectacular would be the rapidity of global demographic shifts in the years following World War II. It had taken the United States 150 years to become urban. In cities like São Paulo and Mexico City, Abidjan and Seoul, the same history would be compressed into a decade or so.

Rural to Urban Shift

By 1950, United Nations' estimates placed 28.4 percent of the world population in cities. By 1980, that figure had reached 41.3 percent. And, by the year 2000, according to UN projections, it will reach 51.3 percent. Before the children born in 1985 become adults, half of the world's population will be urban. And half of this half will be located in cities with over a million inhabitants.

Identifying the rapidity of this process of urbanization too easily and too exclusively with the generic factors of industrialization and

Westernization can be misleading. Urbanization, we need to recall, has a long history in the so-called Third World. The world was dotted with great cities long before modern technology created the assembly lines and empire-building expanded the port cities of Asia and Africa to meet Western colonial demands. And, in fact, even today only a small proportion of urban dwellers works in industry. The life of most Third World cities centers around public administration and commerce.

Two other factors must be remembered in the pace of urban growth. The sheer rapidity of natural population growth in the Third World is unique in human history. And that growth accounts for three-fifths of the urban increase on average (Gugler 1988: 12-15).

And the remaining growth? The "push-pull" forces that promote in-country step-migration from the rural areas, towns, and small cities to the large urban centers.

Latin America in many ways is typical of this in-migration impact. It has become the most highly urbanized region in the developing world. Between 1960 and 1970, the hemisphere's total population increased approximately 2.8 percent annually. But its rural regions grew by only 1.3 percent annually. Urban population increased from 103 million to 158 million (48.4 percent in 1960 to 55.9 percent in 1970). From 1950 to 1970, claims one source, rural migration accounted for twenty-five to fifty percent of the region's urban growth.

Northern Hemisphere to Southern Hemisphere Shift

The world urban center of gravity is moving as well. Urban growth in the old centers of Europe and North America accelerated from 1920 to 1980. Europe moved from an urban population of 46.2 percent to 75.9 percent, North America from 51.9 percent to 73.7 percent. But the years since then have shown a leveling off in urban growth patterns. By AD 2000, predicts the UN, Europe will have moved to 88.4 percent and North America to 80.8 (Palen 1987:4).

In startling contrast is the rapidity of urban growth in the countries of the southern hemisphere. Africa has quintupled its urban community, from seven percent at the beginning of the twentieth century to 28.9 percent in 1980. And by the turn of the century, it will jump again, at almost a fifty percent rate, to 42.5 percent urban. "For every urban African in 1985 there will be two in the year 2000" (Monsma 1989:20). By the end of the 1990s, more than 345 million Africans will be living in cities (Dogan and Kasarda 1988:292).

Asia continues its upward urban spiral as well. Minimal in-migration leaves its nations with the smallest proportion of their people in urban places (twenty-seven percent by 1980). But by 2000, it will likely hit forty percent, a 665 percent growth change since 1920. By comparison its rural growth over the same period was only 95.6 percent (Costa, Dutt, Ma, and Noble 1989:5-6). By the beginning of the twenty-first century, six of the ten largest cities in the world will be in Asia — Shanghai (25,900,000); Tokyo/Yokohama (23,800,000); Bei-jing (22,800,000); Bombay (16,300,000); Calcutta (15,900,000); and Jakarta (14,300,000) (Barrett 1986:45-46).

Emergence of the "Mega-City" Phenomenon

At the beginning of this century there were only twenty cities in the world with a population exceeding one million. As of 1980 that figure had reached 235, with some 118 located in economically less developed areas (Palen 1987:4). Since 1950 there has been a tenfold increase in the population living in such cities.

In 1950, only two cities, London and New York, were over ten million. As of 1980, ten cities had reached that size. By the end of this century, if the Lord tarries, there will be twenty-five cities like that — and five cities over twenty million.

Africa is a unique illustration of the phenomenon. The average size of its largest cities is a little more than 950,000, population figures still smaller than the urban growth in Latin America and Asia. Fourteen countries have no cities with a population of more than 500,000.

Yet here too the rapidity of the mega-city growth is staggering. In 1950, only nine cities had a population of more than one million. But by 1990, there will be thirty-eight cities in that category. And, of the thirty-eight, seventeen will have between two and four million people, and eleven will exceed four million. Cairo, the largest of the continent's urban centers, will reach nearly ten million. Kinshasa, Zaire will be the second largest with over five and a half million, and Jos, Nigeria will be the third with 4,156,000 (Dogan and Kasarda 1988:291-92).

Much of the world's mega-city growth is tied to the recent emergence of the "primate city," whose population growth and influence far exceed those of its closest urban competitor in a nation or region. Bangkok, to cite one example, is over thirty times larger than Thailand's second largest city, Chiang Mai. Ethiopia is ninety-five percent rural

321

and has few towns. But its capital, Addis Ababa, has over 1.5 million people. As of 1980, fifty-seven percent of Kenya's urban population is found in Nairobi, half of Tanzania's live in Dar es Salaam. By 1956, Teheran, with a population of 1,512,000, towered over Tabriz, with 390,000 and Isfahan with 255,000.

Resembling "gigantic heads of dwarfish bodies," such cities are less visible in northern hemisphere regions. Recent research suggests that they develop more quickly in small countries (Copenhagen and Vienna are European examples), in countries like those of the Third World where urban growth has been rare and recent, and in former colonial settlements (Spates and Macionis 1982:251). Very often, they are the capital cities.

Where they emerge, they constitute the core of the nation's life, dominating the rest of the country, which slips into a peripheral status.

In Latin America, to illustrate, the aggregate population of such "primate cities" did not exceed eight percent until the twentieth century. By 1950, however, that figure had climbed to thirty-nine percent (sixty-one million people). One estimate, in fact, suggests that by 1980, twelve Latin American countries had over half their population living in "primate cities."

Growth of Non-Christian Urban Population

As cities grow, the percentage of urban Christians decreases. In 1900, argues David Barrett, Christians numbered 68.8 percent of urban dwellers. In 1980, they numbered only 46.3 percent. By 2000, that figure will drop again to 44.5 percent (Barrett 1989:21). According to Barrett's 1986 perspective, "the churches are losing the cities at the rate of 80,900 new non-Christian urban dwellers every day, or one every second" (Barrett 1986:22).

To speak of "losing the cities" in this connection can be misleading to some degree. We need to remember that Barrett attributes the reason for that loss largely to the massive urban population increases we have been chronicling in Third World countries traditionally hostile to Christianity. "What we may call the opposition to Christian world missions has mushroomed phenomenally from five non-Christian mega-cities in the year 1900 to 121 today, and to 510 by A.D. 2050. Non-Christian or anti-Christian supercities are also exploding from nil in 1900 to 20 today, and to 180 by A.D. 2050" (Barrett 1986:10).

This is powerfully demonstrated in those recently emerging urban

322

giants with over ten million inhabitants each. In 1958 Tokyo became the first to reach ten million. Then came Shanghai in 1967, Beijing in 1976, Calcutta and Osaka in 1984, and Bombay in 1985. By 2000, seven Islamic cities will have joined that select group — Jakarta in 1989, Cairo in 1991, Baghdad, Istanbul, Teheran, and Karachi in 1996, and Dacca in 2000.

Adding to Barrett's picture, and coming closer to the real meaning of "loss," is the growing nominalism and erosion of Christianity in the cities of the northern hemisphere. Here the church faces not a pre-Christian urban world (present elsewhere), but a post-Christian one. Re-evangelization has become the church's order of the day.

By 1989, comments one source, while the church in Africa was adding four thousand new members per day, in Europe the church was said to be losing seven thousand per day (Gili 1989:17). Another more conservative source speaks of a net decline each year of 1.8 million (Cotterell 1989:37). An average of five to six percent of Western Europeans attend church regularly, compared with forty to forty-five percent of Americans. Marc Spindler describes the European scene in terms of "a resurgence of paganism" (Spindler 1987:8).

In the British Isles the picture is no brighter. In 1985, a two-year study, *Faith in the City*, was released by the Archbishop of Canterbury's Commission on England's urban priority areas. It found an average of ninety adults attending out of an urban Anglican parish population of 10,560 (0.85 percent). Among them also was a marked middle class overrepresentation and working class underrepresentation (1985:33-35). For every one person who goes to an Anglican church in an urban parish there are ninety-nine who do not. By contrast are "the increasing number of growing and developing Black-led churches — at present over 160 denominations involving perhaps 100,000 people in about 2,500 congregations" (1985:43).

Canada, to cite one final example, has also experienced a growing rate of urbanization. In 1940 only half of its population lived in urban areas. Now cities account for seventy-five percent of its people, and that number, say some, is expected to reach ninety percent by the year 2000 (Tunnicliffe 1990:18). But whether metropolitan area, smaller city, village, or farm, "fewer than five in ten people in each community-size category claim to be committed to Christianity, or to any other religion, for that matter" (Bibby 1987:92-93). The traditional stereotypes of a religiously committed rural area and an urban secular one do not exist in Canada. Fewer than three in ten, no matter where they live, attend services weekly.

From Rural to Urban Poverty

Moving from rural poverty to the cities is not a large leap. It is just that the poor — between one-quarter and one-fifth of the people of the world — are becoming more visible in the city, their needs more pressing on already overtaxed government economies and programs. "Nowhere else is the economic, political and social distance between the few rich and the masses of the poor greater than in towns of the Third World" (Gutkind 1974:35).

It is estimated that half the urban population in the southern hemisphere lives in slums or shantytowns. Africa's cities have become what one author recently called "centers of despair." An estimated seventy-nine percent of Addis Ababa live in slums and squatter settlements, as do seventy percent of Casablanca's residents and sixty-five percent of Kinshasa's. "More than one-third of the populations of Nairobi and Dakar are slum dwellers. In Nairobi, the population of the lowest squatter settlements has been growing more than twice as fast as that of the city as a whole" (Dogan and Kasarda 1988:304). Half a million people live in the mausoleums of Cairo's cemetery, the famous City of the Dead.

Everywhere the pattern is repeated — 415 squatter areas in Manila, representing thirty-eight percent of the population; five hundred *cuidades perdidas* (lost cities) with 2.7 million people in Mexico City; forty-eight thousand by official count (two hundred thousand being the generally accepted figure) living on the streets of Calcutta; 598 *pueblos jovenes* (young towns) comprising fifty percent of Lima's people.

"In the year 2000, 2,116 million or 33.6 percent of the world will be in cities in less developed regions and forty percent (a conservative figure) will be squatters (846 million). This would indicate a world that is about 13.6 percent squatters by the year 2000 — a bloc nearly the size of Muslim or Hindu populations, doubling each decade" (Grigg 1989:42). In this context, urban mission could easily be redefined as "urban-poor mission."

The socio-economic needs are obvious in all this. Behind them are the pressures on the family: increased marital instability; the new urban financial struggles that strain human relationships; the role changes of wives from rural homemakers to second-income earners; families splitting their time between the city and their country roots; kin obligations on narrowed incomes; conflicts between parents and children as rural value systems are challenged by urban ones being adopted by the

324

children; newly emerging patterns of sociability, based now not only on family but on vocation.

And as the poor become visible, they become younger. A Roman Catholic study notes that in Africa "youth are the most affected by the rural exodus and the consequent urbanisation" (Tessier 1983:3). In 1976, more than sixty percent of that continent's population were under twenty-four years of age.

The city dwellers of the United States have a median age of about thirty. In Mexico City, the average age is 14.2. Sixty-eight percent of the urban populations of Argentina, Chile, Uruguay, and Costa Rica are made up of young people between the ages of fifteen to twenty-four. In the more recently urbanized Andean countries, the figure is fifty-one percent. In Brazil, Mexico, and Venezuela it is seventy-five percent.

This new urban generation is less idealistic and considerably more pessimistic. In a way, they symbolize the challenge of urban mission today. Jaded and old before their time, without hope and marginalized by broken promises, they can become easy prey to the temptations of cynicism and meaningless violence.

Into the Twenty-First Century

There are isolated voices that speak of a "decline in the growth rates of cities nearly everywhere. The era of rapid urban growth," they predict, "is about to finish" (Knight and Gappert 1989:45).

But even these predictions are carefully qualified, limited sometimes to so-called developed countries, never suggesting decline, only slowdown. Even with the possibility of slowdown we will still face the reality of an urban future. And we will still face as Christians the problems and challenges created by the city in the decades immediately ahead.

The predictions of Rashmi Mayur, President of the Global Futures Network, may be important to listen to at this point. He argues that "ninety percent of the earth's population will likely be urbanized by the end of the next century. Much of this urbanization will take place," he forecasts, "in 'supercities' in Third World countries" (Mayur 1985:28). Urban populations will continue to grow at almost twice the rate of national growth and large cities at a rate three to four times as high. Especially where a country's capital is also the largest city (a common pattern, we have seen) it will tend to grow disproportionately fast.

With this growth will come an intensification of the problems on the urban agenda. Few countries possess the social controls to regulate growth like the People's Republic of China, where there is a politically enforced system of migration control and urban-rural balance restrictions.

The inability of nations to keep up with runaway urbanization shows no signs of letup. Urban unemployment and underemployment will continue. Funds will continue to be diverted from rural development to the continuing emergency needs of the growing cities. The role of the city as a center of power and prestige will continue to be accelerated, marginalizing the rest of the country into a deeper peripheral role.

Illustrating that growing peripheral tendency will be a new dimension — the role of the city in a global society. The modern world-class city is fast becoming a pillar of the developing global system. Bypassing traditional national boundaries, global interdependence is becoming urban interdependence. We are watching the expansion of a global market, the growth of international organizations of all kinds, and the global restructuring of the city's economic basis from industry to trade, technology and communication. And this is increasing the twentieth-century city's role as a "hinge," connecting local and regional life with the outside world. The city of the twenty-first century is becoming an international, not a national, power center (Knight and Gappert 1989:24-67). We are only beginning to glimpse what "world-class city" really means.

The Churches Look to the Urban Future

One hundred years after the imperialistic sound of Josiah Strong's mission forecast of an urban twentieth-century future, the church looks at another century to come.

This time the church's tone appears more optimistic. There are those who speak of completing world evangelization in order to "present Jesus with his two thousandth birthday present." For others whose mission strategies are structured to "closure" policies, the year 2000 has taken on deep motivational value. A 1989 Global Consultation on World Evangelization, held in Singapore, has spawned an A.D. 2000 movement that, at present sight, appears more inspirational than institutional (Wang 1990:31).

Probably the strongest sign of mission enthusiasm for the urban future remains the 1989 findings of Lausanne II in Manila. For a participant like Samuel Escobar, the Manila experience represented "an immersion into the urban labyrinth" (Escobar 1990:22).

In fact, urban ministry became one of the points around which Lausanne's earlier 1974 vision of holistic mission was reinforced. If Lausanne II is any indication, urban ministry has moved to center stage. Several signs may well be pointing in that direction.

Mobilization of Traditional Mission Agencies

David Barrett and James Reapsome speak of the "hundreds of mission agencies" who "have recently begun urban mission programs abroad, all hinging on their major traditional resource — residential foreign missionaries" (Barrett and Reapsome 1988:115). Some stand out in particular.

Especially noteworthy are those boards like Mission to the World (Presbyterian Church in America) and the Pentecostal Holiness Church whose whole mission strategy has been structured exclusively around church planting in major cities. These plans are being coupled with an innovative use of team ministries.

Other boards are placing a major, if not exclusive, focus on urban ministry. In 1983 Latin America Mission launched a Christ for the City program and targeted ten major Latin American urban centers (including Miami, Florida) for team attention. Less comprehensive but equally exciting is the Great Cities PACT (Plant a Church Together) Program, launched by the Conservative Baptist Foreign Mission Society in the 1980s. With a dual commitment to the concept of unreached peoples and to the evangelization of major or world-class cities, the board over a period of one year seeks to raise $100,000 for a strategic new urban church planting effort (Tuggy 1989:46). By 1989, the program had aided churches in ten countries where the mission was working.

Other signs of commitment are also appearing. SIM International has appointed a missionary facilitator to specialize in urban church research for Africa. A new mission agency, Servants Among the Poor, appeared in the late 1980s, with its focus on church planting among the world's squatters and slums. Still other boards, traditionally oriented to more stable and (until recently) rural tribal societies, are finding that the tribes have moved to the growing cities, and they are therefore rethinking missionary logistics.

New Models for Existing Churches

Concurrent with this shift in northern hemisphere mission board policy is a growing interest of the global church in urban ministry. And, by and large, the models being proposed are more multidimensional, more holistic than in the past.

The eighth Theological Consultation of the Asia Theological Association, meeting in Singapore in 1987, illustrates this new concern for the complexity of the urban task. "We recognize," their statement affirms, "that our ministry demands a clear and intelligent understanding of the complexities of our economic, environmental, social and cultural context. This necessitates our commitment to be identified with both the conveniences and benefits as well as the sorrows and sufferings of urban life and to relate the gospel of Jesus Christ accurately and relevantly. Our gospel must reach the poor, down-trodden and marginalized as well as the rich, powerful, and comfortable sections of urban population" (Ro 1989b:1).

Augmenting that vision for Asia are the multiplication of Christian centers for urban studies in Singapore and Bangkok, the birth of urban ministry agencies in India, and a new focus on industrial workers in Taiwan and Korea. Lay training programs for urban ministry are appearing in Indonesia, Singapore, and Hong Kong. Appeals are being made for an Asian Urban Ministry Association to bring existing bodies together into one evangelical umbrella organization, for the development of an urban ministry curriculum for theological seminaries (Ro 1989b:23-30).

The evangelical churches of Latin America are verbalizing these same commitments for a larger urban mission. A December 1988 consultation of the Latin American Theological Fraternity meeting in Valle de Bravo, Mexico, is a good illustration of this. In its support of a holistic approach to the city, this continent-wide study fellowship of evangelicals drew guidelines for the future from its research of urban ministry models.

Calling on the churches to be agents of transformation, it outlined the process of that transformation in five areas: (1) better understanding by the church of the city's social and economic structures; (2) the incarnation of the church in those social and cultural realities; (3) sensitivity to all social levels in the city, and particularly affirmative action on behalf of the poor; (4) a clearer definition of the prophetic role of the church in the city; (5) a re-emphasis on the church as a community of compassion by way of a Christ-centered message of hope and incarnation ("Seeking the Peace of the City" 1989:22-24).

How representative of existing urban Protestant models is this call for a multidimensional ministry? That is difficult to say. My own judgment is that the growing edge of Latin America's urban evangelical churches, largely Pentecostal and charismatic, still exemplifies a more traditional "fundamentalist" model. It is one that defines urban transformation strongly in terms of individual conversions and responds to questions of urban injustice and systemic change with a call to building new moral communities. It is not a model to be slighted; David Stoll extrapolates that, based on its present growth rate, evangelicals by 2010 will constitute a third of the Latin American population (Stoll 1990:45).

These traditional approaches have not been without innovative experiments oriented to the city. The Lima al Encuentro con Dios (LED) movement of Peru, begun in 1973, is one such. Initiated by the Christian and Missionary Alliance, the model made use of such traditional elements as intensive evangelistic campaigns, team ministries using national and expatriate workers, a highly developed discipleship program, and careful planning. But to it was wedded the construction of a prominently located, architecturally attractive church building capable of seating at least a thousand members (Smith 1983:19-28).

Since its inception the program has grown from one church and 120 members to twenty-five daughter churches and over ten thousand members. Modifications are being tried in Argentina, Brazil, Chile, Colombia, Ecuador, and El Salvador. And, adds one commentator, the national church has become urban-oriented.

From the Roman Catholic church in Latin America has come what some see as still another urban model, the Base Christian Communities (CEBs). Described by Leonardo Boff as a form of "ecclesiogenesis," the CEB movement may number as many as a hundred thousand communities in Brazil and another eighty thousand in the rest of Latin America (Hewitt 1988:163). They are crossing over now into the Protestant camp, with over a hundred in Guatemala alone (Cook 1988:4).

Deeply oriented to the needs of the poor, the CEB typically appears in the shape of small (from five to thirty-five people) assemblies of poor and oppressed lay Christians, oriented toward worship, Bible study, and community service. In community they search for a prophetic word from the Lord for their daily struggles and corporately seek change in their personal and social situation.

They are not without deficiencies recognized by evangelical critics. Many still struggle with recognizing the need for personal conversion, a term like "the poor" in danger of becoming a salvific category in itself. At the same time, in an urban world characterized by massive

329

poverty, they can model the need for moving beyond an almsgiving approach in social action to one of solidarity with the neediest segment of the city's people (Cook 1983:52-53). With modifications, there is far more than merely potential in the movement, for both Catholic and Protestant.

Expanding Research for the Coming Urban Church

Supporting these new models is a new resource tool for the world church, a rapidly growing institutional network of writing and study devoted to the initiation and cultivation of urban ministry.

The tools themselves are not new. In the 1960s the pressures of the civil rights movement and the desertion of cities by white churches spawned at least twenty-seven ecumenical centers in the United States for urban action and reflection. Oriented toward the American social setting, they sought to be an urban resource, an "arena for confrontation, reflection, commitment, skills training and strategy in action to enable the church to perform its mission in an urbanizing society" (Younger 1987:156). By the early 1970s, however, such centers had disappeared for a variety of reasons, social, economic, and theological.

Similar in philosophy and orientation to these North American models has been the Urban Rural Mission (URM) within the World Council of Churches family. Mandated under a different name in 1961 at the New Delhi Assembly of the Council, URM has undergone a number of modifications with time. Its nine priorities have remained directed to the support of people's struggles for justice and self-empowerment, and to the development of solidarity with regional area churches in social contexts of struggle, repression, and marginalization (Lewin 1987:294). Notably absent by evangelical perspective is sufficient connection of the URM's agenda of social change with evangelization and the task of calling men and women to personal repentance and faith in Christ.

In June 1980, that more clearly evangelistic slant on urban mission was added to the social dimension in another ecumenical arena. At the Lausanne-sponsored Consultation on World Evangelization (COWE) meeting in Pattaya, Thailand, the success of a Mini-Consultation on Reaching Large Cities sparked a follow-up program.

Dr. Ray Bakke, the chair of the mini-consultation, was appointed as a Lausanne Associate, with the assignment of coordinating and servicing an extensive program of global consultations on urban ministry

around the world. A strategy was developed that might avoid any
success images and dependency on Western "high gloss 'here's how,'
solution-oriented, prepackaged programs" (Bakke 1984:149).

Since then, Bakke has led such consultations in over one hundred
cities on six continents and "has contributed more than anyone else to
create this awareness" (Escobar 1990:24). His enthusiasm has spurred
networking connections between urban churches and a search for new
information on the needs of the world's cities. Supported by the
Lausanne Committee and World Vision International, he has encouraged implementation of plans for holistic ministry that have sought
to augment the globally endorsed sentiments of the Lausanne Covenant
and its concerns for "responsible evangelism."

In the wake of the Lausanne effort has come a new outbreak of
research and planning on primarily world-class cities. The Foreign Mission Board of the Southern Baptist Convention, USA, has been a leader
in this area. It has initiated a database survey of the 2,200 cities of the
world with populations over a hundred thousand. David Barrett, employed by the Board, has been an active participant in the research and
has begun to write in the area (Barrett 1986; Barrett and Reapsome 1988).

On a much smaller scale we note the work of the urban missions
program of Westminster Theological Seminary, Philadelphia. It offers
the fullest urban seminary curriculum integrated to global issues both
in and outside the United States and sponsors the journal *Urban Mission*,
now entering its eighth year of publication. Oriented more exclusively
toward research is the Institute of Global Urban Studies, associated with
the United States Center for World Mission and under the directorship
of Timothy Monsma. Born in the mid-1980s, it provides consultant and
research services on urban issues outside of North America.

A number of citywide research survey projects have also begun
to appear. Dr. Ralph Neighbour, Jr., using students from Columbia Bible
College, has conducted and published full surveys of the churches of
Brisbane (1987) and Auckland (1989). He is currently at work on a
similar project for Singapore. Daystar University College has just released a summary of its extensive study of Nairobi and its churches
(Niemeyer 1989). One of the most notable efforts in this area has been
the Protestant cooperative project to provide a directory of evangelical
churches and institutions in Mexico City. The first volume, *Mexico Hoy
y Manana*, appeared in 1987, and a second, to concentrate on more
detailed case studies, is in process (Pretiz 1988:6-10).

Urban studies aiming at North America are showing signs of
revitalization. Organizations like the Chicago-based Institute on the

Church in Urban Industrial Society (ICUIS), begun in 1966, continue their ministry. Joining them are urban training agencies of a slightly different sort.

Groups like Toronto's BUILD program (Baptist Urban Involvement in Leadership Development), Philadelphia's Center for Urban Theological Studies, Boston's Emmanuel Gospel Center, and Chicago's Seminary Consortium for Urban Pastoral Education (SCUPE) are much less action-oriented than earlier patterns we have described. Coming after the white departure from the North American city, they appear (some more than others) to be more directly owned and supported by black and minority church constituencies. With the earlier models, they share a concern for racial reconciliation. But, less radical in methods, their agendas are more oriented to the church and church growth in the city than to the urban demands of society prominent in the 1960s.

In the British Isles, similar signs of urban mission vitality are appearing. Models like the Urban Theology Unit of Sheffield appear to be more heavily on the side of urban "social revitalization." Not without this dimension are groups like the Evangelical Coalition for Urban Mission (ECUM) and their challenging journal, *City Cries*. And standing between the two, calling for a "both/and" perspective, is the powerful voice of the Anglican Bishop of Liverpool, David Sheppard. His book reflecting on twenty years of experience in inner-city London, *Built as a City* (1974), wrestles with evangelical sensitivities and mainline social concerns in the context of the decline of church and inner-city life in England.

An Action/Reflection Agenda for the Urban Future

So we move into the urban world of the twenty-first century, waiting for the Lord to change, even end with his coming, our plans. Right is fearful of left, left is disdainful of right. We continue to look at the city with the imperfect theological models we have used in the past. And before us are the unsolved issues and needs of our cities.

1. How will the urban church define its mission in the coming century? Northern hemisphere definitions in the past have continually divided over the extent of the church's proper involvement outside its own institutional circle. Should it focus its attention narrowly on personal evangelism and wait to see urban transformation through transformed individuals? What of the relationship between evangelism and social responsibility in the city, where the vastness of need underlines such a relationship?

The growth of the city in the southern hemisphere, and the emerging sensitivity of those regional churches to that growth, are pressing for a more holistic reflection on urban mission. The voice of the Lausanne Covenant and the Manila Manifesto of Lausanne II echo this demand. Will these definitional tensions be creative or disruptive?

2. What role will the new foreign missionary force emerging from an urbanized Two-Thirds World play in the winning of the world's cities to Christ? If Larry Pate's projections are borne out, by the year 2000 the Western-based Protestant missionary force will total about 136,000 and missionaries from the Two-Thirds World will number over 162,000, 54.4% of the total force (Pate 1989:51).

Robert Schreiter, speaking from the Roman Catholic side, sees this shift in the agents of mission in his constituency as bringing many new possibilities and challenges (Schreiter 1990:5-7). What will it mean in our search for a new praxis of urban mission? For the Anglo-Saxon church and missionary coming from the northern hemisphere, the modern city often has represented despair, doom, and frustration. For the church of the southern hemisphere, the city has been an object of challenge, hope, and enervating change. How will these differing perspectives affect our understanding of urban ministry?

3. What should be the task of the Christian community in the public sector of the world-class city? The global impact of the world-class city in the public sector, as we have noted, has already marginalized rural and small-town interests. And it is now shifting to the periphery even national concerns. Issues of power and powerlessness are becoming urban issues.

In the Anglo-Saxon church world of the past, this larger agenda has been the hallmark of so-called liberal theological concerns. I see it reflected also in the aims of the URM. Linked to the calling of the institutional church by such forces, it has been neglected by evangelical churches who see their institutional mandate in a more limited role. They have properly feared past capitulations to theological liberalism in this area and warned of the limited competence of the institutional church in the public sector. Their warnings have affected the daughter churches of the "mission fields" in a similar way.

Will the new urban directions promote a rethinking of this issue in ecclesiastical camps to the left and the right? Can Christians, exercising their responsibility as a priesthood of believers outside the institutional structures of the church, participate in a new way in urban issues of poverty and homelessness, unemployment and urban slums? Are there other ways for Christians to participate in meeting the needs of the global city without doing it through the church as an institution? The CEBs suggest that possibility.

4. What of the need for urban church planting and growth? Writing in 1970, Donald McGavran noted that "after a hundred and fifty years of modern missions, the plain fact is that Churches have not done well in most cities" of Africa, Asia, and Latin America (McGavran 1970:280). David Barrett's more recent statistics appear to underline that reality. Reinforcing those judgments is the decline of Christianity in the cities of North America and Europe.

As we move into the twenty-first century, predicts Barrett, the need will grow. We will live in a world of seventy-nine supercities (fifty-nine of them in developing countries), each with over four million inhabitants. Our globe will have 433 mega-cities with over one million people in each. Our urban population will increase by 1.6 million people per week. Poverty in our urban areas will continue to expand, producing a "planet of slums" (Barrett 1987:84).

To meet those needs, new churches must be planted on a radically accelerated scale. The day of church planting for the world's cities has yet to dawn. The invisible, unreached peoples of the world's cities must be found — the poor, the industrial workers, the government employees, the new ethnic and tribal groups settling in urban areas. If we are to reach the world of the twenty-first century, we must reach its cities. And that will demand a new campaign of church planting.

For Further Reading

Archbishop of Canterbury's Commission on Urban Priority Areas
    1985   *Faith in the City*. London: Church House Publishing.
Bakke, Raymond
    1984   "Urban Evangelization: A Lausanne Strategy Since 1980." *International Bulletin of Missionary Research* 8 (4):149-54.
Barrett, David B.
    1986   *World-Class Cities and World Evangelization*. Birmingham, AL: New Hope.
    1987   *Cosmos, Chaos and Gospel*. Birmingham, AL: New Hope.
    1989   "Annual Statistical Table on Global Missions: 1989." *International Bulletin of Missionary Research* 13 (1):20-21.
Barrett, David, and James Reapsome
    1988   *Seven Hundred Plans to Evangelize the World*. Birmingham, AL: New Hope.

Bibby, Reginald W.
1987   *Fragmented Gods: The Poverty and Potential of Religion in Canada.* Toronto: Irwin Publishing.

Cook, Guillermo
1983   "Evangelical Reflections on the Church of the Poor." *Missiology* 11 (1):47-53.
1988   "Base Communities in Latin America (with Special Reference to Central America)." Unpublished paper. San José, Costa Rica: CELEP.

Costa, Frank J., Ashok K. Dutt, Laurence J. C. Ma, and Allen G. Noble, eds.
1989   *Urbanization in Asia.* Honolulu: University of Hawaii Press.

Cotterell, Peter
1989   "The Church in Europe." *Evangelical Review of Theology* 13 (1):37-48.

Dogan, Mattei, and John D. Kasarda, eds.
1988   *The Metropolis Era. Volume One: A World of Giant Cities.* Beverly Hills, CA: Sage.

Escobar, Samuel
1990   "From Lausanne 1974 to Manila 1989: The Pilgrimage of Urban Mission." *Urban Mission* 7 (4):21-29.

Fishman, Robert
1987   *Bourgeois Utopias: The Rise and Fall of Suburbia.* New York: Basic Books.

Gili, Juan
1989   "The Challenge of Southern Europe." *World Evangelization* 16 (60):17.

Grigg, Viv
1989   "Squatters: The Most Responsive Unreached Bloc." *Urban Mission* 6 (5):41-50.

Gugler, Josef, ed.
1988   *The Urbanization of the Third World.* New York: Oxford University Press.

Gutkind, Peter C. W.
1974   *Urban Anthropology: Perspectives on 'Third World' Urbanization and Urbanism.* Assen: Van Gorcum and Comp.

Hewitt, W. E.
1988   "Christian Base Communities (CEBs): Structure, Orientation and Sociopolitical Thrust." *Thought* 63 (249):162-75.

Hutcheson, William R.
1987   *Errand to the World: American Protestant Thought and Foreign Missions.* Chicago: University of Chicago Press.

Knight, Richard V., and Gary Gappert, eds.
  1989   *Cities in a Global Society.* Beverly Hills, CA: Sage.
Lewin, Hugh, ed.
  1987   *A Community of Clowns: Testimonies of People in Urban Rural Mission.* Geneva: World Council of Churches.
Mayur, Rashmi
  1985   "Supercities, the Growing Crisis." *The Futurist* 19 (4):27-30.
McGavran, Donald
  1970   *Understanding Church Growth.* Grand Rapids, MI: Wm. B. Eerdmans Publishing Company.
Monsma, Timothy
  1989   "African Urbanization — the Future." *World Evangelization* 16 (61):20-22.
Neighbour, Ralph, Jr., ed.
  1987   *No Room in the Inn . . . Brisbane . . . Resistant or Neglected?* Queensland: Torch Ministries International.
  1989   *A City That Neglects Its Religious Institutions . . . Auckland . . . Resistant and Neglected.* Houston: Torch Outreach Ministries.
Neill, Stephen
  1965   *A History of Christian Missions.* Grand Rapids, MI: Wm. B. Eerdmans Publishing Company.
Niemeyer, Larry
  1989   *Summary of the Nairobi Church Survey.* Nairobi, Kenya: Daystar University College.
Palen, J. John
  1987   *The Urban World.* 3d ed. New York: McGraw-Hill.
Pate, Larry D.
  1989   *From Every People: A Handbook of Two-Thirds World Missions with Directory/Histories/Analysis.* Monrovia, CA: MARC.
Pretiz, Paul
  1988   "Church Planters Needed — Mexico City Directory Reveals Few Evangelicals." *Urban Mission* 5 (3):6-10.
Ro, Bong-rin, ed.
  1989a   *Urban Ministry in Asia: Cities, the Exploding Mission Field.* Taichung: Asia Theological Association.
  1989b   "Urban Cities and the Gospel in Asia." *Urban Mission* 6 (5):20-30.
Schreiter, Robert J.
  1990   "Mission into the Third Millennium." *Missiology* 18 (1):3-12.
"Seeking the Peace of the City: The Valle de Bravo Affirmation."
  1989   *Urban Mission* 7 (1):18-24.

Sheppard, David
  1974   *Built as a City: God and the Urban World Today.* London: Hodder & Stoughton.
Smith, Fred H.
  1983   "Growth Through Evangelism in Lima, Peru." *Urban Mission* 1 (1):19-28.
Spates, James L., and John J. Macionis
  1982   *The Sociology of Cities.* New York: St. Martin's Press.
Spindler, Marc R.
  1987   "Europe's Neo-Paganism: A Reverse Inculturation." *International Bulletin of Missionary Research* 11 (1):8-11.
Stoll, David
  1990   "A Protestant Reformation in Latin America?" *Christian Century* 107 (2):44-48.
Teaford, Jon C.
  1986   *The Twentieth-Century American City: Problem, Promise and Reality.* Baltimore: Johns Hopkins University Press.
Tessier, Roger, ed.
  1983   *Young People in African Towns — Their Pastoral Care.* Eldoret, Kenya: Gaba Publications.
Tuggy, A. Leonard
  1989   "CBFMS Faces the Challenge of Cities." *Urban Mission* 6 (4):43-47.
Tunnicliffe, Geoff
  1990   "Mission Toronto '90." *World Christian*, February, p. 18.
Wang, Thomas
  1990   "Finally, It's Within Sight." *AD 2000 and Beyond* 1 (1):31.
Younger, George D.
  1987   *From New Creation to Urban Crisis: A History of Action Training Ministries, 1962-1975.* Chicago: Center for the Scientific Study of Religion.

Christian Dialogues
with Other Faiths

Charles W. Forman

Futurologists are in a risky business. But if there are any grounds for
forecasting what will happen in the twenty-first century, we may risk
the prediction that it will be a time of growth in interreligious dialogue.
The dialogue movement has sprouted in the twentieth century and may
well bear large fruit in the twenty-first.

Of course past ages have seen various types of dialogue; whenever
one religion was in contact with another, debates, arguments, conversations, or other forms of intercommunication took place. But interreligious dialogue as we now define it is a twentieth-century phenomenon. As now understood, it consists of people who believe in different
religions talking together about their beliefs so that they may understand each other better and learn something from each other. The purpose is mutual knowledge and growing friendship; the clearing away
of prejudices and those ideas which are false or only partly true and in
need of correction. The purpose is not conversion. Of course, as true
believers, the participants probably have a desire each to convert the
other, and that can be understood and accepted. But for the time of

---

Charles W. Forman is emeritus professor of mission, Yale Divinity School.
Born and reared in India and the son of missionary parents, he worked
there as a Presbyterian fraternal worker. The author of *The Island Churches
of the South Pacific* (1982), he has undertaken post-retirement teaching as-
signments in Pacific theological seminaries.

dialogue the goal of conversion is set aside while they together try to
understand each other, learn from each other, and increase in friendship. No doubt, conversion in either direction remains present as a
possibility even though it is consciously disavowed as an intention.

Dialogue, understood in this way, can be seen by Christians as
part of the Christian mission. Mission includes the whole of Christian
outreach to those outside the church, which means it can take the form
of evangelistic proclamation, or of serving human need, or, in this case,
of dialogue. The San Antonio Assembly of the World Council of
Churches' Commission on World Mission and Evangelism declared:
"Dialogue has its own place and integrity and is neither opposed to
nor incompatible with witness or proclamation" — nor, we might add,
with human service (*Current Dialogue*, no. 16, p. 7). Mission encom-
passes a broad range of activities, including interreligious dialogue.

The world today has much in it that is conducive to the increase
of dialogue, now and in the future. First of all, we may note how people
are being drawn together as never before by swift transportation and
rapid communication. The airplane, the radio and television, and most
recently the FAX machine, have made it possible for people on opposite
sides of the earth to be in touch instantly and be in physical contact
within a few hours (though those hours may seem endless on trans-
oceanic flights!). Large-scale migrations of peoples are taking place so
that religions are no longer geographically isolated from one another.
Muslims and Hindus, for example, are living in large numbers among
the Christians of Europe and America. All this makes dialogue more
easily possible. Admittedly, proximity does not in and of itself bring
about dialogue, for people can live close together and yet be isolated
by walls of suspicion, defensiveness, and hostility, as Northern Ireland,
Israel, and Sri Lanka have demonstrated all too clearly. But if the right
attitudes are present proximity will make for dialogue.

A second factor that is conducive to dialogue is the fact that
human problems are increasingly shared, worldwide problems, which
have to be faced on a world scale. War anywhere threatens the peace
of all. Injustice and the rebellions against it make for instability in world
conditions. The destruction of the ecosystem anywhere endangers
human life everywhere. And since people of different faiths find themselves facing common problems, they are naturally drawn toward common consideration of them. The most successful forms of interfaith
dialogue that have taken place have been those dealing with peace,
justice, and the environment.

Further, and as a result of the above two factors, there is a growing sense of common humanity among the peoples of the world. Of course the fact of common humanity has existed as long as there has been a human race. But this fact does not necessarily imply dialogue or cooperation. Over long centuries people have often seen the existence of other humans not as a reason for friendship, but as a challenge, and contact with others has entailed a struggle for dominance and for the control of scarce resources. As with most other species, the sharing of membership in a common species has implied a fight over territory. So common humanity cannot be taken, in itself, as a basis for dialogue, as it has been in statements from certain ecumenical bodies and from the Vatican (Cobb 1982:21-22). But when a particular interpretation is put on our common humanity, stressing our need for each other and our joint responsibilities for this earth, it is indeed a force making for dialogue.

Among Christians, a demographic fact that will doubtless lead toward greater dialogue is the increasing numerical dominance of Asian, African, and Latin American Christians in the worldwide Christian church. These Christians are becoming more and more interested in indigenizing their faith in the lands of their birth, and hence in knowing more about their own social and religious background. This leads them into dialogue with the religions of their compatriots. It is noticeable that many of the leaders in dialogue have been people of Asia or Africa, and that the two men who have successively carried the primary responsibility for dialogue in the World Council of Churches have both been Indians.

A final fact of contemporary life that leads toward dialogue between religious believers is the spread of irreligion in the world. Those who hold to their faith often feel threatened by any decline in religious belief and want to draw closer to other believers for reassurance. Already in the Jerusalem Conference of the International Missionary Council, held in 1928, it was said that the principal rival of Christianity was not the other world religions but the secular outlook that left no place for any religion at all. In a time when widespread secularity seems to leave in many people's hearts no place for God or any transcendent reality, it is comforting to know that the majority of the world's peoples have a strong sense of God or a transcendent realm in accordance with which they shape their actions and attitudes. In this situation religions seek each other, though it may be only from the need to meet a common enemy rather than from a positive desire for each other's company.

For the essential positive motivation to dialogue, both now and in the future, however, we will have to look beyond world conditions.

All the long array of factors noted here, which are in various ways conducive to dialogue, cannot of themselves bring it about. They cannot determine for religious people whether or not they *should* engage in dialogue. For that a religious basis is required, not just a propitious world situation. Religion is a matter of our ultimate concerns and ultimate commitments, and therefore, for any religious person, religion must determine how he or she approaches the world, rather than the world making the determination, though the practicalities of the world situation need to be taken into consideration. Accordingly, each religious person or religious group will have to decide on the basis of its ultimate commitments whether or not to be involved in interreligious dialogue in the future.

For Christians the answer is abundantly clear. They are taught as a basic precept of their religion that God loves all people, and that they are likewise to love them, seeing them as fellow children of God and as infinitely valuable creatures for whom Christ died. Loving them implies taking them seriously, being open to them and interested in them, trying to understand them better, learning from them something about their life — all of which leads to dialogue. Love also implies respect for other people and a recognition of their right to their own selfhood, which includes their own religious convictions. In accordance with this understanding of Christian love, the Central Committee of the World Council of Churches in its first basic statements on dialogue, made at Canterbury in 1969, said: "The Christian mission and faithfulness to the Gospel imply a respect for men of all faiths and ideologies." Moreover, as the Pope declared in 1964, dialogue is to express respect for the freedom and integrity of others, and as he has said more recently, in 1984, dialogue is an action and attitude that implies respect and hospitality, with each partner retaining his or her own identity (Sheard 1987:26, 129, 156).

One thing that love does not imply is agreement with or approval of everything that others think or do. If, for example, others should believe that no particular character can be attributed to God since God is so great as to transcend all distinctive characteristics, even the characteristic of love, it would not be an act of Christian love to agree with them, for this would destroy the ultimate basis for the love with which they are approached by Christians, that is, the belief that God loves them and that we, therefore, should also love them. The fact that love does not necessarily mean agreement with or approval of all varieties of human belief or life has not always been recognized by those involved in dialogue. The Chiang Mai consultation held by the World

341

Council of Churches in 1977 declared that a diversity of beliefs is good
and is willed by God (Sheard 1987:240), without going on to note that
there may be some diversities that are not good and not at all willed
by God. Christ died for all while we were yet sinners (Rom. 5:8), which
means that we are all loved whatever our actions or beliefs may be, but
does not mean that all our actions and beliefs are right.

A second and subordinate reason why Christians are called into
dialogue now and in the future is that they can expect to learn more of
God's presence and activity in the world thereby. God is at work among
people of other faiths as their common creation by God implies, as the
covenant made with all the descendants of Noah indicates, as Mel-
chizedek exemplified, as Isaiah declared in relation to Cyrus and Amos
in relation to the Philistines and Syrians, and as Peter declared about
Cornelius. The Gospel of John teaches that Christ is the light that
lightens every man, though every man does not recognize that light
(John 1:9-10). From all of this it follows that in dialogue with people of
other faiths, Christians can learn more about God's dealings with
humanity and see the light of Christ in new places and new ways.

The criterion by which God's action is to be recognized is, inevitably for Christians, Christ himself. For every person, religious or otherwise, there must be some norm or criterion by which actions are regarded as good or bad, some touchstone by which God's presence is
recognized, and for Christians that criterion is Christ. Karl Barth has
proposed other criteria — conformity with Scripture and with the confessional tradition of the church, enhancement of humanity, creation of
hope, and calling of the church to repentance (Lochhead 1988:38-39) —
but all of these are derived from the criterion of Christ. Using Christ as
the norm does not mean that Christians will be closed-minded in dialogue. They should, as Donald Swearer has said, expect to be challenged
and tested when engaged by the faith of another, just as the adherents
of other religions should expect to be challenged and tested, for otherwise there is no life in the dialogue (Swearer 1977:41). But the challenge
can be seen as coming from Christ, who calls us ever to repentance and
newness of life.

Having seen the strong reasons for dialogue both in the world
and in our faith, we need at this point to recognize how much has been
accomplished by way of laying foundations for twenty-first-century
advances. A vigorous movement of dialogue is well under way. The
world centers for this movement have been Rome, the site of the Vatican's Secretariat for Non-Christians, founded in 1964, and Geneva,
where the World Council of Churches' Sub-unit on Dialogue with

People of Living Faiths was inaugurated in 1971. Actually, the World
Council preceded the Vatican in interest in this field, for in 1955 it
opened the way for dialogue through a worldwide study, sponsored
jointly with the International Missionary Council, on "The Word of God
and the Living Faiths of Men," and when the IMC joined the World
Council at its New Delhi Assembly in 1961, the united body recommended dialogue in the approach to other faiths, as did the World
Council's mission unit at Mexico City two years later. A large consultation on dialogue was held in Kandy in 1967, and then the first major
multireligious dialogue took place in Ajaltoun, Lebanon, in 1970.
Another multilateral dialogue was convened at Colombo in 1974, concentrating on the social problems that religions needed to face together.
Evidently the multireligious setting was too complex for effective work,
and the other dialogues that have been held by the World Council have
each been with representatives of only one other faith, normally Islam
in its different regional manifestations (1972, 1974, 1975, 1977, and five
more from 1986 to 1989, all with Islam, and one, 1978, with Buddhism).
Four so-called dialogues have been held with the traditional religions
of Africa and the Canadian Indians, but these have been in fact consultations among Christians who are in touch with those religions and
want to learn more from them in the process of indigenizing Christianity (1973, 1978, and 1986 in Africa; 1987 in Canada).

All has not been smooth sailing for those in the World Council
who have been interested in dialogue. Heated debates have characterized the major assemblies and the meetings of the Central Committee
and the various units when the subject of dialogue has been raised. The
principal bone of contention has been over the possibility of salvation
through other religions. There is not space here to track the ups and
downs of the debate, but a possible conclusion was reached in the 1989
meeting at San Antonio of the Commission on World Mission and
Evangelism, when it was declared: "We cannot point to any other way
of salvation than Jesus Christ; at the same time we cannot set limits to
the saving power of God" (*Current Dialogue*, no. 16, p. 7).

In the meantime the Vatican's work on dialogue has been pressing
forward. Roman Catholics have been in greater agreement than Protestants on a positive evaluation of other religions, so they have approached dialogue more easily. The Secretariat for Non-Christians
issued a series of guidebooks for dialogue with each of the major world
religions, and these books take the view that all people are seeking God
or the Absolute and that there is divine revelatory activity in every
religion, sometimes seen as a preparation for the gospel. The Secretariat

at first held no dialogues but encouraged bishops to hold them. After 1973 it began to enter the field itself, but nearly all its meetings were limited to Christians discussing dialogue. On only two occasions did it sponsor actual dialogues, one in 1976 with Muslims, held in Tripoli at the invitation of the Libyan governnment, and one in Rome in 1978 with an interreligious delegation visiting from Japan. At first the Catholics hesitated about including Protestants in their meetings for fear of disagreement about the place of other faiths, but more recently both Catholics and Protestants have cordially participated in each other's dialogues (Sheard 1987:56-66, 102-17).

The Protestants involved have been those linked to the World Council. The conservative evangelicals have been wary of dialogue and none of their groups has sponsored or officially participated in any. When the World Council's unit on dialogue was created, a group of leading evangelicals issued the Frankfurt Declaration expressing the fear that dialogue was replacing mission. In more recent years, however, some of their leaders, such as David Hesselgrave and Waldron Scott in America, have suggested that evangelicals should be open to dialogue, and the Fellowship of European Evangelical Theologians has called for dialogue with non-Christians (Scott 1981:66-67). At the great 1989 Manila assembly of the Lausanne movement of evangelicals, Colin Chapman spoke before the whole gathering urging that they not be afraid of dialogue if it means talking and listening to others in order to understand better their worldview (1989:4).

Before leaving this survey of activities we should note that a great deal has been done about dialogue on the national and denominational level. The national councils of churches in Britain, the United States, and elsewhere have had offices dealing with relations to non-Christians and have held small dialogues with them. Some denominations, such as the United Methodists, have done the same, and the American Presbyterians have published a book challenging their members to discussion and cooperation with Muslims (Haines and Cooley 1987). More important have been the manifold activities of several Christian study centers that have been developing across Asia since 1962. These have made dialogue with the faiths that surround them one of their principal concerns.

As we look to the twenty-first century the prospects for dialogue are not as completely hopeful as what this chapter would seem to imply. There is a growth of religious militancy in many parts of the world that makes dialogue more difficult. In some Muslim lands the liberal Muslims who have been most open to dialogue have been cowed into silence by militants. A report on dialogue in Sri Lanka states that it has been on the decline during the 1980s (*Current Dialogue*, no. 16, p. 24). Christianity has also seen examples of growing militancy.

In addition, there is the common and often growing tendency to place preconditions on dialogue, which will limit and hamper it. Sometimes this comes from mystics who believe that discussion should be ruled out in favor of joint mystical experience. A Hindu leader, when invited to a World Council dialogue, said that if Christians wanted to have dialogue it should be

> of the quiet penetrating kind where . . . we recognize each other at the ultimate level of our experience of Brahman by whatever name we may call it. (Rogers 1973:27)

Among Christians one common way of putting preconditions on dialogue is to claim that in order to have real dialogue we should regard all religions as true. This approach will doubtless provide for pleasant conversation, but, if carried through consistently, it will destroy the possibility of challenging discussion since beliefs are seen as true before they are discussed. To say that everything is true kills dialogue.

A more usual precondition advanced by many Christians is the statement that in order to have dialogue we must allow for saviors other than Christ (e.g., Knitter 1985:191-92, 202; Ariarajah in *Current Dialogue*, no. 16, p. 8). This proposal is not so destructive of dialogue as the previous one, and it has frequently been accepted in Roman Catholic circles. Yet it poses perhaps unrecognized problems for Christians who have seen salvation as the work of God's suffering, self-giving love in Christ. If other ways of salvation are possible, it would seem that the supreme sacrifice that God in Christ made on our behalf was not really necessary and was even an affront to our abilities. Furthermore, if it is believed that God's supreme sacrifice of love is indeed the only way for human salvation, but that there may be many saviors in whom that sacrifice was made, then none of them would really be on the level of a supreme sacrifice, for there could be an endless number of further lives God could have. Jesus said: "Greater love has no man than this, that a man lay down his life for his friends" (John 15:13), but if God could have many lives on earth, then God's sacrificial love would never equal the love of a human being who lays down his one and only life for others. Evidently the possibility of other saviors should be kept as a subject for dialogue, rather than being made a precondition for it.

The laudable aim of these preconditions is the elimination of a sense of Christian superiority that will undermine dialogue, and such a sense is surely to be guarded against. But, as David Lochhead has pointed out in a perceptive analysis of the problems of dialogue, even those who believe that all religions provide salvation may develop a sense of superiority toward those who are not sufficiently enlightened to share this belief. An attitude of superiority is a universal human tendency that we must all try to avoid in dialogue. It may be better, as Lochhead says, to make no advance evaluation of other religions as a precondition of dialogue (1988:26, 39, 44).

Christians can be helped in many ways through dialogue. As we have seen, God has been working in all creation and therefore there is much to learn from all human beings about God and about right and helpful ways of human life. Christians who take Christ as the criterion for recognizing God's actions can find new illumination of Christ from the experience of other faiths. Lesslie Newbigin has said that dialogue may cause profound changes in Christians, that they may find that their "appearance of obedience hides the reality of disobedience" (Newbigin 1977:265, 268). Donald Swearer and John Cobb have pointed out lessons that Christians can learn from Buddhism in the process of dialogue (Swearer 1977; Cobb 1982).

Because of the potential for learning on our part, because of the learnings that we trust will be made available to others, and most of all because of the nature of our Christian calling, we can only hope that interreligious dialogue will fulfill its promise and enjoy a continuing and growing place in Christian mission during the century ahead.

Bibliography

Amirtham, Sam, and S. Wesley Ariarajah, eds.
    1986   *Ministerial Formation in a Multifaith Mileu: Implications of Interfaith Dialogue for Theological Education.* Geneva: World Council of Churches.
Chapman, Colin
    1989   "The Challenge of Other Religions." In *Proclaim Christ until He Comes.* Edited by J. D. Douglas. Minneapolis: World Wide Publications, pp. 179-83.
Cobb, John B., Jr.
    1982   *Beyond Dialogue: Toward a Mutual Transformation of Christianity and Buddhism.* Philadelphia: Fortress Press.

Coward, Harold
    1989   *Hindu-Christian Dialogue: Perspectives and Encounters.* Maryknoll, NY: Orbis Books.

Current Dialogue
    1981-   Irregular bulletin published by the Sub-unit on Dialogue with People of Living Faiths. Geneva: World Council of Churches.

Dawe, Donald G., and John Carman, eds.
    1978   *Christian Faith in a Religiously Plural World.* Maryknoll, NY: Orbis Books.

Haines, Byron L., and Frank Cooley, eds.
    1987   *Christian and Muslim Together: An Exploration by Presbyterians.* Philadelphia: Geneva Press.

Knitter, Paul F.
    1985   *No Other Name? A Critical Survey of Christian Attitudes Toward the World Religions.* Maryknoll, NY: Orbis Books.

Lochhead, David
    1988   *The Dialogical Imperative.* Maryknoll, NY: Orbis Books.

Newbigin, Lesslie
    1977   "The Basis, Purpose, and Manner of Inter-Faith Dialogue." *Scottish Journal of Theology* 30:253-70.

Rogers, Murray
    1971   "Hindu-Christian Dialogue Postponed." In *Dialogue Between Men of Living Faiths: Papers Presented at a Consultation Held at Ajaltoun, Lebanon, March 1970.* Edited by Stanley J. Samartha. Geneva: World Council of Churches, pp. 21-31.

Rousseau, Richard W., ed.
    1981   *Interreligious Dialogue.* Scranton, PA: Ridge Row Press.

Scott, Waldron
    1981   " 'No Other Name' — An Evangelical Conviction." In *Christ's Lordship and Religious Pluralism.* Edited by Gerald Anderson and Thomas F. Stransky, C.S.P. Maryknoll, NY: Orbis Books, pp. 58-74.

Sheard, Robert B.
    1987   *Interreligious Dialogue in the Catholic Church since Vatican II: An Historical and Theological Study.* Lewiston/Queenston: Edwin Mellen Press.

Swearer, Donald K.
    1977   *Dialogue: The Key to Understanding Other Religions.* Philadelphia: Westminster Press.

Christian-Muslim Relations

David A. Kerr

A hundred years ago it was commonly argued in the West that Islam could not survive the twentieth century. European colonialism claimed to be the instrument of social and political modernization with global objectives that included the reformation of traditional Islamic societies. In the judgment of Lord Cromer, the British governor of Egypt, "Islam reformed is Islam no longer" (Cragg 1965:67). Variants of this thesis were held within Christian missionary cadres. Reviewing what he termed "the Moslem World in revolution" at the end of the first quarter of the century, the General Secretary of the (Anglican) Church Missionary Society reflected that "The old Islamic system is being left behind by the people who are in many respects ahead of their faith and their Prophet in outlook, culture and civilization" (Cash 1925:133).

The late twentieth century offers much evidence for the rebuttal of such prognoses. Forms of secular nationalism that were attractive to ruling Westernized-Muslim elites have been increasingly challenged by the mass appeal of "Islamic resurgence" movements. These have succeeded in reviving the confidence of many Muslims that the problems of their contemporary societies are best solved through ideological processes of "Islamization" — an elastic term that includes diverse theories and applications of resurgent Islamic identity in a period of

David A. Kerr is Director, Macdonald Center for the Study of Islam and Christian-Muslim Relations, Hartford Seminary, Hartford, CT. He formerly taught in the same field at Selly Oak Colleges, Birmingham, England.

radical sociopolitical transition. Massive criticism of Western society, and characterization of Christianity as the coordinate of perceived Western social ills, form an essential part of the rhetoric of so-called Islamic fundamentalism (Donohue/Esposito 1982).

Earlier twentieth-century Western and Western-Christian triumphalism against Islam seems to have been replaced by apprehension and questions. Are we on the threshold of a recurrent "Crusader age" — the war this time being carried as an Islamic *jihad* against the industrial-military power of the West? Should Western churches throw their moral support behind "First World" strategies to contain further Islamization of the "Two Thirds World"? Most anxiously are such questions asked by Christian minorities in Muslim countries, many of whom see in political Islamization an oppression that threatens the very survival of the church.

This caricature of the international scenario of changing moods and minds evokes the context in which twentieth-century trends in Christian-Muslim dialogue need to be set. Doubt raises its own questions: Are Christian aspirations for dialogue with Muslims anything more than a function of Western liberal Christianity's historical guilt complex, its post-Enlightenment uncertainties, its nervousness about Muslim demands for equal footing in a new world order? If so — and the implication is clear — is not so-called Christian-Muslim dialogue as theologically and sociologically naive at the end of the twentieth century as Western and Christian assessments of Islam's future were at the century's beginning?

These are tough questions to be faced at the outset of any discussion of trends in Christian-Muslim dialogue, all the more so because they are real questions that are often asked of the practitioners of this apparently dubious art. Their poignancy is sharpened in times of international crisis between, for example, the Middle East and the West.

Answers begin to be found as conceptual clarity is brought to the nature of interfaith "dialogue" itself. In its influential advocacy of "dialogue in community" the World Council of Churches (WCC) warns against attempts to define dialogue before it has been "described, experienced and developed as a life style" (Samartha 1977:144). Significantly, therefore, it was in the context of many decades of nineteenth- and twentieth-century Christian experience of dialogue with Hindus in India that Eric Sharpe evolved his typology of interreligious dialogue. He delineated four types: "discursive," which involves mutual intellectual inquiry; "human," which affirms common humanity as the basis of interreligious relationship; "secular," which prescinds issues of faith in preference for joint secular action; and "internal," where the focus is more mystical and contemplative (Sharpe 1974:82-87).

Applying these types to the twentieth-century history of Christian-Muslim dialogue, it is possible to nuance some of the generalizations with which we started. The case of Egypt, the Church Missionary Society (CMS), and ideas of the Muslim intellectual elite should be revisited.

At the turn of the century the CMS team of Douglas Thornton and Temple Gairdner (Vander Werff 1977:187-224) resuscitated the Anglican presence in Cairo by engaging professors and students of al-Azhar University, a bastion of Islamic orthodoxy, in discursive dialogue. In the heyday of British dominion they held their meetings in "Bayt Arabi Pasha," the former home of a famous late-nineteenth-century leader of Egyptian nationalism. Their purpose was to discuss social and national issues within Egyptian society on human and secular levels as a way of reaching deeper mutual understanding between Muslims and Christians. Gairdner, the more patient, discerning, and long-lived of the two, trained himself thoroughly to study the interior life of Islam through intellectual and spiritual encounter with the Sufi tradition with which, evangelical Anglican though he was, he felt some personal resonance. To the end of his life (d. 1928) he was critical of much of the external trapping of Islamic society, but following his participation in the 1910 World Missionary Conference in Edinburgh (Gairdner 1910) he tentatively construed Islam in its most "vital forces" as the Muslims' *preparatio evangelica* (Gairdner 1912:54).

Gairdner's biographer and colleague of many years, Constance Padwick, explored this idea in her study *Muslim Devotions*, based on prayer manuals in everyday use by Muslims in Cairo and other parts of the world. She commended the *lex orandi* of Sharpe's internal dialogue as the way Christians might seek to understand the Muslim mind (Padwick 1961).

Although he was never formally a member of the CMS, Bishop Kenneth Cragg's episcopal tenure in Cairo inspired him to build upon the foundations of Gairdner and Padwick in his own scholarly contribution to Christian-Muslim dialogue, which began, in mid-century, with his classic interpretative study of *The Call of the Minaret*. He interpreted the minaret's call in terms of a Christian responsiveness that would search for "a relationship in Christ with the people of the minaret" (Cragg: 1956/1985).

Though the word "dialogue" is scarcely found in the literary vocabulary of these authors, it serves — as described by Sharpe's four types — to encompass their concepts and practice. To what purpose did they engage in dialogue? Gairdner never doubted that his sympathetic searching of Islam was intended "to try to show his Muslim friend feature after feature, lovely and glorious, of the true portrait" of Jesus Christ (Gairdner 1915:55). Cragg seeks to bring about "the restoration to Muslims of the Christ whom they have missed" (Cragg 1958:220). Both were anxious to preserve the integrity of faithful witness from the least tint of coercive proselytism by setting it above all in an internal, spiritual dialogue with Islam. Equally, both labored under the immense problematic of the secularist character of the Western civilization with which they were identified. Duncan Macdonald — mentor of Gairdner as his teacher in Hartford Seminary, and indirectly of Cragg as his predecessor in Islamic Studies at that same institution — saw the spiritual reformation of the West's "whole materialistic, mechanized civilization" as a potential fruit of Christian mission in the East (Macdonald 1932:330). Conscious of Islam's rebuke of the West, Gairdner introduced the word "retrieval" into missionary vocabulary, though it was Cragg who filled the concept with meaning: "Let it be clear that the retrieval is not territorial. . . . The retrieval is spiritual. It aims not to have the map more Christian but Christ more widely known" (Cragg 1958:230).

Gairdner's Cairo was the city whose intellectual life was dominated religiously by the *salafiyya* movement of Muhammad Abduh (d. 1905) and Rashid Rida (d. 1935). Whether the Christian-Muslim discussions in Bayt Arabi Pasha ever included these two is unknown, though it is scarcely possible that their views were unrepresented. Abduh, the prime mover of religious reform, wrote appreciatively of the precedent sixteenth-century reformation of the Christian tradition, which he judged to be Islamic in essence and instinct, if not in name (Abduh 1966:149-50). Rida wrote disparagingly of Christian missionaries, but like Abduh he saw the need for Muslim cooperation with native Coptic Christians: "In this way religion would be what God had decreed — a source of happiness for human beings, not of misery and suffering, or an impetus to spread discord and hatred among them" (Ayoub 1984:60). Both men were essentially apologetic in their religious impact, but conciliatory toward Christianity, motivated socially by what a later Muslim historian of contemporary Islamic thought termed "some simple yet vague form of concordism" (Talbi 1985:69).

Simplistic it can be, in another sense, to offset one caricature of mission as "hostility" (Lochhead 1988:12-17) by another that construes mission as "retrieval." Yet the case of the CMS approach to Muslims in Egypt is illustrative, in the context of early twentieth-century Christian-

Muslim relations, of an important evolution in missionary practice and missiological thought that Sharpe portrays in the Indian context of Christian-Hindu relations. This maturation merits more extensive scholarly research, the Catholic Church and Reformed Church being especially fecund in the experience of Christian-Muslim encounter.

In this connection the work of two individual thinkers stands out for special mention in evolving concepts of Christian-Muslim history.

The great French scholar Louis Massignon devoted much of his life to a painstaking study of Islamic mysticism (Sufism), which he described as "the essence of the Islamic soul." Within the lives of Muslim (*sufi*) saints he discerned the blossoming of "conspicuous acts of grace, worked directly by the Holy Spirit." Within the evident conflicts of the Christian-Muslim relationship in history Massignon saw inner ties in what he termed "the commerce in spiritual things" — a *commercium in spiritualibus* sustained by the sanctifying bonds of spiritual kinship in the lives of Muslim and Christian saints (Bassetti-Sani 1974:51-58). If this seems to comply with Sharpe's interior type of dialogue, Massignon applied it in a radical Gandhian way to areas of political conflict between Christians and Muslims caught up in French decolonization of North Africa, and between Jews, Christians, and Muslims in Palestine.

Wilfred Smith — the eminent Canadian scholar of Islam, and Christian philosopher/theologian — has also tried conceptually to recaste the historical and theological relationship of Christianity and Islam as two dynamic movements struggling differently but not discretely with "the idea of God in human history." Smith's emphasis lies upon common scriptural, scholastic, ascetic, and cultural enterprises that "are to be understood," he suggests, "as elements of a dynamic whole." It is in his interpretation of "faith," based largely upon semantic exegesis of the Bible and Qur'an, that Smith finds his primary category of kinship between Muslims and Christians (Smith 1981:281), leading him to the conclusion that "a modern historiography, and even a modern theology . . . must approach the question of Muslim-Christian relations in terms of a single complex" (Smith 1981:263).

Mention of the names of Massignon, Smith, and Cragg — each one questionably representative of his particular Christian tradition, but unquestionably influential in the shaping of Christian-Muslim dialogue in the middle decades of the century — turns our attention to more institutionalized trends in Christian-Muslim dialogue since the middle 1960s.

Louis Massignon's influence on Pope Paul VI's interest in Islam

352

has been attested by the leading Catholic historian of Christian-Muslim relations, Youakim Moubarac, himself a Massignon protégé (Moubarac 1977:394). It was during Paul VI's pontificate that the Second Vatican Council, on the insistence of Arab Christian delegates (Moubarac 1977:398), addressed Christian relationships with Muslims. The dogmatic statement on the church, *Lumen Gentium*, declared: "The plan of salvation also includes those who acknowledge the Creator. In the first place among these are the Muslims, who, professing to hold the faith of Abraham, along with us adore the one, merciful God, who on the last day will judge mankind" (Abbott 1966:35). The Council's recognition of authentic monotheism as the spiritual link between the church and Muslims was elaborated in the papal encyclical entitled *Ecclesiam Suam*, which mentioned Muslims' adoration of God as the exemplification of how it is possible for God to be authentically worshiped by those who do not, as Christians and Jews, share the biblical tradition (Moubarac 1977:412-18).

A first draft of *Lumen Gentium* sought to historicize the monotheistic faith of Muslims by acknowledging them as "sons of Ishmael who, recognizing Abraham as their father, also believe in the God of Abraham" (Moubarac 1977:401). This was removed from the final text of the constitution, though it survived in more extended form in the Council's nondogmatic declaration on relations with "non-Christians," the *Nostra Aetate*. This declaration drew an analogy between Muslims' striving for obedience to God and that of Abraham, "to whose faith Muslims eagerly link their own." While respecting the difference between Christian and Muslim views of Jesus, the declaration acknowledged the place Islam accords him as a prophet, its respect for Mary, and its esteem for a righteous way of life, rooted in worship, by which Muslims prepare themselves for "the Day of Judgement and the reward of God following the resurrection of the dead." This led the declaration to conclude: "Although in the course of the centuries many quarrels and hostilities have arisen between Christians and Muslims, this most sacred Council urges all to forget the past and to strive sincerely for mutual understanding. On behalf of all mankind, let them make common cause of safeguarding and fostering social justice, moral values, peace and freedom" (Abbott 1966:663).

Vatican II marked a major threshold in the evolution of Christian initiative in dialogue with Muslims. The institutional application of the Council's vision can be traced in the work of the Vatican's Secretariat for Relations with Non-Christians, renamed the Pontifical Council for Interreligious Dialogue in 1989 (Fitzgerald 1975/1989). Papal allocutions, particularly those of the present pope on his many visits to Muslim countries, elaborate the Council's perspective. If, in the judgment of the present writer, it seems exaggerated to claim that this amounts to "a doctrine of dialogue" (Pruvost 1980:9), there can be little argument that Catholic initiative has stimulated Christian-Muslim dialogue within the Protestant/Orthodox circles of the World Council of Churches (Brown 1989), and among some Muslim religious thinkers and institutions (Talbi 1985:65).

The first secretary of the Vatican Secretariat, Bishop Pietro Rossano, suggested a way of conceptualizing postconciliar trends of Christian-Muslim dialogue. He likened the Catholic situation to a triptych, "a three fold division, giving us the outline of three positions, a central dominant one, and two collateral ones" (Rossano 1981:205). His typology can be extended to embrace WCC and Muslim developments in dialogue over the last thirty years.

The central panel of the triptych represents "the recognition of a spiritual bond which unites Christianity and Islam," from which dialogue proceeds with "a maieutic intention aimed at focussing upon and developing in the Islamic tradition the aspects and points of contact closest to those of the Christian tradition." This has been elaborated in two recensions of Vatican *Guidelines for Dialogue between Christians and Muslims*, published in 1970 (SPNC 1970) and 1981 (Borrmans 1981). The second and more substantial edition, which appeared in English translation in 1990, explains: "The dialogue proposed is meant to take place on the level of human spiritual adventure. . . . We all realize, of course, that Islam, for its part, has a double aim, in that it is both a plan for the everyday life of society and a plan for human religious experience. By taking the first plan into account we have tried to assess here the likelihood and the limits of dialogue today in terms of the second plan, that is, a 'religious dialogue' between Christians and Muslims" (Borrmans 1990:112).

This perspective was fully shared within Eastern Orthodoxy by the Antiochene Bishop George Khodr of Mount Lebanon in his presentation to the 1971 WCC Central Committee on the subject of "Christianity in a Pluralistic World: the Economy of the Holy Spirit" (Khodr 1971). He argued for a Christian dialogue with Islam that would seek to discern and disclose the mystery of the Holy Spirit in the life of the Muslim community of faith. As he anchors dialogue theologically in Christian participation in the life of the Holy Spirit, he exemplifies it historically in Arab culture, which he defines as a spiritual-humanist synthesis of Jewish, Christian and Islamic influences "under the tent of

Abraham," molded by its embrace of universal monotheism, to which the "structure of dialogue" is elemental. "Arabism," he proposes, "on the religious level is the vehicle of biblical catholicity," which he sees confirmed by the fact that "the Qur'an resonates with a powerful sentiment of Christ" (Khodr 1972-73:185-89).

In similar vein, though with a more generalized sense of human values, Bishop Kenneth Cragg encouraged Christians and Muslims at a 1972 dialogue meeting organized by the WCC to engage in "an inter-penetration of sympathy, of awareness, of recognition, and of responsiveness, and the will to a positive discerning of each other, as the necessary context of our dialogue and our common action" (Cragg 1973:139).

At this point it becomes impossible to draw a fast distinction between dialogue as a search for spiritual kinship and as a struggle for human value. Thus the central panel of Bishop Rossano's triptych merges with its first collateral: Christian-Muslim dialogue of human and social focus "with an intentional prescinding of faith" (faith here in the sense of doctrine), which recalls Sharpe's categories of human and secular dialogue. The Vatican Secretariat's concern, to draw Muslims and Christians into joint exploration of both human rights (PISAI 1983) and holiness (PISAI 1985), matched the WCC emphasis on "The quest for human understanding and cooperation." This was the theme of the WCC's first major initiative in Christian-Muslim dialogue (Samartha/Taylor 1973), and it remains central to its current advocacy of *Ecumenical Considerations on Christian-Muslim Relations*: "The problems of the complex relations between religion *(din)*, the world *(dunya)*, and the state *(dawla)* call for greater dialogue, especially among Christians and Muslims living together in the same society. One of the main objectives of dialogue is the common search for a viable model of society and cooperation in building a really human community which guarantees equality for all, safeguards religious liberties and respects differences and particularities" (DPLF 1991:13-14).

Muslim participation in WCC and Vatican dialogue experiments has been a further encouragement of this social-human emphasis. A striking example is evident in the 1976 Arab Socialist Union invitation to the Vatican Secretariat for a dialogue meeting in Libya, the agenda of which centered around religion and ideology, religion and social justice. The conclusion of this conference affirmed that "All the sons of Abraham have the obligation to ensure that their common religious heritage leads them to a rediscovered mutual trust and renewed love for one another," and exhorted its participants ". . . to have the courage

355

so to act that their life and work inspire them to cooperate as brothers in the service of the human family" (PMV 1978:138). If, as was suggested by one of the Catholic participants, Tripoli marked a "charter for Christian-Muslim dialogue today," the clearly stated view of one of the Muslim participants is telling: "Muslim-Christian dialogue should seek at first to establish a mutual understanding, if not a community of conviction, of Muslim and Christian answers to the fundamental ethical question: what ought I to do?" (al-Faruqi 1968:45-77).

The course of Christian-Muslim dialogue through the 1980s has been strongly marked by the social agenda, as intended by a joint planning meeting of Muslims and Christians in Geneva in 1979 that gave priority to issues of human rights, economic development, and technology (Brown 1989:104-9). Cooperation between the WCC and the Vatican Secretariat resulted in five regional meetings of Christian-Muslim dialogue (Benin, Bali, Crete [with Arabs and Europeans], USA, and Tanzania), each of which addressed issues of religion and state, religion and education, religion and family (Brown 1989:133-81).

As truly as it is affirmed that "spirituality" does not exist separately from the lives of human communities in which the Holy Spirit freely works, a perceived tendency toward the secular in contemporary Christian-Muslim dialogue has provoked criticism from friendly and more hostile quarters. David Lochhead's penetrating analysis of *The Dialogical Imperative* obliquely criticizes the WCC for failing to draw out the theological significance of the human rights' orientation of much of its recent concern (Lochhead 1988:72-73). He agrees with John Cobb's view that the religious character of interfaith encounter has been subordinated to an essentially secularist view of human activity in the modern ecumenical movement.

In very different theological perspective the Lausanne Committee for World Evangelism (LCWE) has been sharply critical of what it apprehends as dangerous relativizing of the gospel's uniqueness. The 1974 Lausanne Covenant rejected "as derogatory to Christ and the Gospel every kind of syncretism and dialogue which implies that Christ speaks equally through all religions and ideologies" (Scherer 1987:172). It needs to be said that the Vatican and the WCC have themselves consistently rejected syncretistic dialogue (Samartha 1977:147-49). The real issue of difference in the LCWE approach concerns the relationship between dialogue and evangelism. If the Vatican and WCC speak ambivalently on this critical issue, the Lausanne Committee expresses itself with uncompromising Christocentricity: "Our Christian presence in the world is indispensable to evangelism, and so is that kind of dialogue whose purpose is to listen sensitively in order to understand. But evangelism is to proclaim the historical, biblical Christ as Savior and Lord."

Within this perspective the LCWE's *Glen Eyrie Report on Muslim Evangelism* proposed "an international Christian-Muslim office on human rights" (LCWE 1978:12) — an idea that remains unfulfilled. In the meantime its more recent Manila Manifesto has reiterated the evangelical affirmation "that other religions and ideologies are not alternative paths to God, and that human spirituality, if unredeemed in Christ, leads not to God but to judgment, for Christ is the only way."

The Lausanne position conforms to the third element of the Rossano triptych of post-Vatican II approaches to dialogue with Muslims: one that for doctrinal and political reasons remains deeply skeptical about all forms of dialogue, other than what Sharpe classifies as "discursive" with the explicit intention of evangelization. The most recent papal encyclical, *Redemptoris Missio*, may lend support to this position.

Attempts to summarize religious trends over a century rarely escape inherent dangers of artificiality. This survey of twentieth-century trends in Christian-Muslim dialogue is, I fear, no exception. If dialogue is personal in the sense of taking place wherever people meet each other in search of mutual understanding and trust, with the intention of servicing together the communities they share, and thus giving authentic witness to their faith (Kerr 1987:24), it could have been more illuminating to search for dialogical trends in places other than the constitutions, declarations, and recommendations of confessional bodies. As it is, the institutional perspective indicates a diversity of positions within contemporary Christianity, and an imbalance of initiative between Christian and Muslim institutions.

And so while this claims to be an accurate assessment of institutional endeavors in Christian-Muslim dialogue, it may unwittingly conceal the quality of individual and local expressions of dialogical awareness.

Two examples from North Africa must suffice to conclude illustration of this remark. One of the most articulate and persuasive commendations of dialogue in the early 1970s came from the pen of a Muslim professor of history in Tunis, Mohammad Talbi. "The precise purpose of dialogue," he argued, "whatever the circumstances, is to reanimate constantly our faith, to save it from tepidity, and to maintain us in a permanent state of *ijtihad*, that is a state of reflection and research" (Talbi 1985:70).

Professor Talbi was one of a group of Muslim and Christian scholars who have met over an extended period in North Africa, prompted by the earlier-mentioned institutional dialogue in Tripoli, Libya (1976). Known as the Muslim-Christian Research Group, their work focused on Muslim and Christian understandings of Scripture, in search of a hermeneutics to sustain Christian-Muslim dialogue. The fruit of their labor, published in English under the title *The Challenge of the Scriptures: the Bible and the Qur'an* (MCRG 1989), presents its conclusions in the form of questions: By what criteria can Christians and Muslims interpret their respective scriptures from their (scriptures') specific historicizations so as to address the challenges of the modern age? How do Muslim and Christian understandings of each other's faith help them to reread their own scriptures? In what manner and degree does the experience of contemporary communities cause Christians and Muslims to rethink theologies that have become normative out of past historical contexts? How can a reformed mutual understanding that arises from shared scriptural research be related to the challenge of living in harmony in a plural world? How shall each discern·what God may be saying to the members of one religion through the scripture of the other, not only in scriptural convergences but even more significantly in what is "different and irreconcilable" (MCRG 1989:87-89).

The twentieth century began with Christian prescriptive judgments about Islam and Muslim apologetic retorts, and draws to its close with mutual questions. Some of these, with which we began, are negative in their presuppositions. Insofar as they arise from religious considerations, they tend to reflect the criticism of dialogue expressed within the third panel of Bishop Rossano's triptych. Missiologically important as they may be — and widely as they are asked — they should not obscure the diverse characteristics of twentieth-century Christian-Muslim dialogue that this article has attempted to clarify. Toward the end of the century we find new questions being asked, by Muslims and Christians together, and these may well prove indicative of where Christian-Muslim dialogue will proceed in the future.

If it has taken Christians and Muslims a hundred years of gradual encounter in dialogue through various forms and modes to reach the questions of the North African Muslim-Christian Research Group, this writer judges the effort to have been valuable. Professor Willem Bijlefeld — whose influence in shaping Christian-Muslim dialogue since the 1950s has been pervasive and subtle (Bijlefeld 1959) — concluded his contribution to the formative 1972 WCC consultation of Christians and Muslims with an observation that I hope he may permit me to adopt as the conclusion of this paper: "These questions can be worthwhile only if and when they become our questions. The foregoing discussion has tried to serve the very modest purpose of stimulating you to ask the right questions, trusting that, with the grace of God, you will also begin to answer them" (Bijlefeld 1972:57).

For Further Reading

Abbott, Walter
1966   *The Documents of Vatican II*. New York: Guild Press.

Abduh, Muhammad
1966   *The Theology of Unity*. Translated by Ishaq Musa'ad and Kenneth Cragg. London: George Allen and Unwin.

Ayoub, Mahmoud
1984   "Muslim Views of Christianity: Modern Examples." *Islamochristiana* 10:49-70.

Bassetti-Sani, Guilio
1974   *Louis Massignon: Christian Ecumenist*. Translated by A. Culter. Chicago: Franciscan Herald Press.

Bijlefeld, Willem
1959   *De Islam als Na-Christelijke Religie* (Islam as a Post-Christian Religion: An Inquiry into the Theological Evaluation of Islam, Mainly in the 20th Century). Den Haag.
1972   "Truth, Revelation and Obedience." In *Christian-Muslim Dialogue: Papers from Broumana, 1972*. Edited by Stanley Samartha and John Taylor. Geneva: World Council of Churches.

Borrmans, Maurice
1981   *Orientations pour un Dialogue entre Chrétiens et Musulmans*. Paris: Éditions du Cerf.
1990   *Guidelines for Dialogue between Christians and Muslims*. Translated by Marston Speight. New York: Paulist Press.

Brown, Stuart, ed.
1989   *Meeting in Faith: Twenty Years of Christian-Muslim Conversations Sponsored by the World Council of Churches*. Geneva: World Council of Churches.

Cash, Wilson
1925   *The Moslem World in Revolution*. London: Church Missionary Society.

Cragg, Kenneth
1956   *The Call of the Minaret*. Oxford: University Press (1985, Maryknoll, NY: Orbis Books, and Ibadan, Nigeria: Daystar Press).

1965   *Counsels in Contemporary Islam*. Edinburgh: University Press.

1972   "In the name of God. . . ." In *Christian-Muslim Dialogue: Papers from Broumana, 1972*. Edited by Stanley Samartha and John Taylor. Geneva: World Council of Churches.

Donohue, John, and John Esposito

1982   *Islam in Transition: Muslim Perspectives*. Oxford: University Press.

DPLF (Dialogue with People of Living Faiths)

1991   *Ecumenical Considerations on Christian-Muslim Relations*. Geneva: World Council of Churches.

al-Faruqi, Ismail

1968   "Muslim-Christian Relations: Diatribe or Dialogue." *Journal of Ecumenical Studies* 5 (1):45-77.

Fitzgerald, Michael

1975   "The Secretariat for Non-Christians is 10 Years Old." *Islamochristiana* 1:87-96.

1989   "25 Years of Dialogue: the Pontifical Council for Inter-Religious Dialogue." *Islamochristiana* 15:109-20.

Gairdner, Temple

1910   *Edinburgh 1910: An Account and Interpretation of the World Missionary Conference*. Edinburgh/London: Oliphant, Anderson and Ferrier.

1912   "The Vital Forces of Christianity and Islam." *International Review of Missions* 1:44-61.

Kerr, David

1987   "Christianity and Islam: An Overview." In *Living Among Muslims: Experiences and Concerns*. Geneva: Centre International Reforme John Knox.

Khodr, George

1971   "Christianity in a Pluralistic World: The Economy of the Holy Spirit." *Ecumenical Review*, April, 118-28.

1972-73 "L'Arabite." *Pentalogie Islamo-Chrétien* 5:185-99.

Kimball, Charles

1991   *Striving Together: A Way Forward in Christian-Muslim Relations*. Maryknoll, NY: Orbis Books.

Lausanne Committee for World Evangelization

1978   *Glen Eyrie Report on Muslim Evangelization*. Wheaton, IL.

Lochhead, David

1988   *The Dialogical Imperative: A Christian Reflection on Interfaith Encounter*. Maryknoll, NY: Orbis Books.

Macdonald, Duncan
    1932   "The Essence of Christian Missions." *The Moslem World* 22 (4):327-30.

McCurry, Don, ed.
    1979   *The Gospel and Islam: A 1987 Compendium.* Monrovia, CA: MARC.

Moubarac, Youakim
    1977   *Recherches sur la Pensée Chrétien et l'Islam.* Beyrouth: Publications de l'Université Libanaise.

MCRG (Muslim-Christian Research Group)
    1989   *The Challenge of the Scriptures: The Bible and the Qur'an.* Translated by Stuart Brown. Maryknoll, NY: Orbis Books.

Padwick, Constance
    1961   *Muslim Devotions: A Study in Prayer.* London: S.P.C.K.

PISAI (Pontificio Istituto di Studi Arabi e d'Islamistica)
    1983   "Droits de l'Homme/Human Rights." *Islamochristiana* 9.
    1985   "Holiness in Islam and Christianity." *Islamochristiana* 11.

PMV (Pro Mundi Vita)
    1985   "The Muslim-Christian Dialogue of the Past Ten Years." In *Christianity and Islam: The Struggling Dialogue.* Edited by Richard Rousseau. Montrose, PA: Ridge Row Press.

Pruvost, Lucie
    1985   "From Tolerance to Spiritual Emulation: An Analysis of Official Texts on Christian-Muslim Dialogue." In *Christianity and Islam: The Struggling Dialogue.* Edited by Richard Rousseau. Montrose, PA: Ridge Row Press.

Rossano, Pietro
    1981   "The Major Documents of the Catholic Church Regarding Muslims." *Bulletin: Secretariatus Pro Non-Christianis* XVI/3 (48):204-15.

Samartha, S. J., and J. B. Taylor
    1973   *Christian-Muslim Dialogue.* Geneva: World Council of Churches.

Samartha, Stanley, ed.
    1977   *Faith in the Midst of Faiths: Reflections on Dialogue in Community.* Geneva: World Council of Churches.

Scherer, James
    1987   *Gospel, Church and Kingdom: Comparative Studies in World Mission Theology.* Minneapolis: Augsburg Publishing House.

SPNC (Secretariatus Pro Non-Christianis)
    1970   *Guidelines for a Dialogue between Muslims and Christians.* Rome: Ancora.

Sharpe, Eric
　1974　　　"The Goals of Inter-Religious Dialogue." In *Truth and Dialogue: The Relationship between World Religions*. Edited by John Hick. London: Sheldon Press.

Smith, Wilfred
　1981　　　*On Understanding Islam*. The Hague, Netherlands: Mouton Publishers.

Talbi, Mohammad
　1985　　　"Islam and Dialogue: Some Reflections on a Current Topic." In *Christianity and Islam: The Struggling Dialogue*. Montrose, PA: Ridge Row Press.

Vander Werff, Lyle L.
　1977　　　*Christian Mission to Muslims*. Pasadena, CA: William Carey Library.

Woodbury, Dudley, ed.
　1989　　　*Muslims and Christians on the Emmaus Road*. Monrovia, CA: MARC.

Church-State Relations and Mission

Norman E. Thomas

Futurists believe that accelerating and convulsive changes will characterize our world for decades to come. These will affect profoundly every political institution, and every religious institution in its mission to relate faith to societal issues. Those who enter the twenty-first century can expect a continuation and acceleration of this trend toward *permanent revolution*.

Some trends, if left unchecked in the next century, will threaten the quality of life on this planet, if not life itself. They include what have been called "the four horsemen of the planetary apocalypse": population growth, resource depletion, environmental pollution, and nuclear disaster (*Global 2000* I, pp. 3, 39-42).

How will twenty-first century societies respond to these changes? Not all futurists are prophets of doom. Alvin Toffler in *Future Shock* (New York: Random House, 1970) analyzed people overwhelmed by accelerating change, while advocating a rational response to change that would harness "this wild growth, this cancer in history" (1970:429-

Norman E. Thomas is the Vera B. Blinn Professor of World Christianity at United Theological Seminary in Dayton, Ohio. A Methodist missionary in Zimbabwe and Zambia (1962-76), he is the book editor of *Missiology: An International Review,* and the chairman of major bibliography projects for the American Society of Missiology and the International Association of Mission Studies.

30). A decade later in *The Third Wave* Toffler predicted that like incoming waves on a shore, a new wave of civilization would overtake the earlier waves of agricultural and industrial societies. His vision was fundamentally optimistic. The colliding and overlapping of waves admittedly causes conflict and tension. However, innovations in communications and technology provide new opportunities for an enhanced quality of human life and interactions (1980:344).

This chapter's thesis is that the church's mission in the next century as it relates to politics is best understood in terms of the emerging new political realities that Toffler described as the "Third Wave." It will include devolution of power to the people in communal democracy. These will often be in conflict with the nation-states — remnants of the rule by elites of the older order. The third reality will be the growth of world associations and allegiances (1980:432-62).

We will therefore analyze three emerging political realities: communal democracy, nation-states, and international orders. In the process we will introduce paradigms for response by churches in mission. Regretfully space does not permit a detailed analysis and application of such response to the variety of cultures and polities within which Christians live.

Communal Democracy — The Challenge of Identification

We Are Somebody — The Ethnic Resurgence

Before the industrial revolution most regions of the world were not consolidated into nation-states. Instead, peoples were politically organized into a mishmash of local units variously called tribes, clans, duchies, kingdoms, and so on. Even emperors ruled over a patchwork of tiny locally governed communities. The wave of industrialization changed that. Economies of scale could only be achieved with polities of scale. Thus it was that Germany's 350 diverse, quarreling ministates merged in the nineteenth century into a single nation (Toffler 1980:96-97). The myth spawned by the American and French revolutions was that this was government "of the people — by the people — and for the people." In reality power and decision-making were controlled almost always by a power elite. The rise of new nations after World War II in the Two-Thirds World of Africa, Asia, and Oceania did not change this pattern, as Latin Americans who had achieved nationhood a century earlier could testify.

Today, however, peoples are reasserting their communal identities. With the collapse of the Soviet Union, independence has been achieved by the Latvians, the Lithuanians, and the Estonians, who lost self-rule in 1939. Under the Commonwealth of Independent States, other groups such as the Georgians and Armenians are seeking independence, although they have no living memory of it. Palestinians from Bethlehem to Beirut to Boston affirm that they are one people, one nation, though without a territorial nation-state to call their own.

Where peoples say, "we are somebody," those in power feel uneasy. Where communities want liberation from domination by a few, the powerful feel threatened. Their first response is often repression and a denial of human rights.

The Mission of Identification 2.

With whom shall the church identify in a liberation or human rights struggle? In Luanda, the capital of Angola in Africa, the Portuguese government built an imposing "White House" for the colony's leaders. Colonial governor and Catholic archbishop shared a common facade, symbolizing the union of church and state in the colonial elite. Meanwhile from 1961 to 1975 the Angolan people rose up in revolt against colonial rule. What was to be the church's mission in that revolutionary context?

Often the church's leadership, and much of its financial support, comes from those holding political and economic power. The result may be a struggle for identification in which the church's understanding of its mission is honed as by fire and anvil.

One type of mission through identification takes place if the church sides with the poor and oppressed in their struggle for liberation. In Brazil, for example, the Roman Catholic Church formed thousands of Base Christian Communities during military rule in the 1970s. They were the means by which the poor could share their concerns when those called political radicals were imprisoned, tortured, and often killed. There the church became the voice for the voiceless (Lernoux 1989:121-35). A parallel radicalization of the church's mission in the face of human rights abuses took place in Namibia, El Salvador, and the Philippines, among other countries.

It is to be expected that such missionary responses will be part of the witness of the churches in the coming century. The challenge for the churches in mission to identify themselves with the poor and oppressed will increase in coming years (Escobar and Driver 1978:36-

56). By every measure of material welfare the gaps between the richest and the poorest, both within and among nations, will increase (*Global 2000* I, p. 39). Competition will increase for scarce resources. Faced with seemingly endless social welfare needs, some will propose ignoring the problems of the homeless and the aliens in their midst. Churches in mission, following the example of their Lord, will be called to empty themselves in service to those in greatest need (Phil. 2:10).

A second type of mission through identification takes place as peoples reassert their communal selfhood. Consider, for example, the link between the Roman Catholic Church and ethnic resurgence in Eastern Europe. Historically in Poland, Slovakia, and Croatia ethnic and religious identities were the same and reinforced each other. By contrast, in predominantly Orthodox Romania, almost all Roman Catholics are from the minority Hungarian or German communities. As a result, under communist dominance, the church found its mission as an advocate for suppressed nationalities — in Croatia, Slovenia, Slovakia, Poland, Romania, Lithuania, and the Ukraine. Wherever the church encouraged opposition to political authority, the fusion of religious affiliation and nationality increased. More recently in 1989 Roman Catholic and Lutheran churches in Estonia, Latvia, and Lithuania became central meeting places as the people struggled to restore their national independence.

The symbiosis of Christianity and nationalism in Eastern Europe has taken many forms. In Bulgaria the communists recognized that Orthodoxy was a bulwark of nationalism and offered the churches a privileged position in exchange for docility and cooperation. In contrast, the Roman Catholic Church in Poland became a rival to the party for popular loyalty as it defended the people against the oppression and injustice of the regime.

An equal challenge for mission in the years ahead will be to support the empowerment of peoples. Many are minorities neglected by those in power. Many favor a devolution of power, rather than those strong central governments preferred by nation-state leaders. As we shall see below, this option need not lead to a narrow parochialism. Transnationalism is consistent in the "Third Wave" with direct democracy for local communities (Toffler 1980:454). Churches can play an enabling role if their affirmation of community is both local and global.

Nation-States: The Challenge of Involvement

Is the nation-state an endangered species? Will the centripetal forces of communal interests cause the breakup not only of the Soviet Union and Yugoslavia, but also of such states as India and Canada? Will overarching needs for world peace, security, and justice make the nation-state an anachronism?

Political scientists think not. Yes, new political institutions will be needed to respond to the desires of varied communal groups for increased political power. Yes, our global interdependence will encourage new transnational associations having added authority. But nation-states will not become obsolete as these new political arrangements emerge. The challenge will be to assist them to be open to change and responsive to the needs of all peoples within their borders.

Church-State Alternatives

Many and varied are church approaches to nation-states. Variables include the relative strength of each church within the political community, attitudes toward the church's role in society, and the degree of identification of religious elites with political elites. Four alternatives can be distinguished:

1. *Active identification* occurs when the churches identify themselves with the goals and intentions of the nation-state. When religious leaders share the public platform with presidents, prime ministers, or dictators at independence celebrations and invoke God's blessing they illustrate this type.

2. *Passive identification* occurs when the churches withdraw into the sphere of the so-called "religious" and refrain from any statements on decisions and actions by the state. "Let's not mix politics and religion" is their common appeal.

3. *Critical collaboration* occurs when the churches evaluate political policies in the light of the gospel. Church political action committees, lobbyists, and references in sermons to political issues are indications of this type.

4. *Opposition or resistance* occurs when church leaders propose and support civil disobedience, saying, "We must obey God rather than human rulers" (*Church and State* 1978:158).

Each among these alternatives, however, is part of the classic dilemma faced by activists in every world religion — how simultaneously to be *in* politics (thus, to influence it) and *beyond* politics (thus,

367

to challenge it). J. Milton Yinger, the prominent American sociologist, expressed it well:

> Those who believe that clear separation of church and state increases the power of the church emphasize the freedom from political domination, the freedom to criticize the political process and the secular power structure. There is a danger, however, that such freedoms are closely connected with powerlessness. On the other hand, close institutional connection between church and state scarcely avoids the dilemma, because the union raises the likelihood that the church will be used to lend sanctity to a secular power structure. (1957:117)

South Africa: Useful Paradigms

South Africa today provides useful models for churches of other nations as they face challenges for mission. Charles Villa-Vicencio, in his useful sourcebook entitled *Between Christ and Caesar* (1986), documents how the church of the establishment can become the church in opposition to the state and vice versa. Dutch Reformed Church (DRC) leaders responded to the 1914-15 rebellion by Boer generals accepting a Christian option of "resistance by a conscience which has been enlightened by the word of God" (1986:207-8). Thirty-five years later the DRC became the church of the political establishment providing theological legitimation for apartheid (xv).

The South African enigma of two "nations" sharing a common homeland, with each claiming a divine right to it, is replicated today in other parts of the world (Jews and Palestinians, Roman Catholics and Protestants in Northern Ireland, Armenians and Azerbaijanis, etc.). Churches in mission in such places are called to witness to wider loyalties under God. To the people of his troubled land Archbishop Desmond Tutu wrote in 1978:

> The liberation of blacks involves the liberation of the whites in our beloved country, because until blacks are free, the whites can never be really free. There is no such thing as separate freedom — freedom is indivisible. (1982:87)

Another alternative for the church in mission amidst political tensions is to provide a theological critique of the crisis and various alternatives for Christians. South African theologians provided such a critique in *The Kairos Document: Challenge to the Church* (1985). British historian Robin Hallett suggests that it "presents the apartheid regime with an ideological threat infinitely more powerful than any form of communism is ever likely to do, for South Africa is still a deeply Christian country" (Villa-Vicencio 1986:204).

First the theologians rejected the "State Theology" with its exegesis of Romans 13:1-7 to give an absolute and "divine" authority to the state. Next they critiqued the "Church Theology" of those in critical collaboration with the state who make racial reconciliation their goal and nonviolence the litmus test of Christian action. "Is not the militarization of the state also violence?" they asked. They advocated a third alternative called "Prophetic Theology" and based on biblical understandings of God as the liberator of the oppressed. Identifying the South African state as tyrannical, they called upon Christians to participate in a struggle for liberation and a just society through civil disobedience.

The issues raised in *The Kairos Document* are those which Christians in many lands will face in coming years. With which side should the church identify itself — the power-elite of the nation-state or the powerless? Are churches inevitably involved in politics, inasmuch as silence may be understood as endorsement of the status quo? Do churches have particular responsibilities in autocratic or one-party states to be the voice of the voiceless, or the "loyal opposition"? What are strengths and weaknesses of a position of critical collaboration with the state? Can churches support resistance to political authority — if so, under what circumstances? These will remain lively issues as churches redefine their mission in relation to varied and changing national situations (Escobar and Driver 1978:57-85; Okullu 1984).

Globalization: The Ecumenical Challenge

"The world appears to be on the verge of one of the great economic, social, and political discontinuities of history." In these words Theodore Hesburgh of the University of Notre Dame summarized one of the major conclusions of recent research on international politics (quoted in Bennett and Seifert 1977:194). Traditional structures can no longer handle the new global network of economic relationships. New ecological realities and the modern technology of weaponry demand changes.

Globalization is the term that best describes this new reality. It is the process by which individuals and peoples understand their identity as persons in world community, and their well-being as enhanced by growing interdependence (Robertson 1987:43-47).

Among the needs propelling decision-makers to think globally are the following:

1. *Security.* Security can be achieved only as a common enterprise of nations. No nation can pretend to be secure as long as others' legitimate rights to sovereignty are neglected or denied. No nation can absolutely secure its borders, as international terrorism has revealed.

2. *Law.* To coordinate policies to avoid wars nations need international law. When nations choose to settle disputes peacefully they seek to develop rules of international behavior.

3. *Economic order.* In a world in which the incomes of many transnational corporations exceed those of nation-states, a new international economic order becomes an imperative. For developed nations "economies of scale" are desirable, as the European Economic Community has discovered. For developing nations with limited export markets yet high demands for imports such as technology, and often oil, new regional and global stabilization is essential.

4. *Ecology.* Ours is a fragile ecosphere. While scientists debate the *extent* of changes caused by nuclear disasters or destruction of rain forests, one fact is clear. All agree that threats are global in impact and that controls are needed if a quality of human life is to be achieved in the next century.

The Vision of Shalom

Christians can approach the new globalization of earth's societies with a global theology. The covenant of God is with all creation and all humanity, just as the call to mission (Matt. 28:16-20) is to go into the whole world to proclaim the gospel (Niles 1989:55-69). In doing so Christians may contribute at a point of felt need since "globalization sets in motion the dynamic for a search for ultimate meaning, values, and resacralization" (Shupe and Hadden 1988:xi).

As Christians embrace their mission within international politics they find that they are not the only religious actors. Leaders of other religions also think globally while acting locally. The Unification Church, for example, is a globally oriented mega-organization with an overriding concern, as its name suggests, for the unification of the world. Jews, Buddhists, and Muslims all have world organizations with concerns for peace and justice issues (Robertson 1987:40-43).

Religious networks enhance effectiveness as Christians work with both governmental and nongovernmental organizations. For Roman Catholics the Pontifical Commission for Justice and Peace provides a strategic global focus. It coordinates concerns both of national offices of justice and peace and of Catholic religious orders. The World Council of Churches links Orthodox and Protestant churches. Its departments include the Commission on World Mission and Evangelism (CWME), the Commission on the Church's Participation in Development (CCPD), and the Commission of the Churches on International Affairs (CCIA). For interfaith concerns the World Conference on Religion and Peace provides a global network for sharing peace and justice concerns (Mische 1977:303-17).

Even prior to the formation of the World Council of Churches in 1948, Christian leaders, concerned to build a new world order after the devastation of World War II, proposed formation of the CCIA. Its purpose was to serve the worldwide constituencies of the World Council of Churches and the International Missionary Council (IMC) as a "source of stimulus and knowledge in their approach to international problems, as a medium of common counsel and action, and as their organ in formulating the Christian mind on world issues and in bringing that mind effectively to bear upon such issues" (van der Bent 1986:2-3).

In the past thirty-five years the CCIA has carried out its mandate in many creative ways. Church leaders have been helped to think globally about common concerns at conferences, such as the World Conference on Church and Society (Geneva, 1966). Many delegates returned to urge their governments to ratify the various UN covenants on Human Rights. Concern for conflict resolution has led the CCIA to lobby at the United Nations. This includes support for resolutions favoring Palestinian statehood while recognizing Israel's right of existence as a state within internationally agreed boundaries. In the Sudan civil war the CCIA went further and in 1971 mediated, together with the All-Africa Conference of Churches, an end to the conflict (van der Bent 1986:31, 51).

In 1983 the Vancouver Assembly of the World Council of Churches called upon the churches to engage "in a conciliar process of mutual commitment (covenant) to justice, peace and the integrity of creation." Consciousness-raising efforts during the next seven years enabled church leaders to relate their biblical understandings of shalom to the concerns of both scientists and political leaders over threats to life on this planet. Returning to a biblical model of covenant renewal (Deut. 31:9-13), delegates at the World Convocation on Justice, Peace and the Integrity of Creation (Seoul, Korea, 1990) covenanted to work for economic justice, political security, ecology, and the eradication of racism and discrimination. Through ecumenical cooperation the churches grew in understanding major global issues and in commitment to mission. The complex issues they addressed would have seemed overwhelming to individual churches or national councils (Niles 1989:ix, 70-81).

Conclusion

Alvin Toffler bases his futuring on the "revolutionary premise . . . that what is happening now is nothing less than a global revolution, a quantum jump in history." Although predicting upheavals, turbulence, and perhaps even widespread violence, Toffler is not a prophet of doom. He believes that humanity is capable of choosing a sane and desirable future (1980:28).

Paul Lehmann, the Christian ethicist, concurs. He believes that Jesus Christ is pertinent to an age of revolution in "the power of his presence to shape the passion for humanization that generates revolution, and thus to preserve revolution from its own undoing" (1975:xiii). Pierre Bigo makes the same judgment in *The Church and Third World Revolution*. He criticizes both capitalism and Marxism for choosing that very violence on which the Third World and humanity are foundering. Instead the church in mission, he believes, is to follow Christ in a preferential option for the poor by witnessing to the truth in the power of the Spirit, and by confronting wealth and power "with no weapons save those of the spirit and at the risk of life itself." In this way, he believes, it will change the course of history (1977:296).

Resurgent ethnic loyalties, popular dissatisfaction with secularized nation-states, and emerging global loyalties — these are the multivariate trends for the next century. Churches in mission can expect to be caught in the riptides of competing nationalisms and buffeted by the winds of secularism. They will face a near-global proliferation of church-state tension (Robertson 1987:46). Out of seeming weakness, however, they can become the catalyst for change from parochialism to globalism, and from despair to hope, as they are empowered by the one who said: "In the world you have tribulation; but be of good cheer, I have overcome the world" (John 16:33).

For Further Reading

Bennett, John Coleman, and Harvey Seifert
   1977   *U.S. Foreign Policy and Christian Ethics*. Philadelphia: Westminster Press.

Bigo, Pierre
1977   *The Church and Third World Revolution.* Maryknoll, NY: Orbis Books.
Escobar, Samuel, and John Driver
1978   *Christian Mission and Social Justice.* Scottdale, PA, and Kitchener, Ontario: Herald Press.
The Global 2000 Report to the President: Entering the Twenty-First Century, Gerald O. Barney, study director. 3 vols.
1980   Washington, DC: US Government Printing Office.
Lehmann, Paul
1975   *The Transfiguration of Politics.* New York: Harper & Row.
Lernoux, Penny
1989   *People of God: The Struggle for World Catholicism.* New York: Viking Press.
Mische, Gerald, and Patricia Mische
1977   *Toward a Human World Order: Beyond the National Security Straitjacket.* New York, and Ramsey, NJ: Paulist Press.
Niles, Preman
1989   *Resisting the Threats to Life: Covenanting for Justice, Peace and the Integrity of Creation.* Geneva: World Council of Churches.
Okullu, Henry
1984   *Church and State in Nation Building and Human Development.* Nairobi: Uzima Press.
Robertson, Roland.
1987   "Church-State Relations and the World System." In *Church-State Relations: Tensions and Transitions.* Edited by Thomas Robbins and Roland Robertson. New Brunswick, NJ: Transaction Books, pp. 39-51.
Shupe, Anson D., and Jeffrey K. Hadden, eds.
1988   *The Politics of Religion and Social Change.* New York: Paragon House.
Toffler, Alvin
1970   *Future Shock.* New York: Random House.
1980   *The Third Wave.* New York: Wm. Morrow & Company.
Tutu, Desmond
1982   *Crying in the Wilderness: The Struggle for Justice in South Africa.* Grand Rapids, MI: Wm. B. Eerdmans Publishing Company.
van der Bent, Ans J.
1986   *Christian Response in a World of Crisis.* Geneva: World Council of Churches.Villa-Vicencio, Charles

1986   *Between Christ and Caesar: Classic and Contemporary Texts on Church and State.* Cape Town: David Philip, and Grand Rapids, MI: Wm. B. Eerdmans Publishing Company.

World Council of Churches

1978   "Church and State: Opening a New Ecumenical Discussion." Faith and Order Paper No. 85. Geneva.

Yinger, J. Milton

1957   *Religion, Society and the Individual.* New York: Macmillan Publishing Company.

Gerald H. Anderson:
A Career Dedicated to Mission

Robert T. Coote

Gerald H. Anderson, born in 1930 to Arthur and Dorothy Anderson of New Castle, Pennsylvania, has followed a career defined by and devoted to the worldwide mission of Jesus Christ.

During his college years at Grove City College, Grove City, Pennsylvania, his training pointed to the business world, and his avocation placed him in the position of leader of a local dance orchestra. But even as he graduated with a degree in business administration, Anderson sensed God's call to the ministry. Abruptly changing direction, he enrolled in Boston University School of Theology in 1952. Upon receiving his seminary degree and ordination as a Methodist minister, he was awarded a Fulbright scholarship and spent 1955-56 at the University of Marburg, Germany. This was followed by studies at the universities of Geneva, Switzerland, and Edinburgh, Scotland, and at Boston University, culminating in a Ph.D. in Church History from Boston University in 1960. During the course of these years, Anderson gained ministerial experience in Scotland and New England, and he logged a summer in Alaska with an assignment from the Methodist Board of National Missions to survey the needs of and establish a church in a remote area on the Kenai peninsula.

Robert T. Coote is Assistant to the Director, Overseas Ministries Study Center, New Haven, Connecticut. He formerly served as managing editor of *Eternity* magazine.

In 1960 Anderson married Joanne Pemberton, daughter of a Methodist minister teaching at Providence Bible College, Providence, Rhode Island. Having accepted a missionary appointment by the Methodist Church, the Andersons arrived in Manila in November of that year, and Anderson took up the post of Professor of Church History and Ecumenics at Union Theological Seminary.

In the spring of the following year, Anderson had the satisfaction of receiving his personal copy from McGraw-Hill Book Company of *The Theology of the Christian Mission*. This, the first of a number of multiauthor books that he has edited over the years, featured contributions from twenty-six widely known leaders and teachers in the field of mission theory and theology. Anderson's goal was to provide a collection that would be widely representative and that would present a "catholic and well-rounded trinitarian point of view." He was also drawn by the themes of continuity and discontinuity, witnessed in Scripture, regarding the Christian faith and other faiths in relation to the saving activity of God. These features — a studied "catholic" methodology and commitment to a rigorous trinitarian theology of mission, nuanced by the themes of continuity/discontinuity — were to become the hallmarks of Gerald Anderson's contributions to missiological foundations and spiritual formation.

At Union Theological Seminary Anderson served as academic dean from 1963 to 1966 and then as director of graduate studies from 1968 to 1970. He also produced a number of works in Asian church history during his years at Union. In addition, he become acquainted with Bishop Stephen Neill, and this led to a joint editing venture with Neill and John Goodwin: *Concise Dictionary of the Christian World Mission* (London: Lutterworth Press, and Nashville: Abingdon Press, 1971).

With two young children, Brooks and Allison, the Andersons returned to the United States in 1970, upon Anderson's appointment as President and Professor of World Christianity at Scarritt College for Christian Workers in Nashville. Anderson served Scarritt until 1973, when he accepted an appointment at Cornell University as Senior Research Associate in the university's Southeast Asia studies program.

Midway in his tenure at Scarritt, Anderson and several other mission leaders founded the American Society of Missiology, with the inaugural meeting being held in 1973 and Anderson serving as president from 1973 to 1975. Similarly, he helped establish the International Association for Mission Studies in 1971, serving on the executive committee; from 1982 to 1985 he served IAMS as president.

In 1974 Anderson was recruited by R. Pierce Beaver as the Associate Director of the Overseas Ministries Study Center in Ventnor, New Jersey, where he become Director upon Beaver's retirement in 1976. Anderson has often remarked that if one has a heart for Christian mission but cannot be directly engaged overseas, there is no place more rewarding and stimulating that OMSC, with its constant flow of missionaries and overseas national church workers.

During the mid-1970s, Anderson joined Thomas F. Stransky, C.S.P., in editing the *Mission Trends* series, copublished by the Wm. B. Eerdmans Publishing Company and Paulist Press. With five volumes appearing between 1974 and 1981, these anthologies of missiological literature served tens of thousands of mission professors and students in taking the measure of contemporary theory and practice of Christian mission; the series also served to introduce Western readers to Third World voices.

In May of 1974, shortly before Anderson was to join Beaver at OMSC, an influential group of mission executives, primarily from the historic Protestant denominations, met at OMSC. Many were at pains to heed the call for a moratorium on Western missions. Anderson, however, had already gone on record as advocating a path of accommodation that would not undercut the missionary obligation of the worldwide church, whether in the West or elsewhere ("A Moratorium on Missionaries?" *Christian Century*, January 16, 1974). When "The Future of the Missionary Enterprise" consultation was held five months later at Ventnor, Anderson reiterated his support for a continuing role for Western missionaries. In some ecumenical quarters this earned him a reputation as a conservative, even as Anderson's ecumenical approach to theological issues and to the open fellowship of the Overseas Ministries Study Center in Ventnor prompted a skeptical, arm's-length treatment from conservative evangelicals.

Anderson's *Asian Voices in Christian Theology* (Maryknoll, NY: Orbis Books) came off the press in 1976. Another major editing project grew out of a joint consultation held in October 1979, involving OMSC and Union Theological Seminary, Richmond, Virginia. Joining well-known Protestant and Catholic theologians of mission were several conservative evangelical representatives, prompting Wilfred Cantwell Smith of Harvard University to remark, "Not long ago this sort of conference just would not have happened." Anderson again joined Thomas Stransky in bringing out the proceedings of the conference under the title *Christ's Lordship and Religious Pluralism* (Maryknoll, NY: Orbis Books, 1981).

In 1977 the trustees of OMSC affirmed Anderson's vision to revive the *Occasional Bulletin* from the Missionary Research Library, which then appeared periodically in mimeograph form with a circulation of less than 300 readers. Within four years the circulation of the *Occasional Bulletin* burgeoned to more than 8,000. With an international and multicultural board of contributing editors, representing the full spectrum from conservative evangelical to conciliar Protestant, to Roman Catholic and Eastern Orthodox, the *International Bulletin of Missionary Research*, as it has been known since 1981, is the largest circulation professional journal of mission studies published today.

In October 1983 Anderson was invited by a group of leading United Methodist clergy in Dallas to address an informal breakfast meeting. He took the occasion to reveal his concern over the failure of the official denominational board to balance its agenda with traditional concerns such as evangelism. After years of trying without success to influence the direction of mission within denominational structures, Anderson expressed the view that there was now reason and opportunity to consider the formation of an independent mission agency that would more adequately embrace evangelicals and evangelical concerns. Anderson maintained that such an agency, modeled along the lines of the Church Missionary Society, which though independent serves within the Anglican communion, would preserve evangelically minded missionaries for the mainline denomination. Within a year, United Methodist evangelical leaders from across the nation had founded the Mission Society for United Methodists. Today the Society fields more than eighty missionaries in about twenty countries. The concerns Anderson expressed in Dallas were presented more comprehensively the following March under the title "Theology and Practice of Contemporary Mission in The United Methodist Church." The occasion was the annual gathering of the World Division, General Board of Global Ministries of the United Methodist Church, where he was invited to address the assembly. This chapter in Anderson's career captured the attention of many, supporters and nay-sayers alike. Evangelical Methodists followed the argument in the independent Methodist periodical *Good News* (March-April 1984).

In July of 1984, in Newmarket, England, Anderson served as a respondent at a consultation on Jewish evangelism. The event was held under the auspices of the Lausanne Committee for World Evangelization, and thus attracted the special attention of evangelicals. He concluded his remarks as follows: "The mission to the Jews is the keystone of the Christian mission to all the peoples of the world, and if this keystone is removed, the universal mission of the Church is in danger

of theological collapse. Either all people need Christ or none do. This
affirmation of the Lordship of Jesus Christ is inherent and fundamental
in the New Testament and in the historical Christian faith."

Simultaneously, Anderson has served for more than a decade on
the World Council of Churches' Consultation on the Church and the
Jewish People.

During the early 1980s, the trustees of OMSC undertook an in-
depth study of OMSC's history, ministry, and future prospects. This
eventuated in the 1987 relocation of OMSC from Ventnor, New Jersey
(after 65 years!), to New Haven, Connecticut. Access to the Yale Divinity
School library, and especially the Day Missions Library for missions
research, loomed as a major consideration in the decision. OMSC continues to draw missionaries and national church workers from around
the world and from a wide range of denominational backgrounds, a
reflection of Anderson's early commitment to a "catholic" approach to
issues of global Christian mission.

A particularly noteworthy development, beginning in 1992, is the
program at OMSC for the advancement of scholarship in Christian
Mission and World Christianity, with the support of The Pew Charitable
Trusts. The executives of the Pew program looked to OMSC and the
leadership of Anderson to coordinate this program. Some twenty research grants will be awarded annually. In a related project, Anderson
himself is at work on a *Biographical Dictionary of Christian Missions*,
supported by The Pew Charitable Trusts, to be published by Simon &
Schuster. It will contain nearly 2,000 biographical sketches with bibliographies of pioneers and leaders in Christian missions, from the post–
New Testament generation until modern times, covering all the major
communions, inclusive of the contributions of non-Western missionaries over the centuries.

The editors of the present volume are honored to celebrate the
career of our colleague Gerald H. Anderson. We have come to appreciate him as one of the most single-minded and hardworking advocates
of the Christian world mission that we have known, and a foremost
champion of the theology that sustains that mission. We pray for God's
continued blessing on his servant.

A Select Bibliography of the Works of Gerald H. Anderson from 1958 to 1993*

Books and Monographs

Bibliography of the Theology of Missions in the Twentieth Century. New York: Missionary Research Library, 1958. 2nd ed., rev. and enlarged, 1960. 3rd ed., rev. and enlarged, 1966.

The Theology of the Christian Mission. Editor. New York: McGraw-Hill; London: SCM Press, 1961. McGraw-Hill paperback edition, 1965. Nashville: Abingdon Press paperback edition, 1969. Japanese tr., Tokyo: United Church of Christ in Japan, 1969. Korean tr., Seoul: Christian Literature Society of Korea, 1975.

Sermons to Men of Other Faiths and Traditions. Editor. Nashville: Abingdon Press, 1966.

Christianity in Southeast Asia: A Bibliographical Guide. Editor. New York: Missionary Research Library; New Haven: Yale University Southeast Asia Studies, 1966.

Christian Mission in Theological Perspective: An Inquiry by Methodists. Editor. Nashville: Abingdon Press, 1967.

Christ and Crisis in Southeast Asia. Editor. New York: Friendship Press, 1968.

*Book review articles not included.

Studies in Philippine Church History. Editor. Ithaca, NY: Cornell University Press, 1969.
Concise Dictionary of the Christian World Mission. Coeditor with Stephen Neill and John Goodwin. London: Lutterworth Press; Nashville: Abingdon Press, 1971.
Mission Trends. 5 volumes. Coeditor with Thomas F. Stransky. Grand Rapids, MI: Wm. B. Eerdmans Publishing Company; New York: Paulist Press, 1974-81.
Asian Voices in Christian Theology. Editor. Maryknoll, NY: Orbis Books, 1976.
Christ's Lordship and Religious Pluralism. Coeditor with Thomas F. Stransky. Maryknoll, NY: Orbis Books, 1981.
Witnessing to the Kingdom: Melbourne and Beyond. Editor. Maryknoll, NY: Orbis Books, 1982.
Mission in the 1990s. Coeditor with James M. Phillips and Robert T. Coote. Grand Rapids, MI: Wm. B. Eerdmans Publishing Company; New Haven: Overseas Ministries Study Center, 1991.
Biographical Dictionary of Christian Missions. Editor. In preparation.

Journals, Editor

The South East Asia Journal of Theology. Special "Philippines Issue," 4, no. 1 (1962). Guest editor.
Silliman Journal. Special issue on "Christianity in the Philippines," 12, no. 2 (1965). Guest editor.
International Bulletin of Missionary Research (formerly *Occasional Bulletin*). Editor, 1977 —.

Articles

"The Theology of Mission: 1938-1957," *Nexus* (Boston University School of Theology Journal) 1, no. 3 (1958): 118-22.
"Motives for the Christian Mission," *Motive* 20, no. 3 (1959): 8-11.
"G. Bromley Oxnam." In *Weltkirchen Lexikon: Handbuch der Oekumene,* edited by Franklin H. Littell and Hans Herman Walz, cols. 1094-96. Stuttgart: Kreuz-Verlag, 1960.
"The Theology of Missions: 1928-1959" (Abstract of Ph.D. dissertation, Boston University Graduate School, 1960), *Dissertation Abstracts* 21, no. 4 (1960). Reprinted in *Church History* 30, no. 4 (1961): 484-85; and in *Occasional Bulletin* from the Missionary Research Library 11, no. 5 (1960): 9-10.

"The Challenge of the Ecumenical Movement to Methodism," *Asbury Seminarian* 14, no. 2 (1960): 21-32.

"A Theocentric Approach to the Christian Mission" (Prize-winning essay), *World Outlook* 22, no. 1 (1961): 7-10. Reprinted in *South East Asia Journal of Theology* 3, no. 2 (1961): 10-18.

"The Hope Within You" (Sermon of the Month), *Philippine Christian Advance* (Manila) 13, no. 6 (1961): 6-9.

"The World Council of Churches Assembles in India," *Philippine Christian Advance* 13, no. 11 (1961): 4-6.

"The Minister as Preacher," *Union Voice* (Union Theological Seminary, Manila), March 1962: 35-42.

"Christian Missions and the Meaning of History," *Silliman Christian Leader* (Silliman University Divinity School, Philippines) 5, no. 1 (1962): 3-9.

"The Vatican Council of John XXIII," *Philippine Christian Advance* 14, no. 10 (1962): 4-10.

"The Christian Mission Reconsidered," *Motive* 23, no. 3 (1962): 16-19.

"The Enduring Experience of Easter" (Sermon), *Philippine Christian Advance* 15, no. 4 (1963): 6-7, 14.

"Asian Studies in Church History," *Christian Century*, Oct. 23, 1963, p. 1306.

"The Missionary Message of Christmas," *World Outlook* 24, no. 4 (1963): 7-9. Reprinted in *Examiner* (Manila), Dec. 27, 1964, pp. 3, 58.

"Four Centuries of Christianity in the Philippines: An Interpretation" (with Peter G. Gowing), *Encounter* (Indianapolis) 25, no. 3 (1964): 352-67. German tr., "Vier Jahrhunderte Christentum auf den Philippenen: Eine Deutung," *Evangelische Missions-Zeitschrift* 21, no. 2 (1964): 49-65. Norwegian tr., "Fire Arhundres Kristendom pa Filippinene," *Norsk Tideskrift for Misjon* 18, no. 4 (1964): 193-213.

"Missionary Readings on the Philippines: A Guide," *Occasional Bulletin* from the Missionary Research Library 15, nos. 7-8 (1964): 12 pp. Rev. and enlarged version in *Silliman Journal* 12, no. 2 (1965): 211-27.

"Grasshoppers Against Giants" (Commencement Address), *Silliman Christian Leader* 7, no. 1 (1964): 22-27.

"John Wesley: A Biographical Sermon," *Silliman Christian Leader* 8, no. 1 (1965): 39-45.

"A Select Bibliography on the Theology of Christian Mission," *Study Encounter* (Geneva) 1, no. 4 (1965): 211-16.

"Research Libraries in New York City Specializing in Christian Missions," *Journal of Asian Studies* 25, no. 4 (1966): 733-36.

"The Protestant Churches in the Philippines Since Independence,"
    Manila Chronicle (U.S. Edition, San Francisco, California), Dec. 13,
    1966, pp. 4, 15; also in *World Outlook* 27, no. 9 (May 1967): 12-14;
    and *Philippines Free Press* 60, no. 23 (June 10, 1967): 12, 19-20.
"Kraemer and After: A Survey Article — Studies in Mission Theology,"
    Encounter 27, no. 4 (1966): 355-62.
"Uppsala 1968: The World Council's Fourth Assembly," *Philippine Stud-
    ies* 16, no. 2 (1968): 391-98.
"The Philippines: Bulwark of the Church in Asia," with Peter G.
    Gowing. In *Christ and Crisis in Southeast Asia,* edited by Gerald H.
    Anderson, pp. 135-62. New York: Friendship Press, 1968.
"Providence and Politics behind Protestant Missionary Beginnings in
    the Philippines." In *Studies in Philippine Church History,* edited by
    Gerald H. Anderson, pp. 279-300. Ithaca, NY: Cornell University
    Press, 1969.
"Peace Corps Intrigue in the Philippines," *Christian Century,* Jan. 7, 1970,
    pp. 4-6; reprinted in *Committee of Returned Volunteers Newsletter*
    (New York), 4, no. 2 (1970): 16-17.
Articles in *Concise Dictionary of the Christian World Mission.* London:
    Lutterworth Press; Nashville: Abingdon Press, 1971, "Continuity
    and Discontinuity," "Far East Gospel Crusade," "James B.
    Rodgers," "Laymen's Foreign Missions Inquiry," "Mission Ar-
    chives," "Mission Journals," "Mission Libraries," "The Philip-
    pines," "Preaching to Men of Other Faiths," "Rebecca Parrish,"
    "The Theology of Mission."
"Mission Research, Writing, and Publishing." In *The Future of the Chris-
    tian World Mission,* edited by William J. Danker and Wi Jo Kang,
    pp. 129-40. Grand Rapids, MI: Wm. B. Eerdmans Publishing Com-
    pany, 1971.
"The Singapore Congress on Evangelism," *Encounter* 32, no. 2 (1971):
    156-58.
"Overseas Missions: The End of the Beginning," *World Vision Magazine*
    15, no. 4 (1971): 20-21.
"Some Theological Issues in World Mission Today." In *Mission in the
    '70s,* edited by John T. Boberg and James A. Scherer, pp. 109-28.
    Chicago: Chicago Cluster of Theological Schools, 1972.
"Foreword." In *Theological Battleground in Asia and Africa,* by G. C. Oost-
    huizen. London: Hurst; New York: Humanities Press, 1972.
"Introducing Missiology: Guest Editorial," *Missiology: An International
    Review* 1, no. 1 (1973): 3-5.
"Our Man Marcos: U.S. Investment in the Philippines," *New Republic,*

Dec. 1, 1973, pp. 14-16; reprinted in *Philippine Times* (Chicago), Dec. 15, 1973.

"Interview with an Exile [Raul Manglapus]," *America*, Dec. 29, 1973, pp. 458-500.

"A Moratorium on Missionaries?" *Christian Century*, Jan. 16, 1974, pp. 43-45; reprinted in *Mission Trends No. 1*, edited by Gerald H. Anderson and Thomas F. Stransky, pp. 133- 41. Grand Rapids, MI: Wm. B. Eerdmans Publishing Company; New York: Paulist Press, 1974.

"The President's Ultimate Strategy?" *Christianity and Crisis*, May 27, 1974, pp. 102-4.

"The Church and the Jewish People: Some Theological Issues and Missiological Concerns," *Missiology* 2, no. 3 (1974): 279-93. Presidential address to the American Society of Missiology.

"The Philippines: Reluctant Beneficiary of the Missionary Impulse in Europe." In *First Images of America: The Impact of the New World on the Old*, edited by Fredi Chiappelli, vol. 1: 391-403. Berkeley, CA: University of California Press, 1976.

"Checklist of Selected Periodicals for Study of Missiology and World Christianity Recommended for North American Theological Libraries," *Occasional Bulletin of Missionary Research* 1, no. 1 (1977): 14-15.

"Religion as a Problem for the Christian Mission." In *Christian Faith in a Religiously Plural World*, edited by Donald G. Dawe and John B. Carman, pp. 104-16. Maryknoll, NY: Orbis Books, 1978.

"Supplemental Checklist of Selected Periodicals for Study of Missiology and World Christianity Recommended for North American Theological Libraries," *Occasional Bulletin of Missionary Research* 4, no. 4 (1980): 176-77.

"Response [to Pietro Rossano]." In *Christ's Lordship and Religious Pluralism*, edited by Gerald H. Anderson and Thomas F. Stransky, pp. 110-20. Maryknoll, NY: Orbis Books, 1981.

"Checklist of 40 Selected Periodicals in English from Mission Agencies and Institutions," *International Bulletin of Missionary Research* 5, no. 1 (1981): 27-28.

"Facing the Realities of the Contemporary World in Mission" and "Christian Faith and Religious Pluralism." In *Educating for Christian Missions: Supporting Christian Missions Through Education*, edited by Arthur L. Walker, Jr., pp. 49-71. Nashville: Broadman Press, 1981.

"Why We Need a Second Mission Agency [in the United Methodist Church]," *Good News* 17, no. 5 (1984): 55-62.

"Christian Mission and Human Transformation: Toward Century 21,"
Mission Studies: Journal of the IAMS 2, no. 1 (1985): 52-65. Presidential address to the International Association for Mission Studies, Harare, Zimbabwe, January 1985.

"American Protestants in Pursuit of Mission: 1886-1986." In *A Century of Church History: The Legacy of Philip Schaff,* edited by Henry Warner Bowden, pp. 168-215. Carbondale, IL: Southern Illinois University Press, 1988. Reprinted with emendations in *International Bulletin of Missionary Research* 12, no. 3 (1988): 98-118; also in *An Ecumenical Introduction to Missiology,* edited by F. J. Verstraelen. Grand Rapids, MI: Wm. B. Eerdmans Publishing Company, 1993.

"Reflections on Orlando E. Costas" (Memorial Service), *Judson Bulletin* (Andover Newton Theological School) 7, no. 1 (1989): 18-19.

"Christian Mission and Religious Pluralism: A Selected Bibliography of 175 Books in English, 1970-1990," *International Bulletin of Missionary Research* 14, no. 4 (1990): 172-76.

"Speaking the Truth in Love: An Evangelical Response [to Cardinal Jozef Tomko]." In *Christian Mission and Interreligious Dialogue,* edited by Paul Mojzes and Leonard Swidler, pp. 162-73. Lewiston, NY: Edwin Mellen Press, 1990.

"Moratorium." In *Dictionary of the Ecumenical Movement,* edited by Nicholas Lossky et al., p. 702. Grand Rapids, MI: Wm. B. Eerdmans Publishing Company; Geneva: World Council of Churches, 1991.

"Mission Research, Writing, and Publishing: 1971-1991," *International Bulletin of Missionary Research* 15, no. 4 (1991): 165-72.

"Toward A.D. 2000 in Mission." In *The World Forever Our Parish,* edited by Dean S. Gilliland, pp. 125-40. Lexington, KY: Bristol Books, 1991. Abridged version in *Good News* 24, no. 2 (1990): 21-25.

"Theology of Religions and Missiology: A Time of Testing." In *The Good News of the Kingdom: Mission Theology for the Third Millennium,* edited by Charles Van Engen, Dean Gilliland, and Paul Pierson. Maryknoll, NY: Orbis Books, 1993.

Index

Holistic mission, 50, 133
Holland, Joseph, 211, 214
Hollenweger, Walter J., 49, 52, 252, 261, 265
Holy Spirit, 41ff., 67, 117, 134, 159, 222
Hong Kong, 141
Homer, Norman A., 164 *(bio. note)*, 172
House churches *(and* Household churches), 81, 141
Huber, Mary Taylor, 122
Hug, James E., 211, 214
Human rights, 365
Hutcheson, William R., 335

Ibero American Missionary Congress (COMIBAM, 1987), 131, 135
Idahosa, Benson, 47
Ikenga-Metuh, E., 245, 251
Ilung, Bakole W. A., 317
Immigration, 101, 102
Incarnation, 188, 302f., 312
Inculturation, 207ff.
India, 3, 58ff.
Indian Evangelical Team, 300
Indigenization, 246ff.
Indigenous theologies, 245-52. *See also* Contextualization
Institute on the Church in Urban Industrial Society (ICUIS), 332
Interdenominational Foreign Mission Association (IFMA), 12, 13
International Association for Mission Studies (IAMS), 178, 376
International Bulletin of Missionary Research, 377
International Council of Christian Churches (ICCC), 13
International Health Services, Foundation, 47
International Missionary Council (IMC), 2, 18, 127, 194, 201, 340
International Review of Mission, 21, 29
Isaiah, 182, 184, 221
Islam *(and* Muslims), 19, 59ff., 95, 103, 149, 156, 164ff., 348-62. *See also* Christian-Muslim relations, and Evangelism
Israel (modern state), 168
Itioka, Neuza, 134, 135, 137

Jacobs, Donald R., 235 *(bio. note)*
Jainism. *See* Mahavira
James, St., 165
Jansen, Frank K., 282, 297, 308
Japan, 144ff.
Javouhey, Anne Marie, 291
Jeremiah, 59
Jerome Biblical Commentary, 99
Jesus Christ, 5, 11, 17, 26, 65, 130, 132f., 157, 159, 179, 181, 185, 186, 190, 222, 260, 378
John of Montecorvino, 140
John Paul II, Pope, 130, 154
John, St. (Fourth Gospel), 189
Johnston, Sir Harry, 88, 96
Johnston, William, 210, 214
Johnstone, Patrick, 68
Joint Working Group of the Roman Catholic Church and the World Council of Churches, 39
Jonah, 180, 181
Jones, Alan W., 211, 215
Jones, Cheslyn, 206, 215
Judaism *(and* Jews), 18, 103, 167, 378
Judd, Steven, 130, 137
Jung, Carl Gustav, 152
Junod, Henri Alexandre, 258, 265
Justice *(and* Social justice), 36, 66, 310-17, 370, 371
Justin Martyr, 183

Kaahumanu, Queen (Hawaii), 110
Kachin Baptists (Myanmar [Burma]), missions, 300
Kähler, Martin, 177, 191
Kairos Document: Challenge to the Church, 368f.
Kaiser, Walter, 289, 293
Kaldor, Peter and Sue, 122

(343) so well put this w nth mer ...y

Act 4:12   7.6.1989, San Antonio, Communion q W.n. Mursi (Angli
to   "We cannot point to any other way q salvation
          | than J.C. ; at the same time we cannot set limits to
          | the saving power q God :"

379 " Either all people need Xst or none do" (Anderson)
              That about says it.
          How can we liberals answ. that ? Xuai beam need it
                      Given had it no answer

218 Gr. word for strategy = 'general', a military term. ×

219-20 critique of 'scientific method': its result: alienation. (Guest - Roszak)

253f "High Religion / "folk religion" — cf new age 259
    how folk religion persists in Xianity

× 261f By 2000 60% of Xians will be non western / among the poor.

270 Brunner "The Xch exists to be mission..." cf Moltmann "..."

274 The city as we know it is obsolete (Drucker)

277 "wanderlust tourism" cf cot to Mexico etc.
    " "can the west be converted?" Newbigin

281 The problem of unconscious competition overseas 14 God

296 "Rice Xians"

300 14 on western Gospel of affluence .. enshrined .. closing eyes of man
    to bring glory to GNP .." : the ineffectuality of western missionaries
308 14 Conscience like a "sun-dial" : At nite it says nothing reliable. cf 4   297-300
    " who Bible centred sun-day. Does not lie

306 14 Penicillin : the counterfeit, cf Acts 12? (Sextus of Savaric?)

310 The old definition of 'Evangelism' (mission)

312 "we know the words but not the music" we don't practice what we preach
                                    (home) (overseas)

318 G The City / mission

p 3 The Communist Control of Russia. 70 yrs of Babylon   Israel in

348f World religion (Islam)

349 14 4 definitions of interfaith "dialogue"

~363 "the 4 horsemen of the planetary apocalypse" — pop growth, pollution
    (Rev)   resource depletion
                                         nuclear disast

158 "only upon truth can trust be built"

264 reform | key N.T words
conform | re: apost000life
reform
transform

264 to dev' isms' consumerism etc.
consumerism "

303 "the cross not only gives life / it takes it too
(cross sense etc)

329 "a term like 'the poor' in danger of becoming a salvific category in itself"

346 "the appearance of obedience hides the reality of disobedience" (Neutiger) Pharisees

108 geopolitics
global economics
155 into reverse process
195 consent/aneous "
220 missio Dei
250 diachronically = "thru time"
" synchronically = "a specific pt. in time"

158 ✝ The Evang. vision (St Fr. lecture) "the only reason for being a chy. is the overpowering conviction that the chr + anti is true (Neill
↓ "The Gospel is true for all & so is true at all" (Taylor
✓ 159 not gospel, but Gospel (in NT) sequel
St Fran

St Fran
Serv - 'elitest' evangel - we have it -
49

131 a new approach to Acts 118
133 whole passage

71 Acts 1:8 - Bartholomew/ Thaddeus to the vicinity to Rome. 159
81 Evangelism when verbal witness is banned. ✝ 196 will puts how modern people view "mission"

258 - was it the word 'force' religion that turned them back

42 II D. - esch in Pentateuch ✝ -
but is O.T did not lead to evangelism,
" rather tightening then belts for the "wait"

116 cf II P (: Hab.) wl occasion ✝ "sell out" - God's die
= 119

151 Intro II P - the spiritual aposto? trag (See 151f for an excellent survey of a decaying
152-3 4 ✝ Xianity in Europe. Exactly like U.S)

on

181 on Jonah - not a
"messianity" - that people
of Veragrant

196 Lk 4: 16f the Messh
✝ women & holy.

220 Gen 1-3 " prologue to Script

287-290 I Cor 14: 34-5) re:
" 11) women in
I Tim 2) the Ech

301 Lk 4 "good news for the
(297f) poor

316 Lk ✝ U.B.: 'economics'
OR repentance

159 Gal 1: 11-12

12 1 Lk "Mesh" "God's Gentlemen"
at 5

18 Rom 1: 15-16 today
'Jews ✝

42 Act 2 "other tongue"
✝ Xenolalia

65 Lk Jesus question
Mt 21: 23f

112 Act 15 Lk a new way
to approach the issue

176 Wm Carey on Mt 28: 20
(the) 1851 ✝
best early Gospel handles the
Great Commission difficulty. See 188-9